RUM A LANDSCAPE WITHOUT FIGURES

By the same author

The Return of the Sea Eagle (1983), Cambridge University Press.
Eagles (1989), Whittet Books.
Sea Otters (1990), Whittet Books.
Penguins (1994), Whittet Books.
A Salmon for the Schoolhouse (1994), Canongate Academic (with Brenda McMullen).
Penguins (1997), Colin Baxter Photography Ltd.

Rum

A Landscape Without Figures

JOHN A. LOVE

with line illustrations by the author

ORIGIN

This edition published in 2018 by
Birlinn Origin, an imprint of
Birlinn Limited
West Newington House
10 Newington Road
Edinburgh
EH9 1QS

www.birlinn.co.uk

First published in 2001 by Birlinn Ltd

ISBN: 978 1 912476 15 2
eBook ISBN: 978 1 78885 124 4

British Library Cataloguing-in-Publication Data
A catalogue record for this book is available from
the British Library

Typeset by Carnegie Book Production, Lancaster
Printed and bound by Clays Ltd, Elcograf S.p.A

In memory of my father
Howell Clifford Love
(1910–1955)

The surface of Rum is in a manner covered with heath, and in a state of nature: the heights rocky.

Thomas Pennant, 1772

The island of Rum will one day be considered, if not the most remarkable of the Hebrides, at least a very important field of inquiry.

Edward Daniel Clarke, 1797

We could see among the deserted fields the grass-grown foundations of cottages razed to the ground; but the valley, more desolate than the one we had left, had not even its single inhabited dwelling: it seemed as if man had done with it for ever. The island, eighteen years before, had been divested of its inhabitants, amounting at the time to rather more than four hundred souls, to make way for one sheep-farmer and eight thousand sheep. ... But the whole of the once-peopled interior remains a wilderness, without inhabitant – all the more lonely in its aspect from the circumstances that the solitary valleys, with their plough-furrowed patches, and their ruined heaps of stone, open upon shores every whit as solitary as themselves, and that the wide untrodden sea stretches drearily around ... – all seemed to bespeak the place a fitting habitation for man, in which not only the necessaries, but also a few of the luxuries of life, might be procured; but in the entire prospect not a man nor a man's dwelling could the eye command. The landscape was one without figures.

Hugh Miller, 1845

Contents

List of illustrations   xi

Author's Preface   xiii

PART I Land and Prehistory

1 Wild Heaths and Rude Rocks   3

2 A Home of Men   16

PART II Early History

3 As Complete an Islander   35

4 Piety and Virtue   53

PART III Land and People

5 Voyages of Amusement   63

6 A Clean but Homely Cloth   74

7 Fertile and Fruitful   84

8 Sustenance from the Chase   101

9 A Wool and Mutton Speculation   113

10 A Most Melancholy Cycle   122

PART IV Sheep Farm and Estate

11 All was Solitary   137

12 Depopulation on Such a Scale   152

13 Great but Ineffectual Works   178

14 Sea-girt Solitude   197

PART V Modern Rum

15 From Clogs to Castle   219

16 No Utopia   232

17 How Strange a Cycle   250

Appendix I Catechist's List: Census for the Small Isles, 1764–65   269

Appendix II Muster Rolls of the Rum Island Company of
                Inverness-shire Volunteers   276

Appendix III Passenger List of the Ship *Saint Lawrence*   281

Bibliography   285

Index   291

List of Illustrations

1. Loch Scresort and Kinloch Woods from Hallival

2. Flooding at Salisbury's Dam, 1980

3. Arrowheads found on Rum and Eigg

4. Bagh na h-Uamha cross slab

5. Kilmory cross slab

6. Norse burial cist

7. Norse gaming piece of Narwhal ivory

8. Chambered shieling and cell, Kimory Glen

9. Rectangular shieling

10. Newborn Highland calf

11. Two feral billy goats

12. Red deer hind in Kilmory Glen

13. Deer trap

14. Kenneth Maclean's cottage at Carn an Dobhran

15. Kinloch River in spate

16. Welshman's Rock or an t-Sron

17. Rum pony

18. Rum pony with foals

19. The second Marquis of Salisbury

20. Graveslab at Kilmory burial ground

21. Fishing boat beached off the old pier in Rum

22. Gravestone erected by Murdo Matheson

23. Photograph of Rum in 1886

24. Remains of John Bullough's tomb

25. Ruins of Papadil Lodge

26. Early photograph of Kinloch Castle

27. Ivory eagle formerly in Kinloch Castle

28. Shooting party

29. Lady Bullough

30. Stalker and ghillie

31. The old post office at Kinloch

32. James MacAskill, at the old post office

33. The Post Office as it is today

34. Children and teacher outside the school, 1957

35. School photograph, early twentieth century

Colour Illustrations

1. The Rum Cuillin from Harris

 2. Ard Nev and the Rum Cuillin

 3. Ruined cottage of the Maclean family

 4. Loch at Papadil

 5. Lazybed system, above raised beach at Harris

 6. Sail-training vessel *Captain Scott* moored at Loch Scresort

 7. Aerial view of Glen Dibidil

 8. View of Canna from Glen Guirdil

 9. The Guirdil bothy

10. Watercolour of New Loch behind Salisbury's Dam

11. Aerial view of Kinlochscresort

12. Portrait of Sir George Bullough

13. Painting of the Bulloughs' yacht *Rhouma*

14. Landscape painting showing vicinity of Kinloch Castle

15. Kinloch Castle

16. Main hall of Kinloch Castle

Author's Preface

I first went to Rum in April 1969, with a dozen or so fellow students from the Biological Society of Aberdeen University. We sailed from Mallaig in Macbrayne's steamer, *Loch Arkaig*, and were transferred ashore in the Nature Conservancy's flit boat, inherited from the previous owners and called *Seoras*, after Sir George Bullough. We camped for a week on the island in Kinloch Glen and in glorious weather. We walked to Shellesder and climbed Hallival. Peter Wormell, the warden-naturalist, talked to us about the island, and in return we gave a day's assistance in the forest nursery. Pat Lowe, one of the Conservancy deer researchers living in the Castle Hostel, gave some of us a lift to Harris in his Land Rover. Although the island had been a National Nature Reserve, owned by the Nature Conservancy, for twelve years, it still had the air of a country estate, with George Macnaughton, son of the Bullough's Factor Duncan, then in the role of reserve warden.

Not long after I returned to Rum in 1975, to work with the Sea Eagle Reintroduction Project, George was transferred to Dinnet Moor NNR in Aberdeenshire, prior to his retirement two years later. Immediately I took an interest in Rum's history, learning much about the island and its history from George, from the stalker Geordie Sturton and from Ian Simpson, boatman/handyman, who was to remain on the island for a further decade. I have remained in touch with Peter Wormell and his wife, Jessie, who used to run the Post Office, and who by then were living in Argyll. Although I had met Joey Cameron several times on her frequent visits back to Rum, it was some years before I met her brother Archie, whose reminiscences of his early life on the island are now a classic in Rum literature. Archie and I met up from time to time and corresponded regularly until his death.

I am fortunate to have had the assistance and hospitality of Robin Harcourt-Williams, archivist to the Marquess of Salisbury, whose estate papers are a hugely valuable resource about Rum in the mid-1800s. Although living all his life on the neighbouring island of Canna, the late Ian Mackinnon knew much about Rum that no longer survives on the island itself, and I am proud to have had the friendship and companionship of Ian and his family. The eminent Gaelic scholar, historian and naturalist, the late Dr John Lorne Campbell of Canna, was another great source of information and over the years I have spent many wonderful days in Canna House and its library, with him and his talented wife, Margaret Fay Shaw. Happily, Margaret still lives in Canna House, although the island has now been gifted to the National Trust for Scotland. I am grateful to them all for sharing their knowledge of Rum with me, and particularly to both George Macnaughton and Archie Cameron for having read and checked the chapters I had written about the Bulloughs. Mairi MacArthur kindly read and commented on the entire MS and I am extremely grateful for her comments and advice.

I went to Rum initially on a six-week contract but ended up living there for nearly ten years. I soon realised that there was more to Rum's story than the Bullough family and their short but conspicuous legacy to the island. Their castle, mausoleum etc. are ephemeral compared with the labours of generations gone before, who eked out a living from the limited resources that Rum had to offer. It was a desire to put figures back on to this distant landscape that stimulated my researches over the last two decades. Inevitably I have had to add fresh information, and although more about the Bulloughs especially has come to light in recent years – not all of it, I have to say, authenticated – I have tried to retain these last chapters pretty much as George and Archie had read them shortly before their deaths, for theirs were first-hand experiences that can never be rivalled. Many other people have offered me assistance and friendship over the years, but are too numerous to name here. I may however be forgiven for singling out Helen Matheson in New Zealand, Marigold Gregory (and her late husband, David) in Australia, Ian Fisher of RCAHMS and finally Richard MacIvor, who had lived in Rum longer than most until his tragically early death a couple of years ago – the last link on the island with George Macnaughton and thence back to the Bullough era.

TO AN ANCIENT RACE

In days now long gone before
weary backs, bent and sore,
had trenched the meagre soil.
And on rigs that now scar the slope
scant crops were grown in hope,
with hard, unceasing toil.

Around a tiny flame of peat
the long nights passed with little heat,
in damp and in darkness.
Blackhouses built of stone and turf
lay huddled from the winter surf,
the wind and rain so endless.

In a tiny plot of hallowed ground,
with drystane ruins all around,
stand crude slabs to souls unknown.
Among aged bones at rest for ever
five children who died from fever –
a family tragedy carved in stone.

Defeated eyes turned to gaze their last
on the island that for long days past
was their whole life, their home.
They turned instead to look to the west,
to a promised land offering all of the best,
and a better life to come.

'Neath lofty crags and misty halls,
since ages past nightly haunted by trolls,
empty and still the wasted island lay.
Not one, from hundreds, was permitted
to stay ...

Until one day a tall ship entered the bay,
with laughter, voices – loud and gay.

A castle in red sandstone to please,
with a tower standing proud of the trees,
was built at the head of the bay.

Shots rang out round the hill
as the gentry braved the wet and the chill
to return at the end of the day ...
... to return after stalking for pleasure,
to a world of comfort and leisure,
to brandy and baths too hot.

In mind of their days on the hill,
from the walls hanging so still –
trophies – stags they had shot.

By a tiny remote loch alone
a ruin in wood and in stone
stands – now smothered by trees –
built in that age now gone.
Within its walls once shone
a world it no longer sees.

Only a tomb in sombre Grecian mime
survives unscathed the pass of time,
absurd and alone on the shore.
But drystane ruin and lazybed
are better monuments – to a dead
longer departed:
to return no more.

John A. Love
Isle of Rum, 1975

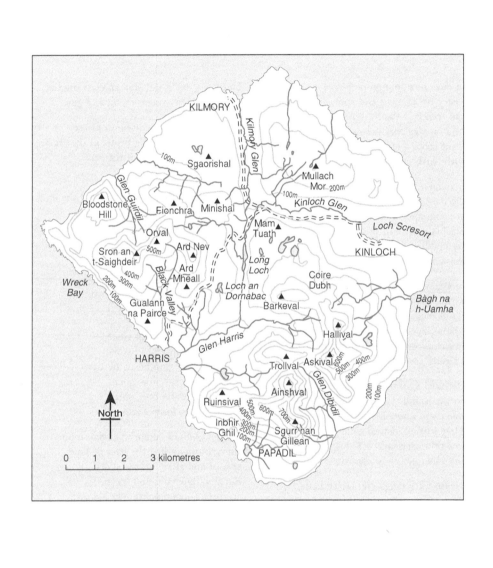

KILMORY

Kilmory Glen

100m

Sgaorishal

Mullach
Mor   200m

100m

Glen Guirdil

Kinloch Glen

Bloodstone
Hill

Fionchra   Minishal

Loch Scresort

Orval

Mam
Tuath

KINLOCH

Ard Nev

500m

Sron an
t-Saighdeir

Long
Loch

Ard
Mheall

Coire
Dubh

400m

Wreck
Bay

300m

Black Valley

200m

Loch an
Dornabac

Barkeval

Bàgh na
h-Uamha

100m

Gualann
na Pairce

Hallival

Glen Harris

HARRIS

Trollval   Askival

600m

400m

500m

Ainshval

300m

Glen Dibidil

200m

100m

Ruinsival

500m

600m

700m

Inbhir
Ghil

400m

North

300m
200m
100m

Sgurr nan
Gillean

0   1   2   3 kilometres

PAPADIL

PART I

Landscape and Prehistory

There is a great deal of stormy magnificence about the lofty cliffs, as there is generally all around the shores of Rum; and they are, in most places, as abrupt as they are inaccessible from the sea.
The interior is one heap of rude mountains, scarcely possessing an acre of level land. It is the wildest and most repulsive of all the islands ... The outlines of Halival and Haskeval are indeed elegant and render the island a beautiful and striking object from the sea.

John MacCulloch, 1824

1   *Wild Heaths and Rude Rocks*

The evening was clear, calm, golden-tinted, even wild heaths and
rude rocks had assumed a flush of transient beauty.

Hugh Miller, 1845

One and a half centuries ago the island of Rum would not have looked
much different from today. Hugh Miller, stonemason, geologist, writer and
evangelist, cast his experienced eye over its landscape and ventured that
the geology was 'simple, but curious'. He likened the island hills, thrust up
through a framework of sandstone, to 'rum-bottles in a cask-basket'. He
surmised that the origins of the island were illustrated by its structure:
'It has left its story legibly written, and we have but to run our eye over
the characters and read.' The layers of sandstone had been tilted up by
volcanic convulsions, he continued, 'tier upon tier, like roofing slate laid
aslant on a floor', which were then broken through by further Plutonic
activity at various stages in its history. Rashly, he then elaborated on this
theory – even although he had been on the island for only a few days – and
his deductions fell wider off the mark.

The geology of Rum is certainly curious, but unfortunately it is by no
means simple. While Miller was correct in the crudest of terms, the exact
details and sequence of events have preoccupied geologists ever since. And
there is still much that remains to be found out.

The island, as we know it today, has taken nearly 3000 million years to
evolve, being sculpted from some of the oldest known rocks – and some of
the youngest – on earth. And these very first rocks are the melted-down
remains of even older rocks, that are now almost impossible to date

precisely. The effects of intense heat, pressure and tension on these most ancient sediments have produced wavy light and dark bands that are characteristic of this coarse-grained rock, known as gneiss (pronounced 'nice'). It makes up much of the Outer Hebrides but in Rum it is limited to the summit of Ard Nev, the slopes of Ainshval and one or two other localities.

Another type of melted or metamorphic rock, known as schist, was formed soon after this time and makes up much of the northern Highlands; none, however, survives in Rum. Elsewhere in the world sediments from this same era exist that were never metamorphosed; they have recently been shown to contain microscopic bacteria and single-celled animals and plants, indicating how – several thousand million years ago – life had already begun to exist on the planet. The north of Scotland then became submerged, allowing the deposition of sediments on the sea-bed that have since become the purple-grey Torridonian sandstones characteristic of north and east Rum. Such neatly layered sandstones and shales also occur in south Skye and Torridon (from where they derive their name) as far north as Cape Wrath.

Hugh Miller first noticed how the sandstone layers on the north shore of Loch Scresort in Rum are tilted downwards to the west. He surmised that they must be several thousand feet thick although today their highest point is only 300 metres above the present sea-level. Miller failed to find any fossils in Rum but elsewhere the petrified remains of primitive shelled animals or molluscs have been discovered in similar Torridonian rocks. Indeed by this time most of the invertebrates we know today had evolved. Those with soft bodies – such as worms – do not leave fossils, of course, but the remains of their burrows can often be detected in the rock, excavated when it was still mud and sand.

Identical creatures have long been known from similar rocks in Greenland (where gneisses are also common) but it is only in recent decades – since the idea of continental drift has been accepted – that we have come to appreciate how the north-west of Scotland once lay very close to Greenland. An ocean, perhaps never much larger than the modern Mediterranean, then separated this land mass from England and the rest of Europe. We have to bear in mind that at this time also these separate halves of Britain lay some 25 degrees south of the Equator – while the Sahara was covered in ice near the South Pole!

About 450 million years ago the ancient Atlantic Ocean began to close. The schists of the Highlands became sandwiched between Greenland and the rest of Europe and buckled to form a huge mountain chain. Cracks and splits created what we now refer to as the Highland Boundary Fault, the Great Glen Fault and also the Camasunary Fault – the deep marine trough that separates Rum from the mainland. Erosion by frost and river action soon took away much of this mountain chain, dumping the sediments in the Moray Firth to form the Old Red Sandstones, rich in fish fossils, where Hugh Miller first cut his teeth as a geologist. We now know primitive amphibians had begun to colonise the land that at that time basked in a hot wet climate. The swamp forests then slowly formed the great coal deposits of central Scotland. About this time (280 million years ago) Africa and then Asia 'collided' with Europe and North America to form a huge supercontinent called Pangea. By now Britain lay near the Equator and endured a hot, arid climate. Rum lay on the eastern edge of an extensive basin occupying what is now the Minch. Sediments draining into it formed a sandy limestone, of which only a scrap persists in Rum, at Monadh Dubh in its north-west corner. Unfortunately, this relic has yielded only imperfect fossils of tiny crustacea and fish, so reveals nothing of the profusion of life that existed in the seas at that time.

Another tiny fragment of even younger sediments, metamorphosed into marble, survives in Rum's east coast near Allt na Ba. (Similar lime-rich rocks protrude below the lava flows of Eigg, some of which have eroded to create the famous Singing Sands in Laig Bay.) Britain's earliest mammal – an early relative of the platypus – has been found in contemporary sediments in Somerset but this era was very much the age of reptiles. Plesiosaurs and ichthyosaurs haunted the shallow seas while dinosaurs and pterosaurs wandered through the coniferous forests on land. A few years ago the bones of a plesiosaur were found at a beach near Flodigarry in Skye and are now in the Hunterian Museum, University of Glasgow. Insects flourished alongside an ever-increasing array of flowering plants. However much of this diverse flora and fauna graced the slopes of Rum, no trace of it now remains; any fossiliferous rocks from this period – if they occurred at all in the island – have long since been removed by the relentless processes of erosion.

It was at this time – towards the close of the age of the dinosaurs about 180 million years ago – that the great continent of Pangea began to fragment. Spain detached from southern Ireland to form the Bay of Biscay, for instance, while North America drifted westwards, thereby forming the Atlantic Ocean and leaving behind an edge of ancient gneisses that are now the Outer Hebrides. Such colossal movements ruptured the earth's crust, resulting in violent volcanic activity. This is referred to as the Tertiary period, and was a major phase in the geological history of Rum and the Small Isles.

Volcanic eruptions occurred both in Greenland and along the west coast of Britain, centred on Rockall, St Kilda, Skye, Rum, Ardnamurchan, Mull, Arran and Ulster. All of these areas are of considerable interest to vulcanologists, but Rum especially so since, over millennia, erosion has left it one of the best exposed Tertiary volcanoes in the British Isles. Its very roots are well displayed in rugged yet accessible terrain. It is also smaller and less complex than Skye or Mull so that the processes which took place in and around its now naked hearth (or magma chamber) are easier to discern. Sir Archibald Geikie went a little too far however when he claimed that Rum presented 'the most stupendous succession of volcanic phenomena in the whole geological history of Europe'.

Rum's huge volcano first became active about 59 million years ago, vomiting lava that might have reached as far as Eigg or Muck but all trace in Rum itself has long since been removed by erosion. There was an extensive upwelling of molten lava in the west of Rum but it never broke the surface. Instead it cooled slowly to form a mass of granite that only later became exposed by erosion to form the smooth, rounded hills of Sron an t-Saighdeir, Ard Nev and part of Orval. This upthrust of granite took with it to the summit of Ard Nev a fragment of ancient gneiss. Another fragment is found on Ainshval but the granite plug of that hill is finer-grained, indicating that it might well have broken the surface to cool even faster. The minerals in these granites give them their characteristic light colour. They have been resistant enough to wave action to form the impressive sea-cliffs of the west of Rum, yet have shattered, through ice and frost action, to create boulder fields and screes on the hills behind.

This early stage of Rum's volcanic activity ended with the uplift of a huge circular block of igneous rock, like some gigantic piston. The friction melted the parent rock around it, acting as a lubricant to elevate it no less than 2000 metres − twice the height of Askival, now Rum's highest mountain. Geologists think that there was not just one single movement but more of a pumping action, making the piston analogy even more apt. This Main Ring Fault, as it is called, is immediately obvious on a geological map but it takes a trained eye to trace it on the ground. From the shore at Papadil it roughly follows the Dibidil path along Rum's east coast and coincides with the south wall of Kinloch Glen. It becomes less obvious amongst the western granites before finally disappearing beneath the sea at A'Bhrideanach, the farthermost west point of Rum.

The consequence of this major event was that the solidifying rock mass, which represents the dying embers of the volcano, was pushed nearer the surface and has since been exposed by erosion. Thus it can be seen that the molten ultrabasic rock, rich in magnesium and calcium, cooled in quite distinct crystalline layers, replenished from time to time with fresh injections of magma. The layering is perhaps best exhibited at the pyramidal summit of Hallival, where the hard, light-coloured bands, termed allivalite, form vertical cliffs, while the darker, more easily weathered bands of peridotite have broken down to form gravel slopes.

The first layers to form were thicker and less distinct and − particularly in Glen Harris – they are rich in another heavier mineral called olivine. Furthermore, being near the floor of the magma chamber with few convection currents, this olivine has crystallised out in long straight crystals to form a rock that is unique to Rum and called Harrisite. The only other comparable material has been found in samples taken back by the Apollo lunar missions; hence Harrisite is sometimes nicknamed 'moon rock'.

Another unique crystal formation can be seen just north of Loch Dornabac, where the olivine and another mineral, plagioclase, radiate out from a central point, looking not unlike giant snowflakes up to a metre across. They rejoice in the incredibly cumbersome geological title 'poikilo-macro-spherulitic feldspars'.

While all this was happening, fingers of lava were being injected into cracks in both the Tertiary igneous rocks and the early sandstones. They tend to radiate out from a point in Glen Harris, suggesting this to have been the centre of volcanic activity in Rum. The only horizontal lava flows that occur in Rum make up the western hills of Orval, Bloodstone Hill and Fionchra. These overlie not only the Torridonian sandstones but also the western granites and parts of the Main Ring Fault, and so must have been extruded late in the sequence of volcanic events. They are contemporary with the lava flows of Canna and possibly emanated from a vent that lay between Rum and Canna. They filled river valleys on top of the sandstones and, along the point of contact, there can be found pieces of carbonised twigs and even the delicate impressions of leaves. It is thought that the episodic volcanic events in Rum spanned one or two million years – sufficient time for forest to clothe the surface of the island before the final eruptions of lava. Even better tree fossils found in the lavas of Mull indicate that the Hebrides were enjoying a sub-tropical climate at the time.

In 1764 the Rev. John Walker 'found a small seam of coal, about 6 inches thick, lodged in a stratum of whinrock, upon the west side of [Rum], but saw no appearance of it anywhere else'. It is to his credit that he discovered it at all. Walker went on to describe the crystallised minerals, often associated with air bubbles or vesicles in the lavas:

The shores of Rum abound with the chalcedony, and blue and white onyx, commonly known by the name of agates or pebbles; and I found also some few fine specimens of the white cornelian. These stones are to be found thrown up by the sea, in the small bays, on the north east side of the island, but in larger masses, and in greater quantity, upon its north coast, facing the Sound of Canna ... The island of Rum affords another stone, very valuable to the Lapidary. Formerly it was considered as a jasper, but by Cronsted the late Swedish Mineralist, it is called petrosilex. It is of a bright green or blue colour; has a degree of transparency, takes a fine polish, and is a very beautiful stone for snuff boxes, bracelets or such like ornaments, and it is found here, in the sea cliffs and upon the shore of the Sound of Canna in great quantities, though abroad it is accounted a rare and valuable stone. I got only such pieces as were fallen accidentally out of the cliffs but by quarrying there might be masses got of a considerable size and of an exquisite colour and polish.

One last geological event occurred before volcanic action ceased in Rum. A crack appeared that split the island along its entire length from north to south. Known as the Long Loch Fault this can easily be traced from the deep cleft of Inbhir Ghil near Papadil. The resistant rocks of Ruinsival obscure this fracture but it re-emerges as the trench within which now lies the Long Loch, leading on to Kilmory Glen before disappearing into the sea at its sandy beach. The rocks to the east of the fault slid sideways several hundred metres, and also slumped somewhat, thus preserving more of Rum's original volcano on its east side but exposing some of the earliest layers on the west.

After the last eruption, Britain continued its drift to northerly latitudes. Twenty million years ago Africa 'collided' with Europe again throwing up impressive mountain ranges, namely the Alps, the Atlas and the Zagros. The event hardly raised a shudder in the British Isles. Meanwhile our west coast began to rise (and still does) while the North Sea coast sank. The climate became cooler and wetter but some exotic mammals such as hippo, rhino, hyena and mastodon wandered our temperate woods and meadows. Two million years ago the fauna became more like those of modern times but the weather continued to deteriorate until ice-caps began to form. At least seventeen glaciations may have struck Britain since then, the earliest being the most extensive, with ice-sheets over 1000 metres thick reaching as far south as London.

In the milder interglacial periods Scotland would have been covered in a tundra vegetation where woolly mammoths and reindeer flourished. The last major cold spell began about 30,000 years ago with separate ice-caps on both the mainland and island hills. Rum's ice, for instance, gradually extended out over the sea to link up the other islands, and sandstone boulders were carried across to Canna where they still sit, dumped after the melt. Another erratic from Rum, of hard, metallic allivalite and known locally as the 'Ringing Stone', lies on a rocky shore in the north-west of Tiree.

Within 10,000 years an ice-cap reached its maximum thickness of 1500 metres and covered most, if not all, of Scotland – again obliterating all plant and animal life. The land surface underneath was scraped bare, or else became covered with 50 metres or more of glacial debris. The weight of ice was sufficient to depress the land so that new shorelines were cut. Once the ice began to melt the land recovered and rose, bringing with it the temporary coastline to leave raised beaches 12 metres and 30 metres above the existing sea-level. Some fine examples can be seen at Harris in Rum.

It was this final phase of glaciation that sculpted into their present form the building blocks of Rum that had been assembled in Tertiary times. The ice-sheet smoothed rock surfaces, knocking off sharp edges by abrasion and creating new ones by plucking away downstream faces. Glaciers altered the contours of valleys to a wider U-shape, depositing glacial till in hillocks and moraines along the valley floor.

As the climate ameliorated meltwater formed new stream courses and carried debris downhill to dump it again whenever the gradient lessened. Arctic conditions persisted on the hills, cracking and splitting rocks with frost action to create boulder fields and screes. On the summit of Sron an t-Saighdeir, for example, blocks have been arranged into stone stripes or polygon formations, typical of Arctic landscapes.

The melt was rapid and within 4000 years the ice disappeared. For a time Scotland experienced cold, dry winters and warm, dry summers. Tundra vegetation developed into heath and grassland with some juniper, birch and willow. Elk, reindeer and lemmings lived in Scotland at this time.

About 12,000 years ago there occurred a short, sharp deterioration in conditions causing a minor ice-sheet to develop in the Western Highlands. Rum was one of the islands that was able to generate its own little ice-cap. Eleven glaciers have been identified; two on the western hills and the remainder on the Rum Cuillin itself. One flowed into Coire nan Grunnd from Hallival to deposit a scatter of huge boulders obvious to anyone now walking the Dibidil path.

The rest of the island would have reverted to tundra again with grasses, sedges and shrubs coming in as soon as the climate improved. Birch would have been an early pioneering species, with hazel and aspen contributing to the forest cover, and willow and alder in the wetter areas. At its warmest, 5000 or 6000 years ago, the climate allowed the tree-line in Rum, and elsewhere, to extend much further uphill than nowadays. Oak and elm would have been able to establish but pine was never as common as on the drier east coast. By this time Stone Age peoples had arrived on the scene but we will take up the human story in the next chapter.

Three thousand years ago, during the late Stone Age and early Bronze Age, Scotland's climate became cooler and wetter, which favoured the accumulation of peat. The area of cultivable land would have decreased, while pine stumps uncovered from bogs in Rum indicate that forests would also have been smothered. Through the Iron Age and Viking times, felling and burning would have accelerated woodland clearance while grazing animals would inhibit much regeneration of trees.

A further deterioration of climate occurred in the latter half of the seventeenth century, which geographers refer to as the Little Ice Age. The Thames regularly froze over and snow fields persisted on the Cairngorms throughout the summer months. In Rum this cold snap would have resulted in poor harvests and hard times for the islanders. Although it may not seem like it the weather conditions in Rum have improved slightly since then.

In 1764 the Rev. John Walker described Rum as:

> an island of an unfavourable climate, being much colder, by reason of the height of its mountains, and much more subject to rains and winds than the neighbouring islands of Egg and Canna, which are lower land. These disadvantages of climate, with its deep wet soil, must prevent it from being ever profitable in the production of corn or cattle.

Subsequent visitors also complained about Rum's climate. In 1772 Thomas Pennant returned from a hike in the hills 'excessively wet with constant rain'. Around 1820 John MacCulloch came ashore at Guirdil in a summer storm and complained:

> if it is not always bad weather in Rum, it cannot be good very often; since on seven or eight occasions that I have passed it, there has been a storm, and on seven or eight more in which I have landed, it was never without the expectation of being turned into a cold fish ... it possesses a private winter of its own, even in what is here called summer.

The *Statistical Account* noted how the late summer and harvest of 1793 were much wetter than any remembered: 'The air is generally moist and the weather rainy ... It is remarked by the inhabitants that the seasons are still becoming more and more rainy.' Fullerton's *Gazeteer* of 1842 described Rum's climate as 'an almost perennial series of storms, fogs and rain'. Eleven years later J. H. Dawson explained: 'As the island forms the only high land between the mountains of Skye and those of Mull, both of which are noted for precipitating torrents of rain on the country around them, it necessarily attracts a vast proportion of humidity.' The prevailing winds in Rum are rain-bearing southwesterlies, straight off the Atlantic.

Daily weather records have been maintained at Kinloch in Rum since 1958, and show the average annual rainfall as approaching 300 cm per year, four or five times that of Nairn on the north-east coast. Some moisture can be detected in Rum on about twenty days every month – about 70 per cent of the year. Fortunately, of course, it is not precipitated with equal intensity through the year. November is the wettest month, September next, but the rainfall can remain heavy through to March. It is not unknown for some rain to fall every day for periods of up to seven weeks.

The island's maximum daily total was measured at 9 a.m. on 16 January 1981, when 91.3 mm had fallen – over 3 inches. That day two huge temporary lochs formed in Kilmory Glen and in places the road was under several inches of water. Runoff can be rapid and every burn or trickle, even the road itself, might swell to gushing. In no time at all the dark, misty hillsides can be disfigured with white scars where previously no streams were visible. The footpaths to Dibidil and Papadil can become impassable within a matter of hours due to burns in spate. It is no wonder that in 1811, when Macdonald inquired of a young islander whether it perpetually rained in such torrents in Rum, the candid reply was: 'No, sir, not always torrents of rain – but sometimes of snow.' But as soon as the rain eases, so does the flood-level begin to fall. There are, of course, respites at other times of the year. May is the driest month when an average of only 129 mm may fall. April, too, might be dry and, so too, surprisingly, February.

February is also the coldest month with a mean minimum temperature averaging 1.9°C. The lowest temperature so far recorded was –9.5°C on 10 January 1982. Air frosts may occur any time from October to May. Being on Scotland's west coast, with the ameliorating influence of the sea, Kinloch in Rum experiences no more than 37 days of ground frost in the year, half that encountered at Nairn on the other side of the country. The years 1963 and 1969 were cold but 1979 holds the record with 69 days of frost; 1971, on the other hand, had only 14 such days.

Despite the weather observation by Macdonald's young man, snow is uncommon on Rum, rarely lying at sea-level for more than a week or two. Patches may persist on the mountaintops throughout most of the winter. In my ten winters in Rum (1975–84) the road to Harris – where it reaches an altitude of 200 metres above sea level – was blocked with drifting snow on only three occasions; once for an interval of three weeks.

The island's geographical position cushions it from low temperatures but, at a latitude of 57°N, nor does it enjoy high temperatures. The maximum ever recorded was 27.5°C on 4 August 1975. Mean maximum temperatures vary from 17° in August to 7° in January. This compares with 30.6° in July at Nairn (about half a degree of latitude further north), and 15° in January. Low cloud over Rum's hills reduces the amount of sunshine recorded at Kinloch to 1100 hours a year, compared with 1300 at Nairn.

In fact, situated in Rum's shaded east coast, Kinloch will be slightly colder than other parts of the island. Certainly it is rare to find snow lying at sea-level at Harris or Kilmory. Rainfall, too, varies considerably across the island: up to 500 cm on the mountaintops but only 180 cm at

Kilmory and 140 cm at Harris. However, exposed to the prevailing southwesterlies, Harris is windier. In 1772 Thomas Pennant had observed that 'what is properly the rainy season commences in August: the rains begin with moderate winds, which grow stronger and stronger till the autumn equinox, when they rage with incredible fury'. Northwesterly gales in January 1989 were sufficiently unusual to bring down many trees at Kinloch.

Gales are recorded at Kinloch on up to 85 days of the year, although the average is only about 40. This can disrupt the ferry services but rarely for more than three or four days at a time. Winds can make winter voyages distinctly uncomfortable. Loch Scresort provides better shelter than is available to either Eigg or Muck. Before 2001 boats could not come alongside any of these island slipways so transfer of passengers to a smaller flit boat was necessary. Canna is the best anchorage of all with the added advantage of a deep-water pier, but its position as the outermost of the Small Isles means that crossings more often have to be abandoned due to rough seas. Fog is a comparatively rare phenomenon on the western seaboard of Scotland – in contrast to the east – but thunder and lightning tend to be more frequent.

Robert Louis Stevenson could easily have been describing Rum when he wrote in *Kidnapped*: 'a wearier looking desert man never saw'. The wet, oceanic climate has had a profound influence on the vegetation of the island. The high rainfall leaches the acid soils and, as a consequence, wet heath and bog consititute nearly 90 per cent of the island's vegetation cover. Geology, too, can have an effect but, except for the lavas around Fionchra, Rum's bedrock does not contribute many nourishing minerals. The hard sandstones in the north and east of the island have weathered reluctantly, to provide only the thinnest of soil; and drainage is poor, encouraging the accumulation of peat. Thicker deposits of peat are found in Kinloch and Kilmory Glens, and at Stable Flats near the Long Loch. In these boggy areas sedges and bog asphodel are abundant, alongside sundew and butterwort that need to augment the scant supply of nutrients by trapping and digesting insects on their sticky leaves.

Peaty gley soils and podzols have developed in places but much of Rum is dominated by purple moor grass (*Molinia*) and deer sedge (*Trichophorum*). Heather or ling (*Calluna*) occurs on drier ground. Any good grassland tends to overlie outcrops of basalt, which breaks down to provide a good nutrient supply. Grass is also found where sand is blown inland from the beaches at Kilmory or Samhnan Insir, but the true machair so typical of Tiree and the Uists is absent from Rum because the sand is more mineral in origin, resulting from broken calcified seashells. Thick glacial deposits overlie the parent rock in the bottoms of the glens and, if not too boggy, can result in a sward of *Agrostis* and *Festuca* grasses rich in herbs. The floor of Glen Harris, for instance, was once heavily cultivated, and since 1971 has been improved by the reintroduction of grazing cattle. The localised outcrop of lime-rich rock at Monadh Dubh has contributed to thin calcareous soils that are otherwise rare in Rum, supporting a particularly rich herbage, with mountain avens (*Dryas*) replacing heather as the dominant shrub.

The ultrabasic rocks that dominate most of Rum are either bare of vegetation altogether, or else weather to form soils that are richer in magnesium than calcium. Wet heath is the most widespread vegetation type but, surprisingly, heather persists in some damp areas. The ultrabasic terraces near the summits of the Rum Cuillin have weathered to provide a coarse, gritty soil that provides the well-drained substrate favoured by Manx shearwaters to dig their nest burrows. The soils are also well fertilised and can support a rich green sward, unusual at such an altitude.

The western granites of Rum are hardly richer in minerals than the Torridonian sandstones, but, being more jointed rocks, they are better drained. Where the boulder fields allow, a coarse peaty podzol has developed and heather flourishes, not unlike the drier moors of eastern Scotland. On the windswept summits of the rounded granite hills the heather is stunted but hardy grasses such as *Nardus* provide useful grazing for deer. The most productive pasture of all overlies the lava flows of Fionchra, Bloodstone Hill and Orval. Basalt weathers to yield minerals that are important for plant growth, while the breakdown of rotting vegetable matter to form humus further enhances the soil quality. In damp flushes the vegetation sprouts earlier in the spring and lingers longer in autumn to provide useful winter grazing for the deer. The steeper rock-faces, well away from hungry deer, also shelter some of the rarer and most interesting of Rum's flowering plants, many of an arctic/alpine nature.

Being an island, Rum is more deficient in animal and plant species than the nearby mainland. Complete lists of plants, insects and other invertebrates have recently been assembled. Summer visitors rarely fail to make acquaintance with Rum's notorious blood-sucking insects: ticks, midges and clegs. In 1845 Hugh Miller noted that 'the armies of the insect world were sporting in the light this evening by millions'. Thirty-five years later Edwin Waugh also experienced the air swarming with stinging insects: 'their vindictiveness was something startling. They came down in murderous hordes upon every exposed bit of skin about you.' More recently Campbell Steven was ferried ashore with a cargo of Westmorland slate destined for the roof of Kinloch Castle: 'The workmen in charge of the unloading, cheery fellows from Ayrshire who had endured a long exile in the island, voiced one unanimous complaint "if it isn't the midges, it's the clegs; and if it isn't the clegs, it's the rain!"' The clegs descended on Steven and his companions in their hundreds, 'suicidal in their thirst for human blood. Frantically we had flailed the air, slapped necks, wrists, legs, moved further away from the trees, all of no avail. Never in our lives had we experienced mass attacks like these.'

The graffiti that once adorned the walls of the Kinloch campsite toilets (before they were painted over) were eloquent testimony to the human suffering midges can cause. There is the tale of the poor unfortunate staked out naked in Rum who died in torment. An old chant collected from the Isle of Eigg by Miss M. E. M. Donaldson and reproduced in her book *Wanderings in the Western Highlands* could almost be referring to this self-same incident:

> Torture, torture, man that be,
> Over there, over there,
> Thou shalt be bound, thou shalt be bound,
> Wasps today, midges tomorrow,
> Eating thee, itching thee, tumouring thee,
> Over there, over there.

Palmate newts are the only amphibian found in Rum, and common lizards the only reptile. In 1625 Father Cornelius Ward was told by the people of Canna that St Columba had cleared Rum of 'all poisonous things'. One toad sought refuge on Canna and was turned to stone; indeed, the islanders had shown him the toad-shaped rock. Various human residents have tried adding frog spawn to ponds in Rum but the water is probably too acid to let them thrive.

Amongst the mammals pygmy shrews occur all over the island, while pipistrelle bats are restricted to the woods and houses around Kinloch, where they are often to be seen flying in mild evenings well into the winter months. Like many Hebridean islands, Rum has its own distinctive race of long-tailed field mouse, supposedly brought by the Vikings. They range all over the island but, even in the absence of any house mice as competition, they rarely venture into dwellings. The same cannot be said for brown rats, which abound everywhere. They feed around the farm, on shellfish by the shore and even on the open hill where they readily supplement their vegetarian diet with carrion; in no time at all the ground beside a deer carcass becomes riddled with rat burrows. The rats also seek unhatched eggs and dead shearwaters near the summits of the mountains – mostly after these sharp-billed seabirds have left for their winter quarters. Although brown hares were released at Kilmory early last century, there are neither hares nor rabbits in Rum now – a feature it also shares with Muck. Both these islands are largely Protestant and were owned at one time by Maclean of Coll. Eigg and Canna, on the other hand, are mostly Roman Catholic and have large numbers of rabbits, which I am led to believe could be eaten on Fridays; but whether there is any religious connection is not certain!

The otter is the only mammal predator in Rum, being quite common around the coast, where it feeds on crabs, fish and even octopus. They like to come ashore to wash the salt out of their fur in freshwater pools and may also venture well inland to the hill lochs. A herd of some 200 feral goats frequent the coastal cliffs from Shellesder, westwards round to Dibidil. The most obvious creature on the island, however, is the red deer, which now numbers some 1500 head. Mortality can be high in cold, wet winters and carcasses of both goats and deer form convenient prey for three or four pairs of golden eagles that nest on the island. Since 1975 white-tailed sea eagles have been reintroduced to Rum from where they are now slowly colonising the whole west coast of Scotland. Red grouse are scarce in Rum so the eagles take a wide variety of other birds, including crows, gulls and ravens, even shearwaters, with brown rats being the only small mammal prey available to them.

Only short-eared owls occur regularly in Rum and – with no diurnal voles in the island – their diet is limited to pygmy shrews, field mice and small rats so they are rarely seen hunting the moors by day. One pair of sparrowhawks often breed in Kinloch woods, where they prey upon the population of small songbirds. Merlin, cuckoos and golden plover might be seen on the inland heath, where only pipits and snipe are at all abundant. Stonechats and wheatears also occur. Besides the Manx shearwaters, Rum holds respectable colonies of fulmars, shags, guillemots, razorbills, kittiwakes and other gulls – mainly along its south-east cliffs.

These then are the resources and conditions in Rum. Meagre and harsh, perhaps, in comparison with other Hebridean islands, but still not so as to deter humans from settling there.

otters

2 A Home of Men

'Uninhabited originally save by wild animals, it became at an early
age the home of men ...'

Hugh Miller, 1845

In 1964 a party from the Schools Hebridean Society were camped in Rum.
On a visit to the beach at Samhnan Insir, at the north-east corner of the
island, one of the boys made an exciting discovery. About 100 metres
west of the ruined cottage, in a hollow scooped by the wind out of the
machair, he spotted an arrowhead of pale green stone and about 2 cm long.
It was the classic shape that archaeologists term 'barbed and tanged' and
had been fashioned out of bloodstone. Beside it lay six scrapers and three
fabricators or 'strike-a-lights', all of bloodstone; three scrapers of chert,
a fabricator of flint, and numerous flakes of bloodstone, chert, flint and
quartz. Lying on the same surface were three beads of different types
and numerous sherds of handmade pottery (undecorated). There were also
later items including two eighteenth-century coins, fragments of iron and
iron slag, lead shot and bronze wire-headed pins. The items are now in
the National Museum of Scotland in Edinburgh, where there is a similar
arrowhead from the same locality that was probably found at the same
time – though not at first reported. (The late Ian Simpson, who worked
as boatman on the island at that time, recalled that two arrowheads had
been found by the school group.)

Bloodstone is a crystalline form of silica associated with the lavas on
the west side of Rum. It originates from a seam about 20 cm thick, near
the summit of Creag nan Stardean. The early geologists called this hill

'Scuir Mor', but it is now commonly referred to as Bloodstone Hill. There was once a small quarry on its north face, near the summit, that was marked on early 6-inch Ordnance Survey maps (1879) and so must date prior to this. It is hardly visible now but a bridle path leads from it, round the head of Glen Guirdil below the slopes of Orval, through Bealach a'Bhraigh Bhig to join the existing Harris road at Malcolm's Bridge; this is still in good repair, being used by the deer stalkers and hill walkers. Bloodstone, often referred to as heliotrope or by the more general term chalcedony, is an ornamental stone that comes in various colours – from almost white, through pale green, dark green and purple. The dark green, fine-grained variety, shot with red spots of oxidised jasper (from which it derives its name), is the most highly valued today. In her book *The Inner Hebrides and their Legends* Otta Swire recounted an obscure story that the red spots were 'blood drops from the Merry Dancers (Aurora Borealis), who are warring hosts under enchantment and have strange powers. Pure green, unflecked stone also occurs which should be treated with respect as such stones may have once belonged to the little people.'

Other small outcrops occur on Fionchra, and in Tertiary volcanic areas outwith Rum, in Eigg and Mull, for instance, but archaeologists now believe that it was from Bloodstone Hill alone that, throughout the Hebrides, prehistoric man satisfied all his needs. Fragments regularly break off from the face of Bloodstone Hill and can be picked up on the slopes or the beach below the summit. Although not as good as flint – which does occur as beach pebbles, albeit rarely, in the northern Hebrides – bloodstone proved an adequate substitute.

Flakes and tools of this conspicuous material have been excavated from other prehistoric sites in the West Highlands and Islands. In 1934, for instance, W. Lindsay Scott excavated a cave midden and burial cairn at Rubh'an Dunain on the west of coast of Skye, only 10 miles north of Rum. The artefacts included some 219 stone tools and flakes, many of which were of bloodstone. Similar early finds were later reported from Torridon, Ardnamurchan and Loch Sunart. When I first became interested in Rum's history in 1976 I paid a visit to the National Museum of Antiquities (as it was then) in Queen Street, Edinburgh to view the Rum arrowheads. Perusing another case of a hundred or more assorted arrowheads, I noticed one that was made of a beautiful dark green, red-spotted bloodstone. This had been found in Eigg in 1882 and presented to the museum by the then owner, Professor N. Macpherson. I drew it to the attention of the curator and it is now included amongst other bloodstone artefacts in a special exhibit. More bloodstone has been found in both Eigg and Canna recently.

In August 1982 a geologist, John Faithfull, was mapping rocks in Coire nan Grunnd, on the eastern slopes of Hallival and had a remarkable chance find: a barbed and tanged arrowhead. One can only surmise that this had been fixed to an arrow lost by some Bronze Age hunter in pursuit of deer or other game. This arrowhead was larger than the Samhnan Insir examples, about 3 cm long and fashioned from bleached white bloodstone.

One day the following summer a Scottish Natural Heritage estate worker, the late Richard MacIvor, was ploughing one of the farm fields at Kinloch. The area had always been known to yield flakes of bloodstone and the late George Macnaughton (son of the Factor and formerly a Nature Conservancy warden for the island) believed that it might have been where, in the nineteenth century, bloodstone from the quarry was worked before it was exported off the island. This time the plough went deeper than before, turning up a profusion of flakes, amongst which Richard MacIvor instantly spotted yet another arrowhead, again pale green and a couple of centimetres long. This was shown to a couple of archaeologists from the Royal Commission on the Ancient and Historical Monuments of Scotland who were surveying the island. In turn, they brought the find to the attention of a colleague in Edinburgh, Caroline Wickham-Jones, who specialised in stone artefacts.

Since the local presence of an abundant, high-quality source of raw material such as bloodstone is a rare occurrence in Scottish prehistory, Caroline Wickham-Jones recognised a unique opportunity to investigate the situation more fully. She drew up a research proposal which was not only approved by NCC (now SNH) but funded by the Historic Buildings and Monuments Directorate of the Scottish Development Department. Her full and detailed report was published as a *Society of Antiquaries of Scotland Monograph* (No. 7) in 1990, from which, with the author's kind permission, the following account is largely derived.

The site lay about 12 metres above sea-level on a coarse gravel terrace at the head of Loch Scresort. It had been subject to many centuries of cultivation, before becoming Kinloch Farm about 150 years ago. Even then the fields have never been used intensively and the plough soil is shallow. The archaeological team began their first season in May 1984 by scouring the surface of the field for bloodstone fragments, and digging out 38 random quadrats, each four metres square. The soil was then sieved and artefacts laboriously separated out by hand. A clear concentration occurred in the south-east corner, up to 1800 pieces per square metre compared with fifty or less elsewhere in the field. This could not have resulted from their being washed downslope since pieces of glass and eighteenth-century ceramics were scattered all over the site. It became obvious that the area had indeed been used for the manufacture of stone tools. Furthermore the quadrats revealed features which could have been prehistoric. Two of these were excavated more fully that year and rubbish pits provided some burnt hazel-nut shells suitable for radiocarbon dating.

Before the discovery of metals, early man could only use natural materials for his tools and implements – bone, wood and stone. In most soils the wood and bone will decompose so only the stone survives. This period in prehistory is commonly referred to as the Stone Age, but archaeologists prefer to subdivide it further – into early, middle and late stages, or Palaeolithic, Mesolithic and Neolithic. Humankind may have first reached Scotland during the mild phases of the Ice Age, but decamped as soon as the climate deteriorated again; the resulting icecaps and glaciers then obscured all trace of occupation, except in the deepest of caves. Northern Britain was still uninhabitable during the Palaeolithic period and only became colonised again during milder Mesolithic times.

Stone tools were pretty crude at first. By the middle Stone Age humans had learnt to chip off tiny tooth-like points of flint, chert or quartz which came to be called 'pygmy flints' or more properly 'microliths'. These served as tips or barbs for arrows, were attached to wooden handles as hand-picks, or else embedded in a line to form a saw-like tool. By Neolithic times stone implements had become quite sophisticated and the use of axe-heads and barbed-and-tanged arrow-heads, such as those that had been found in Rum, persisted even into the Bronze Age.

The abundance of microliths at Kinloch indicated that the site had been occupied much earlier than the arrow-heads had implied, during Mesolithic times. The radiocarbon dates confirmed this. Indeed the hazel-nuts had been collected and roasted 8500 years ago, making Rum the earliest human settlement yet known in Scotland. Of course, when the first peoples came to inhabit the Hebrides, they would have found other places that were much more conducive for settlement; it is only that no radiocarbon dates obtained so far have turned out to be quite as old. Cave middens in Jura, for instance, have been dated at 8000 BP (before the present), and in Islay at 7800 BP. Mesolithic sites in Scotland are also known from Galloway, Fife, in Oronsay, Risga, and near Oban. Colonisation of these places would have been from England and Ireland to the south, small bands of people hugging the coast and hopping from island to island, probably in skin boats rather than dug-out canoes.

In 1982 however, a sedimentary geologist, working for an oil company, recovered a flint tool from a core sample taken from the sea bed in the North Sea between Shetland and Norway. At the start of the Mesolithic period 10,000 years ago Britain was still joined to Denmark and the Low Countries by a land bridge. Some of the northern fishing banks in the middle of the North Sea would then have been islands. Caroline Wickham-Jones, who has examined that interesting flint tool, has surmised that early settlers could have reached Scotland from the Continent by a more northerly route, bypassing south Britain altogether. Thus, Rum could have been reached by quite an early date, though much more evidence is needed.

Britain had finally become an island around the time that Rum first became populated.

Conditions for the preservation of organic substances have been slightly more favourable at Mesolithic sites in Jura and Oronsay, revealing more about the way of life of these first settlers. Mattocks of deer antler have survived that would have been used to dig up edible roots, while hooks and harpoon-heads of animal bone would have been employed in fishing. There is evidence from the Continent that Mesolithic fishermen used nets, but this technology may not have reached Rum until later. The rest of the early tool kit we are already familiar with. Blades and scrapers of flint or bloodstone would have been used in cutting up meat and preparing animal skins, while hammer stones could be utilised in the production of flint tools, of course, and in dislodging limpets from rocks. Limpets might be time-consuming to collect but they are nutritious, twice the calorific value of oysters, and four times that of cockles. Kitchen middens and hearths usually contain abundant remains of shellfish, especially limpets, sometimes crabs and the bones of fish and seabirds. Deer and smaller game would have been hunted with bows and arrows or spears, possibly even snares and traps. Some bones of a dog found at a Mesolithic site near Oban indicates that these animals had already been domesticated and were no doubt used in hunting. These people led a hunter/gatherer way of life, moving on to other caves or campsites as soon as food resources became scarce.

There are caves with middens at Bagh na h-Uamha and Shellesder in Rum that could have offered shelter to early peoples but they have yet to be excavated and dated. In 1949 Drew Smith raked about the floor of the Bagh na h-Uamha cave and mentioned that 'bones of sheep, deer, horse, seal and seabirds abound, together with valves of shellfish in large numbers'. Over several years I myself had picked up more bone fragments there, kicked out of rat burrows and, combined with some more collected by the RCAHMS archaeologists in 1982, they have been examined by Mary Harman. She identified bone fragments of deer, sheep or goats, cattle and a wing bone of a shag. The presence of domestic stock implies that the cave midden had accumulated over a considerable period of time. In 1982, for instance, I turned over a flat stone at the back of the cave which was inscribed with numerous initials and the dates 1842, 1844 and 1845, possibly the handiwork of some fishermen or gillies who had taken shelter there. Some of the bones may have resulted from meals that these men had cooked.

Caroline Wickham-Jones' team believed that the milder climate of Mesolithic times could well have sustained permanent settlement in Rum. Hazel-nuts would have to be collected in autumn, and would certainly keep well; their presence on the site might be suggestive that they formed a convenient food over the winter months. The excavations continued during the summers of 1985 and 1986 revealing a few broken hearth slabs and charcoal, more rubbish pits and a number of stake-holes. The latter tended to occur in several rough arcs of three or four holes each, while another small row suggested a distinct corner. The stakes that they contained probably supported windbreaks or shelters of skins or bark; some of the stones which could have held down the tent covering were still lying nearby. Such shelters are still used by some primitive peoples today.

Excavations also exposed the gully of a small stream or burn that had been filled in, possibly deliberately. Some of the debris contained fragments of pottery, and more stone tools including a broken barbed-and-tanged arrow-head. Rocks, seemingly placed by human hand, might have served as stepping stones across the watercourse or bog. There was also a small pile of brushwood, suggesting scrub being cleared from the surroundings; these organic remains were radiocarbon dated from 4000 BP to Neolithic times. More charcoal was dated at 4700 and 4200 BP suggesting that the site continued to be occupied for several centuries. No traces of dwellings were uncovered from this period but it is likely that the people lived somewhere nearby. Microscopic analysis of the soil revealed a few pollen grains of flax and cereals showing that the area had been cleared for cultivation, an important feature of Neolithic society. By now humans lived in permanent farming settlements.

A fascinating aside of this later material was a dark fibrous smear on the inside of one of the pottery fragments. Under the microscope numerous pollen grains of heather could be seen, with some of meadowsweet, royal fern and a few of cereals. These plants are all normally associated with fermentation, so the pot had probably contained some sort of mead. Dated at 3890 years BP this is one of the earliest discoveries of an alcoholic beverage in British prehistory – a particularly appropriate distinction for an island that rejoices in the name of Rum. Later, the archaeologists were to persuade some interested home-brewers in Eigg, with chemists from William Grant & Sons (the makers of Glenfiddich whisky), to simulate a brew from this recipe, which they politely described as 'non-toxic and quite palatable at 8% proof'.

Over three seasons the archaeological team amassed no less than 138,043 pieces of worked stone, mostly from the Mesolithic. These included 1252 'cores', from which the tools would be fashioned. There were 2575 blades (more of flint than bloodstone and only three of quartz); the narrow ones could be used to produce microliths, and the others retouched to produce a sharp, scraping edge. There were also 1607 pieces which had already been modified into microliths (1155 in all of both bloodstone and flint) or scrapers, borers or leaf-shaped points. The remaining artefacts, mainly regular flakes of bloodstone, would have been considered largely as debris although some could still have proved useful. There were only four arrow-heads, of which all but the one turned up by the plough were broken and presumably discarded.

Detailed study of this material has contributed much to our knowledge of methods of stone knapping by early humans. It was obvious that the Rum folk cleverly modified their flint-working techniques to suit the different properties of bloodstone. Indeed, some of the Mesolithic leaf points were more sophisticated than would have been expected for the period. Thirty-two chunky, waterworn hammerstones were found, their ends pock-marked by use. Antler points – none of which survived – would have been used in more refined retouching to sharpen edges or shape points and arrow-heads. The function of eighteen longer pebbles is more obscure but they may have been limpet hammers.

Finally there were 299 sherds of pottery recovered, 120 pebbles (mostly bloodstone but a few of quartz and agate) and several small pumice stones. Grooves worn into the pumice suggested they were used to smooth and straighten wooden arrow-shafts and bone needles. The acidic soils of the site meant that almost no organic material survived, other than the carbonised hazel-nut shells. Only about 8 g of bone, perhaps from a sheep-sized animal, was discovered, along with two fragments of seashell, a little fossilised dung and one fishbone, probably from a wrasse.

As a break from their labours, the archaeological team visited other parts of the island to search for bloodstone flakes. Already in the 1970s forestry ploughing had turned up some at Rubha nam Feannag on the north shore of Loch Scresort, and at Camas Pliascaig a mile or two further north. The next largest accumulation, including a few cores, was found at Buail' a Ghoirtein just east of the excavation. In the end thirteen different scatters or isolated finds were mapped, all but three of them on the sheltered east side of the island. Clearly the stone-workers preferred to work their material on their own doorstep; their visits to Guirdil beach below Bloodstone Hill seem largely to have been to collect the raw materials. Cores would have been trimmed on the spot, by knocking off an end to leave a flat surface suitable for knapping, so that only the useful material needed to be carried home.

In addition bloodstone from Rum has been discovered at twenty-two other localities away from the island, but all within a radius of 70 km. They were mostly Mesolithic sites, but some of Neolithic and Bronze Age. They are all on neighbouring islands – including Eigg and Canna, even as far out as South Uist – or else peninsulas on the nearby mainland, especially Ardnamurchan and Morvern. None of the sites is very far from the sea. The material is mostly just debris, with cores found only at Acharn in Morvern, Kentra in Moidart and Risga in Loch Sunart, each of which is within easy reach of Rum. The people who lived there could have made special trips for their bloodstone. The scatters elsewhere may have been left by nomadic bands who included Rum in their annual circuit, or else they may have been the products of trade and exchange.

Another important aspect of the archaeological excavation in Rum was an investigation into the environmental conditions and its prehistoric landscape, which places the earliest settlers in the context of the island habitats and resources. Several cores were sunk into the peat at Kinloch, which were analysed alongside earlier results published from the Long Loch area. Pollen grains of plants survive remarkably well in peat and each species or group of species tends to be quite distinctive. Their relative frequencies allow an approximate picture of the prevailing vegetation to be built up; the lower down the core the further back in time.

Although the island would have spawned its own little ice-cap during the last major glaciation, ice from the mainland would also have reached Rum. The weight of ice depressed the island some 35 m below its present level, forming new beaches. Once the ice began to melt, the land recovered; a particularly fine example of raised beach can be seen at Harris, at Rum's south-west coast. Glacial debris was dumped at Kinloch, producing a well-drained terrace at the head of the sheltered sea-loch that was ideal for settlement; more was left in Kilmory Glen but prehistoric remains have yet to be uncovered there. Glen Guirdil, overlying lava bedrock, would also have been reasonably fertile. Elsewhere the soils are relatively poor, acidic and not very well drained, so would have tended to favour the accumulation of peat with blanket bogs in places. It is unlikely that smaller islands such as Canna and Muck supported much in the way of woodland, but one as large and as varied as Rum would have had good cover, at least in the sheltered glens.

As soon as the ice began to melt about 10,000 years ago, sea levels would still have been oscillating and the climate unpredictable. Soils would still have been forming and stabilising so the vegetation may have been slow to establish. Open conditions would have persisted longer than on the mainland, before the first birch, pine and juniper started to take hold. By the time humans arrived on the scene much of the island would have been mainly heath and grassland, with scattered woodland copses. From about 8000 years ago birch and hazel were dominant with ferns, sedges and a variety of herbs as ground cover below the trees. Alder, which thrives in more waterlogged conditions, was by now well established further inland near the Long Loch. By 6500 BP oak had been added to the woods on the drier ground with alder still very abundant elsewhere.

Charcoal from forest fires appears in the peat cores at this time and since alder and hazel are fairly resistant to fire they would have tended to thrive at the expense of other species. The fires were probably natural.

However, humans may have been burning off some scrub to create open areas or to produce early spring growth for deer (if they existed in Rum then) to browse; also, being relatively fire-tolerant, hazel scrub would be encouraged to provide a larger crop of its nutritious nuts. At the site of the Kinloch excavation there is a break in a gap in radiocarbon dates from 7000 to 5000 BP indicating a reduction in human activity. At the same time burning became less obvious in the peat cores but natural fires would have found it hard to take since the climate, and hence the ground, was much wetter.

Cultivation by Neolithic peoples probably began at Kinloch from 4700 BP and was associated with a rapid decline in tree pollen, even alder, as scrub was being cleared to create farmland. The brushwood in the watercourse on the site dates from this time, and it included a variety of tree species: oak, birch, hazel, rowan, crab apple and hawthorn but mostly alder. The weather had become stormy and wet, favouring soil erosion, which is perhaps why the excavated watercourse became clogged up. Inland tree cover was much reduced and blanket bog spread, with heath or acid grassland only on the drier ground. Despite the continued deterioration in climate, cultivation had became intense 3000 years ago and the natural vegetation cover in Rum began to approximate to what exists nowadays. Significant patches of woodland lingered until the end of the eighteenth century but today only isolated relict trees survive where they have been inaccessible to grazing animals; they include hazel, birch, oak, rowan, holly, aspen, hawthorn and sallows, all of which would have contributed to the woodland cover in Rum at one time.

I had mapped out many structures all over the island during my study of the shielings and this was to form a useful background for a more thorough field survey undertaken by archaeologists from the Royal Commission on the Ancient and Historical Monuments of Scotland during the summer of 1983. They could not, however, make any more detailed examination or excavation of any of the antiquities they encountered. Cairns of indeterminate date and function are listed at Guirdil, A'Bhrideanach and Kilmory. One or two mounds of stones on the raised beach at Harris may just be heaps of stone cleared from areas of cultivation – but there is at least one, more structured stone setting nearer the shore, beside some low walls and hut circles, that looks to my inexperienced eye to be a very ancient date (NGR: NM 342955). Two others higher up the slope (NM 344965), to the right of the modern road at a spot called Hugh's Brae, are very similar and I suspect they might be kerb cairns – but at first the Royal Commission preferred to classify them as hut-circles.

Otherwise, Bronze Age remains seem to be scarce in Rum. The transition from the Neolithic is unclear in a remote, uninvestigated locality such as Rum. Bronze tools were unlikely to have been manufactured locally because of lack of resources. Furthermore they would take much longer to reach the island by trade; if indeed the island still supported much of a human population in those inclement times. It is now known that around 1150 BC a period of bad weather in northern Europe – initiated by an eruption of Hecla in Iceland – caused many marginal Bronze Age settlements to be abandoned.

In 1993 David Miller discovered a midden site amongst the boulders of a scree slope at Papadil (NM 365923). It spilled from a small natural 'cave', long used as a shelter by feral goats and obscured by bracken each summer. The midden contained large quantities of shells, including limpets, and a few bones were visible. Miller picked up five small sherds of pottery together with a fragment of a flattish vessel of copper alloy. Caroline Wickham-Jones visited the site the following year and recovered a larger portion of a small, round-bottomed bowl inside the cave. She described the finds in the *Glasgow Archaeological Journal* vol. 18 (1995), pp. 73–5. The bowl would have had an internal diameter of 140 mm and a thickness of 8 mm. It had fired to an orange-red colour with a darker interior. Decoration comprised impressed dots in an undulating line around the upper part of the bowl. There were also dots around the rim, inside which was another impressed decoration apparently made with a fingernail. Inside the base of the pot there were impressions of straw. The outer surfaces of two of the finer sherds of pottery were covered with grass or cereal head impressions. Caroline Wickham-Jones noted how round-bottomed vessels were common in the Neolithic but the everted rim of this one was more typical of the Iron Age or later; the copper find would support this later date.

Skills in working with iron were first introduced to Scotland sometime around the middle of the first millennium BC, probably by a Celtic people originally from the Continent. As they gradually integrated with the indigenous population (rather than conquering them), they introduced several characteristic architectural monuments: timber-laced hillforts, duns, wheelhouses, brochs, crannogs or lake dwellings and souterrains or earth-houses. Unfortunately, Rum is deficient in this proud heritage, boasting only a few crude promontory forts along its coastline. The one at Shellesder (NG 326020) was first recognised and described in 1967. An arc of walling at least 3 m thick was built across the neck of the promontory with an entrance towards the southern end nearly a metre wide. Inside this cliff-girt defence an area about 45 m by 30 m includes at least one oval enclosure about 5 m in diameter. The RCAHMS survey located two less well-preserved forts at Kilmory (NG 350042) and at Papadil (NG 361919). Another natural feature to the east of the raised beach at Harris could have served a similar defensive function. Doubtless Kinloch was also occupied at this time, but any structures have been obscured by modern developments. Until all these areas are excavated we will remain in comparative ignorance of this period in Rum's prehistory.

The first written references to these early Highlanders came from the Romans. Agricola led an expedition north in AD 81, his troops marching through the coastal forests of Angus with a support fleet sailing just offshore. They were subject to guerrilla raids by the local Caledonian tribes who finally amassed somewhere on the slopes of Bennachie, to confront the legions once and for all. It was Agricola's son-in-law, Tacitus, who described, probably with a considerable degree of literary licence, how a warrior lord called Calgacus – 'a man of outstanding valour and nobility' – decried the invading Romans in a diatribe that ended with the now immortal phrase: 'they create a desolation and call it peace'. The battle of Mons Graupius concluded in a hopeless defeat for the Caledonians but, with the threat of winter approaching, Agricola declined to pursue his advantage. Instead he sent his fleet on a sabre-rattling voyage round the north of Scotland. Caledonia, in its hour of defeat, was to remain unconquered and its people 'the last men on earth, the last of the free'.

Using information gleaned by naval expeditions such as this, the Greek scholar Ptolemy was able to produce the first map of Scotland in AD 150. Unfortunately it shows a 90 degree error in orientation that was to be perpetuated in maps and gazeteers for many centuries to come. Although Ptolemy named quite of few of the islands, the precise identity of some remains a matter of debate. 'Scitis' is obviously Skye, 'Malaius' Mull and 'Botis' Bute. T. C. Lethbridge maintained that 'Dumna' must be Rum, with a mistake in the initial letter, and his interpretation is still often quoted to this day. It now seems certain however that Dumna refers to the Isle of Lewis.

Ptolemy portrayed the territories of Highland tribes, amongst them the Caledonians, but by about AD 300 the word 'Picti' first appeared in Roman accounts – probably a nickname for the same people and meaning 'the painted men' from their habit of adorning themselves with warpaint or tattoos. Antiquaries liked to see the Picts as a problematical people but it seems reasonable to think of them as a confederacy of racial and cultural groups (including the aboriginal Bronze Age peoples) with a strong, if not dominating Celtic influence, and bound loosely together by the menace of the Romans.

The tangible artefacts we can assign to the Picts are few, notably the distinctive symbol stones that have been dubbed the finest stone sculptures of the Dark Ages. They are particularly abundant in north-east Scotland but extend northwards to Orkney and Shetland, and westwards to the Hebrides. Two or three are to be found in Skye; but when the Irish monk St Columba visited that island in the sixth century he required the services of an interpreter, so different was his Celtic tongue from that of Skye's

Pictish inhabitants. It is likely that the population of Rum, albeit small at that time, was Pictish in origin.

By the sixth century Scots from Ireland had established a powerful kingdom called Dalriada in Argyll, with Dunadd as its capital. Columba came from Derry in northern Ireland around AD 563 to exile himself at Iona where he established a monastery which was to become a renowned centre of learning and spirituality.

Columba began to spread the Gospel with missions to Skye and to the capital of the northern Picts at Inverness, but it was a colleague, St Donnan, who laboured most in the northern Highlands and Islands. Chapels dedicated to him are scattered from the Outer Hebrides to Wester Ross and are perhaps indicative of his efforts. But he wanted to make his base in the Isle of Eigg and approached his mentor Columba for blessing. The old Abbot of Iona was reluctant, however, foreseeing that Donnan's mission would end only in bloodshed – what the monastic community came to know as 'red martyrdom'. And so it came to pass. Twenty-three years after Columba died, on 17 April 617, Donnan of Eigg together with 150 of his followers were slain. The murderers were probably from the nearby mainland, fearful of a Gaelic expansion from Dalriada into Pictland. That fateful day is still commemorated by the people in Eigg.

Devotion to Columba or Colum Cille lingers even to this day but it was especially strong, not surprisingly, among the generations of monks who succeeded him. Many wrote poetry extolling his piety, humanity and virtue, not least Beccan mac Luigdech, distantly related to Columba through the influential and powerful Irish clan Ui Neill. It may have been as a monk at Tech Conaill in Leinster that Beccan began to develop his bardic skills. At some time before AD 623 he became a monk at Iona, and then a hermit, possibly in Rum.

At this time the Celtic Church was remote from Rome and chose to adhere to the traditional method of calculating Easter Day. It also retained the old tonsure, which shaved the forehead rather than the crown of the head. Under persistent pressure from the mother Church in Rome, the Celtic monks eventually began to come round. The monastery of Durrow in Ireland, for instance, conceded in AD 632 or 633. Its abbot, Cummian, then wrote asking Iona to adopt the new ways in a letter to Columba's successor, Abbot Segene, and in a second to *Beccanus solitarius* – Beccan the hermit – 'his own dear brother in the flesh and the spirit'.

This suggests that Beccan may have been related to the abbot, and seems to have been a figure of some eminence. His being a recluse may bear this out, as 'white martyrdom' was a privilege reserved for those of high sprirtual achievement. Segene must have refused the request for, in 640, the Pope-elect had to ask again. (Iona did not yield until 716.)

Although Beccan was not an uncommon name it is perhaps unlikely

that there should have been two of them associated with Iona at this time.
The poetry of Beccan mac Luigdech certainly indicates a familiarity with
the life of a hermit and the risks of reaching remote islands in small skin
boats. In his *Last Verses (Tiugraind Beccain)* he wrote of Columba:

> – in scores of curraghs with an army of wretches
> he crossed the long-haired sea ...
> He crossed the wave-strewn wild region,
> foam-flecked, seal-filled, savage, bounding,
> seething, white-tipped, pleasing, doleful.

In this recent translation by T. O. Clancy and G. Markus in *Iona: the
earliest poetry of a Celtic monastery* (1995), Beccan then went on to describe
the rigours of Columba's white martyrdom:

> Beloved of God, he lived against a stringent rock,
> a rough struggle, the place one could find Colum's bed.
> He crucified his body, left behind sleek sides;
> he chose learning, embraced stone slabs, gave up bedding.
> He gave up beds, abandoned sleep – finest actions –
> conquered angers, was ecstatic, sleeping little.

It is perhaps more certain that the next brief references to Beccan in
Irish texts refer to the poet, if not the hermit too, as the same person. The
Annals of Tigernach reported how 'Beccan of Rum reposed in the island of
Britain'. The *Annals of Ulster* stated simply that Beccan of Rum 'reposed',
while the *Martyrology of Tallaght* and the *Four Masters* (a compilation
of all the Irish sources available at the time) went as far as 'Beccan of
Rum died in Britain on 17 March'. The dates of all these three entries
about *Beccan Ruimm* (the Gaelic genitive form 'of Rum') ranged from
AD 675 to AD 677. *Tigernach*, however, added that 'a brilliant comet
star was seen in the months of September and October', so the scholar
A. O. Anderson, in his *Early Sources of Scottish History*, took this to indicate
that the actual year of Beccan's death (whether it took place in Rum, Iona
or elsewhere) would have been AD 676.

It is likely that Beccan the solitary found spiritual isolation at Papadil
at the southernmost extremity of the island, and within sight of Iona itself.
Certainly the name translates as 'the dale of the priests' but it is a Norse
word and the Vikings were not to appear in the Hebrides for a century after
Beccan had died. Perhaps his former presence there made Papadil a special
place of pilgrimage for his successors. There is nothing there today that
would suggest a cell or chapel, but it is a well-chosen spot. From the sea
it looks an unlikely landfall but behind the tiny boulder beach, protected
by reefs offshore, hides a sunny little glade and a secluded freshwater
loch. A copse of trees was planted there early last century (to surround a

shooting lodge built on the loch shore), and doubtless in the seventh century a natural scrub woodland thrived there too.

Two Celtic crosses exist on the island today – neither of them at Papadil. In July 1886 the antiquary T. S. Muir visited Rum overnight and in his *Ecclesiastical Notes on some of the islands of Scotland* recorded that

> in a small burying ground, prettily situated on the shore at Kilmory, there is a chapel of which only some obscure traces remain. Near to where it stood there is a slender pillar incised with a plain cross.

The name Kilmory is a dedication to the Virgin Mary, 'Cill' being the Gaelic word for chapel. In 1694 Martin Martin had referred to a chapel at Kilmory, but what Muir described as such can only have been a ruinous blackhouse in the old hamlet around the burial ground. The nearest house is quite a substantial building and does not fit any description of a typical Celtic chapel. It is orientated north/south with a doorway in the centre of the east wall. There is no structure in the area orientated east/west, which tends to be a feature of these early churches.

The cross in the burial ground is still there, prostrate in one corner. But it was another 69 years after Muir's visit before it attracted any more interest. This time it was visited by the Royal Commission on the Ancient and Historical Monuments and Constructions of Scotland (RCAHMCS). This august body, or some individual from it, stayed no longer than Muir, and made straight for Kilmory:

> The churchyard contains a number of plain, unwrought head slabs and a shaft of hard sandstone 4¾ feet high and 9 inches in average width, with thickness of 6 inches, bearing at the top a small incised Latin cross surmounting a circular panel 8 inches in diameter, defined by two incised lines which contains a cross with expanding arms set saltire-wise; towards the base of the shaft are two parallel incised lines.

Obviously Muir's and the RCAHMCS accounts do not refer to the same cross – but they do refer to the same stone. When I first visited the Kilmory burial ground the cross slab of red sandstone was heavily encrusted with lichen on the upper face. Only the plain Latin cross on the underside, completely free of lichen, was visible. This was how Muir must have found the stone and he had probably turned it over when examining the plain cross underneath. In time the encrustation of lichen, by then on the underside and against the ground, was killed off. So when the RCAHMCS arrived it was the face with the Latin cross that was obscured by a thick growth of lichen, but the design on the underside was obvious in all its detail.

The Commissioners must have left the plain cross face down again, which was how it still lay when I arrived in Rum. In the meantime the

complex design on the upper face had become encrusted in lichen again.
This was so profuse that for many years I was unable to make anything of
it. Then in August 1977, one evening just before sunset, I took my mother
to visit Kilmory. Suddenly the light revealed all. Rays from the sun, so
low in the sky, shaved the topside face of the slab and highlighted in
shadow the cross set saltire-wise within its double circle. Archaeologists
refer to this as a 'marigold cross'.

A year later I decided to turn the marigold cross face down again to kill
off the lichen and in January 1980 was able to take a rubbing of the whole
design. This was posted to Ian Fisher of the RCAHMS (as it had since
become), who specialises in early Christian monuments. He assigned both
the plain cross and the marigold cross to the seventh or eighth century,
and suggested that together they marked not only a place of burial but a
place of worship in the secular settlement, a mission probably provided by
visiting monks. It was unlikely to have served as a grave marker, though
latterly it may have come to do so. Ian Fisher also drew attention to several
other marigold crosses of similar design, in both Scotland and Ireland.
Indeed, a small example is preserved in the Isle of Canna.

Ian Fisher also sent me a photograph of another cross slab that had
been found by a group of youngsters four years earlier on the beach at
Bagh na h-Uamha, south of Kinloch. They had reported their find to a
temporary warden supervising the island but – although I was resident in
Rum at that time – I did not hear about it. It was indeed fortunate that
the party's leader, Joe Keppie, had insisted they forward their photograph
to the RCAHMS. The stone had been lying in sand below the high-water
mark but despite numerous searches at low tide I was, for a long time,
unable to find it again. I had been aware that the naturalist Heslop
Harrison had recorded 'an incised cross in the cave' (which gives Bagh
na h-Uamha its name) in the years before the last war, but this cannot
now be found. It was a small stone and easily portable, and is presumed
to have been stolen. 'Its presence', he added, 'indicates that the cave may
have been used as a place of worship.'

Eventually in May 1982, I was searching the beach again and was
attracted to the only stone apparently large enough to fit the description,
lying half-buried in sand. I dug away at its narrow end with my hands and
could feel, with intense delight, a deeply incised cross on the underside.
My friend and I dug out the whole slab, about 5 feet long, but it was too
heavy to transport up the beach. It was certainly not as portable as Heslop
Harrison maintained – unless he was referring to yet another stone. Until
more help could be mustered, the slab was set up on a raft of driftwood to
stop it sinking again.

Two months later I returned with three other friends and found the
stone almost hidden by sand once more, with not a trace of its driftwood

platform. Even in summer and facing east, this beach must experience some heavy seas. The four of us rolled it up the beach on to dry land and a couple of weeks later I returned with a spade and set it upright – for posterity, it is hoped.

Ian Fisher described the design as 'an incised equal-armed cross with triangular terminals, raised on a shaft of the same height'. It is of similar date to the Kilmory stone but shows more similarity to the small cross incised on a stone preserved on the veranda of the Lodge in Eigg. He also thought it possible that Bagh na h-Uamha might have been connected with the hermitage of a Celtic monk; perhaps it was here and not to Papadil that Beccan had exiled himself in the seventh century?

PART II

Early History

Old Kenneth [Maclean] is more than a little proud of his name
and clan, in spite of all the change which has been going on in
the world during the last century. He has seen four new lairds in
Rum in succession in his own life-time; but he tells you with
pride that his progenitors have lived upon the island for eleven
generations, before he was born. He never wearies in talking, in
a dreamy way, of the Macleans of old; the Macleans of Duart,
in Mull; the Macleans of Coll, and of Muck, and of Rum, and
elsewhere – of their power, and their grandeur; now greatly
declined and drowned in the flood of change ... Kenneth is a man
of mark among the simple herdsmen and fishers who dwell in the
straggling line of huts upon the shore of Scresort Bay. In the first
place he is a far-off cousin of the great Maclean; and he doesn't
forget it ... and he is said to know more about the unwritten
traditions of Rum than any man living.

Edwin Waugh, 1882

3   *As Complete an Islander*

Mr Maclean, the Laird, had very extensive possessions, being
proprietor not only of far the greater part of Coll, but of the
extensive island of Rum, and a very considerable territory in Mull.

Dr Samuel Johnson, 1773

The first Scots began to arrive in Scotland sometime before AD 500. They
established a stronghold at Dunadd in Argyll, which became the capital
of the new colony, Dalriada. It was probably to Dunadd that Columba
came in 563 to seek permission from the then king of Scots, Aidan, to
establish his monastic community on Iona. The Dalriadan Scots led a
turbulent history that left them vulnerable to an invasion by the neighbouring Picts in AD 736. Hot on their heels came the Norsemen. The
Vikings first plundered Iona in 794 and, from settlements in Orkney
and Shetland, they repeatedly attacked both Dalriada and Pictland until
the kingdoms united under Kenneth Mac Alpin.

Unrest continued, however, until the tenth century, as the Norsemen
became a dominant force in the Hebrides, yet adopting the Christian faith
of the Scots. While the Norse language predominated amongst the place-
names in the northern islands, such as Lewis and Skye, it was to be Gaelic
that emerged as the native tongue of the Hebrides as a whole. Similarly,
although most of the high hills and some of the main glens in Rum possess
Norse names – Hallival, Askival, Dibidil, Papadil, for example – lesser
topographical features have mostly Gaelic names. It is often suggested

that the hills were known only as navigational aids and that the seafaring Norsemen did not actually settle on the island. But some less obvious features in Rum, such as Camas Pliascaig, also seem to have elements of Old Norse in their names.

Although there are no traces of any homesteads from the period, without detailed archaeological survey and excavation it is impossible to say that there were none. Furthermore, it is highly unlikely that the island, even one as wet as Rum, was not occupied; after all, from AD 800 to 1300 northern Europe enjoyed such clement weather that the Vikings even settled Greenland.

In 1949 a student called Drew Smith found a double stone burial cist just inland from Bagh na h-Uamha which he claimed was of Viking age; its exact location is no longer known although a photograph of the structure survives. There are several such burials known from Eigg and Canna. In Canna, too, are some boat-shaped settings of stones, one of which local legend maintains was the grave of a king of Norway. Just over a hundred years ago two curved pieces of wood about two metres long were uncovered below Laig farmhouse in Eigg and are thought to be the stem and stern posts of a Viking longship. Earlier in the nineteenth century, three burial mounds were excavated at Kildonan on the other side of Eigg, revealing several Viking relics including a silvered bronze brooch, an iron axe-head, two buckles and a beautifully ornate sword hilt – all of which are now in the National Museum of Scotland.

The museum also exhibits a Norse gaming piece or draughtsman that was found in the cave at Bagh na h-Uamha. It was made from the tusk of a whale called a narwhal. About 4.5 cm in diameter, it is intricately carved on one face with an interlaced design. Although Rum may not have proved particularly attractive for cultivation, the Vikings no doubt pursued the deer. Indeed, it seems likely that some hunting party may have been delayed on the hills after dark long enough to hear the burrow-nesting Manx shearwaters begin their ghostly nocturnal chorus. Unfamiliar with these noisy seabirds the Norsemen assumed them to be trolls and named the hill Trollval; today it still holds the greatest density of nest burrows of the whole Rum colony.

There can be little doubt that the Vikings regarded Rum, and its neighbouring islands, as part of their kingdom, which stretched from Shetland in the north to the Isle of Man and Ireland. They may well have subdued the local peoples but they also intermarried with them. When the Scottish throne entered a particularly turbulent period with its own noblemen, the field was left wide open for the emergence of Gaelic/Norse Lordship of the Isles.

Somerled, or *Somhairle macGhiolla Brighde*, the son of a Gaelic warrior named Gillebride, then entered the stage to become a key figure in

Hebridean history. He was a 'well-tempered man, in body shapely, of a fair piercing eye, of middle stature, and of quick discernment'. His rise to power was based on guerrilla tactics and a fleet of vessels, called birlinns, smaller and more manoeuvrable than Viking longships. This fleet, together with Somerled's own royal house, were based on Islay. This build-up of sea power enabled Somerled to extend his hold over the whole of the southern Hebrides. The Norse yet retained sovereignty over Man and the northern Hebrides, which would have included Rum.

Somerled was murdered in 1164 and his territories were divided between his surviving sons. As eldest, Ranald received Kintyre and Islay, and most of the Hebrides to the south of Ardnamurchan; later he was to inherit Garbhcriochan or Garmoran – the 'rough bounds' of Moidart, Morar, Arisaig and Knoydart – together with the islands of Bute and Arran. Another son Dugal inherited Lorne, Jura, Coll and Tiree (though his claim on Mull was later to be challenged by Ranald); and his descendants, the MacDougalls, established fortresses at Dunstaffnage and Dunollie near Oban.

But Ranald emerged all-powerful. When he died in 1207 his eldest son Donald took over most of the estates, and thus founded Clan Donald. Ranald's second son Ruari inherited the Garmoran lands. The brothers were both warlike by nature and aligned themselves to Norway rather than Scotland. In turn, the Scottish Crown was more interested in links with feudal England and the Continent beyond, ignoring the Hebrides to form an independent confederation of lordships, some Gaelic, some Norse. When Donald died in 1250 his eldest son Angus Mor of Islay inherited the dynasty of Clan Donald.

Alexander II, King of Scots, had tried unsuccessfully to subdue the Hebrides and evict the Norsemen, receiving support from the MacDougalls while Clan Ruari remained loyal to King Haakon of Norway. In 1260 his son Alexander III took up his late father's cause once more and encouraged his noblemen to raid the islands at every opportunity. In 1262, for instance, the Earl of Ross laid waste Skye and the surrounding islands, Rum amongst them. His forces sacked villages, desecrated churches and 'in wanton fury raised children on the points of their spears and shook them until they fell to the ground.' Many Hebridean chiefs, notably Ruari, appealed to Haakon of Norway for assistance.

The Norwegian king at once prepared for a major expedition to Scotland. Rounding Cape Wrath on 10 August 1263 to rendezvous with the Manx fleet at Kyleakin, Haakon then sailed south to meet Clan Ruari at Kerrera. His armada now numbered nearly 200 ships and 3000–4000 men. At Oban Haakon clapped in irons Alexander's vassal Ewen MacDougall of Lorne and it was with some reluctance that Angus Mor of Islay and the MacSweens joined the Norwegian force.

The Viking fleet, running short of provisions, anchored off Great Cumbrae in the Clyde. As Alexander had hoped, a westerly gale arose that raged for two days. Many Norse galleys, including Haakon's own, dragged their anchors and were carried ashore at Largs where they were overwhelmed by the Scots.

According to *Origines Parochialis: Vol. II*, Haakon's fleet sought shelter at the 'Isle of Rauney' which is interpreted as the Isle of Rum – doubtless in the safe anchorage of Loch Scresort on its east coast. By the end of October the ships had limped back to Orkney where Haakon fell ill and died in the early hours of 16 December. Alexander's troops, meanwhile, devastated the Hebrides, forcing many of the local chiefs to submit to his rule.

At the Treaty of Perth in 1266 Scotland concluded an agreement with Norway. For an initial lump sum of 4000 merks, and a further 100 merks to be paid annually in perpetuity, the Isle of Man and all of the Hebrides were ceded to Scotland. In granting amnesty to the Island chieftains who had supported Haakon, royal charters were awarded reaffirming their properties in return for fealty to the Scottish Crown. Clan Ruari were allowed to retain Garmoran. Although losing both Skye and Lewis, they acquired instead Uist, Barra, Eigg and Rum, all of which had formerly belonged to the King of Man.

When Alexander III died in a fall from his horse in 1286 and his only heir, his infant daughter, Margaret, maid of Norway, was drowned while returning across the North Sea, the throne of Scotland was contested. The Scottish aristocracy preferred Bruce while King Edward of England, predictably, favoured the weaker John Balliol. The Hebridean chieftains were divided; the MacDougall House of Lorne allied with Balliol, Angus Mor of Islay with Bruce. In an attempt to maintain law and order, John Balliol set up a system of sheriffdoms in 1292: eight davachs of land including the islands of Eigg and Rum were included within the sheriffdom of Skye. But these initiatives proved largely ineffective.

When Balliol finally abdicated, the Comyns took up his cause against the Bruces. Young Robert Bruce killed his rival John Comyn and was crowned in 1306. Three years later he confirmed by royal charter the entitlement of Ranald, son of Alan MacRuari, to lands that included six davachs of Eigg and Rum. Bruce's reputation was sealed when he routed Edward II at Bannockburn in 1314, with an army composed mainly of Celtic lords and including Angus Og of Islay (Angus Mor's son) and Ranald MacRuari.

The MacRuaris were again granted royal charters on their lands of Garmoran and the isles of Uist, Barra, Eigg and Rum, together with MacDougall's forfeited lands in Lorne and part of Comyn's lands in Lochaber. But Ranald MacRuari soon fell out with Bruce and forfeited his territories (only regaining them once David II ascended the throne).

Both Robert Bruce and Angus Og died in 1329, and Angus's son John of Islay fell heir to his father's estates. John married his third cousin Amy MacRuari eight years later, and when her brother Ranald was killed in a feud with the Earl of Ross in 1346 she took over the Garmoran lands, including Rum. John styled himself Lord of the Isles, and created an aggressively Gaelic institution that acted as patron to most of the lesser clans in the west. Over four generations it brought stability to the Hebrides, so much so that the Lordship's main residence at Finlaggan in Islay had no fortification.

Four years later John of Islay divorced Amy – it is said 'without any just reasons or any real cause of complaint against her good faith and faithful conduct'. But he still needed royal approval to retain his former wife's territories, so he married instead Margaret, the daughter of the Regent to the throne. When, in 1372, young Robert II himself was old enough to take over the crown he granted the Lord of the Isles royal charters both on his existing properties and on Garmoran. These lands by then amounted to all of the Hebrides except Skye, and most of the west coast from Glenelg to Kintyre, more extensive than either the ancient kingdom of Dalriada or indeed than Somerled's hard-won realm. However, Robert II did stipulate that John divide his properties between the children of both his marriages. To Ranald, his eldest son by Amy MacRuari (and the progenitor of Clanranald), he conceded half of South Uist, Eigg, Rum, Morar and Arisaig. His brother Godfrey was given the rest of South Uist, Canna, Sleat and Knoydart but in the end Ranald assumed control over them too. Donald, John of Islay's eldest son by Margaret, inherited the rest of the Lordship.

Donald was crowned third Lord of the Isles on the Isle of Eigg and a vivid description survives of the event. Chieftains from all the principal Hebridean families together with the Bishops of Argyll and the Isles attended. Donald stood on the Clan Donald stone of destiny, which had been carried from Islay for the occasion, as he swore to walk in the footsteps and with the uprightness of his predecessors. After mass was said a great feast was prepared that lasted a whole week, with entertainment from poets, bards and musicians.

Eventually Donald retired to a life of religious seclusion and died around 1422, to be succeeded as Lord of the Isles by his son Alexander. His warlike nature made his position seem precarious at times but in 1422 he was still able to bequeath to his fifteen-year-old son, John, the largest dominion in the north – except for that owned by the Crown itself.

James II of Scotland himself had only just emerged from a turbulent minority and was still putting his house in order when, two years later, John, fourth Lord of the Isles first rose up against him. John went down in history as 'a meek, modest man, brought up at court in his younger years, and a scholar more fit to be a churchman than to command so many irregular tribes of people'. Twice though he rebelled against the Scottish Crown and, remarkably, he emerged unscathed – although his son, Donald Dubh, was imprisoned. In 1494 John finally resigned his lands to James IV; it is said they were forfeited although no official document exists to confirm this.

When John of Islay died thirteen years later, in greatly reduced circumstances, he left no immediate heirs. James IV made frequent visits to the Hebrides, and although he conferred knighthoods on some of the important chiefs, he lost all their respect when he appointed a Campbell, Earl of Argyll, as his Lieutenant for the Isles. The Campbells thrived on the embers of the Lordship of the Isles and it was claimed that they often fomented clan feuds to advance their own fortunes.

Whenever the throne of Scotland demonstrated weakness or vulnerability the clan chiefs would attempt to restore the Lordship of the Isles such as on the death of James IV at Flodden in 1513. Although the next Stewart king, James V was, like his father before him, also a minor when he took the throne, he proved to be a harsh and tyrannical monarch. In 1540 he displayed the first real naval presence in the Hebrides, inviting many of the local chiefs on board his flagship only to carry them off to prison in Edinburgh. Some were liberated after yielding up hostages for their future allegiance, while others were detained until James died in 1542. He was succeeded by the infant Mary, Queen of Scots.

Once again the clans rebelled, this time under Donald Dubh, son of John the fourth Lord of the Isles, and who had just escaped from a long imprisonment in Edinburgh Castle. The clans rallied around him and ravaged the lands of Argyll. On 23 July 1545 Donald Dubh mustered his chiefs in Eigg to seek help from King Henry VIII, before withdrawing to Ireland to assemble men and ships. But English gold was slow in materialising and the clans quarrelled over its distribution. This last rebellion fizzled out and Donald died in Ireland shortly afterwards from a sudden fever. He had enjoyed only six years' freedom in his entire life, too brief to achieve the monumental task he had set himself.

John of Islay's death left a considerable power vacuum in the western Highlands and Islands, but then the Scottish Crown totally failed to replace it with anything else. As John Lorne Campbell of Canna commented: 'The Scottish Crown had at last succeeded in shooting down the eagle, but had thereby only let loose a flock of kestrels.' He quoted an account written in 1594 which claimed that 'the kingdom was so on fire with civil wars, was so polluted with massacre and bloodshed, that nought else seemed to exist but a perpetual shambles'.

The clans were feuding bitterly amongst themselves. In 1577, for instance, the Macdonalds were warring against the Macleods over disputed lands in Skye. In March of that year, a band of Macleods landed in Clanranald's Eigg where one of them apparently raped a local woman tending cattle. The menfolk came on the scene and captured the attackers. One account claims that the hands were cut off the man who had assaulted the woman, before the Macleods were bound hand and foot and set adrift in their boat. They eventually freed themselves and reached home to raise a war party to seek revenge.

The Macdonalds were prepared, however, and as soon as the Macleod galley was sighted they repaired to a cave on a remote shore. Although its entrance was narrow, it widened to form a chamber over 70 yards long, large enough for the 395 men, women and children living on Eigg to take refuge. The Macleods searched the island but found no one, except an old woman, whom they spared. In time one of the Macdonalds was sent outside to see if the coast was clear. Unfortunately there had been a light fall of snow in the meantime, so the Macleods were able to follow his footprints back to the cave.

A fire was lit at its mouth and everyone inside choked to death. When James Boswell was told the story in 1773 there were still skeletons in the cave, while in 1814 – 'in spite of the prejudices of his sailors' – Sir Walter Scott took the skull of a young woman home to Abbotsford as a souvenir. In 1845 Hugh Miller poignantly wrote that the floor of the cave resembled a charnel house:

> at almost every step we come upon human bones ... The skulls, with the exception of a few broken fragments, have disappeared; for travellers in the Hebrides have of late years been numerous and curious; and many a museum – that of Abbotsford among the rest – exhibits, in a grinning skull, its memorial of the Massacre at Eigg ... Enough still remains to show, in the general disposition of the remains, that the hapless islanders died under the walls in families, each little group separated by a few feet from the others.

If the entire population of Eigg did indeed die in this tragic incident, as is sometimes claimed, the island was very quickly repopulated, for in 1588 it suffered yet another devastating attack from Maclean of Duart. Yet by 1625 there were still 198 people on Eigg to be converted by the Irish Franciscan mission. As Hugh Miller's companion, the Small Isles minister, John Swanson, had so pertinently remarked regarding the Eigg Massacre: 'the less I enquired into its history ... the more I was likely to feel I knew something about it'.

While the Small Isles have so far played only a peripheral role in the history of the Hebrides, they – and Rum, in particular – assume more importance for one of the Lordship's vassal clans, the Macleans. Their rapid rise to power abounds in rich and vivid, though not always accurate, stories. J. P. Maclean's *History of the Clan Maclean* is a valuable source although at times it is somewhat flawed in its detail. The Macleans of Duart in Mull and a later offshoot, the Macleans of Coll, are central to the story of Rum.

Early in the fourteenth century, Angus Og (Robert Bruce's ally and father of John the first Lord of the Isles) accepted into his service a man called Gillean. Gillean had three sons but there was continuing dispute about whether Lachlan or Hector was the eldest, since this has a bearing on which branch of the Maclean clan is the most senior. Angus gave Lochbuie in Mull to Hector – Eachann Reaganach or 'Hector the Stern'. The other brother, Lachlan, he made Chamberlain of his house. This Lachlan the Wily, or Lachlan Lubanach, later married a granddaughter of Angus, and so acquired lands in Morvern, together with Duart Castle on Mull. Maclean tradition maintains that the brothers had to bully John, first Lord of the Isles, into sanctioning these land deals, which took place around 1360.

Lachlan of Duart's son, Hector Roy, or Red Hector of the Battles, had been made baillie of Coll and Tiree by Donald, second Lord of the Isles. The next Duart chief was Lachlan Bronnach – or 'swag-belly', because of his corpulency. There is a tale that one day he landed on Coll when it was owned by the Norsemen. Lachlan asked of a Maclean woman if he might have some food, but she refused since she did not think him worthy of it. Coll, she said, should belong to his clan, and she lamented that he did not have the courage to take it. Accordingly, Duart returned with a band of warriors and won over the island of Coll from the Norsemen. It was only then that the Lord of the Isles awarded Maclean of Duart a royal charter on the island.

From Lachlan Bronnach of Duart's first marriage his successor Lachlan Og was born. (Lachlan Bronnach also had an illegitimate son, Donald, who was given lands in Ardgour to form a third branch of the Macleans. Two sons from Lachlan Bronnach's second wife, Fionnaghal, were Neil of Ross and Iain or John Garbh – who was later to become the first Maclean of Coll and about whom more presently.) A great-great-grandson of Lachlan Og, Hector Mor, proved both an accomplished politician and a noble warrior, continuing a feud with Maclean of Lochbuie over seniority within the clan and renewing an ancient grievance against the Camerons. He came out in Donald Dubh's rebellion, and was taken prisoner by James V only to be released shortly afterwards. In 1561 he vented his wrath on Maclean of Coll, ravaging his lands and imprisoning his tenantry, bringing the family to the brink of ruin.

Hector Mor's grandson, Lachlan Mor, was to prove the most formidable warrior chief who ever held sway in Duart. He was, however, still a minor and his mother remarried. Somehow he came to the attention of James VI; he was thus raised in the safety of the royal court in Edinburgh while his stepfather ran the estates. At the age of eighteen Lachlan Mor reclaimed his inheritance, kidnapped his stepfather and had him beheaded at Breacachadh Castle in Coll. Although eventually knighted, Lachlan Mor trod a precarious line with the Scottish Crown, made a secret pact with Queen Elizabeth of England and constantly feuded with his neighbouring clans. He will raise his cruel and wily head later in our tale.

The Macleans of Coll – who are central to the Rum story – came into being when Lachlan Bronnach gave Coll to John or Iain Garbh, second son from his marriage to Fionnaghal Maclean of Harris. But, according to one tale, the first Maclean of Coll died young, and his widow remarried Roderick MacNeil of Barra. In another version, recorded by Boswell in 1773 and elaborated upon by Fitzroy Maclean, 27th Chief of the Macleans, in a collection of folk tales entitled *The Isles of the Sea*, it was Iain Garbh's own mother who married MacNeil.

The story goes on: when MacNeil of Barra came to live on Coll with his new wife, he despatched his young stepson to Barra, in the care of a nurse. Being a loyal Maclean the nurse soon discovered that MacNeil intended to do away with Young Coll, so she took herself, and her young charge, off to Ireland. There the boy grew up to be a fine, tall and handsome man, with the nickname Iain Garbh or sturdy John. Eventually Iain Garbh resolved to return to Coll and reclaim his inheritance, first landing on Mull to gather up some of his clansmen to help him. Together they swore to kill the first person they encountered when they set foot on Coll.

Who should Iain Garbh meet first, however, but his old foster-mother. She had aged considerably and did not recognise him at first. His companions urged Iain to keep to his word and kill the old crone but, of course, he could not. Together they set off for Grishipol House, where MacNeil and his wife were at dinner. A battle ensued, with fifty of Iain Garbh's supporters against 120 of MacNeil's. Young Coll found himself in hand-to-hand combat with his wicked stepfather. One of Coll's companions – an Gille Riabhach, the speckled youth – cut off MacNeil's head and the victory was secured. When Iain's mother appeared with her new baby, Iain Garbh stabbed it to death in her arms. He could not afford to spare the child, who in time might seek to avenge his father's death. Iain Garbh then sailed to Barra, which he possessed for several years. This event took place around 1430.

Some time afterwards Iain Garbh managed to secure Rum from Clanranald. Again there is a legend that he swapped it for a galley. But Clanranald held back as soon as he realised that the vessel's timbers were rotten – or 'nail-sick', in the literal Gaelic translation. So Iain Garbh Maclean imprisoned Clanranald on Coll for nine months until he finally confirmed the deal, together with 'a bond of future friendship and perpetual amity' to which subsequent Clanranald chiefs found it hard to adhere.

The earliest surviving account of Rum dates from around 1400, and was written by John of Fordun, Scotland's first historian. He described it as 12 miles long 'with few inhabitants'. The Scots mile was a third longer than the English equivalent, none the less John was well off the mark.

Around 1438, because Clan Cameron had deserted him at the Battle of Inverlochy, Alexander, the third Lord of the Isles, presented some of their lands in Locheil to Iain Garbh of Coll. James II then confirmed to Iain Garbh royal charters on all his lands in Coll, Mull, Rum, Morvern and Lochiel. Coll's only son and heir, also Iain – known as Mac Iain Ghairbh – chose to spend most of his time in these mainland properties in Lochaber. He was killed by Camerons who were attempting to regain their lands, and all the Coll charters on Lochaber were destroyed. Some Macleans managed to rescue Coll's wife and baby son, known as Iain Abrach, and, as a token of gratitude, one of their descendants was to be fostered and educated by the Macleans of Coll for generations to come. Subsequent Macleans of Coll were all referred to by the Gaelic patronymic Mac Iain Abrach, or son of John of Lochaber – an important point which will clear up some long-standing confusion over the ownership of Rum.

In 1493 when John, the fourth Lord of the Isles, had been forced to submit to James IV, he lost effective control of his lands. As a consequence his vassal clans all claimed their independence. As soon as they swore allegiance to the Crown instead, James would issue them with formal charters on all or most of their former lands. Thus the Macleans of Coll could now consider themselves an independent family in their own right. But their erstwhile superiors, the Macleans of Duart, long resented this new arrangement. Iain Abrach's three sons – John, Hector and Neil Mor – were all young at the time of his death, so Maclean of Duart used the opportunity to assume control, albeit temporarily, of the Coll lands.

A new High Dean of the Isles, Donald Monro, was appointed in 1549. One of his first acts was to compile an account of the Western Isles. He travelled extensively but it was probably his clerical colleagues who gave him much of his information. He described Rum thus:

> Sixteen mile northwart fra the Ile of Coll lyis ane Ile callit Rum, an Ile of 16 mile lang, 6 mile braid, in the neirest a forrest full of heich montanes and abundante of little deiris in it ...

Tactfully the Dean said that Rum 'perteins to the Laird of Coll callit Mc ane Abrie ... but obeyis to McGillane of Doward instantlie'. Mc ane Abrie was Maclean of Coll (Mac Iain Abrach) while McGillane of Doward was the land-grabbing Maclean of Duart, who had to give up the claim on Coll soon afterwards.

The fourth John Maclean of Coll died around 1558 and left no heirs so was succeeded by his brother Hector. A learned and talented man, Hector, fifth Maclean of Coll, was known as 'an Cleirach beag', the little clerk or scholar. On one occasion Allan nan Sop, piratical brother of Hector Mor Maclean of Duart, had swooped on Coll taking prisoner Hector, an Cleirach beag. In bondage in Tarbert Castle Hector of Coll composed a tune which he called Allan nan Sop's March; he performed it for his captor with such grace that he was accorded his freedom.

Hector of Coll, an Cleirach beag, married Maeve Macdonald of Islay, by whom his first son and heir, Hector Roy, was born. Although Hector kept an interest in the running of the estate, he officially made it over to his infant son the very next year. He later remarried Finovela MacAllister of Loup and had two sons: Allan, who founded the house of Achansaul, and John, who founded the Macleans of Grishipol. Both were to give rise to important Maclean families in Rum.

As J. P. Maclean, a historian of his clan, reminds us: 'Duart, who was generally acknowledged as chief of his clan, insisted that Coll should follow and serve him in all his private quarrels, like the other gentlemen of the tribe. Coll, however, who now held all his lands direct from the Crown, declined to follow his haughty chief, claiming the privileges of a free baron who owed no service but to the sovereign as his feudal superior.'

So in 1561, while Hector Maclean of Coll was away, Duart ravaged his lands and imprisoned his tenants, reducing the family to the brink of ruin. It was to be several years before Coll was to bring this outrage to the attention of the Privy Council and insist reparations be made.

When old Hector of Coll finally died, his brother, Neil Mor, third son of John Abrach, acted as guardian for the young heir Lachlan. The *Genealogical Account of the Macleans*, written by Allan Maclean of Crossapol sometime before 1833, takes up the story:

> When the said Lachlan Mor [of Dowart or Duart] heard of the Laird of Coll's death, and knowing that his son was very young, about four years, he immediately sent a party of his men with galleys to Coll, in order to take the island by force. This happened the very day that the Laird of Coll's remains were to be put in his grave. On their way to Kilinaig with the interment, being informed that a number of Macleans of Dowart landed at Coll and were on their way after them, Neil Mor and all his men returned. He left his brother's remains at Clabhach attended only with a few men, till he would return. He met his enemies at Struthan nan Ceann near Totronald, where Neil Mor and his men fought bravely and put all their enemies almost to the sword. After this Neil Mor got his brother interred about nightfall.

An amusing legend attached to the story is that while marching to engage with Lachlan Mor of Duart, Neil Mor discovered he had forgotten his flag. One old warrior immediately bared his bald head. 'This will do for a standard, and I promise that it will not go back a foot today,' he exclaimed. Duart's men were routed.

By 1578 Lachlan Mor seems to have been keen to avenge his defeat at Struthan nan Ceann and on 20 April invaded Coll, seized the castle and beheaded his own stepfather, Hector Allanson. Neil Mor fled to Ireland. About the end of 1596, when Lachlan Mor became sorely pressed by his vendetta against the Macdonalds, Neil Mor returned and tried his luck against Duart but was eventually brutally murdered by him.

A Spanish galleon from the defeated Armada, usually called the *San Juan Bautista* but sometimes the *Juan de Sicilia*, limped into Tobermory Bay in Mull in 1588. She was not, however, the pay ship of the fleet loaded with gold for the troops. Furthermore she was erroneously described as the *Florida* by J. P. Maclean in his *History of the Macleans*. The Spaniards demanded provisions from Sir Lachlan Mor Maclean of Duart. In return, Duart was given the services of a hundred Spanish marines from the ship. In November, together with a band of his own clansmen, they 'corned, wracked and spoilled' the islands of Rum, Muck, Canna and Eigg. 'And in maist barborous, shameful and cruell maner, byrnt the same Illes, with the haill men, weimen and childrene being thairintill, not spairing the pupillis and infantis.'

The Spanish captain then demanded the return of his men, but Maclean kept three as hostages to ensure that he was paid for the supplies he had provided. In retaliation the galleon took a Maclean hostage, who succeeded in blowing up the ship, with 300 souls on board. Gaelic tradition has it that one of the Macleans had shown an unseemly interest in a Spanish lady aboard, and the ship was blown up by the page of his jealous wife.

Maclean of Duart, already suspected of being an agent of Queen Elizabeth, was immediately denounced as a rebel for treating with the Spanish against the Macdonalds, who were King James's subjects. He was imprisoned in Edinburgh Castle but got out on bail, which he gladly forfeited. Later, Duart seems to have won a pardon from the king for his massacre in the Small Isles but James was more reluctant to forgive the destruction of the Spanish galleon.

By 1593 young Lachlan Maclean of Coll was old enough to take over his inheritance and petitioned the Privy Council for the return of £20 land in Coll, £12 in Quinish, Mull, £4 in Rum and £4 in Morvern, which Sir Lachlan Mor of Duart possessed yet again. Upon a penalty of 10,000 merks Duart had to yield up the properties he had seized. The old troublemaker was killed two years later, with hundreds of his clansmen, at Bloody Bay off Islay in a fierce battle against the Macdonalds. This long-standing feud broke the power of the Macdonalds and sorely drained that of the Macleans of Duart.

In 1567, when his mother Mary, Queen of Scots, had been made prisoner in England, King James VI was only a year old. His realm was being ruled by a succession of quarrelsome regents, and James was not yet twelve when he took over the throne. Spindle-legged, goggle-eyed and sloppy-mouthed, he was, in fact, to prove surprisingly competent as a ruler. He assumed the Western Isles to be much richer than they actually were, and around 1593 he seems to have had a report compiled on their resources and potential:

> Romb is ane Ile of small profit, except that it conteins mony deir, and for sustenation theirof the same is permittit unlabourit, except two townis. It is thrie miles of lenth, and als maekle of breid, and all hillis and waist glennis, and commodious only for hunting of deir. It is perteinis heretablie to ane Barron callit the Laird of Callow, quha is of McClanes kin, but is possest and in the handis of Clan-Rannald. It is ten merk land, and will raise 6 or 7 men.

Clanranald owned Eigg and 'possessed' both Canna, from the Bishop of the Isles, and Rum, from Maclean of Callow or Coll. Clanranald's hold on Rum seems to have been only temporary, and may have been inspired by the belligerent way Maclean of Coll had acquired the island nearly two hundred years previously.

Since Elizabeth had no heirs, James VI was only too aware that one day he would mount her throne. In 1603, as King James I, he finally forsook Edinburgh for London. But he chose not to forget even the furthest-flung outposts of his new kingdom. The rebellious Hebridean chiefs could no longer take advantage of avaricious English monarchs intent upon winning over the Scottish realm. Now instead they were up against the combined resources of a united kingdom. Also, James had set about planting Lowland Scots settlers in Ulster, which created a wedge between the Highland chiefs and their Irish allies. The Western Isles may have become more remote from central government in London but at the same time they found themselves isolated from those who might have aided them to rise up against it.

Only six years after the Union of the Crowns James coerced nine Hebridean chiefs to sign the Statutes of Iona (1609) in which they agreed to swear allegiance both to the Monarch and the Episcopalian Church. Since these same Celtic nobles were renowned for their 'extraordinair drinking of strong wynis and acquavitae', they were forbidden to import wines and spirits. In addition they were prohibited from bearing firearms and had to limit the size of their households. As a measure of the Maclean of Duart's continuing influence, if not preferential treatment, his immediate entourage could consist of eight gentlemen, while Macdonald, Macleod of Harris and Clanranald were limited to only six each, Mackinnon and Lachlan Maclean of Coll to only three each.

Furthermore any gentleman worth in goods up to sixty cows had to send their eldest sons to be educated in the Protestant Lowlands. This was extended in 1616 when the Privy Council demanded that none of the sons could inherit unless they could speak, read and write in English. These acts were not easily enforced and Clanranald, amongst others, remained devoutly Catholic. Many clans were also able to retain weapons. Nevertheless these restrictions spelled the beginning of the end for the Gaelic language and culture, and were to introduce an increasing gulf between the chiefs and their tenants.

Towards the end of the sixteenth century, the reformed Church became interested in a series of maps and descriptions of Scotland by Timothy Pont; indeed it is possible they may even have commissioned them. Pont is rather an enigmatic figure; the son of a Moderator of the General Assembly of the Church of Scotland, he graduated from St Andrews University around 1583 and spent the next twelve years travelling the length and breadth of Scotland making rudimentary, but often quite detailed maps with accompanying notes. He died around 1612 without ever seeing his maps published. His manuscripts fell into the hands of a dealer before passing, in the 1630s, to the Blaeu family of Amsterdam. Volume V of Joan Blaeu's *Atlas Novus* was published in 1654 and contained forty-nine of Pont's plates, making Scotland one of the best-mapped countries of the day.

Pont's manuscripts eventually found their way to the Advocates' Library in Edinburgh – now incorporated into the National Library of Scotland. Like all his maps, Pont's survey of the Small Isles portrayed as many settlements and churches as physical features. Unfortunately Rum was orientated upside down with Canna wrongly placed to its north-east instead of to the west. Pont portrayed the Harris and Kilmory rivers and the Rum Cuillin, with Bin Moir [Ben Mor] as its highest mountain – obviously Askival. He showed only one loch, named Sandegorry, which interestingly enough is still referred to as Sandy Corrie today. The main sea-loch, which he placed in the south-west, was called Loch Screspoirt but the two main settlements he located at Kilmory (with its church marked) and, enigmatically, Kaming. This last must surely be a Dutch cartographer's wild interpretation of Pont's handwritten word 'Glenharie'. Interestingly, too, the north and east sides of Rum were shown to be quite well wooded.

Pont's description of Rum might well have been second-hand, since the crudeness of his map suggests he himself may never have visited the island. Much later, his account was published in *Geographical Collections* relating to Scotland, Vol. II, compiled by Walter Macfarlane:

Rum is ane big Illand being on the Westsyde of Eig and on the
southeast syde of Canna. This illand appertaines to the Laird of Colla,
containing thereintill but two tounes of Cornelands. One of these two
tounes upon the Northwestsyde of the bigg illand of Rum, and another
toune on the West and Northwest syde thereoff. The toune which is
on the Northwest syde thereoff is called Kilmoir in Rum and the other
Glenharie in Rum, the Illand is verie profitable for there is abundance of
butter, cheese and milk in this Illand for there is no Cornelands in it, but
such as doth grow in these two tounes forsaid, but it is verie good for
goods to feed intill the respect that it is full of muires, mossis, glenns,
hills and very bigg mountaines, there is verie manie Deare in this Illand
and certaine foullis which will be taken in these mountaines and are
exceedingly fatt of the fattest birds of foulis which is in all the sea, they
are no bigger than a dove and somewhat les in bigue. Somewhat grey
in coloure of their feathers being of the most delicate birds to be eaten
that is bred within the whole Illand, except that doe taste oyld.

Macfarlane also included the following, obviously derived from the same
source but probably a later translation:

Rum is a big Iland upon the Westsyde of Eig, and upon the southeast
of Canna, it perteyneth to the Laird of Cola, it hath two tounes one
upon the nordwest syde cald Kilmore the uthir upon the southwest syde
called Glenharie, it hath no corneland but about the said two tounis,
the rest is for pasture, it hath great mountayns and many dear, more
it hath certaine wild fowles about the bigness of a dow, grey coloured,
which are scarce in uthir places, good meat they are, but that to them
who are not acquainted, they tast sumwhat wild.

In August 1617 Lachlan Maclean, seventh of Coll, received a charter for
six-merk land on the Isle of Muck – another of the Small Isles, formerly
in the possession of the MacIans of Ardnamurchan – from Andrew Knox,
Bishop of the Isles, on the condition that he and his successors paid 16 bols
of barley annually. This was confirmed in a royal charter from James VI
& I in 1621. Five years later Bishop Thomas Knox reported:

Coll belonging to the Laird of Coll is 8 mylles in lenth, 4 in breid, peyis
to the Bischope with the thrid of the teind of his twentie merk land of
the Quiynische [Quinish] in Mull 100 merkes yeirlie ... Muck, ane
small island conteining only twa tounnes, belonges to the Laird of Coll,
peyies ane chalder of beir.

Lachlan Maclean, seventh of Coll, married Florence Macleod of
Dunvegan. He was a Presbyterian and is thought to be the last laird of Coll
who was unable to write his own name. His eldest son and heir was another

Iain or John Garbh, a temperate, hospitable man of great wisdom and piety, a harpist and a composer of music. The couple's second son was Hector, who in 1632, with the consent of his elder brother, inherited the Isle of Muck. It seems Hector had first trained for the ministry but later commanded a company of Coll men in Montrose's army, distinguishing himself at the battle of Kilsyth. One night a band of MacIan cattle thieves landed on Muck and when the laird tried to stop them making off with his cattle he was surrounded and killed. His son Lachlan fought at Sheriffmuir in 1715. The Macleans of Muck persisted as a cadet branch of Coll until 1799, when Clanranald repossessed the island in payment of debts owed by Lachlan Maclean, sixth of Muck, an absentee landlord, veteran of the American War of Independence (1775–82) and latterly resident Governor of the Tower of London.

John Garbh, eighth of Coll, married Florence, sister of Hector Mor Maclean of Duart. In accordance with family tradition he had made out the estates to his eldest son, another Hector Roy, who proved quite a warrior. He fought at the battle of Inverlochy in 1645 and at Inverkeithing five years later. He got the estates deeply into debt and died in 1676, four years before John Garbh himself. Hector Roy, however, left two sons of his own. Lachlan, the eldest, was a man of culture and a good poet but he followed in the military footsteps of his father. Serving with a Scots Regiment in Holland, he forced many of his tenants to enlist before he was drowned in the River Lochy in 1687. His only son, John, was a youth of great promise but when eighteen years old found himself caught up in a riot in Edinburgh and was killed by shrapnel from a grenade lobbed at the crowd. So his uncle, Donald, became the 12th Laird of Coll.

Donald had been striving to restore the burdened estates all the time his elder brother Lachlan had been in the army, and had been tutor to his young nephew, John, when he was tragically killed in Edinburgh. A devout Protestant, it was he who 'encouraged' his tenants in Rum to turn away from Catholicism; a story which will be recounted in a subsequent chapter. Donald died in 1729, much respected throughout his seventy-three years.

Donald's son, Hector, tall, handsome and dignified, successfully accomplished the restoration of the estates, with a variety of lucrative enterprises including stock breeding, arable farming, fishing, quarrying, distilling, brewing, money-lending and shop-keeping. He was the last Maclean of Coll to retain a harper for the entertainment of his household. He wisely deterred his tenantry from joining the Jacobite Rising in 1745 but his headstrong brother Lachlan ignored this advice and had to be disinherited as a result. Hector was married twice – both Campbell ladies – but left no sons, so his surviving brother Hugh became the 14th Maclean of Coll. When the two ends of Coll, belonging to the Duke of Argyll, fell vacant, Hector Maclean had snapped up the tenancy, prepared to 'go to the length of his tether rather than let a Campbell into Coll'. But when the rents were raised in 1769 his brother Hugh was more reluctant to pay up. Five years earlier Hugh had bought a house in Aberdeen, where his children were educated. He had shared his brother's business acumen and, leading such a comfortable life, saw no need to rack rent his tenants like so many of his peers. In 1779 he became Provost of Old Aberdeen, a generous old man, if somewhat eccentric. Married to Janet Macleod of Talisker Hugh had seven sons and died in 1786.

His eldest son, Donald, had entertained Johnson and Boswell in 1773 (an encounter about which more anon) and was already taking a keen and enterprising role in running the estates – but not as far as encouraging emigration. Johnson found that the people of Coll had 'not learnt to be weary of their heath and rocks but attend to the agriculture and dairies without listening to American inducements'. Soon afterwards Donald, Young Coll, was tragically drowned in a boating accident off Ulva. Hugh's next son, Alexander, was only twenty at the time. Before taking over from his father he went on to study law and served as an officer in a local Fencible Regiment. While in Ireland he intervened with a major on behalf of one of his clansmen who was to be flogged. The pompous major, humiliated in front of the ranks, challenged Maclean to a duel with swords. Alexander Maclean was so well respected by his men, however, that they threatened to kill the major if he harmed him. Prudently the major declined to turn up for the duel.

In his book *Clan Gillean*, the Rev. Alexander Maclean Sinclair, described Alexander, the 15th Maclean of Coll, as 'independent and somewhat quick-tempered, manly, obliging and benevolent, treating his tenants with thorough kindness. He was a chieftain of great popularity.' He married Catherine Cameron of Glendessary, by whom he had a son Hugh, and six daughters; the fourth, Maria, married Alexander Hunter of Edinburgh, who, we shall see, supervised the 1826 clearance of the tenantry in Rum in favour of sheep farming. In 1814 Alexander bought back Muck from Clanranald's executors, intending to exploit its kelp resources. But this speculation, as indeed the kelp boom throughout the Highlands and Islands, was no longer viable and Maclean of Coll soon found himself heavily in debt.

His son Hugh had been born in 1782 and, according to the Rev. Maclean Sinclair, assumed the running of the estates in 1828, but it is possible he took over before this. The historian went on to describe him as a kind-hearted man, well liked by his tenants although a government document of 1849 added: 'Mr Maclean always acted most liberally when he had it in his power to do so but, unfortunately, he has no longer the ability.' Although the Coll estates were already burdened Hugh Maclean added to the debts by purchasing Ben More in Mull and, around 1825, building himself an elegant mansion house at Drumfin (later called Aros House) near Tobermory. He moved there in 1828 and the family never again lived in Coll. His father died at Quinish in Mull in 1835. Faced with severe financial difficulties, it may be more in Hugh's character rather than his father's, and certainly in his tenant Dr Maclean's character, to have instigated the removal of the Rum people in 1826.

Hugh's first wife, to whom he had four daughters, was Miss Janet Dennistoun. Eleven years later in 1825 he remarried Miss Jane Robertson and his first son, Alexander, was born the following year. Alexander, 16th and last Maclean of Coll, is described by J. P. Maclean as 'tall, athletic and kind ... inheriting in a remarkable degree the characteristics of his family, great benignity and kindliness of disposition, which made his forefathers among the most popular landlords of their day.' In 1849 Alexander emigrated to Natal in South Africa where he died in 1875, aged forty-seven, never having married. His next brother John Norman, a distinguished soldier, retired to live in Brighton where he died in 1882, leaving three daughters. When Hugh's two other sons, William and Hugh – also soldiers – died, the family of Coll (*Sliochd Iain Gairbh*) in direct line, became extinct. But we are now ahead of our story.

4 Piety and Virtue

'where convenient means may be had' a school shall be established
in every parish in the kingdom and 'a fit person appointed to
teach ... upon the expense of the parishioners.'

Privy Council of Scotland, 1616

In 1609 James VI had ordered the Bishop of the Isles to meet with several West Highland chiefs at Iona. He decreed that they were to abandon both their warlike habits and their pursuit of Roman Catholicism. But in actual fact these Statutes of Iona – as they came to be known – made little impact. The Hebrides strived to remain true to Rome and, throughout the seventeenth and eighteenth centuries, maintained links with other Catholic countries. An Irish Franciscan College had been founded at Padua in Italy in 1606 which became, according to the late Dr John Lorne Campbell in his book *Canna: The Story of a Hebridean Island*:

> a great centre of Gaelic learning in exile, producing heroic missionaries to work in Ireland and Gaelic Scotland in the darkest days of their history ... Appeal to the Irish Franciscans for help was made at a time when there was not one priest left in the Highlands and Islands and not a single Gaelic-speaking student at the Scottish exiled seminaries in Rome, Douai or Paris. Irish Gaelic speakers at the time could easily make themselves understood in the Hebrides.

The first mission was sent in 1619 but no account of it survives. A more concerted effort was made in 1624 which involved Father Cornelius Ward. Men such as he risked imprisonment from the Protestant authorities and lived in constant poverty and discomfort. Indeed Father Ward spent two years in prison in London on his way back from Scotland in 1629.

Father Ward's report, in Latin, was not published until 1964, with an English précis by Father Cathaldus Giblin. Father Ward reached the Small Isles on 28 August 1625 and Dr Campbell kindly provided me with a translation of Ward's notes by Dom Denys Rutledge. On 11 October 1625 Ward wrote:

> I was glad to be able to cross to the island of Rum [from Eigg] with his [Clanranald's] brother and other gentlemen. This island, a little under 12 miles in length, has three villages; it is all so wild and mountainous as to make habitation difficult. We were compelled by the wind to stay here till the fourth day, during which time one of the two better class of the village, with his wife and son and fourteen others, were delivered from the darkness of unbelief and added to the roll of the faithful.

In the Minutes of the Synod of Argyll (1639–1651), we are told:

> Because that the four yles of Muk, Canna, Rowm and Eig are in the sea far distant from any continent and that it is thought they are nearer the yle of Skye than any other place, therefore it is thought necessare that they be annexed to Megneiss in the yle of Skye and that the minister to come to these yles to preach to them and catechise them so oft as possibly he can.

(The separate parish of the Small Isles was formed when the islands were removed from the parish of Strath in 1726; at first they tended to be referred to as the 'Short Isles'.)

In 1652 Father Dugan visited Eigg and Canna and brought over 900 people to the Church. In 1671 Father Francis MacDonnell recorded that 'There are other islands belonging to Clanranald, namely Canna, Rum, Eigg and Muck, in which there are not less than 1000 souls, all Catholics.' Rum was by then in the hands of Maclean of Coll (although Clanranald would still have been reluctant to accept this).

The proprietor of Rum, Donald Maclean of Coll (1656–1729), converted to the 'true' religion early. Several accounts survive of him forcing the tenantry in Rum to do the same. One account has it that it was his son Hector and this may well be true since it seems to have been common practice for the eldest son of Maclean of Coll to take on the running of the estate at the earliest opportunity. The Proceedings of the General Assembly Committee of the Church of Scotland (10 May 1726) record the incident: 'Hector Maclean of Coll ... was pleased himself to go with a Protestant Minister to the Isle of Roum, and by God's blessing they have brought over the inhabitants ...'

Father Tyrie's Report on Catholicism in the Scottish Highlands (1737) goes further:

> The inhabitants were all Catholics, but their proprietor, who is a heretic, compelled the men to attend the preaching of the minister maintained by the government for this and the two forementioned islands. The women, however, are for the most part still Catholic; nor did the proprietor trouble to bring any pressure to bear on them, being content that the men attend the minister's services. This instance illustrates the great power of a chief over his subjects in the Highlands, in that the fore-going gentleman forced his retainers to hear the minister preach, all against their will ... It was the father [i.e. Donald] of the present Maclean of Coll who compelled the Catholic men of Rum to attend the minister's services. The present laird, however, does not in any way inconvenience his Catholic subjects.

Samuel Johnson (1773) received the story much embellished, or else chose to add the detail himself:

> The inhabitants are fifty-eight families who continued Papists for some time after the Laird became a Protestant. Their adherence to their old religion was strengthened by the countenance of the Laird's sister, a zealous Romanist, till on Sunday, as they were going to Mass under the conduct of the patroness, Maclean met them on the way, gave one of them a blow on the head with a yellow stick, I suppose a cane, for which the Earse had no name, and drove them to the Kirk, from which they have never since departed. Since the use of this method of conversion, the inhabitants of Egg and Canna who continue Papists, call the Protestantism of Rum the religion of the yellow stick.

Apparently the infamous cane remained in the possession of the family until last century.

A final version occurs in a *British Fisheries Society Report* (written by Lord Mount Stuart in 1788) which attempts to correct the details:

> The change of religion in Rume was literally occasioned by the violence of the Grandfather [i.e. Donald] of the present Maclean of Coll though not exactly as related by Johnson. He had a child at nurse in Rume and happening to go and see it of a Sunday, it occurred to him to ask a friend of his, a clergyman who chanced to accompany him, to preach.
>
> A Roman Catholic man present went out of the room, the Nurse also a Roman Catholic, followed him with the Child, this circumstance enraged Maclean to such a degree that running after the man, he beat him most unmercifully with a stick adding 'get back you rascal, to the

Kirk'. This drubbing frightened the inhabitants so much they none of them ventured more to go to Mass.

The hatred [on Canna] to the Rum people ever since they left the Popish persuasion is something remarkable. When a child misbehaves the mother cries 'I'll send you to Rum', a threat from anyone upon any occasion concludes in Rum and Mr MacNeil [of Canna] told me in one of the sermons the Priest said, 'if you commit such crimes the Lord will turn his back upon you then what will you do, where can you go etc?' Upon this a poor man got up and said seriously, 'if there be amongst you any such wicked person, let them be sent to Rum.'

According to Dom Odo Blundell's *Catholic Highlands of Scotland* (1917), 400 Catholics in Eigg and Canna used to have a priest to themselves but by 1763 they were left 'destitute of any spiritual assistance except what the Bishop or his coadjutor could occasionally afford them'.

In 1770 Father Alexander Kennedy visited Muck, which was by then in the ownership of the Protestant Macleans of Coll. The priest was immediately arrested on the orders of Mrs Maclean, the wife of the proprietor (who was then absent from home) and confined in her house for two days. Kennedy was forbidden contact with the islanders until a boat could be found to convey him back to the mainland.

As Father Tyrie had observed, the womenfolk of Rum resisted conversion longer, and the *SSPCK Minutes* of September 1728 record 152 people over the age of five in Rum, 'all Protestant except 6 women'. One of the menfolk also resented the laird's high-handedness, since the Protestant denomination, especially the Free Church, frowned upon frivolities such as music and dance. According to M. E. M. Donaldson in her *Wanderings in the Western Highlands and Islands* he was called *Am Piobair Mor* (the great piper) and 'fled from the tyranny of *Creidimh a'Bhata Bhuide* – the religion of the yellow stick in Rum' to set up home first in a cave on the north side of Eigg and later at Kildonan. Camille Dressler in *Eigg: The Story of an Island* has the correct version. It was Lachlan MacQuarrie who fled Rum to settle at Grulin in Eigg where it was his grandson Donald who was *Am Piobair Mor.* Donald's two sisters resolved to cure him of his other outstanding talent, his capacity for whisky. Dressed in white sheets they gave him such a fright as he returned from the inn one dark night, that he took to his bed with shock and died. He is buried inside the roofless chapel at Kildonan in Eigg but a cairn beside the road to Grulin, below the Sgurr, commemorates this renowned musician.

While the Small Isles nowadays are noted for religious tolerance, we shall return to the theme briefly in considering the Jacobite Risings. Meantime religion also had a strong influence on early education. In 1616 the Privy Council had approved an Act that 'where convenient means may be had' a school shall be established in every parish in the kingdom and 'a fit person appointed to teach ... upon the expense of the parishioners'. Fortunately for the culture of the Highlands and Islands, poverty and apathy prevented the Act from being too effective; none the less the seeds had been sown. By 1650, however, fewer than half of the parishes in Scotland could boast a school, the Highlands – and more so the Hebrides – being the worst off.

The 1690 Act of Settling Schools made better provision for education, fixing a teacher's salary at £5 to £11 per annum. Although it was up to the landowner to provide a 'commodious' school building, the Kirk Session undertook to run the school. Lairds, however, were often still unwilling to discharge their responsibilities, especially in the north and west Highlands where estates were extensive.

The Scottish Society for the Propagation of Christian Knowledge was formed in Edinburgh in 1709, modelled on an English equivalent that had been initiated eleven years before. The Society strove to promote 'Christian Knowledge and the increase in piety and virtue within Scotland, especially in the Highlands, Islands and remote corners thereof'. The sum of £1000 was raised by subscription and the first five SSPCK schools established, including one on St Kilda on 13 April 1710 (with eighteen boys and ten girls). Thereafter expansion was rapid and by 1795 there were no less than 323 SSPCK schools, including ninety-six special spinning and sewing schools, geared especially towards young girls.

Since it was widely believed that most Catholic doctrine in Scotland derived from Ireland and the west, teachers were forbidden to teach either Latin or Gaelic. Thus as one historian has observed: 'children who did not understand English were instructed by teachers who did not know Gaelic' and the efforts were more directed towards 'instructing the children in the principles of Christianity rather than towards elevating their intellectual and secular interests'.

It had been in 1725 that the SSPCK first considered settling a minister in the Small Isles and establishing itinerant schools there; £100 were set aside for the purpose. In 1727 the Rev. Donald MacQueen (*c.* 1700–70) was appointed to the Small Isles, based in Rum, the only island where he had a sizeable congregation. His yearly stipend of 842 merks was paid by all the inheritors of the parish, although the minister rarely visited the Catholic islands of Eigg and Canna. This is perhaps not surprising, when a petition to the Skye Presbytery explained that 'such lodgings as he can be provided with, being at best but one of the small huts they built for the cattle, and he is still worse accommodated than the poorest servant in his Parish.'

Only the year before, schoolmasters had been sent to Muck and Canna 'desiring them to visit the Society's school at Rum, and send hither an account of the state thereof'. This seems to imply that a school in Rum had been established but was served on a part-time basis by a teacher from one of the other islands. (SSPCK records from 1748 show that a school in Eigg and Canna had been 'erected' on 15 May 1728 with thirty-eight boys and thirteen girls.)

On 5 September 1728 the Society had a letter from the Rev. MacQueen claiming

> that he visits the [Eigg and Canna] schools frequently, and finds some of the scholars advance but slowly, being often taken from the school on account of the poverty of their parents; ... recommending Kenneth MacAskill for being Schoolmaster and Catechist at Muck, who has already sixteen schollars there, and John Stewart to be Schoolmaster and Catechist at Egg who entered to his work on the twelfth of June last, and his scholars are yet but few. He desires that if the Society had not already appointed one for Cana they would provide one by Martinmas next and craves books to these schools.

MacQueen noted a population of 856 over the age of five in the parish: 340 in Eigg, all but 10 being Papists; 128 in Muck, 60 of whom were Protestants; 152 in Rum, all but 6 women being Protestants; and 236 in Canna, all but 16 being Papists.

The Society opted to send John Stewart to Canna, leaving Kenneth Macaskill to cope with both Eigg and Muck. Although there is no specific mention of a school in Rum, it was recorded on 1 May 1729 that Allan Maclean was to succeed John MacArthur there.

On 1 April 1731 the SSPCK Committee received a letter

> giving a full account of the state of the Isle of Rum, Muck, Egg and Cana with respect to Religion, particularly that the inhabitants of Egg and Cana, being much addicted to popery and under the management of priests and the awful power of Popish chiefs, there was not any probability of the means of instruction being entertained by them, and therefore the author is of the opinion that the continuing school in Egg can be of no benefit to the Protestant cause, but rather promote the direct opposite interest, and as to Rum and Muck enhabited mostly by Protestants he proposes that one schoolmaster might sufficiently serve both, who might be at Muck in the summer and harvest, and at Rum in winter and spring, the passage betwixt the two being short.

In July 1731 the Rev. MacQueen found Angus Macleod teaching fourteen boys and two girls in Muck, John Stewart teaching ten boys and four girls in Eigg and Allan Maclean with ten boys and four girls in Rum. At the latter school ten children were reading the Bible, one the New Testament, and the rest the Catechism; nine were learning to write and two were studying Arithmetic.

On 19 August 1745 Prince Charles Edward Stuart raised his standard at Glenfinnan to muster support for the Jacobite Uprising from the Highland clans. Young Clanranald arrived with 150 followers, including many Eigg and Canna men under John Macdonald of Laig. The ageing Ranald, 17th of Clanranald, had been restrained by his pragmatic half-brother Macdonald of Boisdale who, only a few weeks earlier, had boldly advised Prince Charles himself to go home; the prince had replied, 'I am come home, sir.'

Hector Maclean of Coll was by now a prominent figure in the local Protestant establishment. To emphasise his loyalty to King George he had sixty Coll men 'volunteer' for the Argyll Militia, fitting them out with uniforms before despatching them to Inveraray. However, the government failed to supply arms so they returned home. Thus while the Catholic islands of Eigg and Canna were committed to the Jacobite cause through Young Clanranald, the Protestant islands of Muck and Rum were not.

The events that culminated in the battle of Culloden the following April are well known. The prince took to the heather and was sheltered by loyal Highlanders wherever he went, despite a price of £30,000 on his head.

Notwithstanding his discretion, Old Clanranald was imprisoned for a short time on suspicion of having Jacobite sympathies while all along it had been his hot-headed son (who had 'come out'), who had been referred to on his arrest warrant. A protest was lodged on behalf of the family that Old Clanranald had not been involved in the Rising and that there was no such person as 'Donald Macdonald, younger of Clanranald', so both were acquitted and their estates returned to them.

Their island holdings of Eigg and Canna were not so lucky, and Dr John Lorne Campbell has recounted the severe reprisals these islands endured in his book *Canna: The Story of a Hebridean Island.*

Throughout this cruel retribution in Rum's neighbouring islands, Hector Maclean of Coll remained loyal to King George. On one occasion, however, during a routine search in Coll, government troops uncovered a cache of arms. Poor Hector only just managed to explain it away to General Campbell, by dismissing and disinheriting his brother Lachlan as 'a wild man, a very idle odd character, and a poet'. Hector died childless and the estate passed to Hugh, a third brother.

In the wake of Culloden, ministers from every parish in Scotland were requested to submit population figures which were collated in 1755 by the Rev. Alexander Webster of the Tolbooth in Edinburgh. The figures were not strictly accurate (since children and old folk were often not included), so Webster had to juggle with the statistics. He estimated a total of 923 for the Small Isles, with 345 in Eigg, 268 in Canna, 206 in Rum and 141 in Muck.

Another, more accurate, census was undertaken only a decade later. The Rev. John Walker received a list of inhabitants of the Small Isles from the local catechist Neill McNeill (see Appendix I). He was, in Walker's words, 'a sensible and careful man', more so perhaps than the Reverend gentleman himself for his published account gave the population of Rum to be 304, but only 297 names appear on the catechist's list. None the less the latter is a very valuable document since it contains the only full list of names of people living on the island before it was cleared, albeit some sixty years later. By contrast, 143 names are given for Muck, 250 for Canna (three less than the published account) and 459 for Eigg (but I have not checked the original list for Eigg).

Apparently the catechist was resident in Canna where he strived to convert the Catholic populace. It seems that the schoolmaster had an ally in one of the two tacksmen in Canna, a Donald Macleod, who wished to sublet his farm only to Protestants and threatened to evict the Catholics. 'Within a year to come', the catechist ventured, 'the priest will not have any house on Cannay of papish families that he can stay in.' Such a situation apparently prevailed in Rum. He continued:

> Rum is an island inhabited by protestants but [for] two men and four
> women, but they came to hear the minister and catechist when either of
> them is here. These papists are none of the natives of the island of Rum.
> They come here from Eig and Cannay. The priest does not come here to
> officiate. The protestants would not allow any of them to after the death
> of three [worthys?] there two years ago. The priest was forced in there
> by contrary winds on his way from Cannay to Eig on a Saturday. He
> took his lodging in a protestant house. The landlady being of his religion
> he offered to say mass on Sunday but the good man of the house would
> not allow him to officiate ... within his dwelling house or any other
> house belonging to him. His wife now is one of the converts in Rum.

Muck, also largely Protestant, was similarly hostile to visits by Catholic priests. The catechist Neill McNeill concluded:

> The whole of the protestants in this parish wish ... catechising [to]
> continue among them. They find it more advantageous to them than they
> thought ... Here in the parish the catechists go twice a quarter to Rum
> and catechise the whole inhabitants of that island. In Cannay when he
> is at home he convenes all the protestants every Sunday [and reads] a
> small proportion of the scriptures to them and catechises them ...

Due to the efforts of such religious zealots, a rift was created between the communities in the four Small Isles. Furthermore, after the heyday of Clanranald, each island fell into quite separate ownership – except for a short period when the Macleans of Coll owned both Muck and Rum – so the Small Isles, despite their later religious tolerance, were never to pull together as a single community.

PART III

Land and People

There is very little arable land ... The little corn and potatoes they
raise is very good; but so small is the quantity of bear and oats that
there is not a fourth part produced to supply their annual wants:
all the subsistence the poor people have besides is curds, milk and
fish. They are a well made and well-looking race, but carry famine
in their aspect ... In the present economy of the island, there is no
prospect of any improvement.

Thomas Pennant, 1772

5   Voyages of Amusement

Foreigners sailing through the Western Isles have been tempted,
from the sight of so many hills that seem to be covered all over
with heath and faced with high rocks, to imagine the inhabitants, as
well as their places of residence, are barbarous; and to this opinion,
their habit as well as their language have contributed.

Martin Martin, 1703

This excerpt is taken from an unusual book that was published in London
in 1703. It described a far-flung corner of the kingdom which, as its author
pointed out, was as foreign to most Britons as any Mediterranean country.
A notable feature of the work, remarkable though its contents were, was
that it had been penned by a local, Martin Martin, one whose first tongue
was the very Gaelic language of which he wrote.

Martin had been born near Duntulm in the Isle of Skye sometime
between 1655 and 1660 when, as Dr Samuel Johnson later came to point
out, 'the chiefs of the clans had lost little of their original influence. The
mountains were yet unpenetrated, no inlet was opened to foreign novelties
and the feudal institutions operated upon life with their full force.' Johnson
carried Martin's book with him on his own travels through the Hebrides
in 1773.

Doctor Johnson was critical of the literary style of the book and was
disappointed that it did not reveal more. None the less, Martin Martin's
Description of the Western Isles of Scotland was a major insight into the
life-style and traditions of his own people. In the fashion of many young
Highland gentlemen of the period, he had enjoyed a university education

in Edinburgh and was able to return to his native island as a tutor, firstly to the Macdonalds of Skye and later to the future Macleod of Dunvegan. In this capacity he was able to travel extensively through the Hebrides, even to remote St Kilda, which was part of the Macleod estates.

Despite the alleged deficiencies in his narrative, Martin presented vivid insights into traditions which at that time still retained elements of ancient pagan rituals. Furthermore, the Highland culture was so distinct from the rest of the kingdom as to repeatedly rebel against it for decades to come. Unfortunately, Martin has relatively little to tell us about Rum, and some of that appears to be slightly off target. He claimed, for instance, that Loch Scresort was unfit as an anchorage, and went on to describe the inhabitants as Protestant. Curiously, this was some time before the famous 'yellow stick' conversion by Maclean of Coll brandishing a cane. He mentioned a chapel – presumably at Kilmory, although no trace of it now exists. Otherwise 'the language and habit [are] the same with the northern isles.'

Martin went on to describe Rum as 'mountainous and heathy', its coast 'arable and fruitful'. Interestingly he noted that 'the north end produces some wood', the rivers afforded salmon and the mountains had some hundred of deer grazing on them:

> The natives gave me an account of a strange observation, which they say proves fatal to the posterity of Lachlan, a cadet of Maclean of Coll's family; that if any of them shoot at a deer on the mountain Fionchra, he dies suddenly, or contracts some violent distemper which soon puts a period to his life. They told me some instances to this purpose; whatever may be in it, there is some of the tribe above-named will ever offer to shoot the deer in that mountain.

Even to this day the green hill of Fionchra in Rum is regarded as something of a sanctuary for deer, one of its corries being especially favoured by hinds giving birth and referred to by the stalkers as 'Maternity Hollow'. They try to avoid shooting deer here.

Although Martin later came under the patronage of the naturalist Robert Sibbald and other London men of science, and went on to study medicine at Leiden in the Netherlands, he died in 1719 in relative obscurity in London.

The impact of his classic book is undisputed but it was only well after Culloden that the government began to take an interest in the estates it had confiscated from exiled Jacobite lairds. The Rev. John Walker was sent north to report, and a meticulous chronicler he turned out to be.

John Walker was born in Edinburgh in 1731 and from childhood had nursed a passion for botany and geology. None the less, he entered the Church of Scotland, taking up his first charge in 1758 at Glencorse, near

Edinburgh. Within such easy reach of the capital and being a friend of Lord Kames, the renowned agricultural improver of the time, Walker was able to fraternise with such distinguished men of science as Benjamin Franklin and Rousseau; he also corresponded with the celebrated Swedish naturalist Carl von Linné or Linnaeus. The Pentland Hills formed a convenient theatre for Walker's enquiries and in 1762 he took a charge at Moffat in the Southern Uplands. According to one of his flock 'the mad minister of Moffat spent the week hunting butterflies and made the cure of the souls of his parishioners a bye-job on Sunday'.

Walker had first ventured north in 1761 and the following year he first set foot in the Hebrides. Meanwhile the Crown was determined that the profits and rents from their forfeited Jacobite properties should be used in 'civilising' their inhabitants and 'in promoting the Protestant religion, loyalty, good government, industry and manufactures'. But first the well-meaning Commissioners had to discover the prevailing conditions in the Highlands and the resources which they contained. So, doubtless to his delight, the Rev. Walker was granted £60 travelling expenses and leave of absence from his parish to undertake the task. At the same time he was to survey religion and education in the Highlands for the Society for the Propagation of Christian Knowledge. He also found time to collect natural history material for Thomas Pennant, who was at the time working on his definitive *British Zoology*.

Walker sailed from Greenock in a customs cutter, via Ireland and Islay. On 25 June 1764 he scaled the Paps of Jura and, from a base in Iona, spent most of July visiting the Inner Hebrides, including Rum, Eigg and Canna. By 16 August he had reached Stornoway, where he collected a further £40 that had been forwarded by his Commissioners. He quit the cutter in Skye to explore the mainland before returning home by early December. Altogether, he proudly announced, he had sailed 1263 miles, rowed in a boat 280 miles, ridden on horseback 1087 miles and walked 528 miles in what must be one of the most intrepid Highland journeys of all time. Meanwhile he had amassed countless specimens of plants, animals and fossils whose carriage home took 'half a year's stipend'. And, of course, he had made copious notes about the people and the conditions that he had encountered.

Walker completed a memorandum for the General Assembly of the Church of Scotland in May 1765 and another for the SSPCK soon after. His vastly more detailed *Report on the Hebrides for the Commissioners of the Annexed Estates* was not finished until March 1771. He gained further leave to explore several unvisited islands that year, for which he was awarded a further 100 guineas. Another payment would be made for a *Natural History of the Hebrides* but, unfortunately, this was never completed. Although his Report was favourably received and he was awarded honorary degrees by both Edinburgh and Glasgow universities, his magnum opus remained virtually unnoticed until finally edited by Margaret Mackay and formally published in 1980. Walker did, however, gain the Chair of Natural History at Edinburgh and in 1790 even took time out from his intellectual pursuits to serve as Moderator of the General Assembly of the Church of Scotland. He had married only three years earlier and, aged sixty-five, he turned blind and died in 1804.

Although a few of his population statistics in his *Report* might be suspect, he made a particularly detailed study of the Small Isles, having received his data from the catechist there. He noted that Rum contained 304 inhabitants; one man of 81, a woman of 89, another of 92 and one of 97.

> The year before I was there a man had died on the island aged 103 ... The island was then accounted populous, as it had not been visited by the Small Pox for 29 years; for by this disease upon former occasions, it had been almost depopulate.

Walker computed, erroneously, that Rum was at least 15,360 acres 'of which there is a very small proportion that has ever been cultivated; not above 1500 acres'. The greater part consisted of

> steep mountains, deep mosses and tracts of land overspread with rocks. It is an island of unfavourable climate ... [which] with its wet deep soil must prevent it from being ever profitable in the production of corn or cattle ... It has once been well wooded, and in some of the steep gullies, inaccessible to cattle, the oak, the birch, the holly and rowan tree are still to be observed growing vigorously ... There is a large herd of red deer kept upon the island by the proprietor, and in all parts there is a great abundance of moorfowl ... The puffin of the Isle of Man [Manx shearwater] also builds here, which is reckoned the greatest delicacy of all sea birds ...

Walker went on to describe at length the geology, recommending Rum as a supply of semi-precious stone for a small but expanding lapidary industry in the south of Britain.

It is not unlikely that the naturalist Thomas Pennant was in part inspired to undertake his own Highland sojourn by the wealth of specimen material and observation accumulated by Walker. His forms the next fruitful account of the Hebrides and he too lingered long enough in Rum to pen a valuable historical sketch. Pennant, born in 1726 at Downing near Holywell in Flintshire, studied at Oxford but did not graduate. However, as eldest son of a landed family he was able to travel extensively both at home and on the Continent. Thus by 1766 he published the first of his multi-volumed *British Zoology*. The following year he was elected a Fellow of the Royal Society and was later awarded an Honorary Doctorate.

In 1769 he undertook a first tour 'to the remotest part of North Britain' during which he kept an elaborate and detailed journal. This was so successful that three years later he set out again accompanied, as before, by a groom and a couple of servants, together with Moses Griffiths, whom Pennant had trained to illustrate his works. On 18 May 1772 he left the Clyde on board the cutter *Lady Frederick Campbell*, and rounded the Mull of Kintyre to visit Gigha, Jura, Islay and Iona. A heavy swell prevented him from setting eyes on Staffa with its famous Fingal's Cave and it was left to his friend Sir Joseph Banks, a month later, to introduce this natural wonder to popular attention. From Iona Pennant sailed on to Canna and

> with a favourable gale through a rolling sea, in about two hours, anchored in the Isle of Rum, in an open bay about two miles deep called Loch Sgriosard, bounded by high mountains, black and barren: at the bottom of the bay is the little village Kinloch, of about a dozen houses ... The lazy inhabitants were sitting around in great numbers expecting our landing with that avidity for news common to the whole country.

Entering one house he found

> an address and politeness from the owner and his wife that were astonishing; such pretty apologies for the badness of the treat, the curds and milk that were offered; which were tendered to us with as much readiness and good will.
>
> Rum, or Ronin as it is called by the Dean [Monro], is the property of Mr Maclean of Coll; a landlord mentioned by the natives with much affection ... The number of souls at this time number 325, of families only 59, almost all Protestant. The heads of families with wives, were at this time all alive except five: three widowers and two widows. They had with them 102 sons and only 76 daughters: this disproportion prevails in Cannay and the other little islands, in order, in the end, to preserve a balance between the two sexes, as the men are from their way of life so perpetually exposed to danger in these stormy seas and to other accidents that might occasion a depopulation, was it not so providentially ordered.
>
> The island is one great mountain, divided into several points: the highest called Aisgobhall; ... The surface of Rum is in a manner covered with heath, and in a state of nature; the heights rocky. There is very little arable land, excepting about the nine little hamlets that the natives have grouped in different places; near which the corn is sown in diminutive patches, for the tenants here run-rig as in Cannay. The greatest farmer holds five pounds twelve shillings a year, and pays his rent in money. The whole of the island is two thousand marks [£250] ... At the foot of Sgor-mor, opposite to Cannay, are found abundance of

agates ... several singular strata such as grey quarz stone ... another mix of quartz and basalts, a black stone spotted with white like perphyry, but with the appearance of a lava; a fine grit or free stone ...

For want of lime [the islanders] dress their leather with calcined shells; and use the same method of tanning it as in Cannay. The inhabitants of Rum are people that scarcely know sickness; if they are attacked with a dysentry they make use of a decoction of the roots of the Tormentilla erecta in milk. The small pox has visited them but once in 34 years, only two sickened and both recovered. The measles come often.

It is not wonderful that some superstitions should reign in these sequestered parts. Second sight is firmly believed at this time. My informant said that Lachlan MacKerran of Cannay had told a gentleman that he could not rest for the noise he heard of the hammering of nails into his coffin; accordingly the gentleman died within fifteen days. Molly Maclean (aged forty) has the power of forseeing events through a well-scraped blade bone of mutton ... but some of these tales are founded upon impudence and nurtured by folly. Here are only the ruins of a church in this island; so the minister is obliged to preach, the few times he visits his congregation, in the open air.

With the weather moderating, Pennant and his party set sail for Skye on 15 July. They also visited Lewis before returning home overland later that summer.

Thus ended this voyage of amusement, successful and satisfactory in every part, unless embittered with reflections on the sufferings of my fellow-creatures. Gratitude forbids my silence respecting the kind reception I universally met with; or the active zeal of everyone to facilitate my pursuits; or their liberal communication of every species of information, useful or entertaining.

It was this 'voyage of amusement' that in turn stimulated Dr Johnson to embark on his own fact-finding tour of the Hebrides. He considered that Pennant had had 'a greater variety of enquiry than almost any man, and has told us more than perhaps one in ten thousand could have done'. Dr John Lorne Campbell has also pointed out how 'Johnson's interest in the Isles was literary, historical and sentimentally Jacobite'. Johnson met Flora Macdonald at Kingsburgh – 'a little woman of a mild and genteel appearance, mighty soft and well-bred' – and he was able to sleep in the very bed that the fugitive Prince Charles had slept in only twenty-seven years earlier. Of Johnson's journey Campbell continues:

The literary aspect of it was due to the publication of the first volume of James Macpherson's alleged translations of the poems of Ossian, which had appeared ten years before, creating a literary sensation. Dr Johnson denied both the authenticity and the merit of the poems, but was interested enough to investigate their background and the possibility of ancient Gaelic manuscripts surviving in the Highlands and Islands.

Johnson's account of his journey was itself to be highly acclaimed. He never reached the Isle of Rum but, while in Skye, Johnson and his companion James Boswell fell in with Donald, the heir to Maclean of Coll's estates. 'Young Coll' as he was known, accompanied them as far as Mull and introduced the intrepid pair to a variety of singularly hospitable hosts, to many of whom the young man was related. Johnson's account, alongside that of Boswell (which was not published until several years later), has provided a fascinating window on Highland society at the time, and on the Macleans of Coll themselves, who were after all central to the story of Rum. All the while they did not ignore the landscape and the lives of the common people. Thus, it is worth dwelling on this epic journey, or at least on four weeks of it. But first some background to the Macleans of Coll, from the late seventeenth century until Johnson and Boswell enter the stage in 1773.

Late in the seventeenth century the Macleans of Coll had opted to align themselves with the Campbells. However, some supported the Stuart rising of 1688 and one of their own sons, Lachlan, even displayed Jacobite sympathies. This was the wayward youth who had put his own brother, Hector of Coll, in one very embarrassing situation with the Hanoverian government.

Hector Maclean managed his estates well enough – stock-rearing, arable farming, fishing, quarrying, money-lending, brewing and distilling. (There were once nine distilleries on Coll.) From these activities the estate was in good heart financially, although rents from his tenants on Coll raised only a couple of hundred pounds annually. Maclean died in 1754, four years after he had built a new castle at Breacachadh on Coll. He was survived by two daughters so, with his Jacobite brother Lachlan disinherited, the estate passed to a younger brother Hugh who had been a successful merchant on Coll. Married to Janet Macleod of Talisker, Hugh had seven sons and a daughter.

Hugh continued his late brother's enterprises, but many of the outstanding rents from his tenants he collected in kind rather than cash. In 1764 the Rev. Walker had observed how in Coll

their chieftain, for whom they have the greatest affection, governs them with great equity and mildness, and lives among them in this remote island, like the master of a family consisting of above a thousand people.

In 1772 Pennant confirmed that Hugh was also mentioned by the natives of Rum 'with much affection'. Soon afterwards Maclean of Coll moved to Old Aberdeen where he was appointed Provost of the city in 1779 and died seven years later.

His eldest son Donald, born in 1752, had been fostered out – as was common custom by Highland chieftains – to a MacSween family then living in Tiree. He was then educated partly at King's College in Aberdeen and partly in England. This was the enterprising young man that Johnson and Boswell met on their travels. He quickly took the two city gentlemen under his wing and greatly impressed them with his knowledge, kindness and hospitality.

Johnson and Boswell had set off from Edinburgh in August 1773 and journeyed through Fife, along the Aberdeen and Buchan coast to Inverness. From there they had climbed over the Ratagan Pass to Glenelg and across to the Isle of Skye. They reached Talisker House on 23 September where their host, Colonel Macleod, introduced them to his nephew, Donald Maclean, the young laird of Coll. Boswell described him as 'a lively young man'. Johnson added that

> as eldest son of the laird of Coll, he was heir to a very great extent of land. So desirous was he of improving his inheritance, that he spent a considerable time among the farmers of Hertfordshire and Hampshire, to learn their practice. He worked with his own hands at the principal operations of agriculture that he might not deceive himself by a false opinion of skill.

Young Coll was sporting in Skye at his uncle's house. When he discovered that Johnson and Boswell were making for Iona, he offered to accompany them and show them everything worth seeing. He suggested visiting Eigg, Muck, Coll and Tiree on route to Mull, where both he and his father had property. The trio set off the next evening and spent a drunken night at Coirechatachan in Skye, but the next few days were particularly wet, which gave Boswell a chance to recover from his inebriation. Thursday 30 September delivered 'as great a storm of wind and rain as I have almost ever seen,' wrote Boswell, 'which necessarily confined us to the house.' On Friday afternoon they made for Armadale to await a boat. The weather detained them again so it was not until early Sunday afternoon that they set sail. The passage was a rough one, with both city gentlemen being violently seasick. Indeed the passage would have been a dangerous one without 'Mr Maclean of Coll, who, with every other qualification which insular life required, is a very active and skilful mariner, [and] piloted us safe into his own harbour,' Johnson recalled. Thus they were forced to bypass Rum and reached Coll, where they had to sleep on board until dawn. They visited the elderly Rev. Hector Maclean on the way to Breacachadh Castle, the seat of the laird: 'a neat new-built gentleman's house,' observed Boswell, although his companion was not so impressed, calling it 'a mere trademan's box'.

Johnson continued:

> Mr Maclean of Coll, having a numerous family has, for some time, resided at Aberdeen that he may superintend their education; and leaves the young gentleman, our friend, to govern his dominions with the full power of a Highland chief. By the absence of the laird's family our entertainment was made more difficult because the house was in a great degree unfurnished; but the young Coll's kindness and activity supplied all defects and procured us more than sufficient accommodation.

They dined in the company of Donald, son of Neil Maclean of Crossapol. This young schoolmaster in Coll matched Boswell in his capacity for punch; fifteen years later he was to become Church of Scotland minister for the Small Isles and wrote a classic account of his parish for the *Statistical Account*.

Next morning Johnson and Boswell were taken to old Breacachadh Castle nearby. 'It has never been a large feudal residence, and has nothing about it that requires a particular description', except perhaps the vault which, Boswell noted, was still used to house local offenders. Their host proudly showed them more:

> Young Coll who has a very laudable desire of improving his patrimony, purposes some time to plant an orchard; which if it be sheltered by a wall, may perhaps succeed. He has introduced the culture of turnips of which he has a field, where the whole work was performed by his own hand. His intention is to provide food for his cattle in the winter. This innovation was considered by Mr MacSween [Young Coll's foster father] as the idle project of a young head, heated with English fancies; but he has now found that turnips will really grow, and that hungry sheep and cows will really eat them.

'By such acquisitions as these,' Johnson remarked, 'the Hebrides may in time rise above their annual distress.' He noted that the island of Coll was very populous. Although the Macleans did not own it all they were prepared to take out a lease on either end of it 'at a very advanced rent' rather than let the Campbell owners get a footing on the island. When these lands came on the market many years later, the Macleans had just purchased Muck so were too much in debt to be able to buy them.

> Mr Maclean the laird, has very extensive possessions, being proprietor not only of far the greater part of Coll, but of the extensive island of Rum, and a very considerable territory in Mull.

Young Coll told his guests that Rum was 'mountainous, rugged and

barren. In the hills there are red deer ... The rent of Rum is not great ...
The inhabitants are fifty-eight families.' It was by now a Protestant island,
only Eigg and Canna remaining Catholic. Johnson lamented that their
stormy passage had forced them to neglect these islands. None the less he
acutely observed how:

> Popery is favourable to ceremony and among ignorant nations, ceremony
> is the only preservative of tradition. Since Protestantism was extended
> to the savage parts of Scotland it has perhaps been one of the chief
> labours of the ministers to abolish stated observances because they
> continued the remembrance of the former religion. We therefore, who
> came to hear old traditions and see former antiquated manners, should
> probably have found them among the Papists.

The travellers were impressed with the reverence with which Young Coll's
tenants regarded him.

> He did not endeavour to dazzle them by any magnificence of dress: his
> only distinction was a feather in his bonnet; but as soon as he appeared
> they forsook their work and clustered about him: he took them by the
> hand and they seemed mutually delighted. He has the proper disposition
> of a chieftain and seems desirous to continue the customs of his house.
> The bagpiper played regularly when dinner was served ... and brought
> no disgrace upon the family of Rankin which has long supplied the
> lairds of Coll with hereditary musick.

Despite persistent storms Young Coll took Johnson and Boswell
on to Tobermory where they spent a night with his aunt, the wife of
Dr Alexander Maclean, the local physician. His daughter sang, played
the spinnet, and recited Gaelic poems by a famous local bard, John
Maclean, who could neither read nor write and had died only a few years
earlier. Miss Maclean translated the poems into English for the benefit of
her guests, one being an elegy on Sir John Maclean, his chief, who was
forced into exile after the 1715 Rising. Johnson praised her as the most
accomplished lady he had encountered in the Highlands.

To counter Boswell's tiresome praise of the fellow, Johnson drily
commented, 'Coll does everything for us; we will erect a statue to Coll.'
Encouraged, Boswell persisted, 'Yes and we will have him with his various
attributes and characters ... We will have him as a pilot; we will have
him as a fisherman, as a hunter, as a husbandman, as a physician.' Johnson
had to agree. 'He is a noble animal. He is as complete an islander as the
mind can figure.' Johnson then added grudgingly, 'He is hospitable; and
he has an intrepidity of talk, whether he understands the subject or not.
I regret that he is not more intellectual.'

On Tuesday 19 October, ready to sail to Iona, Johnson and Boswell finally 'had a last embrace of this amiable young man' who was returning to Skye to conclude his sporting expedition. Within the year, however, young Donald Maclean, whom Pennant had considered 'was almost worthy of an elegy by Ossian', was tragically drowned in that very stretch of water between Inchkenneth and Ulva where he had taken his leave of Johnson and Boswell.

6 *A Clean but Homely Cloth*

... a land still emerging from legend and still poorly endowed with safe roads and comfortable post houses.

Mrs Sarah Murray, 1802

John Knox – no relation to the Calvinist reformer – had made his fortune in the bookselling trade so was able to retire in 1764 when only forty-four. In the next eleven years he made no less than sixteen tours through Scotland. In 1786 he was commissioned by the British Fisheries Society to report on the prospects for fishing on the west coast of Scotland. The Society had been founded in London in 1786, with the fifth Duke of Argyll as its first governor. Its remit was to halt emigration by encouraging the local fisheries and it was responsible for building three canals in Scotland and creating new fishing villages at Lochbay (Skye), Ullapool, Tobermory and Pulteneytown near Wick, each with their own pier, inn, schoolhouse and church.

Thus, at the age of sixty-six, Knox voyaged from Oban to Tobermory, visiting Tiree, Coll, Rum, Skye, Harris, Lewis and Wester Ross, which he described in *A Tour through the Highlands of Scotland and the Hebride Isles*, published the following year. It is a disappointingly scant volume and he had little to say about Rum. On leaving Coll he had to divert there in a fog, on his way to Canna. His vessel entered

> into the only road upon this bold coast, called Loch Skresort. Here we landed at a small village, in a situation not unpleasant. The people were

all busy packing herrings for the winter provision; and more might have been cured if they had been provided with salt.

He concluded Rum to be a considerable island, or rather one continued rock, of nearly 30 miles in circumference. It was the property of Mr Maclean of Coll, contained 300 inhabitants, grazed cattle and sheep, paid £200 rent annually but had neither kelp, free-stone nor lime. A pier was constructed in Rum before the end of the century but was an insignificant 'endeavour' when placed alongside the British Fisheries Society's wider response to the reports of Knox and his successors. Knox died in 1790.

Donald MacQueen had been the Church of Scotland minister in Eigg, and a veteran of the Hanoverian purges in the island until, ten years later, he was moved to North Uist. In his place came Malcolm MacAskill (1723–87) from Rubh'an Dunain in Skye, known as *Am Ministear Laidir* – the strong minister – but who confessed to a wish

that some of my cloth would carry themselves with more decency towards their superiors in most branches of literature, and call to mind that they are only sacred while in the pulpit.

He was also a firm believer in second sight:

MacAskill's wife was a daughter of Maclean of Coll but, according to the late Hugh Mackinnon of Eigg, she had really wanted to marry a Macleod of Dunvegan. The minister and his wife lived at Kildonan in Eigg and had three sons. Donald became a doctor but never practised, while Alan became a master of a ship. Both had inherited something of their father's physique but the youngest, Ewen, was strongest of all. Hugh Mackinnon related how all three visited Rum one day with their father who was to give a service. There were barrels of tar for smearing sheep on the pier and the brothers began to demonstrate their prowess. All three managed to lift one above their head but Donald slipped; the barrel came down on top of him and injured his nose. None of the young MacAskills attended church that day.

When he died in 1787 Malcolm MacAskill was replaced by the Rev. Donald Maclean who, as a young teacher, had wined and dined with Johnson and Boswell in Coll fourteen years before. Born on 12 May 1752 to Neil Maclean of Crossapol and Julia Stewart, Donald had graduated from King's College, Aberdeen, a few months before his encounter with Johnson and Boswell in 1773. He married Lillias Maclean of Gott in Tiree four years later and had two daughters and three sons, one of whom became an army surgeon and the other two ministers like their father. Donald Maclean became licensed as a missionary in Mull in 1779 and served a short spell as chaplain to the Reay Fencible Regiment before

being formally ordained into the Church of Scotland's parish of the
Small Isles in 1787. He was responsible for setting up the Rum Island
Company of Inverness-shire Volunteers – a sort of Home Guard during
the Napoleonic Wars. 'A man of sincere and unaffected piety', he served as
Deputy Lieutenant of Inverness-shire and died in 1810.

Towards the close of the eighteenth century, the monumental *Statistical
Account of Scotland* was being assembled. Its twenty-one volumes, published
between 1791 and 1799, were edited by Sir John Sinclair, a noted
agricultural improver of the period. His intention was to assess the current
state of the country, 'ascertaining the quantum of happiness enjoyed by its
inhabitants and the means of its future improvement'. By badgering church
ministers he had received descriptions of varying quality, from every
parish in the land. The result was an unparalleled corpus of information
for historians, sociologists, geographers and natural historians alike,
presenting an invaluable overview of Scotland two centuries ago, through
the eyes of educated men who lived and worked in the communities of
which they wrote.

Since the Rev. Donald Maclean was parish minister for the Small Isles,
it fell to him to submit its statistical account; and a classic of its genre it
turned out to be. He explained:

> Weather permitting, the minister officiates in Rum once a month; in
> Isle Muck once a month; in Canna once a quarter; and the rest of the
> time on Eigg. He must attend the meetings of presbytery at Skye, and
> of Synod at Glenelg or Skye, and consequently cannot be above a third
> of his time at home. He must, at his own expense, keep a boat of a
> considerable size, and well-rigged, always in readiness to transport him
> to these several islands, which must be a considerable diminution of his
> income – which he admitted to be about £90 per annum.

Donald Maclean resided in Eigg, in a manse that had been erected in 1790.
'A preaching house' was built three years later. Of the 1339 inhabitants in
the Small Isles no less than 540 of them were Roman Catholics, nearly all
residing in Eigg and Canna. It is strange, therefore, that the minister of the
Established Church should be based in Eigg when most of his flock were
in Rum and Muck; but no doubt this was to counter the presence of the
Catholic priest also domiciled in Eigg. In 1802 Sarah Murray confirmed
how 'the worthy Protestant minister's flock on Eigg is but small …
Fortunately for him he is fond of the sea and is reckoned the most skilful
mariner in the Hebrides'. That year he had conveyed Mrs Murray to Rum,
where he preached to his flock in a barn. The Rev. Maclean continued:

> In the course of the last 20 years the dress of this parish, as well
> as the neighbourhood, both men and women, had undergone a very

considerable change. The men in general wear hats, short jackets and long trousers; instead of bonnets, short coats and philabegs [kilts]; and instead of the tartan short hose, stockings are pretty much used.

This was, of course, in response to a government edict after Culloden forbidding the wearing of tartan.

The kerchief, formerly worn by married women, and the tonnac or short plaid worn by females in general, are now almost wholly out of use. Instead of these, caps of various fashions, short and long cloaks, great coats and ribbands, have been substituted. The men, such of them especially as follow the fishing, find the change in their dress highly convenient, and it may be presumed that they borrowed it from the seafaring people who frequented these isles ...

Most of our young women go to the low country for some weeks in harvest; this time they spend in shearing; and with the money thus earned they endeavour to dress themselves after the low country fashion ... They seldom bring home any share of the price of their labour in cash, and they are a means of encouraging an extravagance of dress ... If manufactures, particularly the woollen, were established among us, our young women might find constant employment at home, mutually advantageous to themselves and to the public.

Maclean gave the population of the Small Isles as 1339 and, interestingly, Rum was by then the most populous with no less than 443 inhabitants. Next came Eigg with 399, then Canna with 304 and finally Muck with 193. In the Small Isles as a whole were 240 married couples, 48 widows and 12 widowers. There were just over 5 people to each of the 252 inhabited houses. Tradesmen included 14 weavers, 5 boat carpenters, 5 tailors, 2 smiths and 1 house carpenter. A surgeon, a schoolmaster, a Catholic priest and a Protestant minister all resided in Eigg.

A more intimate snapshot of Rum at the close of the eighteenth century is offered by Edward Daniel Clarke, a chemist and mineralogist who was the discoverer of cadmium. Although part of his diary is published in William Otter's *The Life and Remains of Edward Daniel Clarke* (1825), a transcription of the whole of Clarke's diary is in the library of the late Dr J. L. Campbell and reveals the geologist to have landed at Guirdil on 26 July 1797 – a glen

with high precipitate cliff, almost perpendicular and yet covered with a green verdure, on whose fearful crags sheep were seen feeding ... A few huts, with a small boat or two drawn up on the beach, constitute what the natives term one of their villages ... Immediately several of the islanders came to welcome Mr Maclean, the brother of the laird. We accompanied him into the cottage of one of his brother's tenants

where we were regaled with new mild, oatcakes and Lisbon wine. I was
surprised to find wine of that species, and of a superior quality in such
a hut, but they told us it was part of the freight of some unfortunate
vessel wrecked near the island, whose cargo came on shore.

Two sons of their host took Clarke and his companions in search of mineral
specimens and fossils:

> Returning to Guirdil we found the old man, who received us at landing,
> waiting with his bonnet in his hand, to request that we would honour
> his cottage with a short visit. Mr Maclean conducted us in when we
> were agreeably surprised to find a clean but homely cloth spread upon
> a board between two beds, which served us for chairs, upon which was
> placed a collation of cream, eggs, new milk, cheese, oatcakes and several
> bottles of the fine old Lisbon wine we had before so much relished.

As evening fell Clarke and Maclean, again accompanied by their two
young guides, went to climb the heights of Orval at the head of the
glen. There they inspected an ancient deer trap and discovered that the
deer had died out in Rum only ten years previously. Clarke flushed some
ptarmigan (now extinct in Rum) while a flight of plovers settled close to
him among the stones. 'They were so tame as to admit of my approaching
almost near enough to put my hat over one of them.' I often wonder were
they the golden plovers which still frequent the lower heaths of Rum, or
were they dotterel, a rare and confiding bird which would certainly have
been at home amongst the ptarmigan on Orval's stony summit? Clarke
regretted that most visitors landed at Loch Scresort, so missing by far
the more interesting west side of the island. He idly prophesied that 'the
island of Rum will one day be considered, if not the most remarkable of the
Hebrides, at least a very important field of inquiry'. And so it has proved
in recent decades, functioning as an 'outdoor laboratory' managed by the
Nature Conservancy and its successor bodies.

Mrs Sarah Murray, to whom Sir Walter Scott dedicated *The Lady of the
Lake*, was an indefatigable 52-year-old widow who undertook a 2000-mile
tour of Scotland. Her book, *A Companion and Useful Guide to the Beauties
of Scotland*, was first published in 1799. Her trip to the Inner Hebrides
three years later was included in the 1803 edition. With an observant
yet practical eye she offered advice to travellers 'to caution and enhance
their progress through a land still emerging from legend and still poorly
endowed with safe roads and comfortable post houses'. Mrs Murray was to
remarry later in 1802 and died in 1811. As previously mentioned, she was
able to visit Rum through the good offices of the Small Isles minister, the
Rev. Donald Maclean.

We arrived at the head of the harbour on Rum in the afternoon and left it at six the next morning. The island is so excessively wild and rugged, that I was unable to explore any part of it … This isle is larger than Eigg, but I imagine it is but thinly inhabited. It is let in six farms, at the rent of about £500 a year. Colonel Maclean of Coll is the proprietor.

Rum was next visited by another geologist, L. A. Necker de Saussure, Professor of Mineralogy at the Academy of Geneva in Switzerland. His account first appeared in English in 1822 although his Scottish journey was made in 1807. He landed at Loch Scresort, so faced a long hike to sample the mineral curiosities described by his predecessor, Edward Daniel Clarke. His French account offered more detail than the English edition, but contains little of fresh interest since he used the *Statistical Account* to furnish himself with background information. Furthermore, he seems to have gleaned a distinctly romantic impression of the place:

> The islanders of Rum are reputed the happiest of the Hebrideans; both on account of the low rent which Mr Maclean receives for his farms and because the isle furnishes a great number of large and small cattle, which supply them all with meat. Their principal occupations are the care of cattle, fishing and the gathering of seaweed, which they burn for the purpose of extracting alkali.

Kelp-burning is unlikely ever to have been a major resource in Rum, however, since there are few beaches where it could be easily collected; any that could be gathered would probably have been used as fertiliser on the fields.

The Rev. Maclean had recorded in the *Statistical Account* that the SSPCK ambulatory school in the parish had survived until 1792, when a parish school came to be established on Eigg. (Oddly, the Rev. John Walker, in his detailed report on the Hebrides, dated 1764 and 1771, had failed to record any schools at all in any of the Small Isles.) The number of SSPCK schools in Scotland began to decline in the nineteenth century and were finally wound up in 1890.

The strict anti-Gaelic policy of the SSPCK had been dropped by the end of the eighteenth century. Although the complete Bible had been translated into Gaelic as early as 1690, this was a classical form of the language which soon became outdated. A New Testament in Scottish Gaelic was first published in 1767, with the Old Testament being issued in parts from 1783 to 1801. The Edinburgh Society for the Support of Gaelic Schools was set up in 1811, its 'sole object being to teach the inhabitants of the Highlands and Islands to read the Sacred Scriptures in their native tongue'. Auxiliary Societies were soon launched in Glasgow and Inverness. Their schools were intended to complement the 290 SSPCK institutions then operating in the Highlands and Islands.

The teachers were peripatetic and not intended to stay more than eighteen months at any one location, providing two terms of teaching to avoid interference with farm work – November to March inclusive, and mid-June until mid-September. English reading, writing and arithmetic were taught along with Gaelic. By 1818 the Inverness Society had enrolled 300 scholars in sixty-five schools, with an annual expenditure of £1013, all voluntary contributions.

In a report to the Gaelic Schools Society in 1811 the Rev. Neil Maclean, the Small Isles' new minister, reiterated his predecessor's complaint about the far-flung nature of his parish:

> The parish of the Small Isles, containing a population of upwards of 1500, comprehends four islands, viz. Egg, Islemuck, Rum and Canna, separated by boisterous seas, the navigation of which is difficult and dangerous. In winter and spring it is often totally impracticable to cross from one to the other. During a tract of severe weather in these months, I have been unable for five, six or seven weeks, to get to the remotest of these islands, and even then perhaps at the risk of my life. The clergyman must preach and discharge other sacred duties in all the islands, at all seasons of the year.

In fact, Mr Maclean's successor, 63-year-old William Fraser (1754–1817), was drowned between Arisaig and Eigg, only a year after he took up his appointment.

Nor were the Catholic clergy exempt from privation. In 1822 Father Anthony Macdonald was described as 'often in great danger to health and life, especially in winter storms, which made the crossing from one island to another always a dangerous matter and often impossible.' Despite his delicate health, Macdonald died in Eigg in 1843, in the forty-ninth year of his ministry and seventy-third year of his life. Previously the chapel house in Eigg had been at Kildonan on the east side of the island, while before that Mass used to be said in a large cave, beyond the famous Massacre Cave. Dom Odo Blundell quoted an islander's version of the move to new premises. Donald Mackay told him:

> My grandfather was fiddler to the Laird of Muck [Maclean], and he had so great a reputation as a musician that Clanranald determined to have him on his own property. Said Clanranald to my grandfather: 'If you will settle in the Isle of Eigg, I will give you a fine house and a good croft.' Well, my grandfather went over and had a look at the house, but he was not pleased at all, at all! However it happened that the priest was wanting the big house and croft [at Cleadale] and my grandfather thought that the priest's house and croft would suit him well, so they exchanged and that was how Father Anthony came over to the west side of the island.

In 1842 Alexander Gillis had moved to 'the ancient and interesting mission of the Lesser Isles' (to quote his obituary notice). But the emigration of some of the best of his flock, his meagre stipend and the dilapidated state of his house, not surprisingly, depressed him. In winter his isolation was almost complete, and once no boat could reach the island with supplies for twelve weeks. Notwithstanding, Father Gillis was long remembered for his skill at shinty, it being an ancient custom in Eigg for Protestant and Catholic alike to play the game on the beach at Laig every Christmas and New Year's Day. Almost certainly his counterpart in the Protestant church in Eigg would have severely disapproved of such frivolities as shinty and fiddle-playing.

In his 1811 report to the Gaelic Schools Society the Rev. Neil Maclean stated that Muck had a population of 190, Canna 392, Eigg 445 and Rum 445.

> There is a Society schoolmaster [in Rum] but owing to the extent, the extreme ruggedness and detached nature of the country, much general benefit cannot be expected to result from his labours ... If it were consistent with the plan of your teachers to remove occasionally from one farm to another, I am of the opinion that in Rum most good might be done; but having the school stationary ... not above 40 or 50 or so could conveniently be assembled in one place.

In March 1822 a missionary minister, the Rev. A. Macleod, accompanied Mr Maclean, the tacksman of Kinloch in Rum:

> I have this day examined the School opened here in November last, upon the benevolent scheme of your Society. The number of scholars present are 34 – 10 of them having read with correctness in the New Testament, 6 in the Psalms, and the remaining 18 are making good progress in the elementary books of their native language. The exhibition the young pupils of your happy institution have made here, and in every other place where I have been present at an examination of this kind, must have given heart-felt joy to all who witnessed the same, if ever they revered God or considered religion of any importance for promoting the happiness of the human race.

The following winter (1822/3) Murdoch Ross, the Rum teacher, had forty-one pupils, and in 1833, when the teacher was Alexander Macdonald, there were twenty-one. By 1839 the Society school in Rum and the other Small Isles had closed, although a parish school still operated in Eigg. The Society was then in serious financial difficulties and their schools all over the Highlands had begun to close down. Following the Disruption of 1843 the Society foundered altogether.

Another informative visitor to Rum was John MacCulloch. Born in

Guernsey in 1773, he qualified as a surgeon but instead turned to geology. He came to the Highlands every year from 1811 to 1821 and published encyclopedic letters to his old friend, Sir Walter Scott, in four octavo volumes in 1824. The actual date of his being storm-bound at Guirdil in Rum is unclear, but the occasion provided a lively narrative of the remote community there early in the nineteenth century:

> With the assistance of the villagers ... the boat was hauled up dry and we made our minds to remain a week; by no means an unlikely event. But we should not have been starved, while there was a Highlander who had a potato. We were in at least as much danger of being devoured with kindness. One [islander] hoped that if I visited his neighbour, I should also come to him. 'The house of one [neighbour] was only two miles off; that of another only five.' I could pass one night at Papadill; or one at Kilmorie – 'it was but a bittie over the Hill'. But as it was impossible to go to all, it ended, as was natural, in taking up with the nearest Maclean who spoke the best English.
>
> If I am to be wrecked anywhere I will choose Rum; for the Rumites are not rich. I have spoken of the antiquities of Highland hospitality before ... In ten minutes the potato kettle was put on the fire, and my boat's crew was provided with such fare as the house afforded. I was taken into the parlour ... [given a 'crazy chair'] and regaled with tea. But as the day wore on, the potatoes were eaten, there was nothing to do, and it continued to blow and rain, as if Rum itself would have been blown about our ears.
>
> The neighbours had come to see the strangers; and a considerable ogling began to take place among some of my handsome lads and the damsels. There was an old fiddle hanging up in a corner, very crazy in the pegs and in the intestines, but still practicable. My host could scarcely scrape and the Cremona was not even in scrapeable trim. But at length, by dint of the boatswain's mate, a little philosophy, and a little oakum, the pegs were repaired and the strings eked out, as well as if Stradivarius himself had had the management of the business. ... Little did I foresee, when solving some obscure fluxion in the theory of vibrating strings, that I should ever have fiddled to a ball in Rum ...
>
> A ball here requires no great preparations, it must be allowed. The lasses had no shoes, and marvellous little petticoat; but to compensate for those deficiencies they had abundance of activity and good will ...
>
> But all human happiness must end ... The sun blazed out beneath the cloud, and the fiddle ceased. But I protracted the evil hour as long as I could, in tender pity to the prettiest girl of the party [Peggy Maclean], who had been sudden and quick in falling in love with a

handsome lad belonging to my crew, and was weeping bitterly at the thoughts of parting ...

I had ballasted the boat with as much bloodstone as would have furnished the shops in London. But still it blew hard, and the boat would not scud so I was obliged to throw the ballast overboard ...

There is a great deal of stormy magnificence about the lofty cliffs; as there is generally all round the shores of Rum; and they are, in most places, as abrupt as they are inaccessible from the sea. The interior is one heap of rude mountains, scarcely possessing an acre of level land. It is the wildest and most repulsive of all the islands. The outlines of Halival and Haskival are indeed elegant, and render the island a beautiful and striking object from the sea ... Loch Scresort is without features or character; the acclivities ascending gently from a flat and straight shore. If it is not always bad weather in Rum, it cannot be good very often; since, on seven or eight occasions that I have passed it, there has been a storm, and on seven or eight more in which I have landed it was never without the expectation of being turned into a cold fish ... it possesses a private winter of its own, even in what is here called summer!

It was on one of those occasions when I could not keep the sea, and knew nothing about the land, that I met a young man in the usual shepherd's dress, and accompanied him to his house, to remain as long as it should please the elements of Rum. When shall I go into such a house in England, find such manners and such conversation under such plaids, and see such smoky shelves, covered not only with the books of the ancients but of the moderns; books too not lying uncut, but well thumbed and well talked of.

The irrascible MacCulloch's uncharacteristically sympathetic sketch of Rum's inhabitants – if less charitable about the island itself or its weather – marked the end of an era. Two years after his book was published, the people with whom he had enjoyed the ceilidh, young Peggy Maclean included, were evicted from their native island and despatched to Canada.

Feral Goats

7 Fertile and Fruitful

— all seemed to bespeak the place a fitting habitation for man, in which not only the necessities, but also a few of the luxuries of life, might be procured ...

Hugh Miller, 1845

It is likely that in prehistoric times much of Rum was covered in scrub forest, especially in the north and east of the island and in the more sheltered glens to the south. Woodland clearance probably began with the first farmers in Neolithic times and continued into recorded history. An ancient poetical name for Rum was *Riogachd na Forraiste Fiadhaich*, the kingdom of the wild forest. Even by the end of the seventeenth century, Martin Martin could record that 'the north end produces some Wood'.

The Rev. John Walker (1764) made some astute observations in the light of recent efforts to recreate the scrub forest:

But as the Bulk of the Island is defended from the Strong South West Wind by a ridge of Mountains, it is likely that the Wood would thrive well upon it; nor is it probable that it can ever be turned to so much account, as by being sown entirely with the Seeds of various Timber, and converted into a Forest. It has once been well wooded, and in some of the steep Gullies, inaccessible to Cattle, the Oak, the Birch, the Holly and Rowan Tree, are still to be observed growing vigorously.

By the end of the eighteenth century, however, according to the *Old Statistical Account (OSA)*, any surviving woodland had gone. Only a few relict trees survived beyond the reach of sheep and fire. In the 1820s, when Dr Maclean, the new grazing tenant, built Kinloch Lodge, he shaded it with trees; 'the south side of the lawn is flanked by a garden, and the north side partly by trees and partly by a low-built, comfortable cottage.' This cottage, the oldest in the island but now much altered, functions as the post office-cum-shop and some of the trees still survive behind it. In 1847 Lord Salisbury's Factor had some sallows planted at Kinloch 'to make a fence around the green' and in 1890 John Bullough planted 8000 trees.

There is no longer any trace of Bullough's plantations at either Kilmory or Harris but many do still thrive around Kinloch, such as the conifers on the north side of Loch Scresort and in the mixed woodlands on the South Side and round the village. It is obvious from early photographs of Kinloch Castle that George Bullough must have added many more ornamental trees and shrubs. Now, of course, Scottish Natural Heritage and its predecessor bodies are actively engaged in re-establishing woodland cover across much of the north and east of the island – efforts that would have gladdened the Rev. Walker's heart.

In 1772 Thomas Pennant landed at

> the little village Kinloch, of about a dozen houses, built in a singular manner, with walls very thick and low, with the roofs or thatch reaching little beyond the inner edge, so that they serve as benches for the lazy inhabitants, whom we found sitting on them in great numbers, expecting our landing, with that avidity for news common to the whole country ...
>
> Entered the house with the best aspect, but found it little superior in goodness to those of Ilay; this indeed had a chimney and windows, which distinguished it from the others, and denoted the superiority of the owner: the rest knew neither windows nor chimnies; a little hole on one side gave an exit to the smoke: the fire is made on the floor beneath; above hangs a rope, with the pot-hook at the end to hold the vessel that contains their fare, a little fish, milk and potatoes.

The *Old Statistical Account* told us how the people may have dressed (see Chapter 6) while, about the Canna folk, Pennant added that

> all the clothing is manufactured at home: the women not only spin the wool, but weave the cloth: the men make their own shoes, tan the leather with the bark of willow, or the roots of the *Tormentilla erecta*, and in defect of wax-thread, use split thongs.

At the beginning of the century Martin Martin had been generous in his assessement of Rum, the island being 'mountainous and heathy, but the coast is arable and fruitful'. The old cultivations are still obvious today where the soil had been heaped up, using a *cas-chrom* or 'foot plough', into parallel ridges, *feannagan* or lazy-beds. (The *OSA* mentions only two ploughs – presumably drawn by horses or oxen – in Rum, compared with seven or eight on each of the other Small Isles.) Much back-breaking toil was involved in the construction of these lazy-beds, quite contrary to the name they are popularly accorded today; this derives from an obsolete Old English word meaning untilled or uncultivated, probably referring to the strip of ground on which the bed was built. The parallel ditches between each ridge assisted drainage in the otherwise wet, boggy earth. The meagre soil was fertilised annually with seaweed, a scarce commodity according to John Knox in 1786, and old, soot-impregnated thatch from the houses.

The social structure was a communal one, with the blackhouses grouped together wherever shelter was afforded from the sea winds. The nine townships mentioned by Pennant can easily be identified on a large-scale map of the island, surrounded by field systems of lazy-beds. Because the only major ground disturbance took place at Kinloch and no later crofting settlement has been imposed anywhere else, the village and field pattern is remarkably well preserved. Harris was the largest single settlement, comprising about thirty blackhouses clustered together behind the raised beach. A further twenty or so dwellings can be seen at the mouth of the Kilmory River.

I have traced over 100 blackhouse ruins in Rum, which would easily have accommodated the peak population (using the Rev. Walker's calculation of about five persons per household). A few houses may have fallen into disuse prior to the Clearances, since a small group on Gualann na Pairc, above the Mausoleum at Harris, are partly obscured by later lazy-beds. Most of the houses vary from about 6m to 14m long, by 3m or 4m across, with anything smaller being used as barns or byres. Associated also with most of these settlements or clachans, are small walled enclosures or kailyards where garden produce may have been grown in summer, and stock penned in the winter; as a consequence these would have been richly fertilised and still contain a bright green sward today.

Under periodic runrig, strips were allocated each year and this ensured a fair distribution of both good and indifferent land. It did, however, deter the user from making serious attempts to improve his allocation – since it was only temporary – and, to southern eyes at least, this system was seen to be stifling progress. It demanded a common crop, common rotation and common dates for ploughing, sowing and reaping. To avoid discord in the community these dates had to be strictly adhered to. The *OSA* noted:

> the seed time begins about the first of April and the harvest about the 12th of September. In Isle Muck the harvest was somewhat later, and yet the seedtime somewhat earlier. Last year, 1793, the crop was not all got in till the end of November.

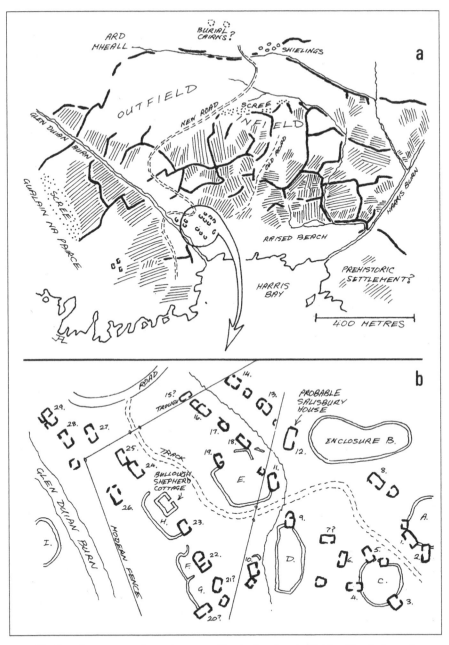

Top Pre-clearance runrig settlement at Harris showing the fields of lazybeds, each surrounded by stone and turf dykes.

Bottom Sketch map of Harris village with about 30 blackhouse ruins, associated byres and enclosures. One house (number 12) is of dressed stone, probably built or at least renovated by Lord Salisbury. Another – Harris bothy (at H) – was built later by the Bulloughs and is still used as a byre or stable.

The *OSA* listed that 'barley, oats, potatoes, flax, kails, and a few other garden stuffs' were grown in small quantities in the Small Isles. The *New Statistical Account (NSA)* added that

> sea-weed, both that which is cut, and that which is cast ashore by the winter storms, is the chief manure. With the aid of this, the people generally raise as many potatoes (on which they for the most part subsist) as are requisite for their maintenance during the whole of the year – each family requiring some 240 to 320 bushels.

Potatoes were introduced into the Hebridean diet around the middle of the eighteenth century. The best arable land around the settlement – the infield – could bear crops every year provided it was tilled and manured each spring ready for sowing three weeks later. The old six-rowed or bere barley rarely yielded as much as four-fold in the Highlands. After one crop, that land would then be sown with oats for a further two or three years, rarely yielding more than three to one. The *OSA* mentioned how

> in Canna, great oats answered pretty well; on Eigg, the cultivation of this grain has been attempted for two years past, but did not succeed. After it comes to the ear, it is lodged, and great parts of it rots on the ground, owing to the frequent and heavy falls of rain. [The situation must have been much worse in the wettest parts of Rum!] On barley and small oats, the rain has often a similar effect, though not in an equal degree. It is with reason believed, that green crops would answer better. The crop seldom affords the inhabitants a competent subsistence.

The outermost poorer land (yet still within the head dyke), termed the outfield, could only be tilled every other year or so, lying fallow between times. Fixed dates were also imposed for taking the stock to the hill pastures to prevent them damaging the growing crop. In winter, once the crops were harvested and the stock had returned from the hill grazings, the animals were allowed access to the stubble. Once this was exhausted they had to make do with whatever else was available, sometimes even venturing on to the beach to browse cast seaweed.

Walker computed that less than 1500 acres of Rum was cultivated (the *OSA* reckoned 1000 acres). He noted that

> as for corn, there is no more of it raised than what serves the people for bread a few months in Winter.

The *OSA* later explained how

> for several years past, a considerable quantity of meal has been annually imported [to the Small Isles], it having been necessary to feed their

cattle with a greater part of their own crop during the winter season, especially when severe ... It is an island of unfavourable climate.'

Walker added '[which] with its wet deep soil must prevent it from being ever profitable in the production of corn or cattle'.

The climate was obviously deteriorating for, in 1772, Thomas Pennant was more blunt:

There is very little arable land excepting about the nine hamlets that the natives have grouped in different places; near which the corn is sown in diminutive patches, for the tenants here 'run-rig' as in Cannay ... The little corn and potatoes they raise is very good; but so small is the quantity of bear [bere barley] and oats that there is not a fourth part produced to supply their annual wants: all the subsistence the poor people have besides is curds, milk and fish. They are a well made and well-looking race, but carry famine in their aspect. Are often a whole summer without a grain in the island; which they regret not on their own account, but for the sake of their poor babes. In the present economy of the island, there is no prospect of any improvement.

... Notwithstanding this island has several streams, here is not a single mill; all the molinary operations are done at home: the corn is graddan'd, or burnt out of the ear, instead of being thrashed: this is performed two ways; first by cutting off the ears, and drying them in a kiln, then setting fire to them on a floor, and picking out the grains, by this operation rendered as black as coal. The other method is more expeditious, for the whole sheaf is burnt, without the trouble of cutting off the ears: a most ruinous practice, as it destroys both thatch and manure, and on that account has been wisely prohibited on some of the islands ...

The quern or bra is made in some of the neighbouring counties in the mainland and costs about fourteen shillings. This method of grinding is very tedious: for it employs two pairs of hands four hours to grind only a single bushel of corn. Instead of a hair sieve to sift the meal the inhabitants here have an ingenious substitute, a sheep's skin stretched round a hoop, and perforated with small holes made with a hot iron. They knead their bannocks with water only, and bake or rather toast it by laying it upright against a stone placed near the fire.

... In every farm is one man, from his office called *Fear-euartaich*, whose sole business is to preserve the grass and corn: as a reward he is allowed grass for four cows, and the produce of as much arable land as one horse can till and harrow ... Very few poultry are reared here, on account of the scarcity of grain.

MacCulloch drily commented that

> in such a climate and with a soil of almost the worst qualities, it is not
> surprising that there is but little cultivation in Rum. Even that little is
> too much.

In common with much of the Hebrides however – as the Rev. Walker
had observed – Rum was less suited for crops than as pasture for stock.
Macfarlane's *Geographical Collections* has a reference from the sixteenth
century:

> The Illand is very profitable for there is abundance of butter, cheese
> and milk in this illand, for there is no cornelands in it, but such as doth
> grow in the twa tounes forsaid ...

In 1764 the Rev. Walker noted that 'flying bent grass', much favoured by
cattle and sheep, grew in abundance in Rum:

> from the middle of May to the end of July, it affords the richest Summer
> feeding that the Sheep have in the high Countries, but when it grows
> long, they shun it, as they do all Grass of a great height.

In 1811 MacDonald was very dismissive of the husbandry:

> In point of agriculture [Rum] is one of the most backward of all the
> Hebrides ... The proprietor attempted to introduce sheep instead of
> black cattle and horses but although they took well the inhabitants were
> prejudiced against them and soon returned to their ancient habits. In an
> agricultural light, therefore, Rum is a blot on the map of the Hebrides,
> and its population, however simple and virtuous, are in their present
> state a dead stock to the community and to themselves.

When Johnson and Boswell met him in 1773, young Donald Maclean of Coll,
the proprietor of Rum, had studied farming in England and 'was resolved
to improve the value of his father's lands, without oppressing his tenants,
or losing the ancient Highland fashions'. It was probably Young Coll's
efforts to which MacDonald referred, but the sheep he was unsuccessful in
introducing would have been a Lowland breed, probably Blackface, intended
to replace many of the old-fashioned animals that were there previously.
The *OSA* recorded that in 1791 'one farm in Eigg was begun to be flocked
with black faced sheep ... They seem to multiply and thrive well.'

Thomas Pennant had mentioned how

> the mutton [in Rum] is small, but the most delicate in our dominions
> if the goodness of our appetites did not pervert our judgement: the
> purchase of a fat sheep was four shillings and sixpence: the natives kill
> a few, and also of cows, to salt for winter provisions.

Interestingly, he added that 'the Canna folk supply themselves with wool from Rum at the rate of eight pence the pound'. Apparently, the laird had got rid of sheep from Canna since he deemed them unprofitable; he kept only a few to furnish mutton for his own table.

After reiterating how Rum was more fitted for pasture than crop, the *OSA* (1796) confirmed how 'there is a considerable number of small native sheep'. This would have been the rare breed that today we refer to as Hebridean. They are small of stature, often black or brown with a very fine wool that would have rendered them rather vulnerable to the wet West Highland winters; they may even have had to be wintered indoors. They often sport four, even six, long protruding horns. The *OSA* went on:

> their flesh is delicious and their wool valuable. A quantity of it is sent yearly to the Redcastle market near Inverness, where it often sells at 14 shillings the stone, while other wool sells about half that price. The island seems best calculated for rearing sheep, being almost wholly covered with hills and high mountains, but the proprietor's attachment to the inhabitants, has hitherto prevented its being stocked with them only.

Mrs Murray recorded yet another attempt to improve the stock in Rum. In 1801 Colonel Maclean [of Coll]

> insisted that one of the farms should be stocked with sheep. The farmer, with much reluctance, complied with his landlord's injunction, but instead of stocking his farm fully, he only put one half of the number of sheep the farm would feed; notwithstanding he sold the wool of the half flock of sheep the first year for £50 and the rent of the whole farm was only £60.

Pennant described the traditional 'souming'. This he considered

> an absurd custom of allotting a certain stock to the land; for example, a farmer is allowed to keep fourteen head of cattle, thirteen sheep, and six mares, on a certain tract called a 'penny-land'. The person who keeps more is obliged to repair out of his superfluity any loss his neighbour may sustain in his herds or flocks … No hay is made on the island; nor any form of provender for winter provision. The domestic animals support themselves as well as they can on spots of grass preserved for that purpose.

Sheep, then, do not seem to have been numerous in Rum before the Clearances and would have been kept as much for domestic use: milk as well as mutton and wool. The Rev. Walker mentioned 'the only articles exported from the Island are some Black Cattle and Horses'. Pennant confirmed how 'a number of black cattle [were] sold, at thirty or forty shillings per head, to graziers who come annually from Skie and other places'.

In 1807 Necker de Saussure added that

> the isle furnishes a great number of large and small cattle, which supply them with all their meat. Their principal occupations are the care of cattle, fishing and the gathering of seaweed.

The *OSA* gave the price of horned cattle to be about £3, sheep about 4 shillings and horses £3 10s. each.

The black cattle being referred to would have been smaller versions of the hairy, Highland cattle we know today. It seems to have been Queen Victoria who introduced the fashion for the familiar red beasts that now figure so prominently on calendars, postcards, etc. The *OSA* noted that 'the horned cattle of Canna and Isle Muck grow to considerable size, owing to the fineness of their grass'.

Pennant also noted 'an abundance of mares and a necessary number of stallions; for the colts are an article of commerce, but they never part with the fillies'. Dr Johnson commented how 'the horses are very small but of a breed emminent for beauty. Colonel [Donald] Maclean not long ago, bought one of them from a tenant, who told him that as he was of a shape uncommonly elegant, he could not sell him but at a high price, and that whoever had him should pay a guinea and a half.' A few years later the *OSA* confirmed that 'horses are reared for sale in Rum only: they are hardy and high mettled, though of small size'. Because Muck was also a property belonging to the Macleans of Coll, the people there, according to the *OSA*, were allowed summer grazing for their horses in Rum, as well as a great part of their fuel.

In his book *Ponies: Past and Present* (1900) Sir Walter Gilbey recorded that Lord Salisbury (father of Lord Cecil) thought Rum ponies in 1845 very like Spanish horses, and

> saw no reason why they should not be descended from the Spanish Armada horses which were wrecked on that coast. ... My father's theory about the Spanish Armada receives curious corroboration in the well known fact that a galleon lies sunk in Tobermory Bay: while in the 'Armada' number of the *Illustrated London News* which was published in 1888 ... there was a small map which showed the storms off the North and West of Scotland, which are almost exactly coincident with the occurrence of this particular type of pony, though no place was so favourable for breeding a type as a remote island like Rum.

This may have spawned a widespread belief that is still quoted to this day, but in fact the same claim is made for the ponies of Eriskay, Connemara and elsewhere – indeed, any inexplicable feature of northern Britain including Fair Isle knitting patterns!

The manifests for the Armada ships in 1588 show that there were no intact horses aboard, only a few geldings and mules to be used as pack-horses; in order to conserve water these had been jettisoned in the North Sea, before they ever reached the Hebrides. The Spanish cavalry – men and horses – had been left standing in the Netherlands while the storms blew the Armada through the Channel and into the North Sea.

The Rev. Walker gives another hint as to how the popular tradition might have arisen. He recounted how Clanranald had been a colonel in the Spanish service and, not long before he was killed at the battle of Sheriffmuir in 1715, had brought some Spanish horses to South Uist. 'These, in a considerable degree, altered and improved the horses in that and the adjacent islands.'

There has been much speculation as to the origins of Hebridean ponies. Undoubtedly prehistoric farmers brought ponies with them, and they also have much in common with Celtic ponies. Furthermore there will have been some interbreeding with Norse beasts during the Viking occupation. Certainly the chestnuts with silver mane and tail, so prized amongst the Rum stud today, bear a remarkable resemblance to Haflingers, while the typical mouse-dun colour with black eel-stripe is also found in the slightly smaller Fjord ponies of Norway, the Faroes and Iceland. The zebra stripes on the forelegs are also thought to be a primitive feature. Generally the Rum ponies are just over 13 hands high, thickset and stocky, with a large head and flowing mane and tail – useful against the notorious midges! Lord Salisbury's son also noted how

> every one of those I bought in 1888 had hazel, not brown eyes; and though only a small boy in 1862, when six or seven of those ponies came to Hatfield, I can remember that they also had the hazel eye.

James MacDonald had noted of the Hebridean pony how

> it is small, active and remarkably durable and hardy. In general the tenants pay no manner of attention to the stallions and the mares, but leave them almost entirely to chance. In summer and early autumn, one half of these horses and mares range freely and unconfined amidst mountains whence they are not brought to different farms and hamlets for work until the harvest is ended, the crop to be carried home, and the peat and fuel to be saved.

Just how widespread ponies or garrons were throughout the Highlands and Islands is suggested by the naturalist William MacGillivray in 1831:

> Horses were formerly kept in immense numbers which have, of late

been greatly reduced. They are small, but not diminutive like those of the Shetlands, robust, hardy, active, patient, docile, peacable and easily maintained ... The breed is by no means fine, the head being invariably large and the pile shaggy. There being few roads, horses are very seldom shod.

The Rev. Walker noted how 'there is a great number of Goats kept upon this Island', presumably for their milk, but, he goes on:

here I found an Article of Oeconomy generally unknown in other Places. The people of rum carefully collect the Hair of their Goats, and after sorting it, send it to Glasgow where it is sold from one shilling to two shillings and sixpence a pound, according to its Fineness, and there it is manufactured into Wigs, which are sent to America.

Eight years later Pennant mentioned that only 'a few goats are kept here'. After the Clearances they may have been left behind to fend for themselves, though the Salisbury papers (see later) reveal goats to have been released into the wild in the mid-1800s. The goats – whatever their origins – took to the inaccessible sea-cliffs, where they have reverted back to the wild type: long, shaggy coats of brown or black with long, upswept horns. About 200 still frequent the coasts of Rum, for some reason choosing to have their kids in February. Many die in the harsh winter weather so some nannies can breed again six months later. Goats do not like the rain, and usually seek shelter in the sea-caves.

In 1772 Thomas Pennant visited Jura – an island so similar in topography to Rum – where he saw

some sheelings or summer huts for goatherds, who keep here a flock of eighty for the sake of the milk and the cheeses. The last are made without salt, which they receive afterwards from the ashes of sea tang, and the tang itself which the natives lap it in.

He later landed 'on a bank covered with sheelins, the habitations of some peasants who attend the herds of milch cows'. Shielings were an important part of pastoral life in Rum too, and often attract the attention of modern visitors and hillwalkers; they soon came to preoccupy me while I lived on the island so I may be excused for dwelling a little on the topic. The shieling system, or transhumance, is a worldwide phenomenon, according to Professor R. Miller in *Scottish Studies* (1967); it is found

wherever climate or topography cause a seasonal variation in the value or availability of pasture, so that man and his flocks and herds must move their base at least twice in the course of the year in order to win the maximum use of the land.

This is distinct from nomadic pastoralism and has arisen, quite independently, in the Alps for instance, the Dolomites, Scandinavia and even the High Atlas – where the dominant factor is a highly seasonal incidence of rainfall. In the British Isles shielings are to be found in the Brecon Beacons of Wales, Cornwall, Ireland and the Highlands and Islands. Ancient Irish laws, dating from the seventh to the ninth centuries, describe going out from the winter residences to the summer pastures, and testify to the antiquity of the shieling system. Indeed, Miller suggested that transhumance may be as old as cultivation itself, since it was necessary for the stock to be removed a safe distance from the growing crops. Later, as enclosures and field systems developed and cattle could live in rotation with arable crops, many shieling areas could themselves become permanent farms. This is obvious from an abundance of Lowland place-names with a 'shiel' element, such as Galashiels in the Borders.

The shieling system persisted longer in the uplands, where the terrain was fit for nothing else but pasture; or in north-west Britain where high latitude and oceanic climate leads to impoverished acid soils, etc. The sheer physical limitations of climate, soil and topography led to the rural economy of the Highlands being geared towards stock-rearing – both for beef and dairying. Herds of black cattle could easily be maintained on the hill pastures during the summer before being driven to Lowland markets in the autumn. On mainland Scotland transhumance continued until the eighteenth century – later still in the West Highlands and Islands, even into the present century in Lewis where today some of the shieling bothies are maintained as holiday homes or for shelter at peat-cutting time.

The shielings began to fall into disuse as the ancient runrig system of agriculture became supplanted by 'modern improvements'; better fencing could keep stock away from crops, for example, and the people were being uprooted to make room for larger sheep farms or deer forests. In the case of Rum, they fell into disuse virtually overnight, when the entire human population was 'cleared' to Canada from 1826–8. Lowland shepherds were instead employed to graze the island slopes with Blackface sheep and modified some of the old shielings as pens for fostering lambs, etc. Miller postulated that many of the hill bothies must have been deliberately dismantled during the Clearances but their dilapidated state can easily be accounted for by the ravages of time and the hooves of sheep and deer.

Traditionally the move to the shielings began on May Day – the Celtic festival of Beltane or *Bealltuinn*. (This would be 1 May on the present calendar and to this day most townships in the Uists remove their stock from the unfenced machair cultivations by the 15th.) Spring would not yet have come to the high ground so initially the stock were just moved outwith the High Dyke. In some places a watchman (*fear coimhead*) was often appointed to protect the new-sown crops; he was often allocated the outermost and most vulnerable rigs to ensure his diligence. A dyke of stone and turf, however, proved rather an ineffective barrier to nimble animals. Since the watchmen were often old people, past strenuous work, they disposed themselves about the arable land with enthusiastic young children doing the herding. 'The old men's brains directed and the children's legs kept the cattle away,' as Frank Fraser Darling put it.

A few weeks later the move to the shielings proper began – the great flitting or *Latha dol do'n ruighe*. Often the menfolk had gone on ahead, with the young and yeld animals not required for farmwork; they could then repair and thatch the shieling huts ready for the women and boys arriving with the rest of the stock. The day of the flitting was also referred to as *Glanadh a'bhaile*, the cleansing of the village. When the men returned from the hill, leaving the womenfolk and the children with the stock, they had many tasks to perform. The houses were re-thatched, and the old soot-impregnated roofing material was spread on to the growing crops as fertiliser. The crops were howed, peats cut and stored for the winter, fish dried and leather tanned.

The manufacture of butter and cheese was the principal occupation at the shielings; these commodities formed not only an important item in the diet of the people but also served as currency. The dairy produce derived mainly from the milk of sheep and goats, but milk cows were also kept; the remaining cattle were being grazed for the autumn market. Very little beef was eaten by the Highlanders themselves as Martin Martin observed: 'there is no place so well stored with such quantity of good beef and mutton, where so little of both is consumed by eating'. In seasons of bounty, hoards of butter were buried in peat – whether to improve the flavour or for long-term storage to safeguard against famine is not really clear. Kegs of bog butter have been found on Skye and elsewhere.

The sheep were small 'with white or reddish faces and white wool', according to the *OSA*. The wool was plucked rather than clipped and it was the job of the womenfolk to spin and bleach it; they also gathered herbs and lichens for dyeing. The shielings were usually located within easy reach of the village so that, each day – or once or twice a week – the youngsters could be despatched with supplies of milk, butter and cheese for their fathers at work below.

There are few contemporary accounts of shieling life but that ever-observant travelling geologist Hugh Miller once visited a shieling under the great basaltic escarpment in Eigg. He described the incident in his *Cruise of the Betsey* (1869):

> The shieling, a rude low-roofed erection of turf and stone, with a door in the centre some five feet in height or so, but with no window, rose

on the grassy slope immediately in front of the vast continuous rampart. A slim pillar of smoke ascends from the roof, in the calm, faint and blue within the shadow of the precipice … Save the lonely shieling, not a human dwelling was in sight. An island girl of 18, more than merely good-looking, though much embrowned by the sun, had come to the door to see who the unwanted visitors might be … And as she set herself to prepare for us a rich bowl of mingled milk and cream, John [Stewart] and I entered the shieling. There was a turf fire at one end, at which sat two little girls, engaged in keeping up the blaze under a large pot, but sadly diverted from their rude work by our entrance; while the other end was occupied by a bed of dry straw, spread on the floor from wall to wall and fenced off at the foot by a line of stones. The middle space was occupied by utensils and produce of the dairy – flat, wooden vessels of milk, a butter churn, and a tub half-filled with curd; while a few cheeses, soft from the press, lay on a shelf above. The little girls were but occasional visitors, who had come out of a juvenile frolic, to pass the night in the place; but I was informed by John that the shieling had other inmates, like the one so hospitably engaged on our behalf, who were out at the milling and that they lived here all alone for several months every year, when the pasturage was at its best, employed in making butter and cheese for their master, worthy Mr MacDonald of Keill.

It tended to be the job of the young lads to herd the animals, to prevent them from straying, drag them out of bogs, and often to make the journey home with the produce of the day.

The time spent at the shielings was up to two months, dependent upon the weather. Traditionally the day of returning was *Lunnasdal*, August. The night of the flitting, *Oidhche na h-Iomraich*, was marked by great excitement. Crowds from the village ascended to help. After the final milking everything was packed. Grass and heather bedding was carried outside and burnt. The turf roof was dismantled to prevent it damaging the wooden roof struts in the winter gales. If timber was scarce, as in islands such as Rum, the people would take home their roof beams for safe storage. Old cows set off, followed by the other stock, and finally the people carrying all their belongings back home.

My survey showed that Rum possessed a fine array of shieling ruins, no two alike. Indeed, the only consistent feature of hut design appears to be the great variety of form. They usually occurred singly or in small groups of three or four, rarely as many as eight or nine. The oldest type seems to have been conical in shape, built completely of overlapping stone slabs and covered in turf. With the walls gradually closing in – a technique known as corbelling – the huts became an almost conical beehive structure.

Alexander Carmichael referred to this as *Both cloiche*, a stone bothy, to distinguish it from *Both cheap*, built entirely of turf.

In an article in *Scottish Studies* (1982) about the 400 or so shielings in Rum, I referred to these conical beehives as cellular huts. About 28 per cent of those in the island were of this type. All but one had collapsed inward so it was impossible to determine the interior height. All were either circular or oval and few exceeded 3m in diameter. They tended to be commonest where there was an abundant supply of stone, such as scree slopes. Many shielings also tended to be in sheltered nooks and crannies, close to freshwater and, of course, to areas of good grazing – mostly within the 50 m and 350 m contours.

By far the most common type of shieling hut in Rum was a chamber (44 per cent of all those on the island). The basic unit seems to have been a low circular or oval wall of stone. No obvious roofing slabs lay within so the structure was probably completed with a framework of timber overlaid with turf. The chambered huts ranged from 1m to 5m across but the larger constructions probably served as enclosures rather than dwellings and so probably never supported a roof. More than half of the chambers had one or two small cells attached, while a few had a small detached cell nearby; these were built of corbelled stone, rather like the cellular huts described above. The entrances, from the main chamber, were small but sufficient to admit a small adult or youngster who may have used it as a sleeping cell. More likely, however, the cells could have served for storage of dairy utensils and produce although recent research into shielings in Skye indicate that they may have been used for smoking the produce (Roger Miket, pers comm).

The remaining 28 per cent of the 377 huts I located in Rum were basically rectangular in plan, with the walls thicker and more substantial than the other two types. Most measured some 3m or 4m long by 2m across; they had an obvious door and some had two, usually facing east away from the prevailing winds. About half of them had associated cells attached or nearby. A distinctive feature of many was a line of kerb stones within, demarcating about half of the floor space which, when filled with heather, would function as a bed, much as Hugh Miller described.

While it is possible to state with some confidence that none of the shielings in Rum was occupied beyond 1828, it is impossible to say when the huts were first constructed. The cellular design is obviously an ancient one, being employed by Celtic monks in the sixth century, and most probably modelled on earlier prehistoric structures. I suggested a crude chronology of design based on the degree of mounding obvious beneath the shieling huts – debris from previous use. Few of the cellular structures were mounded but one-quarter of the chambered ones and nearly half of the rectangular ones were set up on mounds accumulated from previous

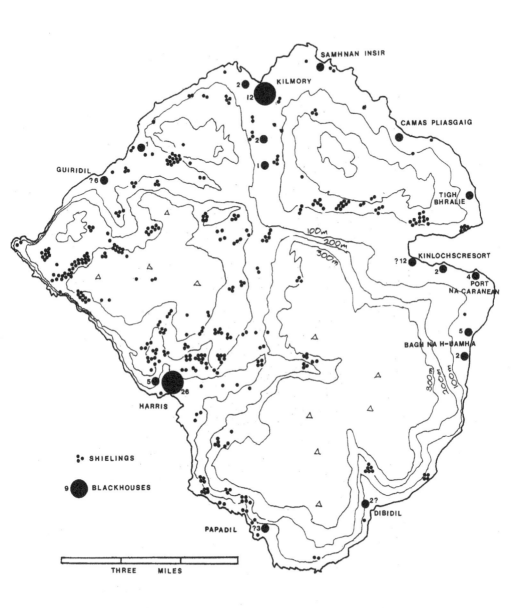

The distribution of blackhouses and shieling ruins on the isle of Rum,
as surveyed by the author.

structures. Excavation of these mounds in Skye has confirmed the remains of earlier structures beneath.

Several accounts advocate how idyllic shieling life could be, the only holiday the people could afford. Indeed on fine summer days it may well have been enjoyable, but more often than not in the Hebrides, it can be cold, wet and miserable. Also, prior to the 1745 Rising, clan feuds were commonplace. The remote shielings to which the women and children repaired in the summer doubtless provided some refuge from raiders. Some of the shieling groups in Rum are remarkably well concealed, especially if they had once been covered with fresh turf. Others are in secure positions, such as those built between the huge boulder blocks on the slopes of Barkeval. One or two are conveniently close to natural caves in boulder fields and the groups around An Dornabac are within easy reach of a cliff-girt prominence. The promontory fort at the summit of An Sgurr in Eigg may well have served as a spectacular refuge for the inhabitants of the shielings in the vicinity.

Rum Cuillin

8   *Sustenance from the Chase*

During the summer [the people of Rum] live entirely upon animal food, and yet are healthy and long-lived ...

Rev. John Walker, 1764

The good Reverend went on to note how

The year before I was there a man had died in the Island aged 103, who was 50 years of age before he had ever tasted bread; and during all the remainder of his long life, had never eat of it from March to October, nor any other food, during that part of the year, but fish and milk; which is still the case with all the inhabitants of the island.

Fish was, then, a mainstay. In 1845 Hugh Miller was told how

The expatriated inhabitants of Rum used to catch trout by a simple device of ancient standing, which preceded the introduction of nets in to the island ... The islanders gathered large quantities of heath, and then tying it loosely into bundles, and stripping it of its softer leafage, they laid down the bundles across the stream on a little mound held down by stones, with the tops of the heath turned upwards to the current. The water rose against the mound for a foot or eighteen inches, and then murmured over and through ... Next a party of islanders came down the stream, beating the banks and pools, and sending a still thickening shoal of trout before them, that, on reaching the miniature dam formed by the bundles, darted forward for shelter, as if to a hollow bank, and stuck among the slim hard branches, as they would in the meshes of a net. The stones were then hastily thrown off, – the bundles pitched ashore, – the better fish, to the amount not unfrequently of several score, secured, – and the young fry returned to the stream, to take care of themselves, and grow bigger.

It is likely that this would have taken place at the mouth of the Kinloch and Kilmory rivers, which have numerous brown trout and also see a small run of sea trout on high tides. In his book *The Limping Pilgrim* Edwin Waugh describes a similar fish-trapping tradition for the little lagoon in front of the present school. He called it *Reigan-na-Pol* or 'the best of pools'; the Ordnance Survey's old name book has it as *Raonapol*.

> The pool is fed by the streamlet which wanders down the mountain side through the little ravine. When the tide is out the pool is not more than twenty yards across; and it empties itself into the sea by a short channel about two yards in width. When the tide is in, however, the influx of water from the bay increases the pool very considerably, and, at the same time, brings into it fish from the sea, which are easily caught by netting in the narrow channel, before the water retires. It seems not unreasonable to suppose that it was because this pool was a kind of natural trap for the fish that come and go with the tide, that it first got the name of 'the Best of Pools'.

Martin Martin attested how in 1703 the rivers on each side of the island afforded salmon. A river fishing tradition persisted into the nineteenth century. In March 1847, it is recorded in the Salisbury papers how a number of salmon one and a half feet long were spotted in the Kilmory River. In March 1850 the local carpenter counted thirty-seven large fish and innumerable smaller ones in the Kinloch River and had never seen so many before. Bag nets were employed just off-shore for salmon but in October 1852 the fishermen were discharged for failing to catch any. This and the Kinloch rivers still held enough interest in 1854 for Lord Salisbury to construct two fish-ladders, the second consisting of no fewer than twenty-four pools (on the Kinloch River?). Although the Guirdil burn was deemed too steep and rocky, the other main rivers seemed well stocked with spawning fish and Salisbury's Factor even considered breeding salmon. The *New Statistical Account (NSA)* mentioned 'several freshwater lakes of considerable dimensions'. Small trout are abundant in some of them. This century at least, the hill lochs were stocked with brown trout.

But all this later activity was directed more to sport fishing. Before the Clearances the islanders themselves tried to exploit the sea fishing, especially herring. The *OSA* noted how herring are usually caught in Loch Scresort during the month of August,

> but the inhabitants being ill-provided in fishing materials, seldom catch

a competency for their own families … The only harbour in Rum is Loch Scresort, on the east coast thereof … Near the head and on the south side of this harbour, a pier was begun a few years since, which is still carried on but not finished. This is sustained a statute labour. This harbour, to be frequented, needs only to be better known.

The *NSA* added:

Upon the east side, there is a good, safe and commodious harbour, for all manner of shipping; and lately an excellent quay has been made there by the present tacksman of the island.

Although this quay dries out at low tide, it was not for want of a suitable harbour that fishing from Rum remained poorly developed. When John Knox arrived there in 1786 he found the people

all busy in packing herrings for their winter provision; and more might have been cured if they had been provided with salt. Mr Maclean, the proprietor of Coll, informed me that he was determined to give the inhabitants of that island every assistance for promoting the fisheries. I hope he will extend his benevolent endeavours to this bay also, erecting a small key [which he did, according to the *Statistical Accounts*], and supplying the people with salt and casks, for which they would pay ready money. By means of this aid, they would furnish all the inhabitants of the island in herrings, or white fish through the whole year.

However, as the *OSA* observed,

the salt laws are an object of great complaint in this parish, as well as in its neighbourhood. The late alterations in these laws have facilitated the getting, at a moderate rate, salt for curing fish; but still the custom-house forms, to which every purchaser of salt must submit, may be considered as a real grievance. If a person wishes to procure 2 or 3 barrels of such salt, to cure fish for the use of his family, he must enter it in a custom-house, if it should be 50 miles distant; he must grant bond and security for it. The fish so salted therewith, he must proceed with to a custom-house, however distant; there he must unship and repack it, and all this trouble and expense for a few barrels of his own family use.

In 1797 Edward Daniel Clarke elaborated:

A slight alteration in the excise laws, respecting the article of salt, would produce a very rapid change in favour of the Highlanders. For want of this necessary article some hundreds of them, during the present year, will be compelled to manure their lands with the fish they have taken; if they were permitted to manufacture it themselves, all Europe might be supplied from these islands, with the fish they would enable to cure. But, as the law now stands, the natives are constantly in perplexity and distress ...

The nearest custom-house to the island of Rum is Tobermory. When they arrive there, they are under the necessity of entering into a bond with regard to the salt they purchase, and make oath, under heavy penalties, that every grain of salt they take home, is to be altogether and entirely appropriated to the curing of fish. When the operation of curing the fish is completed, if a single gallon of the salt remains, they must make another voyage to the custom-house, with the salt and the fish they have cured; display both before the officers of the customs, and take up their bond. But if any part of the salt thus purchased is found afterward in their house, they become immediately subject to penalties, sufficiently burdensome to ruin them entirely, or effectually to put a stop to their future industry.

According to John Lorne Campbell 'Highland fisheries were hamstrung by the government's duties on salt, designed to protect the English saltmakers'. This ludicrous salt tax stifled the fishing industry, not just in Rum but throughout the Hebrides until its repeal in 1817.

The *OSA* related that cod and ling were most commonly caught off the coasts of Canna and Muck, these fishing grounds being 'more convenient to the harbours in these islands'. There is also an interesting reference to *cearban* or sunfish that appeared around the Small Isles in May, and sometimes remained until July. 'Their liver alone is useful for making oil, some of them yielding 12 barrels. This oil is also most frequently exported to the Clyde markets.' *Cearban* is the Gaelic for basking shark and there is no record of how these were hunted, but the practice was revived after the Second World War by the late Gavin Maxwell to be recounted in his book *Harpoon at a Venture*. The waters around the Small Isles were the centre of his operation.

Doubtless shellfish would have been gathered from the Rum shore but in the Highlands and Islands they tended to be looked upon as an inferior food only to be eaten in times of hardship. In March 1849 mention is made in the Salisbury papers of an oyster bed that was 'doing well' but the crows were taking some. Whether this was natural or specially cultivated, these shellfish were probably for the table of the big house. Two months later we are told that the Factor could get no oysters from Loch Hourn on the mainland but three bushels were obtained from Arisaig. In 1845 Hugh Miller was presented with a bucketful of razorfish, probably collected from the sands of Loch Scresort exposed at low tide. 'Winkles' or dogwhelks are still sometimes gathered off the rocks there by present-day islanders to export as a small supplement to their income.

The *OSA* also mentioned that around the Small Isles

the amphibious animals are seals and otters; the blubber of the one is made into oil, and the skin of the other is sold for fur, at a price proportionate to its size; some of them have been sold for above 12s sterling. Though the grown up seals feed at sea, they suckle their young on shore. There are two distinct species of seals, a smaller and a larger; the smaller brings forth its young about the middle of summer, and the larger about the middle of harvest. It is said the young are fully fat, and often killed, before they bring them to the sea.

These observations on breeding are consistent for the common seals that occur most frequently around the harbours of Eigg and Rum where they pup in June. Grey seals occur on the wilder, rocky coasts of Rum and Canna where they breed in October; they have become commoner in recent years probably due to a relaxation in persecution elsewhere. Otters are most often seen along the northern and eastern shores of Rum – often in broad daylight – but also occur on the other Small Isles. Earlier in the last century the shepherd at Kilmory in Rum used to shoot otters for their skins and, it was said, the income paid for his holidays to the mainland. The nail holes where he stretched the pelts to dry can still be seen on the back of the stair door of his cottage, where the deer researchers are based today.

Another form of seaware important to the islanders were Manx shearwaters, pigeon-sized petrels that come ashore to their nest burrows during the summer months; they spend the winter at sea often, according to modern ringing techniques, as far south as the coasts of Brazil and Argentina. The Rum colony is unique in that the birds choose to breed, not on coastal cliffs but on the tops of the highest mountains: Barkeval, Hallival, Askival and Trollval. This last hill has some of the highest densities of nest burrows, which may well have been occupied for a thousand years or more; the name is Norse and, since the Vikings would not have had much experience of shearwaters in their native land, they assumed these noisy, nocturnal creatures underground must have been trolls.

Why these seabirds should nest at such altitude is a matter of debate. The usual reason given is to escape the rats so abundant along the coast. The work of Bob Swann and his friends on Canna has demonstrated how rats can be destructive to nesting shearwaters, but in Rum rats occur all over the island and venture to the hilltops to scavenge the eggs and dead young of the shearwaters. I have long held the view that the rain-soaked seacliffs of Rum are not suitable for burrowing birds (puffins and storm petrels, for instance, are rare), whereas the coarse, gritty soils on the steep slopes of Rum's hilltops can be excavated to form drier, better-drained nest sites. This idea was given some credence recently by the meticulous postgraduate studies of Kate Thompson.

The Rum shearwater colony is also noteworthy for being one of the largest in the world; recent estimates put the number at 60,000. To visit the colony at night in midsummer when hoards of non-breeding shearwaters augment the regular population is something all visitors to Rum should experience. It is not surprising that so many birds, having nested up there for so long, have enriched the soils to form such a green and luscious sward and one that red deer are intrepid enough to seek out.

Early accounts often referred to shearwaters as gannets, solan geese or even puffins (the first scientific name of the species was *Puffinus puffinus*). As long ago as 1549 Dean Monro, for instance, recounted how 'many solan geise are in this Ile'. Timothy Pont's account from the end of the sixteenth century told of

> certane foullis which will be taken in these mountaines and are exceeding fatt, of the fattest birds or foulis which is in all the sea, they are no bigger than a dove and somewhat less in bigue. Somewhat grey in coloure of their feathers, being of the most delicate birds to be eaten that is bred within the whole illand, except that doe taste oyld.

A later version has it that

> more it hath certaine wild fowles about the bigness of a dow, grey-coloured, which are scarce in uthir places, good meat they are, but that to them who are not acquainted, they tast sumwhat wild.

Whether it is meant that shearwater flesh is oily or wild, the taste is very much an acquired one, especially by today's standards. To the ancient Rumaich, however, they were obviously a delicacy, as they were in Eigg until comparatively recently. They had made a welcome supplement to a rather monotonous diet, so in Rum at least, frequent mention of them is made in the literature. In 1764 the Rev. John Walker recounted how

> the Puffin of the Isle of Man also builds here, which is reckoned the greatest delicacy of all seabirds. It is rarely to be met with in other places, and keeps the sea all the year round except in hatching time. It builds in holes under ground and we found its nests among the loose rocks above a mile from the shore.

Although aware that Dean Monro had mentioned 'gannets', Thomas Pennant failed to encounter any during his visit to Rum in the summer of 1772. It was, however, 'excessively wet' when he climbed Hallival so he got no further than Coire nan Grunnd. Twenty-five years later Edward Daniel Clarke observed solan geese around his boat off Canna 'raising themselves to a great height in the air, and then plunging into the sea'.

From this description of the birds feeding these really were gannets and not Manx shearwaters. The *OSA* for Rum, however, added some interesting observations about what might be shearwaters:

> The puffins are found in considerable numbers, which, though sea fowls, lay and hatch sometimes at a great distance from the shore, even near the tops of high hills. Their young, before they leave the nest, are as large as the dam, transparent with fat, and delicious to the taste of many. It is believed, that the young puffin becomes so weighty with fat, as to be unable to take the wing and leave its nest: To remedy this inconvenience, the old puffin is said to administer sorrel, to extenuate, and render it fit for flying. It is, at any rate, a known fact, that sorrel is commonly found to grow near the puffin's nest.

Dean Monro hinted that in 1549 it was not only seabirds that were eaten by the islanders:

> In this Ile thair will be gottin about Beltane [1 May] als mony wild fowl nestis full of eggis about the mure as men pleases to gadder, and that becaus the fowls has few to start them except deiris.

Martin, Walker and Pennant also stressed the abundance of moorfowl, while the *OSA* reported how 'grouse are found in Rum and Eigg'. Red grouse will never be abundant in Rum for the heather cover is poor and the climate too wet. Red grouse were still common in 1871 and in 1889 John Bullough released about 200 pairs to augment the local stock. Judging by the game bags, this practice must have continued over the next decade. 1892 saw over 800 brace being shot, with nearly 700 in 1905. By the time records ceased to be kept in 1939 over 16,000 grouse had been shot, and the island is unlikely ever again to have supported more than fifty or sixty pairs. Partridges were also introduced and in 1849 were said to be 'doing well' even as far afield as Kilmory and Harris; they may have then died out. Bullough reintroduced some more and although twenty-seven were shot in 1893 they seem to have gone by 1909. Similarly, pheasants were released late in the nineteenth century and although as many as eighteen were bagged in 1903 they too died out soon afterwards. Ducks, even corncrakes (eleven were shot in 1908) were also considered fair game.

The *OSA* also reported that

> in some of the high hills of Rum, ptarmigan are found. In respect to size, they are somewhat less than grouse; and for security against birds of prey, they assume the colour of the ground; in cold seasons they are white as snow; in other seasons they are spotted white and blue, like the craggy cliffs among which they live.

At about the same time, in 1797, Edward Daniel Clarke encountered ptarmigan near the summit of Orval:

> [They] came so near me, and appeared so little alarmed at my intrusion, that I nearly took one of them with my hand … While I was thus employed upon the broad and bleak top of this mountain, which consists entirely of loose fragments of stone, destitute of any other verdure than a few patches of moss, I heard behind me a low, plaintive, and repeated whistle which, upon looking around, I perceived to originate in a flight of plovers, which had settled close to me among the stones. They were so tame as to admit my approaching almost near enough to put my hat over one of them …

While golden plover are still common in Rum today it sounds very much, as I have mentioned before, as though Clarke's plovers were, in fact, dotterel. These lovely Arctic waders, confined to breeding in Scotland only on the highest tops, are now rare vagrants to Rum – as are ptarmigan.

The main quarry afforded by the bleak moors of Rum, however, were red deer and in this respect the island has a particularly rich history. The first mention of deer in Rum is by Dean Monro who, in 1549, noted 'abundant little deiris' there. The report for James VI soon afterwards (and reproduced in Macfarlane's *Geographical Collections*) added that the island was 'permittit unlabourit' or left untilled, suggesting that Rum may have been maintained as a hunting preserve. Certainly at a court in Inveraray, Argyll, one infamous rogue – 'a common slayer of deare' called *Raghnall mac Ailein mhic Iain* or *MacRaghnall*, from Borve in Benbecula – was charged with having shot '6 deare in the Ile of Rowme' in the autumn of 1632, and then again the following season 'with a gun slew other 6 deare'. (In fact, it seems that the Protestant establishment was determined to pin something on this fervent Catholic.) So it is possible that the poetic name for Rum – *Rioghachd na Forraiste Fiadhaich* (kingdom of the wild forest) – may have more to do with deer than trees; it could just as easily translate as 'kingdom of the deer hunt'. Another name for the island that appeared in Gaelic poetry is *Rum riabhach na sithne* (brindled Rum of the venison).

In 1703 Martin Martin wrote how Rum's mountains had some hundred of deer grazing them and added:

> The natives gave me an account of a strange observation, which they say proves fatal to the posterity of Lachlin, a cadet of Maclean of Coll's family; that if any of them shoot at a deer on the mountain Fionchra, he dies suddenly, or contracts some violent distemper, which soon puts a period to his life. They told me some instances to this purpose: whatever may be in it, there is none of the tribe above-named will ever offer to shoot the deer in that mountain.

In 1764 the Rev. Walker observed how there was still 'a large herd of red deer kept upon the island by the proprietor' but eight years later Pennant noted only eighty left. The *OSA* claimed that there was a copse of wood in Rum that afforded cover for their calves from eagles and other predators. Edward Daniel Clarke put the extinction of deer in Rum as 1797. He claimed that

> The natives themselves destroyed several of them; but the principal cause of their extirpation must be attributed to the eagles, who devoured not only the young, but the old ones themselves. One would think it incredible that an eagle should venture to attack so large an animal as the stag of the great red deer. The mode in which the natives account for it is that the eagles plunged upon the head of the intended prey, and fastened between his horns. This drove the stag to madness, and he would speedily rush headlong down a precipice; when the eagle disengaging himself during the fall, would return at leisure to mangle the carcase of the expiring victim.

The late Seton Gordon in his classic book *The Golden Eagle* also had this story, adding that the eagle might cover the eyes of its prey with its wings so that the confused deer ran blindly over a cliff and killed itself. How this folk tale arose may not be quite as fanciful as it sounds. A student researching red deer in Rum in the 1980s witnessed a recently fledged golden eagle stoop at a full-grown deer. It managed to plant its talons so firmly in the back of the astonished quarry that the bird was carried some distance before it managed to disengage. One can quite imagine that a panic-struck deer, with vision obscured by the flailing wings of the eagle, might run inadvertently over a precipice. Such events are exceedingly rare however; golden eagles usually confine the occasional attack to deer calves only and are highly unlikely ever to bring their prey to the point of extinction.

It is likely that organised hunts for the clan chiefs would have contributed to a decline but as the human population on the island was increasing so, too, would the local demand for venison – whether obtained legally or not. Human want probably put an end to the deer in Rum. Again, it was Dean Monro who first gave us an account of the hunting in Rum:

> ... deir will never be slane dounewith, but the principal settis man be in the height of the hill, because the deer will be callit upwart, ay be the Tainchell, or without tynchell they will pass upwart perforce.

Settis is often interpreted as *saitts* but is merely an archaic spelling for *seats*; these were the deer traps while the actual hunt he called the *tainchell* or *tynchell* (possibly deriving from the Gaelic *tiomchioll*, meaning a circuit). The *OSA* gave an account of the operation:

Before the use of firearms, their method of killing deer was as follows: On each side of a glen, formed by two mountains, stone dykes were begun pretty high in the mountains, and carried to the lower part of the valley, always drawing nearer, till within 3 or 4 feet of each other. From this narrow pass, a circular space was inclosed by a stone wall, of a height sufficient to confine the deer; to this place they were pursued and destroyed. The vestige of these inclosures is still to be seen in Rum.

The *NSA* reiterated some of the detail and added some of its own:

About the centre of the Isle of Rum, long dikes may still be traced, which, beginning at considerable distances from each other, gradually approach, until at last they draw pretty near to one another. These are said to have been intended as toils for deer, which were once, as is well known, numerous in that island. To these enclosures the inhabitants collected them, and, forcing them by degrees to their narrowest recesses, they were finally caught by their pursuers. The places where these enclosures were made still maintain the names of *Tigh'n Sealg*, that is, the hunting houses; so that it is likely that at the termination of the dikes, houses were erected, into which the deer were constrained to enter, and in this manner a number of them would be at once secured.

As with most of Rum's ancient Gaelic place-names there is now no record of where these hunting houses occurred. There has been much speculation and one unlikely suggestion was that some dykes along the clifftop at Wreck Bay served to force panicked deer over the edge, to be dashed to death on the rocks below. Edward Daniel Clarke's account gives us a first clue:

We soon found ourselves in the centre of the crater of Oreval ... The bottom of the crater, like that of most extinct volcanoes, was occupied by a pool of water, surrounded by a morass. All the interior parts of the crater itself, that is to say, its sides diverging towards the pool, were destitute of any sort of vegetation, and consisted of loose, incoherent matter, which lay in strata one over the other, and occasionally, being detached by rain, had fallen towards the bottom.

From the summit of Orval one might interpret there to be a crater to the east – Monadh Mhiltich, which lies between Minishal and Ard Nev – and to the south in Glen Duian (also known as the Black Valley). However, only the former has a pool: Loch a'Ghille Reamhra (loch of the fat boy). This is likely to be the spot that Clarke described, but in 1980 I found the remains of deer traps in both 'craters'. I had long been aware of two stone and turf dykes running along the ridge between Orval and Ard Nev; the gap between them seems to have channelled the deer to a grassy slope amidst loose screes at the foot of which lay one or two faint v-shaped enclosures (NM 342993).

A more convincing structure in a better state of preservation, and functioning in a similar manner, is to be found on the south slopes of Orval (NM 329987). The *Nardus* heath on the summit forms attractive grazing for deer and a narrow strip extends down the steep south-easterly slope. Its edges have been built up with boulders from the loose scree on either side to clear an easy passage for stampeding deer. These walls converge towards a complex dry-stone enclosure. This is obscured from view at first by the gradient of the slope so that, all of a sudden, the animals would find themselves being forced through a narrow gateway, first into a rectangular enclosure some 8–19m long, and ultimately into a larger circular enclosure. This measures about 12m or 13m in diameter, with high stone walls which, even in their present ruinous state, attain a height of 2m or more. Built on the inside of this wall are several vague circular cells each about 2m or 3m in diameter, possibly refuges where a few waiting hunters could slaughter their unfortunate quarry.

I describe the structures in the magazine *Deer* (1980). The Glen Duian example, in particular, seems unnecessarily tall and elaborate to function purely for domestic stock and, at 470 m above sea-level, it is higher than all the other shielings I found in Rum. Its use as a deer trap would seem consistent with both archaeological and documentary evidence. Clarke went on to describe its use:

> Near the bottom of this crater, Mr Maclean showed me the remains of the snare used for taking the red deer, at a time when they were exceedingly numerous upon this island. About ten years ago they became perfectly extinct in Rum ... The mode in which these snares were constructed is this: a wall or rampart of stones was erected along the side of the mountain, flanking a considerable part of it near its base; at either extremity of which a pit was formed, concealed by a circum-ference of the same stones which formed the rampart. In this pit the hunter stationed himself with his gun. A number of people were then employed to alarm the deer, who instantly taking to the mountain and meeting the wall, ran along the side of it till they came to the pit, in which the sentinels were posted, who easily selected one of them as they passed, and levelled him with his musket.

Dean Monro described how in Jura deer were driven by men and dogs through the narrow isthmus at Loch Tarbert. There is an old reference to another island deer hunt among the Red Cuillin of Skye when 'a thousand head of deer were killed' while in North Uist, near Lochmaddy, is a place named *Suidheacha-sealg*, the hunting seat (NF 890671). In the nineteenth century there were said to be some ruinous dykes still visible on Ben Griam in Sutherland, and also in the Forest of Dunrobin, but I know of no stone enclosures that are so well preserved as the ones in Rum. They are clearly one of the island's major archaeological monuments.

The Rev. Dr Robertson, in his *Agriculture of the County of Perthshire* (1799), told how

> the natives hunted the deer by surrounding them with men, or by making large enclosures of such a height that the deer could not overleap, fenced with stakes and intertwined with brushwood. Vast multitudes of men were collected on hunting days who, forming a ring or 'tinchell' round the deer, drove them into these enclosures which were open on one side ... The enclosures were called in the language of the county 'elerig'.

According to W. J. Watson in *Celtic Review* (1913), this place-name is not uncommon in Perthshire and in Argyll, while there is a Carn Elrig in the Cairngorms. Gavin Maxwell wrote *A House Called Elrig* in southern Scotland where he spent his boyhood. Bogs and, in the case of North Uist perhaps, lochans were sometimes employed to help trap deer and in Sutherland there is 'bog of the high deer trap', *Feith na h-ard Eilreig*.

When Hugh Miller visited Rum in 1845 not only had the deer gone, but so too had the people. He noted along a distant hillside

> the ruins of a grey-stone fence erected, says tradition, in a remote age, to facilitate the hunting of deer; there were fields on which the heath and moss of the surrounding moorlands were fast encroaching, that had borne many a successive harvest; and prostrate cottages that had been the scenes of christenings and bridals, and blythe new-year's days; – all seemed to bespeak the place a fitting habitation for man ... but in the entire prospect not a man nor a man's dwelling could the eye command. The landscape was one without figures ... Uninhabited originally save by wild animals, it became at an early period a home of men, who, as the grey wall on the hill-side testified, derived, in part at least, their sustenance from the chase ... Then came the change of system so general in the Highlands; and the island lost all its original inhabitants, on a wool and mutton speculation, – inhabitants, the descendants of men who had chased the deer on its hills five hundred years before and who, though they recognised some wild island landlord as their superior, and did him service, had regarded the place as indisputably their own.

PLATE 1. The Rum Cuillin from Harris in the winter of 1982, looking down on the Bullough mausoleum and the Harris Lodge, both overlying the ancient lazybed system highlighted in the snow. The raised beach is also visible with the hills (left to right) Barkeval, Hallival, Askival, Trollval and Ainshval. (photo – J. Love)

PLATE 2. The smooth, rounded, granophyre hill of Ard Nev in the foreground contrasts with the rugged outline of the ultra-basic Rum Cuillin beyond – Barkeval on the left, with Hallival behind, then Askival, the highest summit, and Ainshval to the right. (photo – J. Love)

PLATE 3. The ruined cottage of the Maclean family above the secluded sandy beach of Samhnan Insir, where two arrowheads of bloodstone were found by a school party in 1964. (photo – J. Love)

PLATE 4. The lonely loch at Papadil tucked behind the boulder beach, with Muck behind and the Isle of Mull in the distance; Iona is out of view to the right. (photo – J. Love)

PLATE 5. The lazybed system enclosed by low turf walls which lies on the slopes above the raised beach at Harris: a modern sheep fank is visible in the centre distance, and the ruins of the pre-Clearance village to the right. (photo – J. Love)

PLATE 6. The sail-training vessel *Captain Scott* (now based in the Arabian Gulf) moored in Loch Scresort at sunset in August 1975 conjures up images of the vessels that would have anchored here to remove almost the entire population of Rum to North America between 1826 and 1828. (photo – J. Love)

PLATE 7. An aerial view of Glen Dibidil and the bothy with the conical peak of Trollval behind and Ainshval to its left. (photo – J. Love)

PLATE 8. The author's dog Rona at the head of Glen Guirdil with Bloodstone Hill on the left, Fionchra on the right, framing the Isle of Canna and the hills of South Uist on the distant horizon. (photo – J. Love)

PLATE 9. The Guirdil bothy (now reroofed) at the foot of Bloodstone Hill. (photo – J. Love)

PLATE 10. A watercolour by an unknown artist of New Loch, behind Salisbury's Dam, looking down Kilmory Glen to Skye, executed before the dam burst. (courtesy of the Marquis of Salisbury)

PLATE 11. An aerial view of Kinlochscresort showing Kinloch Castle surrounded by trees, with the post office and farm on either side of the river to its right. Looking up Kinloch Glen can be seen the pointed summit of Fionchra, with Minishal and Sgaorishal to its right. (photo – J. Love)

PLATE 12. Portrait of Sir George Bullough looking down from the balcony of the main hall of Kinloch Castle. (photo – J. Love)

PLATE 13. A painting of the Bulloughs' yacht *Rhouma* hanging in Kinloch Castle. (photo – J. Love)

PLATE 14. A landscape painting in Kinloch Castle showing its vicinity devoid of trees; the copse behind the post office originally surrounded the old Kinloch Lodge. (photo – J. Love)

PLATE 15. Kinloch Castle from the gazebo after a snowfall in January 1979. (photo – J. Love)

PLATE 16. Lady Bullough's portrait dominates the varied décor of the main hall of Kinloch Castle. (photo – J. Love)

9   *A Wool and Mutton Speculation*

The lairds, instead of improving their country, diminished their people.

Dr Samuel Johnson, 1773

The Royalist army of King Charles II included many clansmen. After their defeat at the battle of Worcester in 1651 a large contingent of Macleods were sold as slaves by Cromwell to the cotton plantations of South Carolina. Captain Porringer was then despatched in a man o' war to harry the Hebrides to deter the menfolk from ever again enlisting in the Royalist cause. Later, in the aftermath of the 1715 Jacobite Rising, no less than 800 more Scots captives were transported to the plantations as slaves.

In the spring of 1739 Captain William Davison took his ship, the *William*, into Bracadale in Skye and, under cover of darkness, kidnapped some of the inhabitants. He then sailed on to Finsbay in Harris where, the next night, he added more to his human cargo. There were about forty men, but no less than sixty were women and children, with the majority of children being under ten years of age. The *William* paused at Rum where five of the children, too young for the captain's purpose, were put ashore. Four more folk were left at Canna, along with the corpse of a young woman who had died on the ship.

Before setting off across the Atlantic the *William* berthed at her home port of Donaghadee in Ireland, where the prisoners managed to escape. This brought them to the attention of the authorities and although the local magistrate accorded them their freedom few ever found their way home again. What happened to the eleven put ashore on Rum, Canna and

Jura seems not to have been recorded. Nor is it clear whether this was an isolated incident or whether the *William* was the only such outrage to come to light. The *William* incident indicates the cheapness with which some Highland chiefs already held their clansmen. With a grim foretaste of the Clearances, the common people were coming to be seen as a mere encumbrance upon the chiefs' estates.

Where once a proud Highland chief, such as MacDonnell of Keppoch, could admit that his rent roll consisted of 500 fighting men, by 1773 Dr Johnson could only lament how:

> There was perhaps never any change in national manners so quick, so great and so general as that which has operated in the Highlands by the late conquest and the subsequent laws ... The clans retain little now of their original character. Their ferocity of temper is softened, their military ardour is extinguished, their dignity of independence is depressed, their contempt for government subdued, and their reverence for the chiefs abated.

The defeat at Culloden in 1745 had not only put an end to Jacobite aspirations, but it resulted in new laws that disarmed the Highland clans, abolished their national dress and terminated the patriarchal and judicial powers of their chiefs. As John Prebble observed, in his powerful book *The Highland Clearances* (1963), only a few clans had taken part in the uprising, but all felt the impact of the defeat. The new law and order imposed upon the north and west of Scotland finally made redundant the chiefs' need for the military service of their clansmen. Aristocratic tastes and aspirations acquired during their education in the south had instead made commercial profitability the prevalent motive behind the management of their estates. Already they were losing much of their influence over their people and Dr Johnson observed astutely how 'as they gradually degenerate from patriarchal rulers to rapacious landlords, they will divest themselves of the little that remains'.

Rents of tenants, who had formerly been clansmen, were increased; those in Skye, for instance, were trebled during the last quarter of the eighteenth century. Black cattle remained the only marketable product with which they could be paid. On the coasts, herring fishing was encouraged although this did not prove a popular occupation amongst Highlanders; pastoralists did not easily adapt to the ways of the sea. Indeed, Alexander Maclean tried to create a fishing village on his own island of Coll in 1787, but his tenants were reluctant to give up their land, which they perceived as guaranteeing not only a livelihood but also a traditional assurance for the future. He lamented

> that tradesmen of all descriptions are not to be got without procuring

farms for them, and no sooner is this procured them that they become farmers solely.

Increasing industrialisation had created an insatiable demand – and higher prices – for meat to feed an ever-hungry labour force. Cattle prices doubled between 1700 and 1760 and had doubled again, to about £4 a beast, by the 1790s to remain high during the Napoleonic Wars. But the forfeited Jacobite estates had demonstrated how the traditional runrig settlements in the Highlands could be run more economically as large, single farms. As that great agricultural reformer Sir John Sinclair of Caithness had concluded in 1795:

> The Highlands of Scotland may sell cattle at present, perhaps from £200,000 to £300,000 worth of lean cattle per annum. The same ground will produce twice as much mutton, and there is wool into the bargain.

New hardy breeds such as the Blackface and Cheviot were already fast replacing the native Hebridean variety, which Sinclair condemned as 'of an inferior naughty size', and sheep would soon start replacing the people themselves.

As long ago as 1695 an 'act anent lands lying runrig' had been passed to discourage this ancient system of agriculture but in the Highlands it had largely been ineffective due to the harsher terrain and the poverty and conservatism of the people. Even the potato, first introduced in South Uist about 1743, was resisted at first. But it was being grown in Skye and at Arisaig by the 1760s, and was soon widespread. By 1840 potatoes were to form over three-quarters of the Highlanders' diet. With a little fish and milk they provided healthy, if monotonous, fare. Furthermore, they required much less land to grow than cereal crops. This remarkably productive convenience food, together with the general availability of smallpox inoculation by the 1790s, was to encourage a great increase in the human population of the Highlands and Islands.

Voluntary emigrations from the islands had been taking place for several decades, as pressure on land increased. Between 1780 and 1790 some 238 folk are said to have quit the Small Isles and 183 of them made for the New World. Among them were three MacInnes brothers from Rum, whose father had been boatman to the chief of Clan Mackinnon and one of the men who had helped row the fugitive Prince Charles from Skye to the mainland in 1746.

Lachlan MacQuarrie was typical of many early emigrants from Rum. He was already well advanced in years when he left in 1791, along with his three sons and two daughters, to begin a new life in Nova Scotia. The forests would have been a completely new experience for him, and the harshness of the winter – drier maybe, but very cold with snow and frost.

Otherwise the landscape might not have looked too unfamiliar and there would already have been Gaelic-speaking communities well established. MacQuarrie's eldest son Angus was already forty-two and married to Una Macdonald from Eigg; they had six children. Another son, Allan, was thirty-eight and married to Janet Maclean with seven children; he died in 1813. Old Lachlan's other three children – Neil, Marion and Flora – were all over thirty when they too quit their native island of Rum for the New World.

Once the Napoleonic Wars began in 1793 traffic across the Atlantic ceased for a time. The Highlands had long proved a fertile recruiting ground for the British Army, starting with the Black Watch Regiment in 1739. Highlanders had fought overseas in the Seven Years War, and then the War of Independence. It is said that the Highlands, with a population of some 300,000, furnished 74,000 men for the Regular Army, the Fencibles, Militia and Volunteers.

The Fencibles were regular troops enlisted for service at home and for the duration of hostilities only. Eleven from the Small Isles joined the Breadalbane Fencible Regiment in March 1793, for instance. The Scotch Militia Act was passed in 1802. Each county had to provide a fixed quota, selected by ballot, from men aged between eighteen and fifty, who were then committed to a three-year engagement. A variety of excuses were acceptable for exemption, such as trade commitments and apprentice training. Alexander Hunter, the agent who supervised the clearance of Rum in 1826, also explained that during the Napoleonic Wars the men of the island

> all married very early in order to have the number of children requisite to exempt them from the militia; boys of 16 and 17 married, which is the cause of the great increase in the population.

It was not long before their commitments stretched the Militia's role as home guard so that third line forces became necessary. This new service did not press anyone to overseas service; it was entirely voluntary and under the command of the Lord Lieutenant of the county. Being only privately raised and funded, there was no full-scale issue of arms or any official training; as an anti-invasion force they might be considered the equivalent of the Home Guard in the Second World War. About 200 companies of Volunteers were eventually raised throughout Great Britain, forty of them in Scotland, although it is unlikely that more than half of the 130,000 men involved could ever have taken the field.

As Deputy Lord Lieutenant of Inverness-shire the Rev. Donald Maclean of the Small Isles was charged with supervising the Militia Act. On 30 September 1803, following a resumption of hostilities with France, he formed The Rum Island Company of Inverness-shire Volunteers, with himself as Captain. Alexander Maclean of Rum was enrolled as Lieutenant, John Maclean as Ensign or Second Lieutenant and Donald Maclean as Sergeant on permanent pay. Three other islanders were then enlisted as sergeants, two as corporals, three as drummers (one on permanent pay), and no less than seventy-eight privates or gunners.

This part-time force – after 1805 referred to as The Rum Island Company of Volunteer Infantry – were expected to muster whenever required for training and exercises. Nine days' duty were put in before its first Christmas, with wages of 9s. 5d. per day for the captain, 5s. 8d. for the lieutenant, 4s. 8d. for the ensign, 1s. 6d. for the sergeants, 1s. 2d. for the corporals and 1s. each for the privates. The men were paid for eighty-five days in 1804, when clothing to the value of £3 3s. 9d. was issued to each sergeant, £1 12s. worth to each corporals, £2 3s. 6d. to the drummers, and £1 10s. to the rank and file. Eighty muskets, bayonets and 'sets of accoutrements', forty pikes, a drum and sticks, and a cask of cartridges were issued the first summer, having been despatched north from Edinburgh Castle; the freight amounted to £5 15s. Carriage on a further five casks of blank and ball cartridges from Fort William to Rum came to £3 6s.

In the summer of 1805 the men were on permanent duty at Kinloch for thirty days, two of them spent on the march. Their subsistence allowance included one penny a day for beer! The captain augmented his own wages by tending to the troops as clergyman for four days at 10s. a day. Thereafter duty was reduced and in the autumn of 1808 thirteen days, half of the annual commitment, were spent on permanent exercise at Kilmory. Records cease after 1811, presumably the force being demobbed.

Muster rolls for the period 1803–11 survive in the Public Record Office at Kew and show how some forty-seven men served throughout the entire period of the Regiment's existence. There was a turnover, however, among the others and in all 131 names appear. These include fathers, with sons of fifteen or more who were eligible to be recruited. Since each muster roll remained at seventy-eight or seventy-nine, obviously not all the menfolk could be taken on at any one time. These lists are however a valuable record of the island population at this time since – with the exception of the Catechist's list for the Rev. Walker – no other such complete record exists prior to the first Clearance in 1826 (see Appendix II).

To the commandant, the Rev. Donald Maclean, such islanders might ultimately become vital recruits for the British Army. In his role as Deputy Lord Lieutenant of Inverness-shire he became worried seeing so many Highlanders opting to leave for the New World, at the behest of disillusioned tacksmen and unscrupulous emigration agents:

Thus we shall be deprived in future emergencies, of their valuable services, towards keeping at a distance the inveterate enemies of all we hold dear – and towards checking a spirit of licentiousness at home.

The Rev. Maclean was one of several influential men who undertook to pontificate upon the mania for emigration which had gripped the Highlands. He insisted that he was

> no enemy to a well-regulated emigration of a poor and dispossessed population, but in the present case they are not the poorest and most indigent only that prefer to emigrate, but likewise the more wealthy and substantial who want not the necessities of life and might raise comfort, by the same measure of industry, which they must exert in a distant land.
>
> Aventious designing men, little attached to their Country's prosperity, actuated by love of lucre or other selfish views, who make a trade of conveying emigrants to any part of America, are the most powerful known instigation to emigration – may I not say, the enemies of our country. They send out emissaries among our people, instructed to raise in them a spirit of discontent and dissatisfaction with their present situation, which they infamously brand with the disgusting name of slavery, and to invite them to a land of freedom and happiness. This ruinous villainous plan is carried on with secrecy and art until they extort promises and engagements from the deluded people.
>
> The people are made to believe … all who settle in His Majesty's colonies will have out of His Majesty's stores provisions for twelve months after landing gratis, as well as lands rent-free for ever.

By now though the Hebridean chiefs had identified another resource to exploit on their coastal properties: kelp. When burnt, this seaweed yielded a high-quality soda ash that could then be used in the manufacture of glass, soap and bleaching agents. Kelp gathering was very labour intensive but provided a means, albeit a backbreaking one, whereby an ever-increasing but impoverished tenantry could pay rent. It required no great skill nor capital investment on the part of the landlord and every year's harvest was renewed again in time for next season. Within two decades the burning of kelp and other seaweeds became highly lucrative, with prices peaking at £20 or £25 a ton. With their extensive, shelving beaches, North Uist, Barra and Tiree were productive areas, while the mainland shores and the islands of Mull and Skye were less important. The rocky coastline of Rum on the other hand was totally unsuitable, although a little could be gathered on Eigg and Canna. In 1814 Maclean of Coll purchased the Isle of Muck in the hope of exploiting its kelp resources.

Seaweed was no longer allowed to be 'squandered' on the land as a vital, natural fertiliser and, predictably, landowners went to great lengths to encourage their tenantry to gather it. In many localities small farms, previously held by families, were split into many separate holdings, each occupied by a single tenant or crofter but alone unable to afford them a viable living. Thus crofts, which are such a dominant feature of the Highlands today, proliferated.

Aghast at the depletion of their labour force through emigration, the lairds used all their influence to be obstructive, and in 1803 encouraged the appointment of a government Select Committee to look into emigration. This august body included 'a nice mixture of evangelical reformers, government spokesmen and Highland lairds'. They recommended the regulation of passenger numbers in transatlantic ships, and a minimum ration of food to be issued to each person. The Committee also expressed concern about the poor conditions aboard. All of this resulted in an increase in the fare to Nova Scotia, from £3 10s. to about £10, placing it firmly out of reach of many prospective emigrants. These moves became law with the Ships Passenger Act of 1803, and were specifically intended to deter – what the kelping magnates advocated – excessive numbers of people voluntarily quitting their native soil. Within twenty years, however, the price of Hebridean kelp slumped to only £3 a ton. Kelping, as one historian concluded, had proved a false promise at a critical moment in the history of the Highlands.

Gradually, too, opposition towards emigration declined, probably because the kelp boom was over and cattle prices were low; official disapproval ceased altogether after 1815. Indeed, the exact opposite policy came to be pursued in an indecent haste to exploit the land for sheep. Dr Johnson, as early as 1773, had observed how 'the lairds, instead of improving their country, diminished their people'. Hugh Rose, a Factor of the Countess of Sutherland, saw

> the depopulation as callous and cruel. For let once the natives of these countries be extirpated or dispersed, it is believed that no set of people whatsoever, from any other quarter of the globe, would be got to inhabit them.

Life in the New World was not a bed of roses, however. John Maclean was last bard to the Macleans of Coll. Born in Tiree in 1787 he published a volume of verse in 1818, before emigrating to Nova Scotia in 1819 – a decision he soon came to regret.

The poet lamented:

> 'S i seo an duthaich 's a bheil an cruadal
> Gun fhios do'n t-sluagh a tha tigh'nn a nall.
> Gur h-olc a fhuaras oirnn luchd a'bhuairidh
> A rinn le'n tuairisgeul air toirt ann.

> This is the country where there is hardship,
> Though the people coming across don't know it.
> It was evil they brought on us, those enticers
> Who contrived through fairy tales to bring us out here.

In 1880 and 1881 the poet's grandson, the Rev. A. Maclean Sinclair, published forty-seven of his hymns and forty-four secular poems, the latter collection being entitled *Clarsach na Coille*. Born in 1840, the Rev. Sinclair inherited, like so many of his family, much of their forebear's poetic genius. His own son, of the same name and also a minister in Nova Scotia, was a Gaelic scholar of note who later furnished me with useful information on the Rum Clearances.

But the old Maclean bard's cynical poetry did nothing to stem the flow to the New World. Donald, son of Lachlan Maclean, came from Rum around 1820 and took a farm near Maclean's Point at North Ainslie in Cape Breton. Eventually he was able to buy another 200 acres for his own son Lachlan. Roderick Maclean emigrated from Rum in 1822 with two sons and a daughter. He was allocated 200 acres in Cape Breton: 'it is a beautiful farm now but one can see that it took many a hard and heavy blow to give it its present pretty face'.

No longer, however, were all of these early departures voluntary. By now, considerable fears were being expressed that tenants were being forced to leave so that the land could be turned into one vast sheepwalk. 'Should this grow general,' someone was moved to comment,

> and all our gallant Highlanders desert us, I fear all the sheep that can be introduced and reared will form in their stead a sorry defence against our enemies.

Since the Clearances, as they were effected in Rum, were an apocalyptic episode in the island's history, it is worth providing a little context to fully understand them. The first Blackface or Linton sheep from the Borders had been introduced to Perthshire around 1750, and to Cromarty and Argyll about ten years later. But other breeds were quickly being improved by judicious breeding. The wool yield of Blackfaces increased from 2 lb to 3 lb in 1790 to over 4½ lb by 1831. Carcass weights increased by some 60 per cent between 1790 and 1884. The native breeds were puny by comparison and usually had to be wintered indoors. Their wool was unusually fine and soft but was useful only in stocking manufacture, an outlet which began to disappear by 1815. Furthermore, the native sheep became ravaged by scab and liver fluke introduced by the Lowland breeds. The hardy blackface from the Scottish Borders was found to be particularly suited to the harsh Highland climate.

The Napoleonic Wars had not only increased the value of kelp but also of wool. The rugged, manual labour of factory workers demanded warm, durable clothing for which the fleeces of Cheviots, and especially Blackfaces, were ideal. Furthermore sheep required much less manpower than cattle-rearing, which had been the mainstay of the Highland economy up till then. The price of wool had first begun to rise about 1770 and by 1820 it had quadrupled. The workers also demanded protein. Cattle prices remained buoyant at first, but it soon became evident that sheep were more economical. Sir John Sinclair believed that 'under sheep the Highlands would be six, if not ten times more valuable than under cattle, if proper breeds were introduced'. James Macdonald explained:

> Sheep cannot be cultivated to a profit unless in large flocks ... Small capitalists cannot thence manage them; and thus arises the necessity of large sheep farms.

In 1785 James Anderson observed:

> The proprietors find their lands overstocked with people, who are mere cumberers of the soil, eat up its produce, and prevent its improvement, without being able to afford a rent nearly adequate to that which should be afforded for the same produce, were their fields under proper management. Countries that are naturally calculated for grazings, as is the case with a great proportion of the Highlands of Scotland, can be managed at little expense by a few people.

Clan chiefs and landlords alike set about moving their clansmen and tenants aside so that their land could be deployed more profitably under sheep. Their methods left a lot to be desired and often were tantamount to cruelty. The most notorious of the Clearances were perpetrated in Sutherland, especially Strathnaver, in 1814 and 1819. The geologist John MacCulloch found in the county of Sutherland 'a solitude like that of a grave ... it is silence and death; but only because it was once life and motion'. He appreciated the hardships of the old way of life and, as a friend of the Earl of Selkirk, was optimistic about the new improvements. In 1822 Bishop Ranald Macdonald of the Isles wrote that:

> Midway between the Outer Isles and the mainland of Scotland are the Isles of Eigg, Rum and Canna, called the Lesser Isles, where there are 500 Catholics, of whom many emigrated this summer to America.

There were Clearances in Lewis and Skye from 1823, Rum and Bracadale in Skye in 1826, Rum again together with Muck, also Ardnamurchan and Arran in 1828; and so it went on until sheep – like the kelp before them – finally became less profitable too.

10 *A Most Melancholy Cycle*

The people of the island were carried off in one mass, for ever, from the sea-girt spot where they had been born and bred, and where the bones of their forefathers were laid in the ancient graveyard of Kilmory. The wild outcries of the men, and the heart-breaking wails of the women and their children filled all the air between the mountainous shore of the bay.

John MacMaister, shepherd, 1828

Hugh Maclean, 14th of Coll, living in retirement in Aberdeen, had always been reluctant to raise rents on his lands; a move which, with other 'harsh usages' perpetrated by other lairds, usually forced the tenantry to leave the country. He realised that there were too many people on the estate, but, like his forebears, Maclean was of independent character and greatly beloved for his benevolent and generous disposition.

His twenty-one-year-old son Alexander, although a lawyer by training and a soldier by profession, had stepped competently into the shoes of his dead brother, Donald – the 'Young Coll' of Johnson and Boswell. In common with his father's policy and that of a few of his fellow Highland lairds, he remained hesitant about instigating some of the 'new improvements' – notably those we have come to call the 'Highland Clearances'. Eventually in 1823 he applied for government assistance to transport his Rum tenantry to Canada, but his request was refused. In 1811, James Macdonald published his *General View of the Agriculture of the Hebrides* and reported how Alexander Maclean of Coll had also attempted to introduce Lowland sheep in Rum. Although the new breed took well, 'the inhabitants were prejudiced against them and soon returned to the ancient habits'. In 1802 Mrs Murray had been told the same story. Apparently Maclean of Coll had insisted

> that one of the farms should be stocked with sheep. The farmer with much reluctance complied with the landlord's injunction but instead of stocking his farm fully, he only put one half of the number of sheep the farm would feed; notwithstanding he sold the wool of the half stock of sheep the first year for £50 and the rent of the whole farm was only £60.

James Macdonald further observed that Maclean of Coll

> might let as a sheepwalk his large island of Rum containing upwards of twenty thousand Scotch acres, at a profit of several hundred pounds per annum, to two or three farmers instead of the present three hundred and fifty inhabitants who possess it for a mere trifle, could he find any means of providing for these poor people consistent with his patriotism and humanity. But although he has been for some years looking out for eligible situations for these persons who are more and more crowded every year, and consequently must gain by being removed from an island on which they cannot possibly raise a comfortable subsistence, yet he has not hitherto been successful.

James Macdonald was critical of Maclean of Coll's current policy:

> The proprietor's humanity prevents him from depopulating [Rum], although his good sense must convince him that his benevolence is, in the long run, cruelty to the poor creatures whom he feeds at his own expense ... In point of agriculture, Rum is one of the most backward of all the Hebrides, and its population, however simple and virtuous, are in their present state a dead stock to the community and to themselves.

Maclean's finances had suffered a severe blow when a brief kelping speculation on the Isle of Muck failed drastically. In 1814 he had bought the island from Clanranald's executors for £9975, which he was paying up in three instalments. By so doing he could not take up first refusal on the Campbell properties on Coll, which were put on the market for £8000. Potash from the burning of seaweed, and used in southern factories to manufacture glass and soap, had been in high demand but already the price was dropping from a peak of £23 per ton (it reached only £3 by 1835). He found himself in heavy debt and it may have decided him to hand over the running of his affairs to his son Hugh (born in 1782). Dr Johnson had been told how it was 'a custom in this family that the laird resigns the estate to the eldest son when he comes of age, reserving to himself only a certain life-rent'. (Johnson's Young Coll had himself inherited thus in 1771.)

> My father [Hugh observed] has not yet by raising his rents and other harsh usages forced his tenants to leave their country as the many other proprietors have done; in fact there are actually at present too many people in the estate, and more of the ancient attachment subsists between him and his tenants than most Highlanders can boast of.

Alexander Maclean died in 1835 and is buried in the family tomb at the east end of Crossapol Bay on Coll. When the bard John Maclean, by then living in Nova Scotia, heard of the death he composed an eloquent eulogy – probably the last lament to be composed by a family bard for his chieftain:

> ...'S iomadh cuimhneachan cairdeil
> Bh' aca 'n oidhch' ud mu'n armunn nach beo.

> ... Many were the affectionate memories
> That night of the chieftain no longer alive.

The bard's respect and affection were genuine, his words spoken from the heart.

Hugh Maclean may have been of a more mercenary disposition for he would pay more heed to James Macdonald's harsh advice. In the meantime, he built himself an elegant mansion in Tobermory and moved there permanently in 1828; the family were never again to reside in Coll. With such extravagances Hugh added to the debts of an already over-burdened estate. He experimented with pig farming in Coll, where his Factor was Donald Campbell, a notorious evictor who cleared several townships for sheep.

Rum was leased to Hugh's kinsman by marriage, Dr Lachlan, son of Charles Maclean of Gallanach, Coll. Charles was said to be descended from Donald Maclean, 12th of Coll, and his grandfather had fought at Culloden, presumably with his chief's disinherited son, Lachlan. Born in 1760, Dr Lachlan's father Charles was, according to the Rev. A. Maclean Sinclair, well educated, 'a clear-headed and shrewd man'. For a short time he lived as a merchant in Glasgow before returning to Coll where he ran a shop at Arinagour. In addition he made a handsome profit from the kelp business which enabled him to rent the farm at Gallanach; Maclean of Coll also employed him as an estate factor. Dr Lachlan's mother was Margaret, the daughter of Neil Maclean of Crossapol, whom Boswell had found to be 'a most industrious man ... with the highest rented farm of any of [the tenants]. Upon this he has always lived creditably for one of his station.' Neil also had two other daughters and seven sons, one of whom was his heir – Allan Maclean of Crossapol – and another Donald Maclean, the Small Isles minister who contributed to the first *Statistical Account (OSA)*.

In 1787 Charles and Margaret had a daughter and, two years later, Lachlan was born. (Another daughter, Isabella, was, in 1822, to marry the second Rev. Donald Maclean who contributed to the *New Statistical Account*.) Lachlan graduated in medicine at Edinburgh in 1810 but preferred to follow an agricultural career. At first he was appointed manager of Lochlash estates in Wester Ross before taking a lease at Talisker in Skye in 1817. *The Historical and Genealogical Account of the Clan Maclean* (1835) described him as

> a gentleman of much general information; he devotes his time chiefly to the pastoral and praiseworthy pursuit of sheep farming, of which he is considered one of the most practical judges in the land.

Dr Lachlan also owned land in Mull which he sold to his father in 1825 so that he could take over the sole tenancy in Rum. The Rev. A. Maclean Sinclair wrote in his book *Clan Gillean* that Dr Lachlan has been 'severely blamed for the evictions which took place on that island'.

In a memorandum he wrote in 1872 (which is quoted in the *Celtic Monthly* of 1901) Dr Lachlan defended his motives:

> In the first place I will explain how I was induced to take the Island of Rum. For some years before I took the lease of it, the inhabitants became very unreasonable, and would not pay for rent what was reasonable, but what they pleased. At last it was resolved to let the whole island to one person. The proprietor was to pay the passage of all who chose to go to British America – to which the people had agreed the more readily as a considerable number had some years previously emigrated and settled, and wished their friends to follow them. Their arrears of rent were also given up to them. The island was advertized, and understanding that a Club were [about] to offer for it, who would show no sympathy for the people, and happening to be in Edinburgh at the time, I made an offer which was accepted. This was in 1825, and the following year, 1826, I took possession. I bought, or rather took at valuation, all their livestock and everything they had to dispose of. About 130 of the inhabitants being poor, they did not take the benefit of this generous offer. These remained on the island for two years, and were all employed by me and fairly paid. Hearing reasonable accounts from their friends, they at last followed – their passage being paid, to which I contributed £150. I was always an advocate for emigration – if done in a kind and liberal way, as in this case. All were well pleased. They had a great advantage in the fact that the proprietor encouraged them for many years previously to educate their children, I may say at

his own expense, so that all of them could read and write. This was the system on all the property of that exemplary proprietor, Alexander Maclean of Coll, who went under the name of the last of the Lairds, as he was in reality the last Highland Laird who knew and practised his duty to his tenants. He gave up the management to his son, who was kind and amiable, but wanted steadiness and judgement, and very often forgot his promises.

At Whitsun in 1825, before Dr Lachlan went to live in Rum, its native population were given a year's notice to quit. Most went in 1826 and the remainder departed two years later. The late Hugh Mackinnon of Eigg, as related by Camille Dressler in her recent history of that island, told of a tradition that, prior to their departure, the last of the Rum folk sought to leave a lasting sad memorial in the land of their ancestors. In one last gesture of grief and defiance they rolled an enormous boulder – probably the *Clach Cuid Fir*, the manhood stone – to a prominent place by the track up Kinloch Glen, where it still stands unexplained but obviously not the glacial erratic it might appear to be. No one in Rum remembers this remarkable and poignant tale. Archie Cameron merely referred to the feature as the 'Rocking Stone' (but I prefer the interpretation of the sleepy student who called it 'a glacial errotic').

The evictions taking place in Rum were by no means unique. Muck was also to be cleared of 150 folk in 1828, and in 1854 it was sold to Captain Thomas Swinburne, RN, of Eilean Shona in Loch Moidart. In 1827 Eigg was bought from Clanranald for £15,000 by Dr Hugh Macpherson, Professor of Greek at Aberdeen University. Clanranald also disposed of Canna in 1827, to Donald MacNeil, whose father had been renting it for many years; later 200 people were cleared off.

Hugh Maclean of Coll had appointed his brother-in-law, Alexander Hunter, WS and partner in a reputable Edinburgh law firm, to supervise the clearance of the Rum folk in 1826. The following year Hunter was called to give evidence before a government Select Committee on Emigration where he loyally claimed that the emigration did not take place in consequence of any act of the landlord in the improvement of his estate; Hunter conceded only that the Act enabled him to do so:

> In an island for sheep alone you could hardly suppose it possible that they could raise as much grain as would feed so large a population, therefore the proprietors got little or no rent – the tenants were obliged to lay out the price of their sheep in supporting themselves.

Had there not been any emigration, he reasoned,

> the population would have gone on increasing, and of course as the population increased, the rents would diminish

'The system in the Highlands is very much like the Irish,' Hunter maintained.

> The son or the daughter of one of the crofters marries, and the father allows him to build a hut at the end of his [own] hut, and gives him a cow etc.; he is not a tenant or a crofter at all, he is living on the bounty of the other.
>
> The landlord was bound by humanity to support the population. Why, a man cannot allow his population to starve! ... It wasn't the introduction of sheep-farming that made it desirable for these people to emigrate since, in the island of Rum it is all sheep-farming; it never was anything else, nor is it adapted for raising crops.
>
> These people owed a great deal of arrears of rent and Maclean of Coll agreed to give them their arrears of rent and to advance a certain sum of money in order to assist them out, and to give them a little money in their pockets when they arrived [in Cape Breton] ... Instead of a population of 350 people, there is a population now of 50, and one person has taken the whole island as one farm. Of course he is enabled to pay a higher rent, as he has not to maintain so many people.

Thus Maclean of Coll's agent strived to justify an Act that, overnight, deprived Rum of virtually all its inhabitants.

'And were the people willing to go?' asked one of the Select Committee.

'Some of them were,' came the reply. 'Others were not very willing; they did not like to leave the land of their ancestors.'

Many years later one of the shepherds employed to look after the 8000 Blackface sheep which took the place of the people, was to be more forthcoming. John MacMaister from Argyll stood on the shores of Loch Scresort as the Rum folk departed:

> The people of the island were carried off in one mass, for ever, from the sea-girt spot where they had been born and bred, and where the bones of their forefathers were laid in the ancient graveyard of Kilmory. The wild outcries of the men, and the heart-breaking wails of the women and their children filled all the air between the mountainous shore of the bay.

The whole scene was of such a distressful description that the old man never forgot it to his dying day.

The cost to Maclean of Coll was on average £5 14s. per head. In addition each adult was given a weekly allowance of 11 lb oatmeal, 3½ lb bread or biscuit, 1½ lb beef, ½ lb molasses, ½ lb pease or barley, ¼ lb butter with 35 pints of water free. Coll was able to reduce his expense considerably by substituting more oatmeal for the beef, 'since they live on oatmeal, in fact potatoes, principally'. A few had salt mutton and potatoes of their own. An Act of Parliament had decreed that each emigrant was provided with a minimum of twelve weeks' allowance of food, so that some would be left over on arrival until the people were settled.

Hunter then went on to explain how a similar emigration – not at the landlord's expense – had taken place four or five years earlier. Thus when the people landed in Cape Breton

> they were met with a great number of friends, who had gone from the neighbouring islands a few years ago. The friends of those who had no money assisted them, and they became labourers to their friends; and those who had money got grants of land.

Seed potatoes were provided although it was known they did not keep well on the voyage. As Hunter explained:

> If the islanders arrived in Cape Breton by early June they could raise a crop that year and there would be no expense feeding them for the first 12 months. They could get their seed from friends already there.

In fact, the people did not leave Rum until 11 July 1826 and the voyage took thirty-seven days. Hunter was careful not to remind the Select Committee of this but added that he had received one letter from those who had gone out, stating that they were perfectly satisfied.

Three hundred people were ushered aboard two ships whose names were not recorded. Nor do passenger lists survive. Dr John Lorne Campbell offered to contact a friend in Nova Scotia to investigate the matter for me. The Rev. Donald Maclean Sinclair, son of the author of *Clan Gillean* and a descendant of Maclean of Coll's bard John Maclean, unearthed a letter to his father, dated 31 March 1897, from a James Maclean. The letter reads:

> Allan and Roderick Maclean with their wives and children and all they had, left Skye and went to Kilmory, Rum, the inheritance of their forefathers, where for five or six generations, got very numerous and were well known as *Sliochd Ailean agus Clann Ruarie MacGilliospuic*, until the Curse and Scourge of the Highland Crofters, Dr Lachlan Maclean of Gallanach, evicted them all in 1826 and took the island to himself: two ship loads viz. the *Harmony* and *Highland Laddie* landed them in Cape Breton that summer. The few that remained went to C.B. with the Muck people in 1828. Dr Maclean was turned out of Rum in 1839, bankrupt and penniless, much worse off than the comfortable people he turned out of Rum 13 years previously. He then went to Australia (General Lindsay gave him means), taking his eldest son, Daniel, with him, then 14 or 15 years [old], came back in 1842 and left his son abroad, much against the boy's will ... Dr L's mother was a sister of Allan of Crosspoll, that was all the connection to the family of Coll.

Official Nova Scotia records confirm that *Highland Lad* and *Dove of Harmony* entered Cape Breton in 1826 but no passenger lists have yet been traced. Documents go on to reveal that when *Harmony* berthed the following year with 200 more Scots, twenty-two of them were suffering from measles and no less than eighteen more had died on the voyage. The cause of such dire fatality – by no means unusual on emigrant ships – was 'readily traced to the confined, crowded and filthy state of the vessel'.

The whole of Rum was left with only 50 souls, according to Alexander Hunter; Dr Lachlan confessed to 130, which would concur with the known peak of population in Rum at the time (443 given in the *OSA* in 1796). Their days were numbered, however. In 1828 together, it now transpires, with about 150 folk being cleared from Muck – another of Maclean of Coll's properties and which was just about to go on the market – they too were shipped to Canada in the *St Lawrence*. This event is also confirmed by the Rev. Sinclair's letter and by Dr Lachlan himself. Interestingly, Bill Mackinnon of Michigan, whose ancestors from the Small Isles were aboard the *St Lawrence* on that very trip, tells me that this was the same vessel on which Herman Melville undertook his first voyage, between New York and Liverpool, as a seaman in 1839. His experiences with the captain and crew were so brutal that he featured them in his third novel, *Redburn*. Although Melville, the author of *Moby Dick*, was well able to embroider his tales, it makes one wonder what the emigrants had suffered aboard the same vessel eleven years earlier.

The *New Statistical Account* (1845) summarised the whole tragedy. At least 400 people from Rum had

> found it necessary to leave their native country, and to seek new abodes in the distant wilds of our colonies in America. Of all the old residenters, only one family remained upon the island. The old and the young, the feeble and the strong, were all united in this general emigration – the former to find tombs in a foreign land – the latter to encounter toils, privations and dangers, to become familiar with customs, and to acquire habits to which they had formerly been entire strangers.

This frank statement was submitted to the *New Statistical Account* by the Small Isles Parish Minister, Donald Maclean – a different man and no immediate relation to one who contributed the Small Isles section of the previous *Statistical Account* (*OSA*). Born in 1793, third son of Allan Maclean, farmer at Kinlochscresort in Rum, Donald Maclean was a graduate of King's College, Aberdeen, and became ordained into the ministry in 1818; in September of that same year he was appointed to the Small Isles and four years later married Isabella, sister to Dr Lachlan Maclean of Gallanach. The first Rev. Donald Maclean was thus uncle to the wife of this second Rev. Donald Maclean.

And thus the second Rev. Donald Maclean became brother-in-law to the tacksman in Rum who was to perpetrate the clearance in the first place. There is little in the minister's tone in the *New Statistical Account* to imply that he at all disapproved of the act – but then he dare not speak ill of his relative. He was also a substantial farmer in his own right, cultivating the Glebe, Sandavore and Castle Island on Eigg. But the locals never forgot his association with the Rum and Muck Clearances and the fact that – as Parish Minister – he had not spoken out against the deeds. Perhaps a guilty conscience led to his seeking solace in alcohol.

In 1834 he was charged with adultery, attempted rape, indecent exposure, assault, drunkenness on foot and on horseback, and neglect of duty! The case dragged on for years until in 1838 the Rev. Maclean turned up drunk at the General Assembly of the Church of Scotland in Edinburgh, where his appeal was to be heard. Not surprisingly his appeal was unsuccessful; he was deposed and died the next year – on a steamboat sailing between Glasgow and Greenock. His wife lived on until 1881 and together they had six children. Their eldest son was born in the year of the Rum Clearance and died at the age of twenty.

As recently as 1744 the population of Cape Breton was little more than a thousand, with not a dozen Scots among them. At first most emigrants landed at Pictou, some at Prince Edward Island. The first coming directly to Cape Breton were some 300 folk stepping ashore at Sydney. By 1815 the population was estimated at 6000, and by 1838 no less than 35,420. In 1821 Boards of Land Commissioners were set up, presenting to those settlers applying a 'ticket of location'. Up to 1827 land was granted free: 150 acres to each head of family and 50 to each child, to a maximum of 200 acres free; over this, payment was made of 5 shillings for each 50 acres (P. & J. Lotz, *Cape Breton Island*, 1974).

The early life of Cape Breton's settlers was a harsh one. The forest had to be felled and cleared away to provide land for cultivation. Blight and frost destroyed the crops – potatoes and grain being the mainstay of the settlers' diet. Early government records in Cape Breton are full of pathetic pleas for relief, which present tragic glimpses of the misery and starvation. The bard John Maclean summarised the hardships in another bitter poem:

> Gur h-iomadh ceum anns am bi mi 'n deis laimh
> Mu'n dean mi saibhir mo theachd-an-tir;
> Bidh m'obair eigneach mu'n toir mi feum aisd'
> 'S mu'n dean mi reiteach air son a'chrionn:
> Cur sgonn nan teintean air muin a cheile
> Gu'n d'lasaich feithean a bha 'nam dhruim,
> 'S a h-uile ball diom cho duch a sealltainn,
> Bidh mi 'gam shamhlachadh ris an t-suip.

Many a labour I'll be involved in
Before I can make my living secure;
My work will be exhausting before
I get any returns from it and
Before I make a clearing for the plough.
Piling tree-trunks on top of each other
In bonfires, has strained every muscle
In my back; and every part of me
Is so black that I'm just like a chimney sweep.

Records in Cape Breton of the fortunes (or otherwise) of the Rum folk are incomplete and tend to be scattered throughout the official archives. At first the register of marriages and deaths kept in Cape Breton was only optional. On 13 June 1876, for instance, at Port Hastings, is recorded the death from consumption of Margaret Mackinnon, who had been born in the 'Isle of Roome' to John and Christy Maclean. Another settler, Donald Maclean, son of Roderick and Sarah Maclean, died in 1876 aged sixty-eight; his family came to live at Brook Village in Cape Breton.

One of the best-researched family histories, compiled by their descendants, is detailed in J. P. Maclean's *History of Inverness County*. Hector Maclean from Guirdil in Rum was married to a Mary Mackintosh from Eigg. With six of their children the couple left for Cape Breton in 1826, leaving behind a daughter, Mary, who was betrothed to James, the third son of Allan Maclean of Crossapol. James was then Factor of Rum and Muck living at Kinloch in Rum. One of Allan Maclean's sons was, of course, the second Donald, the Church of Scotland minister for the Small Isles. Hector purchased 347 acres at Whale Cove, which he divided amongst his first three sons, and an adjacent lot for his fourth son, Charles. The eldest, John, became known as 'the Banker' because of his notable thrift and rare knack for saving money. Eventually he was able to send his own eldest son to study medicine at Harvard.

In Rum, in the year of the clearance, John's sister Mary was wed to James Maclean. James was found a post as Factor at Gallanach in Muck, where he remained until 1836. Two years later James and Mary, with their two sons Hector and John, emigrated to Melbourne in Australia. The two families retained sporadic contact for several decades thereafter. In 1874, from Margaree in Cape Breton, John 'the Banker', by then eighty years old, was replying to his nephew who had become manager of a sheep farm at Longerenong in Victoria:

I was delighted to have heard from you. Indeed I had almost despaired of ever hearing from you again.

I am proud that after many years of total ignorance of each others circumstances and condition a letter comes from you giving the cheering information of your enjoying health and prosperity, the greatest boons that Providence bestows upon his beings. I thank you most sincerely for sending me your likeness and that of your fair consort. I shall prize it as one of my most precious jewels. In fact it recalls to my mind very vividly the remembrances of other years.

... The names of the most of your children are easily understood by us all. I am glad that you chose good true Scotch names. They have not been forgotten by you even among strangers. Let the names of many of the departed be remembered by us at all times.

My dear daughter Mary Ann, the youngest, died three years ago at the age of 22 years. A better girl never breathed the air of Heaven – she died happy. Enclosed please find her likeness.

... I am getting feeble myself now. My race is almost run.

... Be careful to answer this as soon as you receive it. I cannot live long now – so let us remember each other while we are here ...

Your affectionate Uncle,
John Maclean

This letter was found nearly a century later, at the back of an old desk at Longerenong by David Maclean Gregory, great-grandson of John in Australia. David then undertook a lengthy quest that culminated in the two families re-establishing contact and exchanging information on their antecedents from Rum. David and his wife Marigold, a cousin – also of Rum descent – were able to visit Rum, where I was privileged to meet them, shortly before David's tragically early death from illness.

Another of the Rum emigrants to settle in Nova Scotia was Lachlan, the son of Alasdair Maclean. Born in 1763 he became ground officer in Rum for thirty years. With his wife and two children, Donald Ban and Marion, he was forced to emigrate in 1826. Before they left, Donald had married Christy Maclean, daughter of John Mor of Kilmory in Rum. They had eleven children, all brought up near Strathlorne at Fort Cape in Cape Breton. The eight sons were a striking family – all large, fine-looking men of very considerable physical strength. Two grandsons became teachers in Inverness County, the first locals to qualify under the original Education Act for Nova Scotia. The burly sons obviously took after their mother's people. Allan Maclean had been a descendant of the fifth Maclean of Coll himself and moved from Skye to Kilmory late in the seventeenth century. Allan's son, Lachlan, was also a man of great strength, a trait which he had passed down his line. John Mor, his grandson, was a strapping six feet four and a half; he married twice and had ten children before dying at Kilmory at the age of only fifty-five. His fourth son, Murdoch Mor, had also inherited the family physique. His first son, John, was born on 10 July 1825 and a year later many of the family, together with most of

Rum's inhabitants, were cleared from the island to Cape Breton. Murdoch Mor's half-brother, Donald, was for some reason allowed to stay behind in Rum.

John grew up in the harsh environment of this young colony, his homestead lying on the shore of Lake Ainslie. His neighbour was the Rev. Norman Macleod. This fanatical cleric became dissatisfied with the Church in his native Sutherland and had emigrated to Cape Breton in 1817. There he had assembled a staunch band of disciples, all Highlanders and victims of the Clearances. Macleod, large and powerfully built with a voice like thunder, was the terror of evil-doers and once condemned a boy suspected of theft to have the tip of his ear cut off! Yet he was a stout friend to all who strived to do well, and they all regarded him with unbound devotion.

The summer of 1848 brought a miserable harvest, together with a letter from the Rev. Macleod's son Donald in Adelaide. The man extolled the virtues of the new continent but Macleod, who was then sixty-eight with a wife crippled from rheumatism, gave the matter little more thought. The following year a second letter came. This time seeds were sown. Macleod's wife had improved in health, and some 300 settlers expressed interest in what the minister told them of Australia. He therefore instructed them to construct two ships and on 28 October the 236-ton *Margaret* set sail with 130 on board. A further 188 followed soon after in the 179-ton *Highland Lass.*

Those of Macleod's flock who remained in Cape Breton eventually heard that the ships had reached Melbourne. This town was gripped with gold fever so the prospects for suitable settlement were far from ideal. So the voyagers pressed on to New Zealand, where they set up a small colony called Waipu, near Auckland. Their favourable reports stimulated more of the Cape Breton Scots to build other ships. In 1856 188 set sail in the 217-ton *Gertrude*, with 66 others in the 99-ton *Spray*, and 129 more on the *Breadalbane* in December 1857.

All the while John Maclean stood on the shore and waved goodbye to his friends, and watched many of the houses around him fall into ruins, the land reverting back to forest. No sooner had the *Breadalbane* sailed over the horizon, than the remaining settlers began building yet another ship. There was a mighty felling of timber that winter and every able-bodied man set to the task. Finally in September 1858 the *Ellen Lewis* was launched, 336 tons of sound Cape Breton oak.

That year John Maclean's son Allan died, and he finally resolved to quit. With his wife and four surviving children, the thirty-five-year-old Maclean boarded with the last of Macleod's flock, 180 brave souls in all. The *Ellen Lewis* left Cape Breton on 17 December 1859. The voyage around the Cape of Good Hope before eventually reaching New Zealand – 12,000 miles in all – took 150 days. The pace was leisurely since the comfort and the safety of the passengers was paramount – a far cry from the crowded, filthy emigrant ships which had first brought them from Scotland. The ship was crewed by those amongst them who were familiar with the ways of the sea.

They found Waipu to be a large and thriving colony and were welcomed with open arms by their friends. The fertile coast was by now well populated so many of the new settlers had to set up home on the hill slopes overlooking the bay. But the climate was mild and warm, the soil fertile and the prospects encouraging. Sadly twin girls, born to John Maclean's wife, died in 1863.

The Rev. Norman Macleod, the founder of this remarkable colony, died six years after John Macleod's arrival. He was aged eighty-six, a strong, determined man of astonishing principles, foresight and vigour. For long, Gaelic remained their first and, in many cases, their only language. It provided little barrier to the young New Zealand men who gravitated to Waipu seeking wives. One old woman recalled how her suitor had first given her a wink. She winked back. He gave her a squeeze. She squeezed him back. She said 'Iain, mo ghaol' and taught him to say 'Seonaid, mo ghaol' back. And that was that. They were wed soon afterwards!

Thus, John Maclean's family became first-generation settlers in New Zealand. He had been but a year old when he had departed Rum, and remembered little of it. However, he epitomised the bold pioneering spirit that had provided the Rum emigrants with a determination to face their future – wherever in the world they ended up. Only one family remained behind on Rum.

PART IV

Sheep Farm and Estate

Uninhabited originally save by wild animals, it became at an early period a home of men, who, as the grey wall on the hill-side testified, derived, in part at least, their sustenance from the chase. They broke in from the waste the furrowed patches on the slopes of the valleys – they reared herds of cattle and flocks of sheep – their numbers increased to nearly five hundred souls – they enjoyed the average happiness of human creatures in the present imperfect state of being – they contributed their portion of hardy and vigorous manhood to the armies of the country – and a few of their more adventurous spirits, impatient of the narrow bounds which confined them, and a course of life little varied by incident, emigrated to America. Then came the change of system so general in the Highlands; and the island lost all its original inhabitants, on a wool and mutton speculation – inhabitants, the descendants of men who had chased the deer on its hills five hundred years before, and who, though they recognised some wild island lord as their superior, and did him service, had regarded the place as indisputably their own.

Hugh Miller, 1845

11   *All was Solitary*

All was solitary. We could see among the deserted fields the
grass-grown foundations of cottages razed to the ground; but the
valley, more desolate than that which we had left, had not even
its single inhabited dwelling; it seemed as if man had done with it
forever.

Hugh Miller, 1845

The *New Statistical Account* of the Small Isles was written in 1836 by the
Rev. Donald Maclean (1793–1839). Unfortunately his description of the
Small Isles does not compare with that of his namesake in the first *Account*
and is disappointing in its detail. It stretches to ten pages, two of which are
devoted to a verbatim report on the so-called Massacre Cave on Eigg, with
a third on the geology of the Sgurr of Eigg. The Rev. Maclean confessed
that Parochial Registers had never been regularly kept in this parish and
gave the population of the Small Isles in 1831 as 1015 souls, adding 'some
years previous it was much greater'. (In fact, only ten years earlier it had
peaked at 1620, the subsequent reduction being almost entirely due to
substantial Clearances on the isles of Muck, from 321 inhabitants to 155;
Canna, from 436 to 264; and Rum, from 394 to only 134. Eigg with a
population of 452 in 1831 had been reduced by a mere seventeen, to 435.)
Maclean reported:

> There are no villages; and no inns, excepting one in the Island of Eigg.
> In each of the islands there was formerly an inn. There is no packet,
> nor any regular means of communication with the post-office or the

mainland from any one of the islands ... A road has been carried across the Island of Eigg by the statute labour of the inhabitants. There is no church on any of the islands. In Eigg we assemble in the schoolhouse for public worship; but in the other islands we sometimes meet in the fields, when we cannot conveniently get a house to receive us. The manse was erected in the Island of Eigg in 1790. It has often been repaired, but it is so much exposed to the winter gales, and so high above the level of the sea, that it is hardly possible to make it comfortable, or to keep it so for any length of time ... The stipend is one of the small livings, and Government pays £64 16s. annually.

Since the Rev. Maclean was married to the sister of the Dr Lachlan Maclean who had cleared both Rum and Muck, it is perhaps not surprising that he was not offered a house and often had to preach in the open when he visited these islands; his own island of Eigg was predominantly Roman Catholic, and neither would he have been particularly welcomed by the Roman Catholic community on Canna.

The minister then verged on libel in his comments about the fifty-year-old schoolmaster, John Murray, who had been teaching on Eigg for nearly twenty years and was to soldier on for another twenty:

There is but one parochial school in the parish. It is on the island of Eigg. The house was built in 1829, and made very comfortable. The salary was, the same year, increased from £18 to £30. The school fees may amount to £10 a year. The present schoolmaster is not noted for attention to his scholars, or diligence in the discharge of his duty. He seldom has more than from 20 to 30 scholars, and often he has none, the parents witholding them from the school, as knowing that they make no progress in their education under him. Excepting in the Island of Muck, where the Gaelic School Society has had a teacher for the last three years, there is no other school in any of the islands.

Maclean was lavish, by contrast, in his praise of his brother-in-law, Lachlan:

In the Island of Rum, a good dwelling house with splendid offices was erected by Dr Maclean, the present tacksman, in 1826, who spared neither pains nor expense in draining, fencing and planting around his residence, at the end of the harbour. His improvements have been carried on, on a very extensive scale. They exhibit both taste and judgement, and to reward his diligence, his plantation of trees is now in a forward and thriving state.

Kinloch House was situated at the head of Loch Scresort, behind what is now the modern post office/shop; only the old gate-posts survive. Half an acre of sycamore, beech, ash and wych elm which Maclean planted around the house still thrive.

> The other islands [the minister's account continued] may be said to be as nature left them, saving that in Eigg tolerable farm-houses are to be found ... With the exception of Mr MacNeil's house on Canna, there are no other mansion houses. He is the only inheritor that resides within the bounds of the parish.
>
> There are about 600 persons above six years of age in this parish who can neither write nor read. The number of poor upon the roll in this parish is 10 ... We have no beggars. Among the inhabitants are some artisans, such as weavers, boat-buildiers, smiths, tailors, and one shoemaker: but although these devote some of their time to the various employments of their calling, yet they chiefly depend upon their agricultural occupations for their subsistence.

Each family was said to require some 240 to 320 bushels of potatoes to live on throughout the year, and manured their fields with seaweed cast up on the shore by winter storms.

> The rearing of black cattle and sheep was said to be the prevailing occupation in the Small Isles ... From 300 to 400 heads of black cattle are annually sold in the parish to dealers at home, who again bring them to the south country markets for sale. The number of sheep pastured in the Island of Rum alone is about 8000, which are all of the black-faced kind, and which are likewise all salved or smeared.

In 1823 Dr Lachlan, the tenant in Rum, had married Isabella Mackenzie, the eldest daughter of Captain Donald Mackenzie of Hartfield, Applecross in Wester Ross. (Donald Alexander, the first of their eleven children, was born in Skye shortly before they moved to Rum.) The creation of a sheep walk on the island, however, came at a bad time, for the price of mutton and wool was in decline. Dr Lachlan also became involved in an expensive lawsuit and was 'reduced to poor circumstances' as a result and, some claim, he became an alcoholic. As the Rev. Maclean Sinclair's correspondence from Cape Breton informed me:

> He was turned out of Rum in 1839, bankrupt and penniless, much worse off than the comfortable people he turned out of Rum 13 years previously. He then went to Australia (General Lindsay gave him means), taking his eldest son, Daniel, with him, then 14 or 15 years [old], came back in 1842 and left his son abroad, much against the boy's will.

Three or four years later Dr Lachlan returned to Scotland to set up in medical practice in Tobermory. His eldest son, Donald, sometimes referred to as Daniel, ended up in the gold diggings in Australia after he left Melbourne in 1846 and was not heard from again. Another son, something of a Gaelic scholar, became a distinguished diplomat in India; two other sons were army surgeons, another a civil engineer abroad, while a sixth died young; there were also five daughters. Interestingly, one of the daughters, Annie Flora, married a grandson of Dr James Anderson who had compiled reports on the Hebrides for the British Fisheries Society in 1785.

Dr Lachlan himself moved from Mull to Greenock, where he practised for ten years, but by 1859 he was farming 400 acres on Kerrera near Oban, where he occupied a substantial stone house which is still standing. He retired to Oban, where he died on 29 November 1881 from 'decay of nature' at the advanced age of ninety-two, while his wife – 'an excellent woman' – passed away three years later. Curiously, her passing was reported in the *Oban Times* although that of her husband was not.

There is next to no information surviving about these early attempts to graze sheep in Rum. It is left to the next visitor, Hugh Miller, the Cromarty stonemason turned geologist and evangelist, to describe the scene. Miller had been at school in Cromarty with John Swanson, who was later to become Free Church minister for the Small Isles. Born in Gravesend, Kent, in 1804, and son of a Scots sea captain, Swanson spent two years as a grocer, then became a schoolmaster at Nigg before finally being ordained to the Church of Scotland in 1839. Notoriously anti-Catholic, he published a pamphlet against popery in 1843, when he also opted to 'come out' in the Disruption along with one-third of his disillusioned colleagues to form their own Free Church. By so doing they all cut themselves off from state funds, stipend, home and security. Swanson was sent to serve the Small Isles parish and held fervent meetings in a thatched cottage near Eigg manse, whose ruins can still be seen. The Free Church scraped together sufficient funds to purchase a small yacht, the *Betsey*, in which Swanson – from a seafaring family and with only a single crewman – cruised around the other Small Isles to preach to his flock. In 1842 he took up a post in Nigg and died there twenty-seven years later.

In his book *The Cruise of the Betsey*, Miller described how in July 1844, he accompanied the Rev. Swanson out of Tobermory bound for the Small Isles. The two men shared a tiny cabin – 'about twice the size of a common bed and just lofty enough under the beams to permit a man to stand erect in his nightcap'. In Eigg Swanson delivered his sermon in Gaelic, a language the minister had to learn on taking up his appointment. Being a geologist, Miller was particularly fascinated by the remarkable rock formation there called the Sgurr.

The next port of call was Isle Ornsay in Skye before the little boat turned back towards Rum in the worst of weather:

The gale, thickened with rain, came down, shrieking like a maniac, from off the peaked hills of Rum ... but the *Betsey*, with her storm jib set, and her mainsail reefed to the cross, kept her weather bow bravely to the blast, and gained on it with every tack.

The weary sailors dropped anchor in Rum at five o'clock in the morning, and at ten the minister held a service ashore.

The gale still blew in fierce gusts from the hills, and the rain pattered like small shot on the deck. Loch Scresort, by no means one of our finer island lochs, viewed under any circumstances, looked particularly dismal this morning ... Along the slopes of the sandstone ridge I could discern numerous green patches, that had once supported a dense population, long since 'cleared off' to the backwoods of America, but not one inhabited dwelling; while along a black moory acclivity under the hills on the other side I could see several groups of turf cottages, with here and there a minute speck of raw-looking corn beside them that, judging from its colour, seemed to have but a slight chance of ripening ... Bad as the morning was, however, we could see the people wending their way, in threes and fours, through the dark moor, to the place of worship – a black turf hovel, like the meeting house in Eigg. The appearance of the *Betsey* in the loch had been the gathering signal; and the Free Church islanders – three fourths of the entire population – had all come out to meet their minister.

The Monday morning dawned breezy but clear so Miller resolved to cross the island to Scuir More or Bloodstone Hill in search of minerals, with a young islander as guide. Attaining the crest of Bealach a'Bhraigh Bhig, between Orval and Fionchra, they first caught sight of Scuir More 'standing up over the sea, like a pyramid shorn of its top. A brown lizard, nearly five inches in length, startled by our approach, ran hurriedly across the path.' Descending through the 'swampy valley' of Guirdil, Miller comments

The Scuir is a precipitous mountain, that rises from twelve to fifteen hundred feet direct over the beach. McCulloch describes it as inaccessible, and states that it is only among the debris at its base that its heliotropes can be procured; but the distinguished mineralogist must have had considerably less skill in climbing rocks than in describing them!

There is a solitary house in the opening of the valley, over which the Scuir More stands sentinel – a house so solitary that the entire breadth of the island intervenes between it and the nearest human dwelling.

Miller and his party sat down on the summit to rest and, 'on hospitable thoughts intent', the shepherd and his wife, who lived in the cottage below, climbed up to join them with a bowl of milk, bread and cheese. After searching for agates and heliotropes, the *Betsey* party set off home.

> The entire population consisted of but the sheep-farmer and a few shepherds, his servants ... But depopulation on so extreme a scale was found inconvenient; the place had been rendered too thoroughly a desert for the comfort of the occupant; and on the occasion of a clearing which took place shortly after in Skye, he accommodated some ten or twelve of the ejected families with sites for cottages, and pasturage for a few cows, on the bit of morass beside Loch Scresort ... We reached the cross valley [Kilmory Glen] in the interior of the island about half an hour before sunset. The evening was clear, calm, gold tinted; even wild heaths and rude rocks had assumed a flush of transient beauty; and the emerald green patches on the hill-sides, barred by the plough lengthwise, diagonally and transverse, had borrowed an aspect of soft and velvety richness, from the mellowed light and the broadening shadows. All was solitary. We could see among the deserted fields the grass-grown foundations of cottages razed to the ground; but the valley, more desolate than that which we had left, had not even its single inhabited dwelling: it seemed as if man had done with it for ever. The island, eighteen years before, had been divested of its inhabitants, amounting at the time to rather more than four hundred souls, to make way for one sheep-farmer and eight thousand sheep. All the aborigines of Rum crossed the Atlantic.

The incident Miller was referring to resulted in the row of five ruined houses at Port na Caranean, at the end of the modern South Side Nature Trail. There are also some remains of older blackhouses. The 1841 census, three years before the cruise of the *Betsey*, lists the five families, all from Bracadale in Skye. There had been a clearance there in 1826 and a Matheson family tradition puts the date of their arrival in Rum as 1827. However, the birth places of the various children listed on the census returns would indicate that the families arrived sometime between 1832 and 1838. Kenneth Campbell, Angus Maclean and Murdoch Macrae all settled as crofters, with their families, in Kinloch itself. John Matheson, Donald Matheson his brother, John Gilles his brother-in-law, Norman Macdonald and Angus Macleod set up house at Port na Caranean. The site may have been significant since, being so near the mouth of Loch Scresort, it overlooks Skye and Bracadale itself.

If the census ennumerator began logically at the westernmost house and worked along to the one furthest away from Kinloch, Norman Macdonald, a mason, would have lived in the most substantial of the cottages; it is certainly the best constructed and has a fine free-standing chimney in the east gable. Each house is unique in its design, about 30 ft long and 10–12 ft wide; one has no windows, two a single front window and two (including Macdonald's) have two front windows. One cottage has only low walls of undressed beach boulders so they have been built into two peaked gables to give extra height; three houses have flat gables. Two had fires against the west wall, but Macdonald's chimney was in the east wall. Each has a kailyard nearby, enclosed by a dry-stane dyke, while Macdonald's has a byre built against his west wall; his neighbour to the west has a free-standing byre in front of the house. There are lazy-beds behind and traces of peat cuttings to the east.

The Gilles family had moved into Kinloch further along the shore by the 1851 census and what might have been their house, the easternmost, is the poorest preserved. The other four cottages remained occupied until John Gilles, and his brother-in-law Donald Matheson and their dependants, all emigrated to Canada the following year. With them went six other families including two more of the Bracadale folk from Kinloch: Kenneth Campbell, his wife and eight children, and elderly widower Angus Maclean, with his sister Margaret (who was possibly the childless widow of Angus Macleod of whom there was no further account). John Matheson and Norman Macdonald had moved from Port na Caranean to Kinloch by the 1861 census. These families are mentioned again when I deal with Salisbury's ownership of Rum, and John Matheson finally died at Kinloch in 1885 aged ninety-one. His death certificate gives the cause as 'old age and catarrh, no medical presence' and his descendants claim he was buried in an unmarked grave at Kinloch. (There is such a grave in the South Side wood near the Nature Trail but the late Archie Cameron knew this to belong to a sailor whose body was found washed up on the beach early in the twentieth century.)

Nearer Kinloch at Carn an Dobhran lived the family of Allan Maclean, an original Rumach left behind after the Clearance, and John Russell, a crofter from Argyll. The Russells and one of Allan's sons, Kenneth, remained on the island for many years and will feature in later accounts. According to the 1841 census about eight other households lived at Kinloch itself: the three from Bracadale already mentioned, Alexander Cameron, a crofter, and Alexander Macdonald, an agricultural labourer, with John Mackinnon as boatman, and two shepherds (namely Duncan Fraser and Walter Cowan, who was probably by then head shepherd or manager and will be mentioned later).

Single shepherd families were outposted at Harris (Donald Macgregor) and Papadil (Alexander Mackinnon). At Samhnan Insir lived Archibald Maclean, a carpenter, another of the original Rum family left behind after the Clearance – perhaps a younger brother of Allan (mentioned above). At Guiridil assistant shepherd William Macrae boarded with the family of Duncan Livingston, shepherd, while two other shepherd families had cottages at Kilmory – Alexander Chisholm and Adam Lauder – alongside that of Hector Mackinnon, a pauper.

But to return to Miller's visit. That evening, after their hard day's labour, the *Betsey* 'fared richly' on tea and trout, before departing Rum next morning for Glenelg where the Rev. Swanson had to attend a Presbytery meeting the following day. Hugh Miller could only conclude:

> It did not seem as if the depopulation of Rum had tended much to any one's advantage. The single sheep-farmer who had occupied the holdings of so many had been unfortunate in his speculations, and had left the island: the proprietor, his landord, seemed to have been as little fortunate as his tenant, for the island itself was in the market; and a report went current at the time that it was on the eve of being purchased by some wealthy Englishman, who purposed converting it into a deer forest.
>
> How strange a cycle! Uninhabited originally save by wild animals, it became at an early period a home of men, who, as the gray wall on the hill-side testified, derived, in part at least, their sustenance from the chase. They broke in from the waste the furrowed patches on the slopes of the valleys – they reared herds of cattle and flocks of sheep – their numbers increased to nearly five hundred souls – they enjoyed the average happiness of human creatures in the present imperfect state of being – they contributed their portion of hardy and vigorous manhood to the armies of the country – and a few of their more adventurous spirits, impatient of the narrow bounds which confined them, and a course of life little varied by incident, emigrated to America. Then came the change of system so general in the Highlands; and the island lost all its original inhabitants, on a wool and mutton speculation – inhabitants, the descendants of men who had chased the deer on its hills five hundred years before, and who, though they recognised some wild island lord as their superior, and did him service, had regarded the place as indisputably their own.
>
> And now yet another change was on the eve of ensuing, and the island was to return to its original state, as a home for wild animals, where a few hunters from the mainland might enjoy the chase for a month or two every twelvemonth, but which could form no permanent place of human abode. Once more, a strange and surely most melancholy cycle!

The wealthy Englishman who had his eyes on Rum as a sporting estate was none other than James Cecil, the second Marquess of Salisbury, who purchased the island in 1845. By now red deer had been extinct for many decades, with other fish and game far from abundant. So Salisbury had to

PLATE 1. An evening shot from Hallival, looking over Loch Scresort and Kinloch Woods to the sloping sandstone terraces of Mullach Mor, with the Isle of Soay and the Cuillin of Skye in the distance. (photo – J. Love)

PLATE 2. Flooding at Salisbury's Dam and in Kilmory Glen behind, in September 1980, when four inches of rain fell in 36 hours. (photo – J. Love)

PLATE 3. The pale-green arrowhead found at Samhnan in 1964 with one of the more typical dark-green and red-spotted bloodstone (right) found in Eigg in 1882. (photo – National Museum of Scotland)

PLATE 4. The Bagh na h-Uamha cross slab as the author re-erected it above the high water mark, with the snowy slope of Hallival behind. (photo – J. Love)

PLATE 5. The Kilmory cross slab as it lies in the burial ground. The photo was taken in July 1983 after the author put the slab face down to kill off the lichen encrustation and reveal the marigold cross; there is a plain Latin cross on the other face. (photo – J. Love)

PLATE 6. In 1949 Drew Smith found what he took to be a Norse burial cist just inland from Bagh na h-Uamha, but its exact location is now unknown. (photo – J Drew Smith)

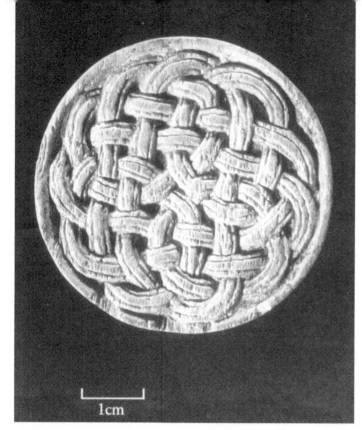

PLATE 7. Norse gaming
piece of Narwhal ivory
found in the cave at Bagh
na h-Uamha. (photo –
National Museum of
Scotland)

1cm

PLATE 8. A typical
chambered shieling
and cell on the north
slope of Kilmory Glen.
(photo – J. Love)

PLATE 9. A well-preserved rectangular shieling above the path between Dibidil and Papadil; it may well have been restored as a bothy by the Welsh mason and his assistant while they were building for Lord Salisbury the huge dyke visible on the clifftop. The Isle of Eigg lies in the distance. (photo – J. Love)

PLATE 10. A newborn Highland calf at Harris in Rum in May 1979. The breed kept on the island before the Clearances would have been similar but black in colour. (photo – J. Love)

PLATE 11. Two feral billy goats on the clifftop near Kilmory in May 1978, with a fishing boat out at sea. These goats may have been left behind after the Clearances but fresh stock was certainly introduced in Salisbury's time to deter sheep from grazing dangerous cliffs. (photo – J. Love)

PLATE 12. A red deer hind in Kilmory Glen in August 1977, with the hills of Hallival and Askival behind. Red deer were reintroduced by Lord Salisbury. (photo – J. Love)

PLATE 13. The well-preserved deer trap running down the south-facing slope of Orval into Glen Duian; the wall is constructed from boulder scree, leaving a clear glassy run down to the dry-stone corral at the bottom. (photo – J. Love)

PLATE 14. Kenneth Maclean's cottage at Carn an Dobhran (now wooded) on the south shore of Loch Scresort. (photo – J. Love)

PLATE 15. The Kinloch River in spate on 2 January 1977, with the farmhouse to the left. (photo – J. Love)

PLATE 16. Welshman's Rock or an t-Sron from the sea, showing the constriction in the green path across its face that the Welsh quarryman was charged to widen – unsuccessfully however, so the path was diverted over and behind the hill instead. There is a silhouette of a human face in the vertical rock against the skyline. (photo – J. Love)

exploit the grazing potential of the island in the meantime. We have full records of Salisbury's efforts, much of which might have been procedures developed under Dr Lachlan Maclean's direction. So they may approximate to the regime imposed immediately after the Clearances, but about which we know so little. One principal difference is that by Salisbury's time sheep numbers had been reduced from the initial, over-optimistic 8000 Blackface to some 5000 or so. It is likely that the grazings in the island of Rum had deteriorated steadily since the Clearances, and initially may have been dependent on arable land that had been worked by the inhabitants.

The *New Statistical Account* described Rum as

> lofty and mountainous; and although a few of the hills are green, yet most of them exhibit a rough, abrupt and craggy appearance. From the rocky materials of which they consist, they are especially in winter during snow, dangerous and unsafe for shepherds, who frequent them in quest of sheep, so that on more than one occasion, some of them have been lost. Upon the east-south-east and north-east sides, the ground is covered for the most part with heath, strong heather and coarse grass. The soil is soft and wet, composed of peat earth over a substratum of rock. On the west and north-west sides, it is almost all covered with a green sward; the grass is fine and exhibits a striking contrast to the other parts of the island. Some of the hills are here green to the very summits.

Thus the best grazings would be found on the site of the old cultivations and in the west of the island, around Guirdil, where the vegetation overlies the mineral-rich basalt rock. The whole island, probably in Maclean's time and certainly in Salisbury's time (according to the Rum Archive held at Hatfield House and upon which much of the following chapters is based) was divided into nine hirsels of sheep. These were Kinloch, Samhnan Insir, Kilmory, Guirdil (2 hirsels), Harris (2 hirsels), Dibidil and Papadil. (It was only after about 1855 that the last two were split.) Ten shepherds were employed, one to each hirsel so that two shepherds lived at Harris, Guirdil and Papadil.

A house at Papadil was rebuilt in 1847, presumably the one whose ruins still stand there near the remains of the Lodge built at the end of the nineteenth century. New cottages were built at Dibidil in 1849. These houses were remote, reached only by a rough, hill footpath some 5–10 miles from Kinloch. If two shepherds were based together they were either both single or else a single man lodged with a married one.

Extra hands were required at gatherings and at smearing, usually being hired from Skye at 8*d.* or 9*d.* a day. Presumably the farm labourers and cottars around Kinloch would be pressed into service at such times. The shepherds were allocated oatmeal in addition to their £10 a year wage (£20 for head shepherd), and were also allowed to keep a cow or two. Initially they also kept a few wethers for sale or for their own larder but Salisbury considered this to be an invitation to pilfering from his own flocks and it was disallowed after 1847. None the less sheep still disappeared and the men from Skye employed in draining were suspected – in collaboration with the shepherds. By 1855 losses became so great that the entire workforce was dismissed.

The shepherds' contracts were renewed each Whitsun, at the end of May, if their work proved satisfactory, and they had to be prepared to move from one hirsel to another according to the whim of Salisbury or his agent. November is probably the best time to begin to describe a shepherd's year in Rum during Lord Salisbury's period of ownership. The month begins with smearing; a tedious process of rubbing a mixture of tar and butter into the fleece, to deter flies and parasites. A highly skilled man could anoint twenty sheep in a twelve-hour day, although the average was nearer ten. This procedure has long been replaced by dipping into a potent chemical bath.

Smearing was a costly business and was not without its unforeseen problems. In July 1859 44 barrels of American tar and 1½ tons of grease/butter were ordered for the Rum sheep stock. In 1852 the price was recorded at 32s. per barrel of tar, 70s. per cwt of butter and 45s. per cwt of grease. Once (in October 1846) the cargo steamer delivered the wrong kind of tar, so more butter had to be procured as a substitute, and this was scarce even in a city the size of Liverpool. In November 1846 the arrival of extra hands for the smearing was delayed by stormy weather, while two of the local shepherds had not returned from delivering the cast ewes to Liverpool. It was usual to accomplish the smearing by 8 November or else 'the sheep do not get the good of it, neither does the wool grow as well', according to the Factor. In 1846 the Harris, Kilmory and Guirdil hirsels were not done until 18 November, and a second gathering was required to get in 'any that may still be white'. That year there had been plenty tar but butter was in short supply. On 11 July 1853 it is recorded that the Factor ordered four casks of 'Begg's dipping composition', perhaps as an experiment, but its success was not reported.

The next activity was to put the rams or tups out to the ewes, usually the third week in November. Old tups were replaced in July, some being sold as new stock was bought in from markets in Fort William or from the estate of a Captain Campbell in Mull. On 14 October 1848 fourteen tups were dead on arrival in the steamer, which the Factor put down to 'tremors caused by overheating from the engine room'. Salisbury's frosty response was 'I've never heard such nonsense!' On one occasion a Southdown tup was said to be still suffering from the boat journey 'and won't look at any sheep'.

After they had performed their task, the tups were sometimes housed and fed for a short time. Initially the 200 tups on the island were kept for the remainder of the time at Papadil, well away from the ewes, but later they were found to be more conveniently held at Kinloch. All the other stock remained outside throughout the year and losses could be high.

The first lambs could be expected in the third week of April. Lambing percentage varied between hirsels and averaged 70 per cent over the whole island. In mid-May the stock was gathered in so that the lambs could be marked and counted. It is these May returns which have been used to calculate the lambing percentages. A gathering again took place in June/July to mark the lambs. In Rum the left horn bore the mark 'Rum' and the right one the number of the hirsel, beginning with Kinloch as number 1 and working round the island clockwise to Samhnan Insir as number 9.

Clipping began in early July (although in 1853 it began much earlier, by 23 June) to try and avoid the maggot fly that was so rife at the time in Eigg and Muck. A good man might be expected to clip 80–90 sheep in a day. The Samhnan Insir fleeces were often impregnated with sand from the beach and dunes, especially after the dry summer of 1857; they had to be beaten out and packed separately and yet still attracted complaints from the wool dealer. In 1859 Cheviot and cross wool was in particularly high demand, fetching much higher prices than Blackface wool.

The two markets important for all dealing with sheep and lambs in the Highlands were Inverness (held on 8 July) and Fort William (held on 13 July). In 1852 lambs were selling at £8 the clad score. In 1859 wether lambs were sold through an agent, Mr Gibbon. Forty clad score were disposed of at £9 each; thus £360 was paid to Gibbon, which the island Factor resented. He was convinced he would be able to dispose of the lambs himself in the future, thus avoiding paying commission to a middle-man. The Rev. H. Beatson in Eigg took twenty-one lambs in November 1845, while in 1852 and 1853 a Mr MacAskill of Rhudonan (Rudh'an Dunain) in Skye bought the clad and shot lambs. In July 1859 all the inferior ewes and wether lambs were sold to a man from Barra, who also took eleven yearling tups and twenty old ones. In May 1845 it is recorded how scores of lambs died in transit, from braxy and fly-strike.

The steamer usually came in the autumn, loaded with stores for the island and ready to take off stock and wool. In July 1959 it was timed to arrive just before the full moon on 12 September, so that stock could be loaded at the quay on the rising tide. Sometimes, however, the steamer had to leave early because the tides threatened to ground her with a full load, or else the tides delayed her arrival. Once a sheep that had died during loading was sold to the steamer crew. In October 1853 the steamer was late and twenty lambs died in the meantime. The Factor preferred to have the wether lambs taken off the island as soon as possible after being separated from the ewes.

In November 1846 the steamer docked on a Saturday but the men could not be sent out to gather the sheep until the Monday morning, presumably reluctant to work on the Sabbath. They returned at 5.30 after dark and when the sheep were counted through the fank there were only 221. The steamer could take 400, along with forty bales of wool, so it was detained until Thursday while the men went out to gather more sheep. Usually the Factor would despatch the shepherds to gather a week before the steamer was due.

At first the estate boat, *Ramsgate Packet*, transported the stock to Liverpool, but latterly a steamer had to be hired specially. This was probably a much less satisfactory situation, there being enough problems with weather and tides, etc. In August 1861 bad weather prevented the Factor from completing his sheep account, intending to ship out seventy-five bags of wool and 300 ewes. It was unlikely that a steamer would be available for hire so a sailing vessel might have to be used instead. On 13 September it was proposed that the sheep could be transported by a local boat to Arisaig, and from there walked to Perth. The Factor thought that this was impractical as they would require three boatloads, and a small local boat might be delayed by storms. In the end Salisbury proposed waiting until the next year. On 9 December the Factor wrote to him:

> I am sorry the cast ewes were not taken away as they were all got ready by the time I mentioned. I hope better arrangements will be entered into another season. It takes a full week to gather and draw the cast ewes from the flock and they lose condition when close-herded for exportation.

On 17 April next he had to report that the deaths in the ewes were mainly amongst those awaiting export: '700 will be cast this year including those from last year'. By 5 June he was again lamenting 'the excessive loss amongst last year's cast ewes awaiting export', so that by the time the steamer came they loaded only 595 ewes and sixteen three-year-old wethers (together with eighty-two bags of wool). The vessel had arrived early but the tide was ebbing fast and darkness overcame the loading so that eleven sheep had to be left behind. Such were the problems of transporting stock from a Hebridean island, problems that are hardly less in the Small Isles even today, since only Canna has a deepwater pier.

These were the practical considerations of running a sheep farm on a remote Hebridean island. How did the island match up in terms of performance? The island was heavily stocked. Sheep numbers varied from about 5000 to 7000, with 2000 or 3000 lambs born each season. Nearly all the breeding ewes were Blackface, although in September 1848 some

250 Cheviot ewes were brought to the island. Fifty were run at Harris, and 100 each at Guirdil and Kinloch. Their lambing percentage was very low and in the space of less than a year nearly one-quarter of the ewes had died: 47 per cent at Harris, 37 per cent at Guirdil and 30 per cent at Kinloch. By January 1850 the Factor had to conclude that the Cheviots were not doing well, due to the severe climate. Earlier, in February 1846, perhaps after experimenting with alternative breeds, the previous Factor had concluded that 'the Southdown x Leicester sheep are constantly housed and fed. I think Southdowns a hardy sheep when inured to the climate but the Leicester will not stand our wet climate.'

At smearing in November 1848, at lambing the next spring and again at shearing in July 1849, records were kept so that a prize could be awarded to the most attentive shepherds:

NOVEMBER 1848

Hirsel	stock in hand at smearing	deficient	stock in hand at shearing	deficient	total deficient	remarks
Papadil	280	18	242	13	31	1 in 9
Harris	1906	9	1494	38	47	1 in 40
Guirdil	1625	41	1498	36	77	1 in 20
Kilmory	665	4	593	29	33	1 in 20
Samhnan Insir	523	0	453	0	0	best shepherd
Kinloch	598	4	517	6	10	1 in 50

It is not surprising that Samhnan Insir should boast the best shepherd, since it is all low ground with few cliffs and easy to patrol. Papadil, on the other hand, has dangerous rocks and is quite precipitous. Surely the results do not reflect so much the best shepherd as the best hirsel for shepherding.

NOVEMBER 1848

Hirsels	breeding ewes in hand	lambs bred	lambing percentage
Guirdil	1261	857	68
Harris	1411	1002 most lambs	71
Kilmory	508	332	65
Samhnan Insir	385	257	67
Kinloch	450	222	49

The overall lambing percentage in Rum was 67 per cent. To assess it against that for other parts of the Highlands, we can use F. Fraser Darling's *West Highland Survey*, albeit calculated 50–100 years later. In fourteen years between 1911 and 1944, in the Outer Hebrides, he found an average of about 71 per cent, and a range from 63 per cent to 82 per cent. Thus Rum was probably about average for a west coast sheep walk. Lambing success on the island varied from year to year – from 54 per cent in 1859 to 71 per cent in 1855.

Harris in Rum produced the most lambs because it had the most sheep, and its lambing percentage was only marginally better than that of Guirdil. Grazing was probably slightly poorer in all the other hirsels, and certainly the north and east of the island would be wetter. Prior to 1855 Papadil held only the tups (about 200) throughout the year and about 1400 wethers in late summer. Only later were 300 breeding ewes hefted there.

Hirsel	total stock	blackface ewes	others
Kinloch	c.650	c.350	100 ewe hogs, 200 tups
Samhnan Insir	c.400	c.300	50–100 ewe hogs
Guirdil	c.1100	c.850	c.250 ewe hogs
Harris	c.1650	c.1300	c.350 ewe hogs
Dibidil	c.700	c.550	c.150 ewe hogs
Papadil	c.375	c.300	c.75 ewe hogs
whole island	c.4875	c.3650	c.1025 ewe hogs, 200 tups

Adult sheep mortality in Rum was probably higher than many other sheep farms in the west:

Hirsel	% lambing	% mortality		No. of shepherds
		ewes	others	
Kinloch	68	10.4	20.8	2
Samhnan Insir	65	11.7	25.37	1
Kilmory	67	7.8	22.8	1
Guirdil	77	9.0	26.7	2
Harris	68	7.5	29.3	2
Dibidil	48	8.6	20.5 }	
Papadil	71	8.6	20.1 }	2
whole island	70	7	c.25	10

Some 9 per cent of ewes died each year, most of them during lambing (April to July inclusive). Amongst non-breeding stock mortality was spread throughout the year, although slightly more deaths occurred in the winter months (October to February inclusive).

Doubtless mortality also varied from year to year. The agent could not remember a colder and wetter December than 1845, for instance; disease (braxy) was rife and the hogs lost condition. Between smearing and early January 1850 a great number of ewe hogs had died from braxy, principally in Harris and Guirdil, although deaths thereafter were fewer than in any previous January. In June 1855 some ewes and lambs were smitten with maggot, which was also rife in Eigg and Muck at the time.

Losses occurred due to accidents amongst the rocks and crags. Sheep were often tempted by lush grass growing on dangerous slopes and it was considered best either to erect dykes on the clifftop to prevent access and to introduce goats to graze off these precarious grasses. On 5 May 1846 a billy goat, six nannies and six kids were turned out at 'Strone' and 'Papperdale'. It was feared that they might not have survived the winter but five were seen the following August. Although we know from Walker's account in 1764 that goats were kept on Rum, the fact that some had to be turned out in 1846 at all suggests that none of them had survived.

Sheep also died from disease or exposure. The climate of Rum can be exceptionally inclement and was a major factor in the island's relatively poor performance. In June 1855 the sheep were in surprisingly good condition considering the severe winter and the dry spring; only the Samhnan Insir flock was poor, apparently because they had been allowed to graze too much on the low ground, which was spent. Two years later, after another severe winter, the sheep were in poor condition, their wool had not risen and they had to be left unshorn. Salisbury maintained that this was because the island was overstocked, although his Factor disagreed. The 1858/9 winter caused fewer deaths than normal because the pasture was still good and more care had been taken in culling the old ewes. The next winter was an especially harsh one. The 1861 autumn was very wet, with hardly a week of dry weather since mid-July. Snow was not a major event in Rum, but exceptionally heavy falls in January 1852 smothered many sheep; one drift 12 feet deep contained no less than twelve sheep, nine of which were dug out alive.

12 Depopulation on Such a Scale

It did not seem as if the depopulation of Rum had tended much
to anyone's advantage. A report went current at the time that
the island was on the eve of being purchased by some wealthy
Englishman who purported converting it to a deer forest.

Hugh Miller, 1845

The father of the new owner of Rum had been James, seventh Earl and
first Marquess of Salisbury, born in 1748. Although he served as George
III's Lord Chamberlain, he was – like his father before him – very much
overshadowed by his wife. Lady Emily Mary was the flamboyant daughter
of the Irish Earl of Downshire. Considered the premier Tory hostess of
the day, she dressed and entertained extravagantly. At her request, much
of the stately home at Hatfield was redecorated in fashionable Jacobean
style, with her own portrait (painted by Sir Joshua Reynolds) taking pride
of place in the King James' Drawing Room. She was also an enthusiastic
sportswoman and her hunting always attracted much comment from polite
society. A family history of the Salisburys recounts that

> a hundred stories are told of her eccentricities. She rode around the
> estate scattering guineas to the poor from a velvet bag held by her
> groom; she led gambling parties … which lasted till the dawn, when
> the floor was ankle deep in discarded packs of cards; she hunted the
> hounds herself until she was nearly eighty. Half-blind she was strapped
> on to the horse which was led by the groom; when they came to a fence,
> 'Damn you, my lady, jump!' he used to say.

The first Marquess had married in 1773, and his only son, James Cecil, was born eighteen years later. James grew up nursing an ambition to be a soldier, but being the only son and heir, his parents would not allow it. He was short and stocky, strong-featured with an aggressive countenance. Inheriting much of his mother's vigour and enthusiasm, he could expend it only in public life. He was elected to the House of Commons but on the death of his father in 1823, he succeeded to the peerage and entered the House of Lords. Before he was thirty-five James, the second Marquess, was made a Privy Councillor and, twice in later life, served as Lord Privy Seal.

Two years before coming into his inheritance, James Cecil had married Francis Mary Gascoyne, herself an heiress to large estates in Lancashire and Essex. Tall and graceful, with fine eyes, wavy dark hair and a sweet smile, she was also deeply religious, talented and intelligent. For the third successive generation, a Salisbury peer was to be eclipsed by a charming and accomplished spouse. Francis Mary Gascoyne was a close friend and admirer of the ageing, but still influential, Duke of Wellington (a cousin of her husband's), and it was he who on 22 February 1821 gave her away at the wedding in her father's home in London.

James Cecil's elderly, eccentric, widowed mother continued to dwell with her son and his young wife, at the seventeenth-century stately home, Hatfield. Her death was dramatically appropriate to one who had led such a colourful life. On the night of 22 November 1835 her apartments in the west wing caught fire. The blaze spread quickly. Help was impossible and James Cecil had to be physically restrained from dashing into the flames to rescue his elderly mother. It was only a change of wind direction and the bursting of a huge lead water tank in the roof that prevented the fire engulfing the rest of Hatfield House. According to *The Book of Hatfield*, 'the mercurial Lady Emily had perished, terribly but magnificently, in wind-tossed flames against a winter sky'. But it was a further two weeks before the Dowager's remains were recovered from the charred remnants of the west wing.

Apparently her extravagant gambling had led her deeply into debt and her death helped avert a financial crisis. The Marquess restored the damaged building and took the opportunity to change much of the decor into Elizabethan style which was once more so much in fashion. He also created the maze and terraced gardens around the house.

Sadly James Cecil was soon to suffer another bereavement. His wife, who had never enjoyed good health, died in October 1839 after a prolonged illness and at the early age of thirty-seven. In his widowhood, Salisbury grew more domineering. He had long shared a vigorous opposition to the Liberal movement, but now he developed a deep disillusionment with Disraeli as leader of the Tory party. In these liberal times, much influenced by the French Revolution and later, at home, by the Industrial Revolution, the Tories rarely won office. Thus, James Cecil was never able to make his mark in national politics – as his son Robert Cecil, three times Prime Minister, was later to do. Instead, James Cecil's energies found fulfilment in the autocratic management of his own estates. He was Colonel of the Militia regiment at Hatfield – the nearest he came to satisfying the military ambitions of his boyhood. In other local affairs he became 'the general, self-appointed dictator of the Hatfield district', as the family biographer Lord David Cecil recently described him.

> James Cecil was a shrewd businessman. On the death of his wife he had inherited her Lancashire and Essex estates and, in 1845, also received considerable compensation for loss of properties, due to the widening of Cranbourne Street in London. Like so many of his contemporaries, he had long nursed a desire to own a sporting estate in Scotland. So, that same year he diverted £24,455 of his London windfall towards the purchase of the Isle of Rum, in the Inner Hebrides.

On 23 July 1845, the *Inverness Courier* carried the news:

> The Marquis of Salisbury is reported to have purchased the island of Rum for the sum of £24,000 in order to form a shooting ground or deer forest ... In consequence of two great emigrations of the people in 1826 and 1828 the population was reduced from 400 to 100 or 130.

It was while paying his first visit to his new island estate that the Marquess learnt of an imminent visit to Hatfield by Queen Victoria. Hastily he returned south and, with only eleven days until the royal occasion, he initiated many last-minute improvements to the house and grounds, redecorating the State bedrooms and erecting new gates. In honour of the Queen and her consort a great ball was held at Hatfield, where a great ox weighing over a hundred stone was roasted. The leftovers were later distributed to the local poor and the house was thrown open to the public: thousands flocked to see where the royal couple had banqueted and slept.

Such lavish entertaining was typical of James Cecil, probably an inheritance from his mother. On such occasions, even retainers and tenants were liberally plied with beer and roast beef. One guest recalled how prayers were first said in the chapel. 'Dinner takes place in the old Elizabethan Hall. The band of the Militia ... plays during the meal in an outer apartment. Each lady as she passes into the Dining Hall is presented with a handsome bouquet.'

The year after Queen Victoria's visit, James Cecil married again. He was by then aged fifty-six and his new wife only twenty-three. She was Lady Mary Sackville-West, daughter of the fifth Earl de la Warr, and a lady of both sharp wit and high ambition. (After Salisbury's death in 1868 she remarried to become Countess of Derby.)

James Cecil had had seven children by his first marriage, but only five survived to maturity. His eldest son, James, suffered at birth from a nervous disability which rendered him an invalid and blind until he died aged about fifty. A second son had died in infancy, so it was to be the third Robert Cecil, born in 1830, who was to succeed as the third Marquess in 1868. Soon afterwards Robert Cecil disposed of the Rum estate. By his second marriage, James Cecil had three sons, one of whom, Eustace, spent his honeymoon in Rum, in the autumn of 1860 – in none too pleasant weather.

The owner of Rum, James Gascoyne-Cecil, as the second Marquess had styled himself, was, according to one of his granddaughters,

> obstinate in adhering to his views, uncompromising in the defence of his rights, and resentful of all outside interference. He had a dominating sense of public duty and an unhesitating readiness to accept responsibility in the performance of it.

But while traditional in politics, he was also progressive in outlook. He modernised agricultural methods and machinery on his estates, and built new improved cottages for his workers, whom he paid more generously than other landlords of the day. He encouraged the location of the railway station near his home in Hatfield so that he might fully benefit from it himself. He initiated night schools for boys on his estates – but, typically, would deduct 6*d.* from their wages for each evening they failed to attend. Despite this occasional bullying he was not disliked by his workforce who, it is said, appreciated that he had their own interests at heart.

Although his advice on all questions of estate management was widely sought and valued, his well-to-do contemporaries considered him 'irrascible, high-handed and egotistical. On his own ground he was domineering and quarrelsome. He had little respect for the opinion of others and a high respect for his own.' Nothing we know of the way he managed his estate in Rum does anything to alter this picture of his character.

Since the Marquess visited the island for only a month or two each year, he appointed an agent or Factor to represent him and to report back to him. The first to take up the post was H. M. MacDougall, an elderly businessman who in 1838 had headed an Australian company formed by the Society of Gentlemen. As such he had been entrusted with capital of £20,000 with a personal salary of £300 per annum. The venture folded, however, and MacDougall ended up living in Tobermory. He took up his new position by May 1845, and by November had moved into his house in Rum.

The previous tenant, a Mr MacGregor, had employed Walter Cowan, a middle-aged shepherd from the Borders, as his manager. Cowan was never to accept MacDougall being appointed in his stead. He had lost his wife, Catherine Henderson, a couple of years before and her crudely carved headstone still stands in the burial ground at Kilmory. Some errors in the inscription are presumably the work of a less-educated stonemason, since letters Cowan sent to Salisbury would indicate that the shepherd himself was quite literate, even articulate. (Interestingly, the name of the island is spelt 'Rhum' – an early date for an inaccuracy that was to be perpetuated for so long.)

Curiously, too, Cowan's wife was referred to as Mary in the 1841 census; one of his daughters is called Catherine, however, so may have been given one of her mother's Christian names. This child seems to have had a twin (also aged eleven) called Frank or Francis, while an elder child in the household was named Christian, or Chrissy-Anne, and aged twenty-two. Cowan's age was given as thirty-nine, and his wife a year younger. Two years later, on her gravestone, she was said to have been forty-nine. This is probably correct since ages written down on census forms were not always accurate.

A resentful Cowan was the first problem with which MacDougall had to contend. The shepherd complained to Salisbury that

> I do not know how a man can give orders to shepherds what is to be done when he does not [know] himself ... and if Lord Salisbury does not grant me the sole charge of the sheep stock ... I am determined to leave the island.

Three days later Cowan was to complain that MacDougall had allowed one of the shepherds to leave the island on business, during the busy time of tupping, and without Cowan knowing about it. He reported that MacDougall no longer communicated with him and that the Factor himself had departed the island to visit friends in Mull. Furthermore, MacDougall did not allow the shepherds any tallow for lighting their homes, hiding it in his own house until able to take it off to Mull with him. MacDougall's response was predictable. Cowan was refusing to follow his orders, having been 'too long absolute here to make a good obedient servant'. When the Factor requested that the shepherds control their dogs by tying them up when not working, it was Cowan's son who refused. 'Young Cowan is more fit to be a Tailor or a Dancing Master than a shepherd.' Another sarcastic, but more cryptic, comment was directed towards Cowan's daughters.

Cowan was not alone, however, in his criticism of the Factor and the conditions in Rum. When others in his employ began to complain, his Lordship countered:

> With regard to the men who grumble at work, I am sure the wages are sufficient with the other advantages they possess. If they had higher

wages I should impose higher rents which would come to the same thing, and they are at liberty to take themselves and their families off the island if they do not like the terms ...

Like so many landlords of the time, Salisbury obviously considered his power absolute. In December 1845 MacDougall reported: 'Your Lordship wishes to know the people constantly at work. The men at the Point [Port na Caranean] are very diligent and wish to be employed.' Norman Macdonald from Bracadale, aged fifty-five – 'a good mason [who] can still clip and smear' – was unable to work at that time because of ill health.

All others are trenching except John Gilles and son. They prefer the fishing which they are commencing. He is one of those that should be sent about his business. He is too great a politician and very often puts bad notions in the heads of others.

On 4 January 1846 Salisbury demanded the names of the troublesome labourers and threatened them with immediate discharge. He asked that they be told that they must be prepared to leave at the expiration of their term.

MacDougall fuelled his Lordship's intentions on 9 February by informing him how such discharges could be effected:

Crofters require 40 days before the Term – any paying rent require warning served by a Sheriff Officer. Shepherds and other servants who pay no rent, a verbal notice is sufficient, given in due time.

By 18 March Salisbury was informed by his lawyers that they 'have written by the Post to the Highlands to take the necessary steps to give the tenants on the island legal notice to quit'. The lawyers then made certain recommendations on the new terms Salisbury should offer his staff. The shepherds' wages, for instance, should be 'the same as in southern Scotland', suggesting that they were receiving less! Cowan was recorded in 1845 as receiving a wage of £6 per half year, his son as an assistant shepherd £5. 'I shall see how the matter stands with them,' MacDougall replied, 'but I have my doubts the crofters will neither quit nor come into the new agreements this year ... I fear Cowan will be troublesome, however.' In March, two years later, the assistant shepherds were still receiving £10 annually with an allowance of meal.

Salisbury disapproved of his staff being allowed to keep sheep of their own – 'being a temptation to dishonesty' – preferring instead to pay them a little extra money. Besides dissatisfaction with their work, Salisbury was worried about sheep losses. He was told of no less than a hundred unaccounted for on his last visit, with a further 245 missing and 150 dead. MacDougall proposed that

> the sheep losses will be reduced if some of the worst [cliff] passes are inclosed. During an experience of 40 years in managing stocks, one other farm excepted – I have never met with such accountable losses as here.

Cowan tried to put the blame at MacDougall's door to which Salisbury replied:

> Your letters of 12th and 15th December have reached me. You will recollect that the abuse of the person placed over you is no excuse for your own negligence.

To MacDougall he wrote:

> I cannot but express my great dissatisfaction at the account which you give me of the stock under your superintendence. You seem to treat it with much unconcern as if every part of the property was safe and no loss had been suffered. We do not in this part of England usually consider the loss of 25 sheep as a mere trifle ... the death of 150 is a very large average and far exceeding that which is usual on those Highland properties with which I am acquainted.

Clearly Salisbury held MacDougall ultimately responsible. In November 1845 (only months after the Factor had taken up his appointment) MacDougall received a curt note from his employer:

> I have to acknowledge receipt of your letter of the 4th November. It does not convey any precise information as to what is going on at Rum. You neither state the number of men at work with the digging, nor the quantity of work done. Nor do you give me any account of the number of sheep to be smeared or the losses by death and otherwise. In the meantime I am by no means satisfied with the state of the sheep which came here [to Hatfield] from the island.

Four months later Salisbury was

> by no means satisfied with the progress you have made in obeying my instructions ... I give you full credit for your good intentions and am not surprised that you should feel at a loss how to adopt a system of management entirely new to you.

Several weeks later, on 8 March 1846, Salisbury had decided:

> It is evident that your continuance in my employment for another year could only lead to disappointment to me and vexation to yourself. I have

therefore come to the resolution of replacing you at the expiration of the period of our engagement.

Salisbury then set about seeking a replacement. On 22 March Alexander Mackenzie wrote to accept his new appointment. In the meantime MacDougall was reluctant to relinquish his Factorship. On 4 April he remonstrated:

> With a view to vindicate my own character which I am aware has been misrepresented to your Lordship. I took the liberty of inclosing for your Lordship's perusals, a few testimonials from some of the most influential and practical men of the district wherein I then resided ... Believe me, my Lord, I would not take four times my salary and pass another year, as I have done the last, and all owing to these people and I can further say that they are dear Pets to your Lordship.

Salisbury returned the references promptly but was unswayed, commenting, 'in announcing our agreement I did not mean in the slightest degree to cast any imputation on your character'.

MacDougall had certainly inherited an awkward situation with Cowan's resentment of him, which must have put additional strains on his relationship with the rest of the labour force. Salisbury had reacted in typical autocratic fashion by issuing them with an ultimatum: 'take it or leave it!' Some of the islanders did leave, some were dismissed. MacDougall survived that first crisis, but being an elderly widower he might have found life in the island difficult. In December 1845 he had intended bringing his sister or daughter back from Tobermory 'so that I may not feel the long winter nights too wearisome'. In the end they were unable to make the trip because of bad weather. Notwithstanding, MacDougall was far from the efficient and experienced Factor that Salisbury needed – one that he was fortunate to find in his successor. The estate records change abruptly from being a complete shambles to being tidy, methodical and informative. The new Factor, Alexander Mackenzie, submitted monthly stock returns, wage accounts and corresponded regularly.

MacDougall's replacement was a forty-year-old former soldier from Dalkeith, near Edinburgh. Mackenzie travelled direct from the Portobello Barracks in Dublin, with his wife Sarah and sixteen-year-old daughter, Elizabeth. They had to spend five days in Glasgow on the way, reaching Rum towards the end of April 1846. MacDougall by this time had left Rum but Mackenzie met him in Tobermory to sort out some personal matters that necessitated the old Factor returning to Rum at the end of May to lay claim to numerous items of his own. 'Mr MacDougall left here on the 26th,' Mackenzie reported to his employer,

and for all the good he has been since my arrival on Rum, he had as well (perhaps better) been away. It was as much as I could do to avoid having words with him.

By this time MacDougall's arch-enemy Walter Cowan had died in a drowning accident. It had happened on 17 May 1846 but it was several weeks before his body was washed ashore at Strath in Skye. Although his second wife and family had already departed Rum, Cowan's remains were taken back to Kilmory for burial beside his first wife; he is not mentioned on the headstone. His widow pressed Lord Salisbury for the wages due to her late husband and on 3 October received the sum of £3. The following February the family tried to claim some sheep but the new Factor, Mackenzie, refused to entertain them. The son, Francis, even tried driving the sheep from Kinloch, intending to sell them and claiming that the family had been given the sheep by Mr MacGregor, the previous tenant of the island.

Mackenzie, meanwhile, was installing himself and his family in their new home. He possessed

> all the necessary utensils for cooking, crockeryware and other useful articles. Bedding, bedspreads, chairs, tables and fire irons I have not, these being supplied in the Barracks.

It was several months before a boat arrived in Rum with a cargo of furniture from Salisbury.

The Marquess must quickly have come to appreciate the youthful vigour and military efficiency of his new agent. Besides acceding to the request for furniture, Salisbury also provided mathematical instruments. Several years later he was sending regular bundles of old newspapers to his Factor. Another welcome diversion for Mackenzie was entertaining the occasional learned visitor to Rum. On the night of 30 July 1856 he was host to the antiquarian T. S. Muir. In his book *Ecclesiological Notes on some of the Islands of Scotland* Muir recalled how the geologist MacCulloch had considered Rum 'the wildest and most repulsive of all the islands'. 'Wild undoubtedly it is,' Muir added,

> and, if responsible for conditions not properly its own, repulsive too, very likely, when it pours and the wind is ahead. Had the doctor been with me on the day that I crossed over from Kilmory, at the north-west side of the island, to Kinloch-Scresort on its east, with my coat in my hand, I daresay he would have altered his opinion, for the serenity and sunshine made all around on the way beautiful. Rum, however, contains nothing at all interesting to the ecclesiologist or antiquary, apparently. In a small burying-ground, prettily situated on the shore at Kilmory, there was a chapel, of which only some obscure traces remain. Near to where it stood there is a slender pillar incised with a plain cross.

Another one of cross form, made of slate, stands by it, inscribed: Catherine Henderson, ob. 5 May 1843 and her husband Walter Cowan Manager Rhum.

Surprisingly Muir's transcription of the stone is inaccurate; in fact, it reads:

Sacred to the memory of Catherine Henderson who departed this life upon the 5 day of May 1843, aged 49. This stone erect here by hir belovied ied husband Walter Cowan, manager Rhum.

Also had he examined the slender cross slab more closely and cleared away its encrusting lichen on its other face, he would have discovered a more interesting marigold cross. Muir left the next morning for Skye but doubtless Mr Mackenzie the Factor enjoyed his company.

In 1858 Mackenzie reported to Lord Salisbury:

My old dog is dead. If your Lordship has one which you do not much prize, either pointer or any other kind which will find [grouse]. The shepherd [who was at the time at Hatfield with sheep] can bring it with him. It may also help me to get at the snipe and woodcocks; even a dog serves to relieve the solitude of the hills.

Salisbury despatched a spaniel (which Mackenzie found would not follow him on the hill) and a pointer, which served him very well 'for I am a very bad shot'. Indeed, when the Factor later asked if he might shoot a beast for the household, his employer agreed to a fallow deer but quipped, 'unless you can shoot it yourself, I do not know how it is to be got!' Several years later Mackenzie approached Salisbury again:

I hope before my return to the island your Lordship will give me a better rifle to take with me. The one I got is worthless now ... Among the defects the hammer will not always fall when the trigger is pulled, the cock is worn out.

In his letters Mackenzie was including many anecdotes about the weather. His very first winter had seen very deep snow, the most for twelve years. December 1848 was exceedingly stormy and there had been many wrecks in the area. July 1857 had been the driest in his experience, while the winter of 1858/9 was very mild with no frost since November. February and March saw 'more fog than is usual ... None of the heath was able to be burnt because of the wet.' The following winter was a complete contrast, however, being very severe, while September 1861 saw the hay cut but not secured, the potatoes failing and no peats taken in. On 21 September 1858 Mackenzie reported:

We have fine views of the comet every night for the last week. The nights are clear. It appears after sunset in the northwest in the evening and in the northeast in the morning before sunrising. I think astronomers would be glad to view it from here.

This was Donati's Comet, one of five new ones reported that century; more significant than its brightness had been its several tails which changed shape from time to time.

Late in 1859 Mrs Mackenzie was taken ill and went to Sheffield, the family home, for medical treatment. Salisbury considerately recommmended that Mackenzie himself should join her for the winter. By March she had recovered somewhat, 'though still weak', and it seems that she might have remained in a mainland nursing home thereafter. By this time Mackenzie's daughter, Elizabeth, a teacher, had married a seaman called Page, so was able to live with her father in Rum, until the spring of 1861.

The Marquess was not above offering medical advice when the occasion demanded. He once recommended that a young shepherd who was dying of a chest inflammation to be treated with

> mustard plasters and repeat them as need be. If resorted to at first they rarely fail. In default of mustard, scraped horse radish will answer equally well. Neither should be kept on at one time long enough to take off the skin. They should be repeated often in fresh places.

Despite the mutual respect, and even affection, that Salisbury and his Factor displayed in their correspondence, Mackenzie was not immune to his employer's quick temper. On one occasion he was criticised over his deployment of a Welsh miner engaged in building the track to Papadil. On 31 October 1848, the Marquess demanded that he should not be distracted by the path round the Strone (now referred to as Welshman's Rock). It was more a job for the winter, while Papadil had to be tackled in the summer. 'This comes,' admonished his Lordship,

> of your upsetting my arrangements upon a nonsensical pretext of not being able to lodge him at Papperdale, which I had ordered you to do, because you wanted to lodge your stonewall builders there. You are constantly placing me in the difficulty of either giving you no discretion at all, or leaving every one of my arrangements set aside. Its just the same with the roads ... They not being finished by the time I arrive next year is tantamount to asking for your dismissal.

Nor did Mackenzie avoid his own labour problems. Some were doubtless spawned by Lord Salisbury's dictates from Hatfield, while others were a product of the prevailing conditions at the time – a growing, ever-hungry population in the Highlands, the Clearances and the potato famine. Mackenzie appears to have emerged from the situation with commendable diplomacy.

On 10 August 1846, for instance, Neil Maclean had to be dismissed for not pulling his weight. He stayed on with his brother-in-law Peter Maclean, and in January of the following year requested permission of fish offshore. Salisbury refused, unless he fished for the estate. As Factor, Mackenzie was asked to see that Neil left his brother-in-law's house. So instead the fisherman lived aboard his boat, which was anchored in Loch Scresort. An irate Marquess sought legal advice but all he seems to have achieved was forbidding Maclean to come ashore, and the ultimate outcome is not recorded; Neil was still living with his brother-in-law by the next census in 1851.

Salisbury's reluctance for his staff to have any sort of independence from the estate resulted in the islanders losing small patches of land which they had previously cultivated as crofters. In January 1847, they petitioned the landlord:

> Because of the difficulty which have occurred as to the dispensation of providence regarding the failure of the potatoes crop, [we] humbly request that your Lordship will have the goodness to allow us to have the ground which was formerly held as it would be a considerable assistance in witholding us from being involved in debt ... at the same time we promise as in dutybound to attend to your Lordship's service punctually ...

Signed:

Donald Matheson	Kenneth Maclean
John Matheson	John Mackinnon
Norman Macdonald	Kenneth Campbell
Angus Macleod	Angus Maclean
John Russell (snr)	Malcolm Macrae
Donald Maclean	John Gilles

Predictably, Salisbury refused the request, as he could not allow them 'to place any dependence on the occupation of small farms'. Only two months later Mackenzie reported to Hatfield that

> accounts from the neighbouring islands are very distressing. Skye appears to be the worst off in this neighbourhood; Uist and Barra are also in a bad state. There are no complaints among our people here, but I doubt that their wages for the last half year in some cases, will all be expended to purchase meal. They have generally as many seed potatoes from last year's crop as will do for seed.

The previous summer in the Hebrides had been an unusually wet one. In his newspaper *The Witness* Hugh Miller had reported:

> In the course of a week, frequently in the course of a single night or

day, fields and patches of this vegetable [the potato] looking fair and flourishing, were blasted and withered and found to be unfit for human food.

The *Inverness Courier*'s correspondent observed a similar tale of woe from Skye, Knoydart, Lochalsh and Kintail:

In all that extensive district he had scarcely seen one field which was not affected – some to a great extent, and others presenting a most melancholy appearance as they were enveloped in one mass of decay.

The 1846/7 winter set in early and proved both cold and stormy, with frequent gales and snow storms. The effectiveness of the potato blight varied from area to area, some being worse affected than others. It is probably true to say that Rum was cushioned from its worse effects since the islanders were dependent upon the estate for most of their needs. Had Salisbury consented to the extra plots for cultivation the potatoes would still have been blighted.

What was needed during these times of extreme hardship was a suitable substitute. Meal proved inadequate as it was deficient in vitamin C, and cases of scurvy were occurring in the Highlands where it had been unknown for over a century. Fish would have proved both nutritious and rich in vitamins so it was a pity that Salisbury had been so reluctant to encourage those, like Neil and Peter Maclean, who wished to pursue this occupation; Peter had sold his boat. Early in 1846 Norman Macdonald, John Gilles and their sons (all living at Port na Caranean) were fishing with some success. But they appear not to have received any encouragement and indeed may have had to cease altogether due to Salisbury's edict on independent enterprise. By November 1846 it was reported how no vessel on the island was fit for sea.

By the beginning of the next year some of the islanders were hard-pressed financially, probably due to the need to buy in food. In February William Elliott threatened to leave unless his wages were increased to £20 annually, with the customary 6½ bolls of meal. The reason he gave was that he had recently been moved from Harris and was lacking in sufficient grazing for his cows. Remarkably Salisbury consented to this wage rise as he was 'extremely well satisfied with his exertions'. Elliott, however, eventually left the island in May 1848 as he could not agree with Mackenzie: 'I am here counted as a disturber of the peace', he claimed.

Hector Campbell, the single shepherd at Guirdil, was unlucky in his request. He wished to move from his lonely cottage but had to stay where he was for the time being, without any increase in pay, despite being 'our best cragsman'. Eight years later, as a 29-year-old widower, Campbell was being employed at Kinloch as Head Shepherd.

Salisbury responded to this unrest amongst his staff by reminding them, through Mackenzie, that shepherds were employed on a short-term contract only, and had to be prepared to leave the island at its expiry. A new contract of employment, drawn up in March 1847, is worth quoting in full:

It is agreed that in the future, no parties in the island of Rum shall be considered as Crofters or entitled to possess any land in that capacity. The people on the island are to be considered as in the services of the Marquess of Salisbury engaged by the year on the following terms and conditions:-

1) They are to receive the money, wages and allowances in meal after mentioned ...

2) Each is to be allowed a free house and garden with pasturage for a cow on such part of the island (as near to their houses as possible) as may be pointed out by the Marquess' overseer.

3) The people are to be at all times at command of the Marquess' overseer and to be employed at such work as he may point out either on land or at sea.

4) The Marquess to be entitled to stop the wages or other allowances to the people in the event of their not attending to the instructions or disobeying the orders of the overseer and that to an extent not exceeding one shilling a day and to dismiss anyone guilty of gross neglect of duty or disobedience.

Only one replacement hand was necessary as a consequence of this contract. Norman Macrae, the unmarried shepherd at Harris, left the island. Apparently the turnover in single shepherds was quite high, as Mackenzie had noted: 'for want of domestic comforts, no young man will remain longer than his term binds him'. The new Harris shepherd was young Allan Matheson, son of John Matheson, but he was dismissed in October for being idle. He found a job on a visiting schooner but met with an accident. After a spell in Glasgow Infirmary he returned to Rum to recuperate. In November 1848 he left with Neil Gilles to seek employment in Glasgow. Neil soon returned when his father became very ill with consumption; by January 1849 John Gilles had recovered.

In 1867 Allan Matheson returned to the old family church at Bracadale to marry Kirsty Cameron. They went to live in Tobermory where five children were born. The younger sons, Donald and Neil, later emigrated to New Zealand but were tragically killed in the ANZACs during the First World War, Neil at the Gallipoli landings. Their father, with their eldest brother, also called John, had meanwhile moved from Mull to Inverness where the old man died in 1911. Young John's son, Kenneth, became a doctor in Argyll before becoming a prisoner of the Japanese during the Second World War. He survived to practise in Inverness until his death in 1963. His own son, Allan, who had been a schoolfriend of my own, also became a doctor but died still a young man in Keith, Aberdeenshire. His younger brother Roderick was amongst the first commandos ashore at Port San Carlos during the Falklands war in 1982 and, since he was fluent in Spanish, acted as interpreter at the eventual surrender of the Argentinian General Menendez. A distinguished pedigree indeed, from a young man whom Lord Salisbury had dismissed from his employ for being idle!

By July 1847 Rum's population had consisted of twenty-one families, totalling 118 people. Fever and smallpox became rife in Eigg the following February, with some sickness also and one fatality in Rum: Murdoch Macrae, who was over ninety. By March 1848 two extra families had arrived with an increase in population to 125. The next December proved a wet month and Mackenzie was concerned about flooding in Kinloch Glen. Many ships had been lost in the storms, and one 500-ton barque *The Snowden of St John's*, New Brunswick, had its mast and rigging torn away before going aground off the mouth of Loch Scresort. By this time the estate had its own boat (see next chapter), which towed the wreck into Rum harbour for the sum of £20. A month later, duly repaired, it resumed its voyage to Liverpool with a cargo of salt, and with young Allan Matheson (back from Glasgow) as one of its crew.

While on the subject of wrecks it is worth mentioning that in January 1850 a boat was lost off Lewis with a crew of five; one body was found on the shore by the Harris shepherds and taken to Kilmory for burial. On 18 July 1852, a foggy Sunday morning, a schooner struck rocks between Guirdil and Harris and sank, only its rigging showing above the water. Its crew of six seem to have survived although the owner/captain was not insured. On 3 December 1853 a schooner sailing to Ireland with barley was dismasted off Eigg. The crew took to the boats and came ashore on the north side, but they lay out on the hill all night, supposing the island to be uninhabited.

Early in 1849 young Allan Maclean, the son of Archibald the carpenter from Samhnan Insir, was wed and sought a house in Rum. By August, however, he had decided to emigrate to America with some of the Canna folk.

John Russell, son of the gardener at Kinloch, was lucky enough to find suitable employment on the island, first as an agricultural labourer at £4 a year, and eventually as a schoolteacher. In April 1846 the factor had written to Lord Salisbury:

> I am requested by Russell the gardener to state to your Lordship that he has a son, who is competent to teach the children in the island

reading, writing and accounts. The Free Church minister [on Eigg] has nominated him to the appointment. The people agree to pay him £10 and provide for his board.

Mackenzie respectfully suggested that Lord Salisbury might like to make up his salary to £14 or £15 per annum. Rather gruffly, his Lordship replied:

I do not know who this son of his is nor how can he be on the island without being one of my servants. The subject of education is an important one, and whatever I ultimately determine on the subject, whatever schoolmaster is employed shall be nominated by me, and only me. It is my intention to keep clear of any of the disputes between the Established and the Free Kirk or any other religion, and I certainly will not allow the minister of any denomination to advance a person as schoolmaster.

None the less the 22-year-old was duly employed, under the direction of the parish schoolmaster in Eigg, with his salary paid by Lord Salisbury. The following month Mr Murray wrote from Eigg to seek some remuneration as parish schoolmaster from Salisbury, to which his Lordship responded:

I presume that there are duties attached to the office, and that Mr Murray is required to give at least some attendance upon the inhabitants of Rum. As I have never heard his name mentioned and as I do pay a person to do that which he professes to do, I must decline the payment ...

The new dominie John Russell found his school in a very bad state of repair, and submitted a list of articles required to Mr Mackenzie, the Factor. On 2 August 1848 Russell gave a report on his twenty-seven pupils to Lord Salisbury:

First class: 4 boys between 12 and 13 years. They can read, parse and construe with tolerable accuracy any piece of Modern History composition in prose. As some of them have only attended occasionally since the beginning of April, their stages of progress in Arithmetic are various. Some have advanced as far as the 'Square and Cube Root' while others are as far back as 'practice'. They have committed to memory a considerable portion of Reid's Rudiments of Geography and can trace on the maps many of the places therein described. They can write a comparatively plain hand and repeat the Westminster Shorter Catechism.

Second class: consists of 6 boys and 3 girls (ages varying from 7 to 11 years). They can read very correctly and their knowledge of Geography and Arithmetic is proportionably to that of the First Class. They write Text and Half Text lines. They have some knowledge of English Grammar and can repeat the above said Catechism.

Third class: consists of 5 boys about 6 years of age. About this time last year they could scarcely pronounce monosyllables [presumably English since for most of them Gaelic would be their native tongue] but can now read the Bible and spell correctly. They write on slates.

Fourth class: consists of 2 girls and a boy. They can read easy passages of Scripture and spell dissyllables.

There are other 6 young ones that have entered School about the beginning of June. Hence the total number of weekday scholars is 27. The average number of Sunday scholars is 30, two of the eldest boys have left entirely while others only attend occasionally.

John Russell, junior

In December 1849 Russell asked leave to continue his studies at Moray House in Edinburgh, after which he would be entitled to a government subsidy on his salary. Salisbury agreed but expressed concern that the government would take the school under its direction, and repeated his refusal to have dealings with either the Established or Free Church of Scotland, himself being a member of the Church of England. Russell returned in July, but the children had had no teaching since he had gone to Edinburgh eight months previously.

In the meantime Salisbury had begun work on a new school. By October it was ready for slating, though lead was required to put round the chimney. The floor was laid in December and Mackenzie reported that 'it will be a very comfortable house when thoroughly dry'. The new school was finally opened at the start of the New Year 1850, though 'it will stand without paint or tar until your Lordship decides which is to be used for the outside boarding'.

Two years later Mackenzie's daughter Elizabeth was employed as schoolteacher, being paid £8 11*s.* 4*d.* per year with an additional £4 5*s.* 8*d.* as Inspector of the Poor. In September 1853 the salary was increased to £15 per year, and Salisbury was by then paying a statutory contribution to Mr Murray on Eigg as parish schoolmaster, £3 10*s.* 8*d.* with an additional 15*s.* as Inspector of the Poor. Finally we learn how on 7 April 1857 John Murray, for forty years parish schoolmaster in Eigg, resigned his charge at the age of seventy. He approached Lord Salisbury to contribute an annual allowance and part of his salary as a retirement pension, but predictably Salisbury refused. The post of Inspector of the Poor fell vacant and

Mackenzie proposed Russell in opposition against the Factor in Eigg. 'I do not expect to be successful,' Mackenzie confessed to Lord Salisbury, 'but I did not wish to let the Eigg party have all their own way!'

The Rev. Peter Grant (1796–1864), the parish minister, took the opportunity to petition for a new church in Eigg. The west end of the ground floor of the schoolhouse, then used as the schoolroom, had been intended originally as a place of worship; the other end, then used as a kitchen, was appropriate as a school, with the upper floor of the building serving as a dwelling place for the master. A new church could be built for £148, with an additional £255 for slates and joinery. A new manse and schoolhouse had been built in Eigg by July 1860.

In January 1849 Hector Mackinnon, the crippled pauper at Kilmory, was discovered to have a relative of his wife – from Canna – living at his house. Mackenzie warned him that if he again encouraged anyone not of his own family at his house, he faced eviction. Salisbury demanded that a house be found for him in Kinloch, and in March 1850, once the new Rum school was opened, Mackinnon and his family were moved to the old schoolhouse.

For some reason Lord Salisbury and his Factor harboured a deep suspicion of Canna. In August 1846 MacDougall complained that the Canna folk were still landing to cut peats on the Rum shore at Kilmory. In October that year a number of Small Islanders were employed draining but a month or so later MacDougall intended

> paying off the Canna people and only retain[ing] Robertson and his party from Eigg as they are the only men who seem to understand draining properly. I have had to be constantly watching the Cana [sic] people and sometimes had occasion to use harsh language to get the work done in any kind of workmanship.

On 27 November 1848 Mackenzie reported to him that:

> MacNeil of Cana died at Oban I believe on the 10th inst. If there was anything to apprehend from the depredations of the Cana people before, I fear there will be more now ... I have given strict orders to the shepherds on that side of the island opposite Cana to lose no time in acquainting us if any landing is attempted by any of them except at Kinloch.

Nor had Salisbury's high-handed attitude to his own staff diminished in any way. Donald Macrae departed in January 1850, the reason not being stated. A few weeks later Alexander Chisholm, the sixty-year-old shepherd, was dismissed. He begged leave to stay but his Lordship responded: 'I cannot permit any person to remain on the island of Rum except those who are my hired servants, and Mr Mackenzie has declined to engage you for another year.' One of the Russell boys, Hugh, left in April for Greenock, to learn shipbuilding; Salisbury declared he would not stand in his way to get on in the world. 'I shall, of course, when he leaves, not let him settle on the island again.' Whether he did in the end opt to leave, or whether Salisbury allowed him back, is not known but he does appear on the 1851 census. In May the following year he again wished to quit his post as shepherd at Harris. Salisbury admitted that Russell could do better as a miner or fireman on a steamer.

The 1851 census revealed twenty-five families totalling 161 people, more than Salisbury could either employ or tolerate. The potato famine had served to underline in the eyes of many Highland landlords that the crofting system, as it was then, was a redundant way of profitably organising their estates. A few lairds handed out large sums of money, even to the verge of bankruptcy, to prevent their tenantry from starving. In 1850 Macleod of Dunvegan's Factor in Skye warned that several great and famous landlords would 'very soon bid adieu to their properties' and join the growing list of historic families who had already sunk in a sea of debts, unless a very large number of people were not at once removed from the Highlands.

Rum had escaped the worst of the famine but its population, like that elsewhere in the Highlands, was increasing all the time. A new wave of emigration fever was sweeping the north in 1850, which perhaps influenced Lord Salisbury to effect a clearance of his own. So acute was the suffering around this period that many Highlanders were only too willing to quit their native land, and Salisbury found no shortage of volunteers in Rum. In December 1851 a list was drawn up bearing no less than fifty-seven names and in the following month agents were approached in Greenock, about transport across the Atlantic. But there was still some indecision in Rum as to who would take up Salisbury's proposal. Some were at a loss to know whether they should bother to plant their gardens for another season. Salisbury, on the other hand, had the financial aspects on his mind:

> The question now remains what amount of pecuniary assistance they will require from me, and that will vary according to their means. I cannot recommend them to go unless they have something beyond their passage, money or friends who will assist them when they get out.

'I should think it absurd', he adds, 'for old Maclean, who is I believe one of them, to undertake such a journey.' Old Archibald Maclean, the carpenter, was determined, however, and featured on a fresh list of sixty-three names dated 23 February. A new family had been added, that of Norman Macdonald, his wife, four sons and two daughters, but Kenneth and Catherine Maclean (brother and sister) withdrew as they did not wish their eighty-year-old father Allan to be left on the island on his own.

Mackenzie relayed to Salisbury the decision of the emigrants to go to Hamilton in Upper Canada:

If his Lordship donated articles of clothing, they would require no further aid in money. They time their departure for the end of April or early May so that they would receive half a year's wages which together with the money from selling their cows, will provide adequate funds.

Lord Salisbury granted some skins to make clothing for the men. He noted that it would cost £5 extra for the steamer to stray from her regular course to pick up another eight or nine families who were quitting Eigg.

On 22 March the old carpenter, Archibald Maclean, was persuaded to withdraw his name and those of his family, deciding instead to go to Canna 'where they expect the proprietor to do something for them'. Salisbury dictated that the daughters able to go into service must remain behind in Rum, rather than go to Canna, while if the younger son found employment on the estate boat, 'he must not loiter about the island'. Old Maclean may have resented these stipulations for, in the end, he did emigrate with the rest of his family. Norman Macdonald and his dependants remained behind. 'The eldest son is a general useful man,' decided Mackenzie, 'and I propose him to take charge of the Kinloch hirsel [of sheep] in the room of Angus Gilles, who will leave with the others.'

By 5 April Salisbury was understandably impatient:

Your list of intended emigrants appears to vary in every letter and becomes so confused that it is impossible to come to any definite result. Now, as it is favour I do them to assist them at all, I must have a definite list from which, when approved, I will allow no variation … They must leave the island or any that cannot provide themselves elsewhere will be treated entirely as paupers and put in such houses as may suit me, not allowed to keep cows etc. Mind to explain that I have a desire that they should emigrate. It is a favour I do them to assist their wish.

He disapproved of the vessel calling for them at Rum, as some might change their minds at the last moment: instead he was prepared to negotiate a fare per head as 'steerage passengers' on a regular steamer to Glasgow:

It will be expedient that [Mackenzie] should see those that emigrate safe on board the immigrant vessel at Glasgow. No money to be given until they are on board. You had better lose no time in sending an answer to this letter, I have no doubt the list will be considerably diminished. You will have to take great care, that the owners of the steamer to Canada do not impose upon the emigrants and if necessary call in the supervision of the Government Agent as to provisions etc.

On 18 May 1852 Mackenzie left for Glasgow with the emigrants:

> They sailed from here on Thursday night about 12 o'clock and cleared out at Greenock yesterday. They sailed in the barque *California*. The fares for the adults £3 15s. – half price between the ages of one and fourteen ... The people went off in good spirits.

The families who departed were:

> Kenneth and Christina Campbell, 6 sons and 2 daughters.
> Donald and Ann Maclean, a young son and daughter and baby boy.
> John and Margaret Mackinnon, 4 sons and 2 daughters.
> John and Flora Gilles, 4 sons and 3 daughters.
> Donald and Christianna Matheson, 3 sons and 2 daughters.
> Peter and Margaret Maclean, 2 sons and 2 daughters.
> Angus Maclean and his sister Margaret.
> Archibald and Christina Maclean, 2 sons and 4 daughters.

The steamer fare to Glasgow had cost 5s. per adult, half-price for children, and once in Quebec it cost a further £1 6s. (13s. for a child) to Hamilton. Salisbury had paid each employee their wages due, including a £5 gift for old Archibald Maclean the carpenter. The Marquess had doubted the wisdom of the people taking too many belongings, 'except perhaps woollens', but gave each person several articles of clothing – shirts and Chinese gowns and frocks, blue bonnets for the boys, shawls, flannel petticoats and shoes. Altogether the assisted emigration had cost Lord Salisbury £291 3s. 6d. The conditions were certainly much improved than during the 1826/8 eviction, but again the island had lost much of its youth. Seven families remained behind in Rum, most of them middle-aged or elderly, although some had children of working age. Those remaining were:

> Norman and Anne Macdonald, 4 sons and 2 daughters (2 of them
>   employed on the estate).
> Allan Maclean, the aged widower, his son Kenneth and daughter
> Catherine, both in their thirties.
> John and Euphemia Russell and 2 teenage sons.
> John and Margaret Matheson, 3 daughters, a young son and a baby girl.
> The widow Flora [Sarah?] Mackinnon and 3 young children.
> Angus Maclean, nearly 80, and his daughter in her thirties.
> Allan Macrae, his widowed mother and an orphan boy.

More staff had to be engaged but when one of the new shepherds turned up drunk at Hatfield with a consignment of sheep he was instantly dismissed. In October 1852 Mackenzie acquired a bag net and employed some men in fishing salmon round the island. They were unsuccessful, complaining that it was not the proper kind, and the men were eventually discharged.

December proved a dismal month for the islanders. Mrs Russell took ill and had to be sent to the mainland for medical treatment. This cost £5, excluding her board, and may well have been the first time Effie had been off the island. The daughter of the skipper of the estate boat was also ill on the mainland, while the cripple's widow, Sarah Mackinnon, fell off the edge of the shore embankment in the dark and bruised her thigh. Two years later she and her family considered emigating to America with some of the Canna people and asked Salisbury for some remuneration. He agreed to a small sum for the widow and her youngest child, refusing the older daughters since he had 'no desire to encourage young able-bodied persons to go to America. If they wish to go they can always work their passage over.' The widow decided to stay in Rum.

Mackenzie the Factor was recruiting some new shepherds in October 1853, with some predictable interference from his employer:

> As to your proposal to have a South Country shepherd it is entirely inadmissable. The Highlanders, it is true, are indolent to the greatest degree, but I have no reason to doubt their honesty. I am sure they know their business as shepherds.

He went on to complain about sheep losses and rustling, and within a year or two would greatly alter his opinion of Highland shepherds. His patience was again tried when Russell, Matheson and Kenneth Maclean objected to £1 having been deducted from the wages, reducing them to £9 per annum. 'Shoes and all other necessary articles are much higher in price,' was the response. Where once 10*s.* they were now 12*s.* Salisbury complained to Mackenzie that he had never heard a more unreasonable request. 'They are a dissatisfied set of people and do not know when they are well off ... You have a much higher allowance of labourers than the extent of your land entitles you to employ.'

Labour relations came to a head early in 1855 when the sheep numbers were found to be deficient by ninety animals. The Head Shepherd, 33-year-old widower Hector Campbell from Bracadale in Skye, was held responsible. He submitted a letter of resignation, to which he appended that his house was so damp anyway that it was affecting his health. Salisbury insisted that a stranger was appointed in his stead and that the rest of the shepherds be dismissed as well. Mackenzie resented them all being sacked just prior to lambing. The rather hasty Marquess was well aware of the inconvenience, but when robbery has been carried out to so great an extent, it is next to impossible that all should not have been concerned in or at least have had a guilty knowledge of it. I can fix upon no one individual, therefore all must go. As it is we have the satisfaction of knowing that we are the laughing stock of every Scotch farmer for our losses.

Diplomatically, in a letter to Salisbury dated 15 March, Mackenzie pointed out that the population on the island was gradually decreasing. Thirty-year-old Allan Macrae, son of the late widow Mairi, had recently obtained a situation in Glasgow; there had also been two rather serious accidents. Hector Campbell, the disgraced Head Shepherd, had fallen off a ladder in the hay loft, fracturing an arm and dislocating a wrist. Old Norman Macdonald the retired mason, who lived in a slated house near the quay, fell over the breastwork opposite his door, severely bruising his right side and suffering a contusion of the head. Campbell was taken to Skye for treatment but storms prevented Macdonald receiving any medical help.

On 31 March 1855, just before quitting the island, Hector Campbell asked Lord Salisbury for a reference. This he duly received, with a note to the effect that

> I have done it as favourably as I can consistently with truth – but it is impossible to conceal the part of the defalcation of so many sheep with justice to your future employers.

The reference itself was more blunt:

> Hector Campbell has been with me the greater part of time I have possessed Rum, first as Under Shepherd then as Head. I believe him to be perfectly Master of his business and he gave me the great satisfaction until the year before last. I have no reason to suspect his honesty but there has been a diminution of my flocks for the last two years which is quite unaccounted for, and in consequence of the extent of which, I have resolved to discharge all my shepherds. I have no grounds for charging any one of them with dishonesty. Hector Campbell gave me notice to quit my service before I carried my resolution into effect.

Whether Campbell managed to secure an alternative position with such a reference is not known. His replacement in Rum was Peter MacIntyre, a 37-year-old married man from Mull, with a young daughter and two younger sons. At once he pointed out that it was impossible to know where to begin if all the old hands were to be removed. Mackenzie again tentatively approached his crusty employer, suggesting that two of the shepherds were kept on. James Stoddart was a single man based at Kilmory who had been taken on only the previous year, while Alexander Mackenzie from Guirdil was married with no children but had an elderly, widowed

relative lodging with him. Salisbury flatly refused with the lame excuse
that to retain only them would cast stronger doubts upon the honesty of
the others.

By June all the old shepherds had indeed been replaced. Only Mackenzie
lingered for a while in his lonely house at Guirdil. His replacement was
coming from a remote corner of Mull and had been delayed by bad weather.
The rest of the new men also came from Mull, except for the Kilmory
shepherd, Murdo Matheson, a Lochcarron man who had been employed on
Eigg for two years. Matheson was later to quit the island in tragic circumstances, as we shall see presently. The labour force consisted of:

Name	Position	Wages	Cows	Bolls meal
Peter MacIntyre	Head	£20	2	6½
Charles Robertson	Kinloch	10	1	6½
Murdo Matheson	Kilmory	10	3	13
John Mackinnon	Samhnan Insir	10	lives with brother	
Lachlan MacDougall	Guirdil	10	4	13
Donald Macdonald	Guirdil	10	lives with MacDougall	
Angus Fletcher	Harris	10	3	13
John MacIntyre	Harris	10	lives with Fletcher	
John Mackinnon	Papadil	10	2	6½
William Mackinnon	Papadil	10	2	10

The Factor immediately appreciated Peter MacIntyre's 'lack of desire to
seek to exhalt his own abilities at the expense of the man he succeeded ...
Campbell's principal fault was not sufficient command of those under him.'
On 2 August 1855, after an unusually successful gathering, Mackenzie
found that there were 500 more sheep than Campbell had counted at the
last gather for smearing the previous November. It seems that Campbell's
only fault had not been sufficient command of Arithmetic!

Jubilantly Mackenzie wrote to the Marquess: 'I am happy to be able to
give your Lordship a highly favourable account. Instead of having a painful
report of a great unaccountable loss to give, there are nearly 500 more than
appears from the monthly report.' This was a rather off-hand summary of
a blunder that had cost so many men their jobs. The deported shepherds
soon heard about the discrepancy and quite justifiably wrote to Salisbury,
asking for the favourable references that had previously been denied to
them. Alexander Mackenzie, formerly of Guirdil, tactfully commented that
'it is very odd that so many hundred sheep would be lost last year, and
found on the same ground this year'. He hoped that Salisbury would keep
an open mind in considering him for employment the following year.

After his first winter, MacIntyre, the new Head Shepherd, expressed his satisfaction with his staff. The single men were requesting a rise of £2 but Salisbury first demanded a statement of their conditions. His Factor replied that the single men lived in the houses of married ones, who could sell calves at a year old to supplement their income.

Thereafter, there were relatively few community matters discussed in the correspondence between Salisbury and his Factor. At the end of July 1861 Archibald Russell, younger brother of the former schoolmaster and son of John Russell the gardener, left for New Zealand (where his descendants still reside today). Archibald married Jane Denley, who arrived in New Zealand in 1862 on a ship that lost almost half its passengers to disease during the voyage. The Russells had five children and eventually settled in a small town called Temuka in South Island where they ran a grocery called Russell's Breadalbane Store.

To replace Archibald Russell, Mackenzie had to hire a man from Soay:

> The only other man available on the island is a son of Macdonald; his two brothers already work here. The parents and his brothers did not wish him to be employed in case they might all be wrecked.

In such a volatile regime the family were understandably reluctant to have all their eggs in one basket, but only a few years previously Salisbury would not have allowed anyone on the island unless they worked for the estate. At that time young Macdonald was employed aboard HMS *Seagull*, which was engaged in survey work around Rum. 'When the work is over Macdonald will, I believe, go to Australia.'

October 1861 saw the return of the potato blight and food shortages. Mackenzie reported: 'This is likely to be a disastrous year for the poor people of the Western Isles. The potatoes are in general an almost complete failure.' He added that there was also a destitution of fuel in Skye because the wet autumn had prevented the people from gathering their peats. The following year was no better. The potatoes again provided a scant crop, being much diseased; the conditions were somewhat drier so benefited the peats.

Earlier, at Whitsun in 1862, four shepherds – Hugh MacDougall, aged twenty-two; Charles Macdonald, aged twenty-three; William Mackinnon and Angus Mackinnon – were sacked for refusing to work. Some replacements were promised from Mull but still had not arrived by June. The following month there was an alarming case of fever in the Russell household, a young niece being delirious for two days. The estate boat was sent to Arisaig for assistance.

The last of Mackenzie's letters to be preserved at Hatfield House is dated 24 November 1862. In April the following year James Cecil, second Marquess of Salisbury, gave up direct management and the island seems

PLATE 17. One of the Rum ponies (Pride III or 'Granny') above Harris in November 1976. Her line tended to share her unusual red colour with silver mane and tail and were all called 'Pride'. (photo – J. Love)

PLATE 18. Two foals with the mother of one, showing the eel-stripe along the back which is typical of the Rum ponies. (photo – J. Love)

PLATE 19. The second Marquis of Salisbury, who owned Rum for a time and whose son became the Victorian prime minister. (courtesy of Marquis of Salisbury)

PLATE 20. Graveslab erected in the Kilmory burial ground by Walter Cowan in 1843 to his wife Catherine Henderson; the inscription has been outlined in chalk for the purposes of the photograph. (photo – J. Love)

PLATE 21. A fishing boat beached at low tide off the old pier in Rum, with the redundant lime-kiln (also dating from Salisbury's time) to the left. (photo – J. Love)

PLATE 22. The gravestone erected in Kilmory burial ground by Murdo Matheson to six of his children who died before the family finally emigrated to New Zealand. (photo – J. Love)

PLATE 23. A photograph that accompanied the prospectus for the sale of Rum in 1886, showing the pier, Lea Cottage (centre) and White House (right); some of the old thatched cottages described by Edwin Waugh in 1882 are also just visible along the shore. The Dibidil path can be seen snaking up the slope behind, with the low Prow of Askival dominated by the summit of Hallival. (photo – Aberdeen University Library)

PLATE 24. The tiled back wall, all that remains of the rock-cut tomb of John Bullough. His body was subsequently moved to the mausoleum where his son and daughter later joined him; the original tomb had been likened to a public toilet, so was blown up. (photo – J. Love)

PLATE 25. The sad ruins of Papadil Lodge, now dilapidated and smothered in rhododendrons; it was said to be haunted by a 'white lady' but perhaps a monk in white robes might be more apt, given its early Christian associations.
(photo – J. Love)

PLATE 26. An early photograph of Kinloch Castle showing the conservatory that once covered the patio on the south wing; the gardens and woodland are yet undeveloped.
(photo in Kinloch Castle)

PLATE 27. The ivory eagle formerly in Kinloch Castle.
(photo – National Museum of Scotland)

PLATE 28. One of Bullough's shooting parties on the steps of Kinloch Castle early in the twentieth century; Sir George is second from left. (photo in Kinloch Castle)

PLATE 29. Lady Bullough in the castle gardens with a stag she had shot on one of the Rum ponies; the identity of the ghillie is unknown. (photo in Kinloch Castle)

PLATE 30. The stalker Calum Sinclair with his ghillie, James MacAskill, in front of Kinloch Castle; the identity of the ponyman is unknown but the pony is one of the 'Prides'. (photo in Kinloch Castle)

PLATE 31. The old post office at Kinloch, the cottage attached being one of the oldest still standing on the island today. At this time – early in the twentieth century – the post office was run by the MacAskill family, James being an estate worker/ghillie. (photo – the MacAskill family)

PLATE 32. James MacAskill and his wife or sister when they ran the Rum post office early in the twentieth century. (photo – the MacAskill family)

PLATE 33. The Post Office as it is today. (photo – J. Love)

PLATE 34. Children and teacher playing outside the school in 1957. (photo by *Scotland's Magazine* in the castle archives)

PLATE 35. School photograph taken early in the twentieth century, the children having been identified for the author by Archie and Joey Cameron. From left to right – back row: Kenneth Thwaite, Isa Morrison, Donnie Cameron, Willie Allan Morrison, Maggie Maclean, Ian Cameron, behind Mary Macinnes, John Ray, Flora Maclean and George Macnaughton – front row: Jessie Morrison, Chrissie Thwaite, Hannah Macnaughton, Calum Maclean and Bobby Ray. (photo in school archive)

to have been rented out to a tenant, a Captain Campbell. By that time the island's population stood at nearly sixty, the Factor considering six families to be 'resident', including Norman Macdonald, John Russell, Allan Maclean (the widower with his son Kenneth and daughter Catherine), John Matheson, Angus Maclean (a widower with daughter) and Sarah Mackinnon with her daughter. Russell was employed as gardener, Norman Macdonald a retired mason, the widow Mackinnon a weaver, and the remainder being cottars. The 'moveable' sector of the community were employees:

Mackenzie the factor with his (new?) wife and stepdaughter.
Peter MacIntyre, head shepherd and his family.
Murdoch Matheson, Kilmory shepherd and family.
Lachlan MacDougall, Guirdil shepherd and family.
Charles Macdonald, Harris shepherd and family.
John MacIntyre, Papadil shepherd and wife.
Neil MacGillivray, Dibidil shepherd and wife.

There were also four other young single men and two maids. The old gardener John Russell, son of William Russell, cottar, and Catherine Maclean, eventually died on 19 February 1869 aged seventy-six. His widow Euphemia or Effie, unable to write, added her mark to his death certificate. Presumably he was buried in the Kilmory graveyard but no inscribed headstone marks the grave. Effie Russell, about twenty years his junior, continued to live in Rum until the 1880s.

Lord Salisbury died in 1868 and soon afterwards his son, the eminent Victorian politician thrice to be Prime Minister, put Rum on the market. He saw little financial return from the island estate, having seen his father pour out so much money and energy, much of it fruitless. But first we will discover just how Salisbury's estate in Rum had functioned.

13   *Great but Ineffectual Works*

The Marquis of Salisbury is reported to have purchased the island
of Rum for the sum of £24,000 in order to form a shooting ground
or deer forest.

Inverness Courier, 1845

On assuming ownership of the island of Rum in 1845, Lord Salisbury
maintained a small paddle-steamer called the *Ramsgate Packet* to transport
passengers, provisions and mail to and from Liverpool. It was skippered by
Captain William Ward, with John Hammersley as engineer, two Englishmen
who, according to the 1851 census return, had their families living in Rum.
Two other mariners are mentioned: Alfred Finch and John Padding.

In October 1846 the steamer arrived in Loch Scresort with 80 tons of
coal, and the following March was sent to the island of Lismore near Oban
for 200 barrels of lime. Apparently the *Ramsgate Packet* also made regular
trips from Arisaig and Skye with shell sand (at 1*s*. 6*d*. a ton) for the fields,
until Lord Macdonald forbade any more loads from Skye in March 1849.
A few loads from Rum's own shore had been tried but there was little
available locally.

In 1846 Captain Ward was authorised to purchase a smack, *Jenny
Lind*, from Campbeltown for £143, and it was towed to Rum by his
paddle-steamer. Ward was also employed in fishing to feed pigs, but was
instructed to buy fish for salting whenever the opportunity arose. In
March 1847 we are told that there was no difficulty in procuring a boat
from Liverpool so Ward was taken off the fishing and sent there. On 15
October 1848 Ward reported:

I write to inform your Lordship of my safe arrival at Liverpool last evening at eight o'clock, leaving Rum on Wednesday evening with four hundred and twenty five sheep and 52 bales of wool and I am sorry to inform your Lordship that I met with an accident on striking a rock coming through the Sound last voyage ... When at Rum I saw that the fore part of her keel is damaged.

Repairs cost £100. On 3 November the same year Ward again had to admit:

I am sorry to have to write to your Lordship of another accident which happened to me. I left Liverpool docks yesterday afternoon ... A steam boat coming up the river and us going down came in contact with each other. She catched us in the paddle box and knocked it to pieces and broke part of the paddle wheel.

The damage took six days to repair and Salisbury was also obliged to pay for the repairs to the other vessel. The lawyers defending Ward in court told Salisbury that 'Captain Ward is exceedingly distressed by the accident which is a very common accident on the river.' Notwithstanding, Salisbury remarked cynically to Ward: 'You must be very unlucky or very negligent as you seldom move now without an accident!' But he retained his services until 1856, when Ward went to live in Greenock.

That same November 1848 the smack *Jenny Lind* also suffered an accident. 'When off the Isle of Muck on Wednesday she was struck with a heavy squall that her mast was broken off about 5 feet from the top.' In fact, it proved a stormy winter, with many ships being wrecked around the Small Isles, including one in Canna. The smack seemed to have been a sturdy little workhorse, however. It returned to Rum on 15 June 1852, for instance, with a load of coal and then next day set off for Arisaig for lime. Later that year, on 9 November, the *Ramsgate Packet* was sold for £600 in cash and a bill of £150, including £28 commission, advertising, etc.

In February 1857 it was proposed to dispose of the smack, too, or else lay off her crew, and rely on passing shipping to provide communication with the mainland. Mackenzie argued that there were few strange boats coming into the bay and pleaded that the only other boat was that used by the shepherds to get at the shore.

With the reduced state of the population there are not enough qualified men to handle this boat in a gale. In the event of your Lordship's parting with the smack, it leaves the painful impression that we were cut off from the world. I hope your Lordship will consider that we are liable to natural diseases and accidents with the rest of mankind.

There had been three fractured limbs in Mackenzie's time, with medical aid from the mainland being summoned on numerous other occasions:

> I cannot forget that my wife has had severe attacks for the last three successive winters ... In the case of a death it is too painful to contemplate the possibility of one or more of the few here being interred without a coffin – or a body, being kept for an uncertain time till one could be got by a chance boat, might have to remain unburied till the sight was revolting.

Salisbury considered that a bargain might be struck with Arisaig boatmen to call once a fortnight. He then quickly changed the subject by adding that there were so many wet days that men could be employed indoors looking after sails, ropes etc. In the meantime Mackenzie sounded out the Arisaig boatmen but preferred to defer the matter until Salisbury next came to the island. The Marquess did not come that year (1857) or the next, but expressed his disappointment that more repairs were needed for the smack and requested that the caulking of the timbers could be done on the island, presumably to save money.

September 1857 saw the whaleboat and the lifeboat lying up on the beach rotting, and Mackenzie thought it would be best to sell them. 'We are in want of a good strong skiff for the shepherds to go round the shore.' More repairs were needed for the smack that month and Mackenzie was still pleading: 'If your Lordship lays up the vessel it is cutting us off from Society.' He relates the case of a shepherd's wife dying in childbed. As it happened the practitioner came too late but had there been no smack she would have died 'leaving the impression that could a doctor been had she might have been saved'.

Exactly one year later (September 1858) and negotiations with the Post Office over boat links with Arisaig having been unsuccessful, Lord Salisbury reluctantly agreed to repairs on the *Jenny Lind*. She had to be furnished with a new sail. One had been already rotten when the vessel was first bought, and it blew away in a gale; fortuitously, as it happened, or else the smack would have been driven on to the rocks.

In March 1860 Mackenzie was seeking a replacement smack because Salisbury was reluctant to have a new one built. An estimate received for a 34-foot boat came to £250. By August a smack was being built of timber: 20 tons weight, coppered hull, partly decked for'ard, finished like a fishing smack with square stern, mainsail, foresail, flying topsail and three jibs – total cost about £170. The new vessel came into service just in time, for Mackenzie described how

> Our poor old *Jenny Lind*, you will have heard, was defunct on the dreadful morning of 3rd October. The hull was broken up into splinters

and the three poor fellows had a most narrow escape for their lives – it is miraculous they were not drowned: the surf and spray must have been awful on the Arisaig shore where the smack was driven on the rock where she was wrecked.

The new smack was capable of carrying 16 tons safely, but on 6 July 1861, her capabilities were exceeded on a passage from Ardrossan with coals. Nineteen tons had been put aboard and all went well until she reached Ardnamurchan Point. Suddenly overtaken by one of those sudden gales so common to the place, the crew could not return to Tobermory and had to carry on to Arisaig. In rolling she shipped water on both sides and about a ton of coals had to be cast overboard to lighten her. 'It is to be regretted that she was not built another foot higher out of the water. In every other respect she is an excellent vessel and sails beautifully.'

She had been rendered safer by 9 December and on 5 July the following year was to vindicate Mackenzie's fears about the island being left with no boat, by running to Arisaig for a doctor when Russell's niece became delirious with a fever.

The first requirement Salisbury found on taking up the ownership of Rum was to upgrade, renew or replace the buildings around Kinloch. Work was already in progress on the farm steading on the arrival of the first Factor, MacDougall, and by early December Cowan had moved into a new house and was 'very snug'. 'I am also into mine,' the new Factor reported to Salisbury, 'and feel myself very comfortable ... A fine flag quarry, found a little way northeast of the Square, has been of great service in flooring.'

Presumably MacDougall was not staying in Kinloch Lodge, which he referred to as 'the Mansion House'. This had been washed over with 'hot lime burned here, the limestone taken from Egg'. There is a lime kiln near the quay so the lime could have been treated there. The mason had near finished the north end and the larder of Kinloch House, although the kitchen at the south end was not completed. The porch was to be roofed over soon. A carpenter called Stalker was employed in the woodwork, obtaining his timber from Glasgow. A dyke was built running up from 'the old house', which may refer to what is now the post office. John Russell and one of his sons were trenching the garden, finding the soil very stony.

Soon afterwards a roof was put on the woman Matheson's house, and a new piggery, granary and smithy were incorporated into the Square. On 3 May 1847 a schooner, *Albion*, arrived at Rum with 20,000 bricks and building materials. Stone for constructing the new quay came from a local quarry, behind the house now known as 'Bayview'. It was decided to place the stone steps leading down to the water line on the seaward side of the quay so they did not interfere with vessels lying alongside the pier itself. In October blasting was carried out to clear rocks which obstructed passage for boats.

Building also progressed outwith Kinloch. In November 1847 the house at Papadil was taken down and rebuilt. Completion, bar the pointing, of a house at Guirdil was achieved by June 1848, within a year, however, the felt on its roof had to be replaced. The following February (1848) a new house was required at Kinloch for Russell the gardener, while another was planned for a shepherd to be outposted at Dibidil.

Surviving plans reveal the Dibidil cottage was to be 36 ft long outside, 18 ft wide with a wall 8 ft high and an additional gable of 6½ ft high. It was to have three rooms. Two measured 14½ ft by 12 ft, one floor flagged to serve as a kitchen, while the third, a bedroom, was 10½ ft by 8 ft. The inside walls were to be plastered. Allan Maclean, the carpenter, estimated his contribution to cost £23 with an additional £30 for timber to board the main room and bedroom, slates, nails, etc. The mason tendered an additional £23. The house was to have a south or south-easterly exposure, placed near a good water supply and have windows which opened. The building eventually built was slightly larger, with main rooms 16 ft by 12 ft, with beds and lobby in a space between them 4½ ft wide. Fireplaces were built into the gables, and a cellar, privy and ashpit was placed at the back. Although finally abandoned early last century this building at the mouth of Dibidil Glen still survives, having been reroofed as a climbers' bothy.

In 1853 a wooden cottage was built for a shepherd at Kilmory, which was thatched with heather. Two years later, just before the Matheson family moved to Kilmory, a young serving girl inadvertently set fire to the thatch and the cottage burnt down; the shepherd was not in residence at the time. In 1856 repairs were effected to the house at Harris. In March 1859 the Mansion House needed some work on it. Two years later Mackenzie again reported:

> I beg to inform your Lordship that the house will require some repairs this summer. It is very damp; the gale of last October, and the rough casting on the south side being loosened, admits the wet. The papering in your Lordship's dressing room is coming off and requires renewing. The wet gets through the front porch … There will also be some painting required.

Work was completed on the new school by January 1850, while John Russell, the father of the teacher, tended the garden of Kinloch House. By 1847 gooseberries, blackcurrants and rhubarb were being grown, although that year they were checked by the frost. Carrots, parsnips and flax were thriving by May but 'the greatest trouble is to keep down the weeds, of which there are an abundance'. Another pest was 'a very troublesome buck that remains about Kinloch. He takes every opportunity he can of coming about the garden and the crofters' ground, and eating up what suits him best.' Salisbury suggested 'you might let the dogs at the deer which does mischief, but not the shepherds' dogs as it would spoil them.'

In June 1849 we discover that 'all the lavender plants were dead except one – one of the rosemarys is dead and others do not look well. Neither do the rose bushes, fuschias and sweet briar seem to thrive. The strawberries and vegetables had been hit by April frosts.' Shell sand, manure, seaweed, stubble mould and fish bones were all administered to improve the soil.

The crofters and shepherds grew a little corn and potatoes but most of the agricultural activities were confined around the farm at Kinloch. Turnips were grown to feed the tups but partridges also ate them; in July 1857 maggots proved a problem. Lord Salisbury recommended turning out ducks, together with seagulls suitably winged, to control the pests. By November 1855 about 5 acres of oats were grown, 12–15 acres of turnips and 3 acres of potatoes, while two years later it was reported that there were only 7 acres of arable land for seeds, oats and potatoes with some of it being enclosed meadowland.

Pigs were being reared at Kinloch as early as November 1845; they were said to be thriving and fond of the shore. A year later a piggery was built at the farm. Twenty-six pigs were fed on waste fish caught or salted locally, but one beast had to be slaughtered when a fish hook stuck in its throat. They often went short of food, with only a few boiled turnips and braxy sheep on offer. Until the granary was built spoiled meal was also fed to the pigs. By February 1848, however, it was decided that there was no profit in keeping them: 'they do not breed and the fishing is unproductive'. Salisbury recommended that they be sold but none features in an agricultural return dated July 1856.

A variety of cattle were kept on the island, and shepherds were allowed to graze one or two as house cows, and to sell the calves and thus supplement their income. Presumably these did not feature in the stock returns for the estate for, in July 1848, cattle only numbered one bull, six cows, six two-year-old heifers, one yearling ox, four yearling heifers and four calves. By August the number of heifers and calves rose, with both Irish and Galloway heifers mentioned as rearing stock.

Some cattle were grazed at Guirdil for, on 18 February 1853, a stot fell over a cliff. By May 1853 Mackenzie was of the opinion that eighty cattle could be wintered; he bought some calves from the shepherds and cottars so that within the year the stock totalled a bull, thirteen cows and eighty-seven yearlings. The rearing stock were sold in the summer and only nine retained. In May 1856 thirty head of cattle were shipped off and none features in the agricultural return for July that year. Thereafter rearing stock rarely exceeded about a dozen head.

In July 1848 there were two horses, four asses and a mule, as well as seven ponies. There were still two or three mules on the island until about 1856; the ponies sometimes numbered as many as ten. One wonders how pure the breed remained for, in December 1845, MacDougall was inquiring about a pair of ponies from Uist and Barra. Six ponies were bought at Falkirk fair the following September. In March 1847 Mackenzie was looking over the pony stallion from Eigg: 'I think him too small and he is grey which is in my opinion an objection. I believe grey horses to have bad eyes.'

In July 1849 'the ponies require shoeing as they cannot now travel the road barefoot – at least until the stones are pressed to a more level surface. The smith from Skye can shoe them.' Five were sold in September 1859, and the ponies numbered fourteen by July 1861. By April 1862 Mackenzie was looking for a market as the ponies were getting rather numerous, 'scattered throughout different parts of the island'.

Lord Arthur Cecil, Salisbury's son, took a particular interest in the Rum ponies and took some to improve the New Forest breed. In Gilbey's *Ponies Past and Present* he wrote:

> When the ponies, mostly stallions, came to Hatfield in 1862, I remember some of them broke out of the station, and it took several days to catch them again. They were almost unbreakable, but my brother Lionel and I managed to get two of them sufficiently quiet for us to ride, though they would not have been considered quite safe conveyance for an elderly gentleman. We were never quite sure of their ages, but they must have been nearly thirty when they died.
>
> The Rum ponies which were much thought of by my father, seem to be quite a type by themselves, having characteristics which would always enable one to recognise them anywhere. Every one of those I bought in 1888 had hazel nut-brown eyes.

The Marquess of Salisbury bought a Highland pony stallion from Coulmore in Ross-shire to head his Rum stud. It was mouse dun with black eel stripe, and was sired by a stallion called Allan Kingsburgh.

Although the Rev. Walker's account indicated that goats had been kept by the inhabitants before the Clearances, there is no mention of them being domestic or feral in Salisbury's time. On 5 May 1846 the Marquess sent a billy, six nannies and six kids to be 'turned out by Strone and Papperdale at the dangerous parts of the rocks'. The idea was that the goats would graze the precipitous slopes and deter the sheep from risking themselves. On 3 April 1847 Mackenzie wrote to Salisbury that a goat had been found floating in the sea; he thought it might be the last on the island as 'I could neither see nor hear of any other being seen for some time. I think it must be convincing proof that sheep must be falling over.' In fact, five goats were seen on the cliffs from a boat on 1 August 1847.

It is likely that the present feral goat population, some 200 animals, is descended from this and later introductions.

In December 1845 MacDougall had proposed that sheep losses could be reduced if some of the worst passes in the cliffs were enclosed. In July 1846 Mackenzie went round the whole island to identify dangerous sections and thought that to make wider sheep tracks would have been impractical. By February 1847 he had changed his mind, convinced that 'the deficiency of sheep was due to them being in parts of the rocks only accessible from the sea'. A fence was proposed to run from Dibidil to Papadil.

Salisbury did employ a Welsh miner called Williams to widen a narrow sheep or deer track several hundred feet above the sea on the Strone, now called Welshman's Rock. 'There was room neither for two animals to pass on meeting face to face, nor for one of them to turn,' wrote Gilbey in *Ponies Past and Present*,

> and as a result in the old days many sheep and deer were killed there. The mortality was especially heavy during the rutting season of the deer, when stags often meet and engage in a combat which ends with one or both of them falling into the sea several hundred feet below.
>
> When the Marquess of Salisbury was proprietor of the island, he resolved to widen the track but no one in Scotland could be found to undertake this dangerous job. In the end he engaged half a dozen slate quarriers direct from Wales.

It is uncertain just how accurate is this account of Gilbey's since the papers in Hatfield House mention only one miner, helped by two local men. Also, there would have been few red deer, if any, on the island when Salisbury undertook the project.

In August 1846 Mackenzie reported that men were employed in building the path to Papadil. Two years later he was taken from the path building to repair walls in the tup park, having done 9 yards at the Strone; a week later he had completed 20 yards with not more than 30 further yards to blast. 'He is well pleased with his assistants Donald Matheson and Hugh Russell.' That autumn they had to return to Kinloch several times because their picks required sharpening; these Mackenzie had to send to Tobermory until in July 1849 he engaged a smith from Skye for the purpose.

In October 1848 Mackenzie had recommissioned the miner to undertake:

1) about 35 yds of tunnel through Strone Point;

2) steps to admit of an easy access for the sheep to the lower platform of grass;

3) 24 ft of wall, 4 ft base and 4 ft high, to prevent the sheep descending through the fissure;

4) steps down the next fissure for the convenience of shepherds;

5) 443 yds of wall to shut up three passages down the cliffs;

6) about 20 yds of hurdles for the purpose of fencing off a dangerous passage round to which the shepherds are obliged to go in a boat to save the sheep. [Some of these hurdles, long discarded, were eventually lifted by lobstermen and taken to Canna where, according to the late Iain Mackinnon, a few still remain to this day.]

7) steps down the cliff to admit of an easy descent;

8) set of steps at the other end of the chasm to allow of the dogs descending on one side so as to drive the sheep up No. 7.

Salisbury added:

if when the miner has completed Strone and you [Mackenzie] are still in distress for want of room at Papperdale, [have him] make a passage at Guirdale on the end of the Bloodstone Park so that the shepherds can go along the shore as projected ... You must not neglect the roads to Guirdale and Papperdale ... also the crossroads from Kilmory and Harris at the fank, to the place where one crosses when going to Bloodstone Rock.

By 23 September the miner had completed the path nearest the shepherd's house and had made good progress with the next stretch.

On 31 October 1848 the miner wished to continue at Strone before going to Papadil and hoped to complete the contract in a year. He was working with especially hard rock so it was difficult to keep tools sharp; twelve borers had to be sent to Arisaig for sharpening. Salisbury, however, demanded that Strone be kept for the depths of winter when the days were too short for anything else, and severely chastised Mackenzie for upsetting his arrangements. The Factor replied that the miner was being hampered by having to send his tools off for sharpening so often. Thus he had been employed blasting drains, much to Salisbury's annoyance. December 1848 brought severe flooding in Kinloch Glen, necessitating rerouting the road to Guirdil.

By February 1849

the miner has cut through at the Strone so as to give a full view of the projecting rock. The appearance of that point is not at all encouraging. There will be great danger working at it.

Salisbury replied, 'Now you will be able to find out if steps can be cut so that a shepherd or a dog can go up or down.' A month later (March 1849) the miner was still trying to cut a path on the Strone. Young Russell asked to be taken off the job as it was too dangerous – even Salisbury was concerned. The miner refused to work there with any new hands so both Russell and Matheson were given extra pay. By 5 April the track on Strone was finally completed as well as the track along the shore [at Bloodstone?] 'Another is being made from the west side which will take about three weeks and allow a man and a dog sending sheep before them with no danger.' Work was then resumed at Papadil, which was completed by May so that he could begin on the Dibidil stretch. Mackenzie had an old hut nearby repaired and roofed as a temporary residence for the miner and his companions. 'Williams is anxious to get the work over. I believe he is heartily tired of it.' In July 1849 a smith was brought in from Skye to keep his tools sharp.

In August 1849 Salisbury sought government aid for his work on the roads, claiming to have spent upwards of £200 already, with a further £320 being required since roads were so vital in the occupation of the island. As he was being taxed for the upkeep of roads he asked that he may receive some benefit in return. He cited 157 yards of road at Strone, 540 yards at Papadil and 945 yards at Guirdil. In October work began on the Harris road.

In April 1850 Hugh Russell, who had been helping Williams the miner, left to take up a job in a shipbuilding yard at Greenock; two years later he was back working as a shepherd at Harris and wanting to quit. Salisbury approved of his leaving, feeling he would do better as a miner or a fireman in a steamer.

The roadworks on Bloodstone Rock may have been connected with the outcrop of semi-precious stone near its summit, but there is little mention of it in the Salisbury papers. In 1847 some samples of 'inferior bloodstone' had been sent to Lady Salisbury in a small box, and the following year a mineralogist was on the island inspecting the outcrop. In May 1849 a buyer, called Mr Martin, had been found for the whole of the Bloodstone suggesting that some effort had been put into its extraction. A quarry is marked on early Ordnance Survey maps and a pony path leading to it is still obvious on the summit of Bloodstone Hill. The only other reference in the papers is that on 2 July 1860 'bloodstone was sent as directed' although the late George MacNaughton remembers that Queen Victoria had been presented, probably by the Bulloughs, with a coffee table, whose top consisted of a slab of Rum bloodstone.

Besides the work on the roads the other major construction project was the modification of existing natural watercourses to improve the Kinloch and Kilmory rivers for fishing. Mackenzie deemed the incorporation of the Guirdil river as impractical. As with the road construction, the descriptions of the damming project is fragmentary in the Hatfield papers and geographical locations are vague.

In February 1847 Mackenzie reported seeing a number of salmon 1½ feet long in the Kilmory River. In September 1848 he was taking levels at the Long Loch, which then presumably emptied south into Harris Glen:

I took the man [Macleod] with me who is doing our mason work. He will undertake to cut a meandering course to fall into the river at the junction of the two streams, build a double wall 14 feet high and puddle between them making them watertight up the outlet at the south end. He states that he could not undertake it for less than fifty pounds.

To this Salisbury replied:

I shall not object to the £50 if the work could be properly done so that there is no impediment for the salmon to run up from Kilmory into the Long Loch – and if he makes the dam he should undertake to keep it [watertight?]. It is not desirable to make the Long Loch deeper than is absolutely necessary. Salmon will not take a fly or bait where the water is too deep.

The intention at this stage seems to have been to dam the southern flow into Harris from the Long Loch. Another dam at the north end would increase the level of the loch somewhat with a new outflow cut beside it to direct the flow into the Kilmory River, thus allowing salmon to run up to the loch from the sea. In March 1849 Donald Macleod was commissioned to undertake the work, with £45 to be paid as soon as it was completed and £5 retained as security for repairs until 31 March 1850.

Mackenzie reported that he started in mid-June, with six hands at first, more if necessary, to finish before the end of July. As an encouragement for the whole scheme, the carpenter saw thirty-seven large fish and innumerable smaller ones in the Kinloch river, never having seen so many before. By 11 October the Long Loch had filled up to the new level but, on 5 December, Mackenzie had to report:

My Lord,
I am sorry to inform your Lordship that the double wall at the Longlock has been swept away by an unusually heavy flood from the hill.

I have been confined to my bed yesterday and Monday and could not venture out today. I caught cold from getting wet feet last week on the hills.

As soon as I get sufficiently well to venture I will go and inspect the Lock and report accordingly ...

On 3 January he was able to explain:

The cut from the Longlock has been deepened very much in some places by the water before the embankment was carried away. A great portion of the bank along the sides of the cut has been washed down and deep holes or pools left in many places where the bottom is soft.

Salisbury saw no objection to the formation of deep pools in the river but continued:

> there were as I told you two defects in the embankment. The first that a trench had not been filled up with clay to prevent the water from getting under and blowing it up. The second that the workment used peat soil instead of clay in the middle of the embankment. You don't say from what cause it gave way. ... The misfortune is that the contractor has received too much money.

The next month another man, a Mr MacPhie from Skye, was contracted to build a new dam and began the work in May 1850. Presumably he completed it to Salisbury's satisfaction. There is, however, a gap of eighteen months in the letters being transcribed into Hatfield's record books.

In February 1852 we find estimates being received for a major new cut at the Long Loch. The proposed watercourse was 280 chains long, 12–16 feet deep and 12 feet wide at the bottom. Sufficient labour was not available locally so had to be got from Eigg, Mull and the mainland. (At least one man from Canna was also taken on, according to the late Iain Mackinnon – his own great uncle.) The intention this time seems to have been to construct a new dam below the Long Loch, thus creating a completely new loch altogether. Mackenzie was keen that the job be started by early April so that it could be completed that summer. Eighty men were required and by July the work was progressing well. By October, however, it was obvious that the job would not be completed in time, partly, it seems, due to labour problems. The embankment was left unfinished over the winter. In the meantime Mackenzie was gratified to see that the Kinloch River was well stocked with spawning fish, and some salmon were caught.

On 27 February 1854, D. Clement the contractor writes from Inversnaid on Loch Lomondside:

> My Lord,
> I take the liberty of again writing your Lordship regarding the Rum work as to what your Lordship stated about the Puddle Bank being too thin. If your Lordship is of [the] opinion that the Puddle is too thin it could be made sufficient by a Puddle dyke and earth bank placed in front of the building which in my opinion would remedy any defect.
>   I take the liberty of enclosing a cross-section of Bulwark and proposed Puddle bank and embankment which your Lordship can please look over. If your Lordship think it right it might be advisable to consult an experienced engineer as to a Puddle bank of moss being ever known to contain water to a depth of 40 feet. If it is thought too slight the

sooner it is rectified the better and it can never be easier done than before the completion of the work. I made the Puddle bed fully as thick as mentioned in the specification and if it turns out too weak I am not to blame but if this answer at convenience will oblige as if this is done I could require to take some tools along with me for the purpose.

From Hatfield on 19 March Lord Salisbury replies:

Sir,

In answer to your letter of the 27 Feb. I must decline to authorise you to depart in any way from your original plan for the formation of the embankment in the Isle of Rum. I have already incurred an enormous expenditure and very great delay has been interposed in the completion of the work. If you alter the plan you must do so at your own risk and your own experience. I am glad to inform you that the last accounts from the Island say that it is in no worse condition than it was when you left it last year.

Gascoyne Salisbury.

It seems there may have been a leak in the embankment over the winter, but it survived and in April Clement was keen to resume the work, content that he may have covered himself for any mishaps by his correspondence with Salisbury. He requested that a balance of £150 be paid but the Marquess refused, considering that the bulwark had not yet been adequately tested. On 7 July Clement visited the island to inspect a leakage in the embankment, and by 3 August the job was considered nearly complete. Soon afterwards it must have collapsed altogether, as indicated in a letter from Lord Salisbury, dated 19 August 1854. 'The interior seems to be filled with any rubbish that was nearest at hand.' Salisbury considered that it would cost more to repair than to build a new one and refused to pay Clement any more money. The Marquess was quick to point out Clement's error:

He not only left no overflow to save it from a flood but during its construction he never entirely stopped the run of water which he could not have done without risk nor did he confine it to one drain or channel which when the embankment was concreted might have been stopped by a sluice or mortared wall, the water consequently rendered his whole work rotten. He was told of this error ... last year. I have no doubt that he left the work last year in despair and only came again this [year] because I foolishly agreed to make him further advances. Mackenzie appears to have exceeded the authority I gave him [by] about £31. The consequence of Clement's error was that the moment any real pressure came against the bulwarks the whole thing gave way.

On 15 September David Clement wrote to Salisbury offering to complete the work if weather permitted, or else give up the whole scheme altogether on payment of £200. He maintained that the thinness of the wall was on the original plan and he was not responsible for it. Salisbury's lawyers replied that no more money would be paid and a large sum was due to his Lordship: 'in short the whole sum of £1700 paid being lost'. If Clement agreed to give up the work 'not desirous of acting harshly', Salisbury was willing to give him £100 on account. Was this a climb-down, with Salisbury admitting some liability?

By 5 October Mackenzie reported:

> nearly the half of Clement's embankment has fallen and now lies levelled to the foundation. The rain fell from Saturday night last till Monday night without ceasing, which filled the dam. The embankment gave way through the night on Monday and the water in its course swept away the Black Bridge … Clement will find it no easy matter to rebuild it should he make the attempt.

In the end Clement agreed to abandon the work on receipt of the £150.

In 1886 the gentleman naturalist J. A. Harvie-Brown visited the site and, in his book *A Vertebrate Fauna of Argyll and the Inner Hebrides*, gave a full, but dangerously inaccurate account of the whole affair:

> Lord Salisbury spent £11,000 [*sic*] on breastworks and cuttings at the head of Kilmory Glen in 1847 [*sic*]. Two days after the contractors had completed the breastwork, and had run away from the scene of their 'extraordinary operations', the breastwork – not erected on the principles of modern engineering – burst away before the eyes of the astonished workmen who were still encamped upon the slope of the hill above the New Loch, and bore down with vast flood and force, widening and temporarily deepening the Kilmory Burn as far as the sea, and making a river bed throughout the whole course of what had been before a mere mountain 'burnie', cutting deep into the fertile haugh in its lower part of the valley, and heaping high the debris all along its course.
>
> Now, the idea of this whole plan and work, had it been conducted on scientific principles, was magnificent … A portion of this breastwork still remains standing. It is 20 feet in height, with a perpendicular and concave side opposed to the vast weight of water, of what for the space of two days had been converted into the New Loch, of at least 1½ acres in extent, and from 20 to 30 feet in depth. The place is a curious circular natural hollow, surrounded on all sides, except at the exit of the burn, by almost, or perfectly, perpendicular cliffs.
>
> The exact object of these constructions, and of certain deep rock-cuttings, leading away from the New Loch or reservoir, was to divert

the whole water of Kilmory Burn, and all the waters above, into the adjacent Kinloch Burn, which runs into Loch Scresort, close to the present mansion house, and also to raise the level, by the formation of the new reservoir or lake, so as to lift the fish up into the Long Loch above, which in turn is fed from numerous tricklets and burns issuing from the forest hills, which would otherwise, as before, have gone down Glen Harris to the west. In order to prevent the water of the Long Loch going down to the west, a similar dam, but on a much smaller scale, and which still fulfills its part, was erected at the exit of the Long Loch at the head of Glen Harris ...

Now, by the failure of the great breastwork to withstand the above accumulated weight of water, and the consequent failure to divert the far better river (really) of Kilmory into Kinloch Glen, the former burn has been doubled in width.

It seems that Harvie-Brown might be confusing the collapse of the first Long Loch dam, when the workmen probably were indeed still camped on the bank, with the more spectacular ruin of the New Loch dam. There is a watercolour painting preserved in Hatfield House, done by one of the Salisbury ladies, of Kilmory Glen with the New Loch completely filled with water. The artist would have had to be quick off the mark to capture this scene if that dam had indeed collapsed within two days. As it was, it may not have survived more than a few weeks, or perhaps months.

'At this stage', Harvie-Brown continued,

since the giving way of the dam – Mackenzie, Lord Salisbury's then factor, spent an additional £500 in making a new rock cutting ... He took the new rock cutting direct from the Long Loch, scraping it out along the hillside, above the site of the New Loch ... to the level of the cutting previously made as the outlet to the New Loch ... Now, to allow our readers, partially at least, to realise the heavy work entailed, all these cuttings are made in solid rock varying in depth from 6 to 10 feet throughout, and the principal cutting 10 or 12 or more feet wide. After all this was done, the final connection between the main and first cutting and Kinloch Burn was put a stop to by his Lordship, so that thus it remains at the present day.

This last effort is mentioned in the Hatfield papers. In March 1855 the man who completed the Long Loch embankment, Mr MacPhie, agreed to tackle the canal, bypassing the dam. He employed twenty-three men initially, more later before giving up. It seems that the Bulloughs completed the cut many years later, so that the Long Loch water could flow into the Kinloch Burn. Many of the dams, and associated fish-ladders which Salisbury also constructed at the same time, are still to be seen. Some have been breached, however, to let water drain back into the Kilmory Burn because of flooding in Kinloch Glen.

All these efforts were directed towards improving the salmon and trout fishing in Rum, but in reality the rivers are subject to such violent spates that successful spawning is largely impossible. Few salmon ever enter the rivers, really just large burns, and sea trout – although they have been caught in the Long Loch – are not abundant. On the other hand, brown trout thrive but only in some of the hill lochs do they ever reach a size worth catching.

Salisbury initiated draining schemes in Kinloch Glen, south of Bloodstone Hill, etc., as much to improve the grazing for sheep as for grouse. Rum is much too wet for good heather to thrive so grouse numbers have never been high. Although partridges were reared and released, thriving quite well both in Kilmory Glen and Harris, there is no mention of grouse rearing. Instead, Mackenzie's letters sometimes made a statement on their abundance. There were 'more grouse' in the spring of 1849, for instance, and they increased considerably that season. The grouse had another good year in 1857, with broods of as many as twelve young being seen; 1858, on the other hand, saw many grouse nests flooded by rain.

Four swans, and some wild and tame ducks, were despatched from Liverpool on the *Ramsgate Packet* in August 1846. 'I wish the swans and the wild duck to be taken to some of the small lochs ... on the east side between the house and Kilmory,' requested Salisbury.

> The object in sending them is to attract wild duck. You will therefore choose the lochs rather retired. They should have roads about them for them to feed and if the willow sets are growing round any of them, these might be good places as they would afford them shelter.

At the same time as he encouraged game birds, Mackenzie and his staff were engaged controlling predators. In February 1847 they were thinning out crows 'by laying out poisoned eggs' and again in June 1849. In April 1848 Mackenzie had reported: 'we have destroyed a number of hawks. I have three alive in the garden.' In March 1850 the shepherds were constantly using arsenic for rats and poisoned eggs against crows, and in September 1853 Kenneth Maclean was paid 5s. 6d. for killing thirty-three rats – quite a handsome fee. Rats were said to be especially numerous in 1859, although otter skins were hard to come by.

In December 1852 two dozen winged-vermin traps and a dozen eagle traps were ordered from Glasgow. In 1860 Mackenzie was condemning his rifle saying it would be a waste of powder to try and shoot the eagles down. 'It is of some importance to kill these birds, they take away many of the lambs when young.' Two years later he reported 'there are three eagles building. I mean to try a rifle shot at them, perhaps I may chance to hit one or more.' Eagles attracted particular attention both because of their alleged depredations upon lambs but also as items of curiosity. In July 1846 an eagle was killed in the nest.

> I wished we have got the old ones. I have two eaglets alive which Campbell [the shepherd] went down to the nest and took out. I will endeavour to keep [them] alive till his Lordship comes. They are of the largest kind.

These were obviously white-tailed sea eagles, being larger then golden eagles and often having two chicks survive in the nest. Later that summer Mackenzie wrote: 'I doubt that I will not be able to get an Eagle. The one at Guirdil cannot be approached and the two men who are making the Papadil road killed the other by throwing stones at it.' The following year 'I only hear of four pairs of eagles on the island. We will endeavour to destroy old as well as young this year.'

In 1848 he noted an eagle nest at Guirdil and another at Papadil. If he was able, he asked Salisbury, could he obtain a live one to send to an ex-officer friend in Yorkshire? On 10 July the following year he acquired no less than three. 'They were all in one nest. I believe they have seldom more than two.' Again these are very obviously sea eagles and there are only two recorded instances of three chicks being reared in one eyrie in Scotland. (When Duncan Macdonald from Skye was employed as a shepherd in Rum in the late 1820s or 1830s he shot three young out of one eyrie in the island, together with both parent birds. The second case was recorded from the Outer Hebrides last century. More recently one of the pairs reintroduced from Norway to Rum reared three young – though not in Rum itself.)

In October Salisbury requested that the eagles be sent south,

> either two or three if you do not want any. They must be addressed to the Zoological Gardens, Regent's Park, London and Ward [the skipper] must take care to deliver them to the Guard of the Railroad, with a request that they may be sent to the station as soon as they arrive. You will take care to cut the feathers of a wing of each.

Mackenzie reported back immediately that the eagles had been sent:

> The one I offered to the gentleman I mentioned to your Lordship sent for it, but unfortunately it got loose and I had to shoot it to prevent it escaping. Captain Ward will be instructed to deliver them according to this order. The feathers are cut.

On 13 October Ward notified Salisbury that the eagles had been delivered. The following year (1850) an injured female sea eagle was sent to Lord Derby who had a small private aviary on his estate at Knowsley in

Lancashire (now a safari park). His Lordship wrote to the Marquess that the eagle's wounds 'will meet with every attention and not prove of any lasting inconvenience to it'. In return he sent some deer to Rum.

Deer were already extinct when Salisbury bought Rum and one of his first acts was to reintroduce them. As early as 3 August 1846 Mackenzie reported that Russell had seen a fawn. On 3 May 1847 the schooner *Albion* arrived with, amongst other things, thirteen fallow deer:

> One buck and one doe were dead and one doe died on passage ... One buck and two does of Reindeer [does this really mean red deer?] were also got ashore, let go from the Quay and took to the hills on the south side of the islands.

On 14 June it was reported that 'two young deer of the larger Variety' were landed opposite Eigg 'where the other three were brought in May'; which might also indicate that the first batch were indeed red deer and not reindeer. He went on 'I have located the fallow deer scattered about the island. Some are at Guirdale, Kilmory and Papperdale and one very troublesome buck remains about Kinloch ...'

Thirteen more deer arrived on 6 October and by the following spring 'the deer are looking well. We do not see the does just at this time. It is probable they are having fawns and keep to the retired places. The red buck is very fine.' By May Mackenzie was lamenting that the deer were very troublesome but strong and healthy. No fawns were expected before next month. In April 1849 the islanders were still much annoyed by the deer, and in July five deer arrived from Liverpool, another had died on the voyage. The stock in hand on the island on 31 July 1848 included thirty-three deer. One fell over the cliff in the following January, at least two more died in March so that by 31 December 1849 the numbers were down to twenty-nine.

In January 1850 a fallow doe died and the following month one buck was found dead, covered with scurf like a dog with mange. Both had been very low in condition. Later a doe with a fawn at foot disappeared. Obviously the fallow were not thriving, lacking forest cover to protect them from the elements. Mackenzie observed that they seemed to be getting smaller. Red deer, once native on the island, were much more suited to the conditions, and few were found dead. In September 1850 and again in April 1852 more deer were sent from Knowsley by Lord Derby. Lord Arthur Cecil (as recounted in Gilbey's *Ponies Past and Present*) remembered them arriving in strong crates on the steamer with their antlers sawn off close to their skulls. That June the red deer had increased with at least ten or twelve being seen; two hinds and a stag seen a few days previously were looking 'very fine'.

In December 1853 the largest red deer stag on the island was found drowned in a salmon net in the Long Loch. Little more is recorded until May 1858 when 'the deer are thriving better than any other animals – a score in one herd'. Mackenzie heard of few dead ones but they were becoming troublesome in the corn fields. In May 1859 'there were 43 of them in the grass fields – some of the bucks seem old enough to kill'. The following year Mackenzie approached Salisbury to take one of the marauding beasts and was allowed a fallow.

A final entry on 24 November 1862 commented:

> the general opinion is that there are not more than one hundred fallows and about 60 red deer – [the shepherds] have never seen finer: some of the stags are really splendid. I saw 25 of the fallow deer in one day in the large park. I fancy they have degenerated, the number of fawns are few in proportion to the number of does. There was one very good buck which I was wishing Mr Talbot to get a shot at, but he could not be seen at the time: he was among the 25 I mentioned.

Bullough continued to import red deer and the island herd continued to increase. The fallow deer, however, died out. In 1882 Edwin Waugh saw some grazing behind the White House at Kinloch, Harvie-Brown mentions a few frequenting the area around Salisbury's dam and the *British Fisheries Society Report* of 1886 also mention some.

Murdo and Christina Matheson

14 *Sea-girt Solitude*

... the wild, sweet, sea-girt solitude called the Isle of Rum.

Edwin Waugh, 1883

Lord Salisbury eventually lost some of his enthusiasm for the island and about 1863 he let the sheep grazings on Rum to a Captain Campbell. The Marquess died five years later. His eldest son was blind and suffered from a nervous disability, while the second had died in infancy. So the estates fell to his third son, Robert Cecil, then aged thirty-eight. The third Marquess had no romantic notions about his island property, fully aware of the difficulties in running it from the south of England and of the losses it incurred. In 1870 he put it on the market.

The buyer was Farquhar Campbell of Aros, presumably the same Captain Campbell from Mull who had been letting the grazings in the meantime and one of the Campbells of Ormsary, an Argyllshire family installed in the middle of the seventeenth century. (James Mor, the first of Ormsary, was a son of the first Campbell of Kilberry who died in 1619.) Within his Rum property Campbell had four crofts, from each of which he derived an average annual rent of £3. Each croft had about 0.2 acre arable, was allowed to graze a cow and calf on common pasture and allowed to cut peats. The 1871 census revealed eighty-one people living on Rum.

Farquhar Campbell had bought Hugh Maclean's former Aros estate in Mull in 1856 but seemed to have been in financial difficulties and maintained a running battle against the local crofters and cottars. In seventeen years he prosecuted almost that number of people in Tobermory Sheriff

Court, mostly for small thefts of firewood; he also contested, unsuccessfully, that anyone had the right to graze cattle on his land. In April 1870 the *Oban Times* reported that villagers interested in regaining their crofts from Campbell were requested to meet and in a body to go and take possession. 'Accordingly upwards of a hundred of all ages and sexes responded to the call, possessing themselves with spades and in the coolest manner possible turned up a small space of each croft, sowed some seed, and then according to their view, became possessors of the soil.' Further agitation followed in October of the year when about 200 people tore down fences in the area. A more violent protest in October led to court appearances for the ringleaders but public opinion was on their side and, in the crowded court room at Tobermory, they received only eight-day sentences for breach of the peace. Alexander Allan, a wealthy young shipping magnate, bought the estate in 1874 and went to great lengths to restore good relations with the resident population.

Comparatively little has come to light about Rum's history under Farquhar Campbell and few visitors seem to have committed their experiences to paper. Robert Buchanan, son of a Glasgow journalist, cruised the Hebrides in his 7-ton yacht *Tern* about this time but his account *The Hebrid Isles* (1872) makes rather turgid reading. He abided by a principle that 'any description of landscape that is not poetical must, for artistic reasons, be worthless and untrue.' None the less he ventured:

> Haskeval and Haleval, the two highest peaks of Rum, throw their shadows over the drifting *Tern*, while from some solitary bay inland the oystercatchers and sealarks whistle in the stillness ... Scattered along the southern side of the bay are a few poor cottages, rudely built of stone and roofed with peat turfs, and at the head of the loch is a comfortable whitewashed house, the abode of Captain Macleod of Dunvegan, the tenant of the island. There is, moreover, a rude stone pier, where a small vessel might lie secure in any weather, and off which a battered old brigantine is even now unloading oatmeal and flour ...
>
> Starvation, however, does not seem the order of the day in Loch Scresort. On landing and making the first hut at hand, we find the cow, with her calf by her side, tethered a few yards from the dwelling, two pigs wallowing in the peat-mire close by, and at least a dozen cocks, hens and chickens running to and fro across the threshold, where a fresh, well-fed matron with a smile for the stranger, salutes us in the Gaelic speech. With that fine old grace of hospitality which has fled for ever from busier scenes, she leads us into her cottage – a 'but and ben'. The apartment into which we are shown, despite the damp earthen floor and mildewy walls, is quite a palace for the Highlands; for it has a wooden press bed, wooden chairs and table, and a rude cupboard shaped

like a wardrobe; and the walls are adorned, moreover, by a penny almanac and a picture cut out of the *Illustrated London News.*

Drink fit for the gods is speedily handed round, in the shape of foaming bowls of new milk fresh from the udder – a cup of welcome invariably offered to the traveller in any Highland dwelling that can afford it. A few friendly words warm up the good woman's heart, and she begins to prattle and to question. She is a childless widow and her 'man' was drowned. She dwells here all alone; for all her relatives have emigrated to Canada, where she hopes some day to join them.

She longs very much to see Tobermory and its great shops – also to look up a distant kinsman who has flourished there in trade. She tells us much of the laird and his family – the 'folk in the big house'; they are decent, pious people and kind to the poor.

The 'laird' was Norman Macleod (1825–88) of Orbost in Skye. A retired army captain, he married a daughter of Major Ewen Macpherson of Badenoch around 1876. Soon afterwards he gave up the tenancy of Rum, sold Orbost and moved to Uiginish in Dunvegan. Captain Macleod had brought to the island several domestic servants, including a forty-year-old widower, Norman Mackinnon, who acted as gardener. From the census, amongst Rum's other inhabitants, we know that only Kenneth Maclean (aged fifty) and his elder sister Catherine survived of the original Rum family left after the Clearances. Old John Matheson, one of the Bracadale men from the Port na Caranean settlement, was still living in Kinloch with his widowed daughter Anne, her daughter and two grandchildren. The widow Effie Russell lived nearby. Effie's brother, Malcolm, lived with his sister, Mary, and although by then in his late sixties, was still making a living as a fisherman in Kinloch, with three other men. Another widow, Sarah or Marion Mackinnon, must have been the one who entertained Robert Buchanan in 1872; she and her late husband Hector, from Canna, had lived at Kilmory in 1841 and 1851. She had been widowed by 1861 and moved to Kinloch with her daughter Flora.

On the far side of the island, Lachlan MacDougall from Mull was the shepherd at Guirdil, with an assistant, William Ross from Skye, living with him and his family. Roderick Macleod was assistant to his father William, and shared the cottage at Harris with both his parents, his own wife, a teenage brother Donald (who would later succeed him) and two sisters. This family came from Scarista, Harris, in the Outer Hebrides. James Chisholm from Bracadale on Skye, his wife and four-year-old son, Kenneth, lived a lonely existence at Papadil. John Macdonald from Lochinver in Sutherland, his Raasay-born wife, her sister, and their six children were all crammed into the Dibidil cottage.

Murdoch Matheson was the shepherd at Kilmory, and his story is one which even today attracts much interest among visitors to the old burial ground there. Born in 1823 at Applecross, his parents managed to give him a good education but he left school to work as a shepherd on an Inverness-shire estate where he met and married Christina Elliot, a dairy maid originally from the Borders. Later Murdo set up as a butcher in Dingwall where, in 1853, his son Dougald was born. The next year he decided to go back to shepherding and the family moved to Eigg, where son James was born. In 1855 Murdo was offered the post of shepherd at Kilmory. Mackenzie, Lord Salisbury's Factor, had noted on 2 June that year when he had hired new shepherds:

> One from Eigg (a Lochcarron man) has been there [Eigg] for two years. I hired him for Kilmory. I regret to have to report that the shepherd's house at Kilmory (the thatched wooden cottage) was burnt – the heather thatch caught fire from the chimney in the departing shepherd's absence while a girl was left in occupation. I am getting one of the bothies fitted out for the family.

According to Matheson's descendants, one of whom has privately published a booklet describing the family's history, his employer was a Dr Macleod, who leased the grazings from Lord Salisbury some years later. Their daughter Rebecca was born on Rum soon afterwards, followed by Matthew (1858), Robert (1860), John (1861), Alexander (1863), Christina-Ann (1865), Murdo (1867) and William John (1869). Archibald Duncan was born in 1870 but died seven months later; another baby, Jessie Margaret, arrived in 1872.

Matheson educated his children with secondhand books supplied by the Ulster Church and a nephew, David Beatson, a divinity student, acted as tutor to them in the summer months. Perhaps he was related in some way to the Rev. Henry Beatson who had been minister on Eigg until 1847. When the two eldest Matheson boys were in their late teens they found part-time employment with an uncle who owned a chandlery in Skye and some fishing boats. Dougald was particularly skilled in the ways of the sea and, being a strong swimmer, had saved some seamen who were wrecked off Rum.

But in 1873 tragedy struck. Some of the Matheson children were smitten with diphtheria and between 7 and 9 September five of them died and were buried alongside their infant brother in the tiny graveyard at Kilmory, close to their cottage. Murdo Matheson erected a handsome headstone to their memory, one of only two modern slabs in the burial ground. But his wife was unable to overcome her grief, and in 1875 they decided to emigrate to New Zealand, where Christina Matheson's brothers and sisters had settled.

In July 1875 they sailed from Glasgow in the *Auckland*. Dougald had once nursed an ambition to become a merchant naval captain, so had learnt logarithms from his father and had studied books on navigation. He amused himself by charting the ship's entire course to Port Chalmers in New Zealand and upon arrival, eighty-eight days later, found that he was only three miles out in his calculations.

Sadly little Jessie Margaret, aged three, died soon after the family arrived. Murdo, with his wife and youngest surviving child, Alexander, eventually settled on Cottesbrook Station, where her brother James Elliot was head shepherd. In November 1875 Dougald, James and Robert journeyed by wagon to central Otago, and were joined later by Matthew. They freelanced as shepherds and drovers, but still returned home to visit their parents. Dougald made several daring trips of exploration to the west coast, where he discovered and named Lake Matheson, a now famous beauty spot below Mount Cook.

In 1885, when Cottesbrook was subdivided, the shepherds were allotted grazings. Murdo Matheson's acquisition he called Hartfield, but the family had to live under canvas until a house was built. His sons James and Matthew returned home to help him. However, Murdo was slow to adapt to his new style of living; rather authoritarian in outlook he became more reserved in later life, not helped by bad attacks of rheumatism. He died at Hartfield on 19 June 1906, aged eighty-four. Christina Matheson is remembered as being kind and gentle, and somewhat superstitious. She continued to correspond with friends and relatives in Scotland, until she died on 2 September 1912, aged eighty-two.

Matthew and Alexander remained unmarried and farmed at Hartfield until 1915. Being the youngest and quite an extrovert, Alexander adapted best to colonial life and delighted in training sheepdogs; he was still winning championships at the age of eighty-six. He shared with his brother a keen interest in Highland dancing and piping. Matthew was more reserved, showed a mechanical bent and was a skilled woodcarver. He died in 1942, aged eighty-five. Alexander died in 1956, aged ninety-three.

Dougald, Murdo Matheson's eldest son, had been allocated a lease of land which he called Attadale. He married in 1897 and had three sons and a daughter. He was active in local politics, and continued his interests in navigation, astronomy, mathematics and surveying. His eldest son, Ian Dougald, died in 1921 at the age of seventeen. Dougald himself died in 1931 aged seventy-eight. His second son, Elliot Hugh, inherited the farm and it is he who has since studiously researched his family history. The connection with Rum has not been forgotten, several members of the family having come to Britain and journeyed all the way to Rum to see the old gravestone at Kilmory. I was pleased to meet Elliot's daughter, Helen, and to show her round the island; she has kindly furnished me with the details of her family's history.

In 1876 and newly married, Captain Norman Macleod, tenant in Rum, received a visit from one Donald Macleod of Drynoch. On 27 September Donald wrote a letter to his mother, a copy of which is lodged in the Rum nature reserve office, and which provides a rare vignette of the island and its tacksman at that time:

Here we are at last in the island of Rum which we reached on Tuesday last. The day was lovely which was a great matter for us as in bad weather the landing at Rum, which has to be done in a small boat, is often not only inconvenient but impossible. About three hours sailing having brought us off this place, as we came round the point we saw the boat from here waiting for us, and when it came alongside we found that Norman 'Orbost' himself was steering. As it was quite calm Mary had no difficulty in getting into the boat and soon we pulled ashore.

Here the first difficulty presented itself as the tide was at its lowest ebb and it was impossible to get to the usual landing place, but we got out on the rocks and soon reached dry land. We saw someone coming to meet us and who was this but young Macleod of Dunvegan who was here on a visit to Norman 'Orbost' ... We were received very warmly by 'Mrs Orbost' ... She is much younger than 'Orbost' himself, indeed quite young, and used to be quite a lady of fashion in Edinburgh. What a different lifestyle she leads here where they so seldom see strangers, and where she has no lady companion, but she seems very happy and contented. She has two nice bairns, one a bright little girl of 15 months and the other a baby of 4 months. The nurse can hardly speak a word of English and ['Mrs Orbost'] does not understand Gaelic which must be rather inconvenient for her.

After lunch on the day of our arrival young Macleod and I went up on the hill to look for grouse and succeeded in bringing home a good bag, not only of grouse but also a snipe and when we were out we saw a herd of fallow deer. The next day we went out deer stalking but though we saw a good many and I had some shots, I was not successful in getting one. The next day I went out again but with even worse luck as I did not even get a shot.

However I was not discouraged, the next day (Friday) I arranged the night before that I would make an early start, as they usually do not rise from breakfast here till 11. I however got off at 8 and Donald the keeper and I set off for Harris about 8 miles off. We saw several deer but were not able to get near them, but at last came on a very fine stag and hind feeding quietly together on top of a high hill just over the sea. I was more than two hours creeping up to them and had to drag myself along on my face, and at last had the satisfaction of bringing down the stag.

It was a fine beast about 19 stone. We were so far from home we had to leave the stag there for the night and next morning we set out with a man and a pony to bring it in. It was a very fine head and as it is my first Norman 'O' opened a bottle of champagne in honour of the stag. 'Orbost' lives here in grand style. The first evening Macleod and Norman said to each other, 'It is time to go and wash our fingers' and came down in full dress kilts – and have done so each night – and 'Mrs Orbost' dresses as for a dinner party. As we had sent our evening clothes to Portree we felt rather at a loss.

Norman 'O' has been much put out about the letters. He sent a boat for them on Thursday last and they did not arrive till Sunday morning. My letter arrived after myself. It must be very inconvenient at times, having no regular post.

The difficulties of mail reaching the island was a perennial problem. On 14 February 1868 the clerk of the Small Isles School Board wrote from Eigg:

Owing to the want of a post communication with this parish, yours of the 21st, 28th Jan and 7th inst. only came to hand yesterday, and although I write this, it is quite uncertain how soon it may find its way out of the island ...

The Rev. Kenneth Macleod (1871–1955) was youngest son of Donald Macleod, schoolteacher in Eigg from 1867 to 1888, and became minister on Colonsay and Gigha. He collected many Gaelic songs in Eigg and collaborated with Mrs Marjorie Kennedy Fraser in their publication. In his book *The Road to the Isles* he elaborated on the difficulties of communication:

In the middle of the nineteenth century a smack crossed from the Island of Eigg to the mainland once a week, weather and inclination permitting, for the few letters and the one newspaper brought by the stage-coach from Fort William to Arisaig: about a fortnight later, somebody sailed across from Rum to Eigg to see if any letters had arrived by the packet boat within the previous month; in the course of another week, more or less, a shepherd from the west side of Rum, looking for a stray sheep, unexpectedly found himself in the seaport clachan of Kinloch, and while there might remember to ask if there were any letters for the neighbouring island of Canna; on the following day the folk of Canna saw a fire on a certain hill on Rum, a sign that their letters had somehow or other found their way to the shepherd's house, and some time before the end of the week somebody, who had probably never in his life received a letter, sailed across the Sound and returned with the mail-bag as soon as he felt in the mood for returning.

Around 1880 John Bullough, an industrialist from Lancashire, took over the shooting tenancy in Rum at £800 per annum, and leased the White House. In April 1881, according to the census returns, William Bullough, an eighteen-year-old mechanic and engineer (and perhaps a grandson), was in residence along with John Ashworth, a gamekeeper. Kinloch House was occupied by the Campbells' manager or tenant, Colin Livingston from Morvern, his wife and family. He was a cousin of the celebrated African explorer and missionary. Livingston's son, Hugh, an excellent piper, was a businessman in London but visited the island from time to time.

John Bullough invited many friends to Rum, amongst them a Lancashire poet named Edwin Waugh. His detailed account forms one-third of a book entitled *The Limping Pilgrim on his Wanderings* (1883). In contrast to his poetic colleague Buchanan ten years before, Waugh provided a fascinating and accurate description of the community living in Rum at that time, full of intimate and colourful detail and verifiable by the census returns which had been completed only a year earlier. Since the book is now very scarce both secondhand and in libraries, it is well worth quoting at length.

Waugh left Manchester for Rum on 28 May 1882, on a train to Carlisle and then to Greenock, where he embarked on a steamer to Oban, Salen and Tobermory. As it continued its voyage north it diverted to land Waugh on Eigg. Here he passed the night in 'a clean and comfortable little inn; and we received some kind attentions of Professor Macpherson who is owner of the island'. Although Waugh first mentioned that 'the *Hebridean* comes puffing and churning up to the pier about once a fortnight', later in his account he implied that its calls were irregular, always by special arrangement, and generally at night-time. 'They have to sound a kind of hoarse horn, or whistle, to let the sleeping inhabitants know that they are in the bay.' The next day he himself sailed to 'the wild, sweet, sea-girt solitude called the Isle of Rum' in a small open boat.

He found a road stretching half a mile from the pier past a cluster of eight or ten thatched cottages called 'The Town'. There was a ford across the first stream (what is now often referred to as the Rockery burn), with a small wooden bridge 'for ither folk'. The road then crossed a level meadow, through a fine clump of trees shading the rear of Kinloch House, the best dwelling house on the island, 'standing at the head of the bay, with its bright green lawn sloping down to the sea.' The large garden contained many excellent fruit trees. Crossing another stream, Kinloch burn, the road continues to the farmstead.

The nearest doctor was in Arisaig, the parish minister – the Rev. John Sinclair (1825–1908) – resided in Eigg. There was no church or chapel in Rum except 'a small, plain edifice of wood, 8 yards long by 4 yards wide which looked like a haystack with two windows in it'. During weekdays a student teacher, William Henry MacDougall, presided over 'about a score of hardy, bare-legged little islanders'; and there, too, on a Sunday, he might have to officiate as minister. The church-cum-school had a slated roof, whitewashed walls and an earthen floor. Wooden forms acted as pews, with a seat beneath the oak pulpit for the precentor and a small table where the 'swells' generally sat. The congregation normally numbered twenty or thirty, not counting the sheepdogs which lay about the floor or outside in the sun. The service was in Gaelic but if any visitors were present it would be followed by another short one in English. The church has since been replaced by a stone building although it still doubles as a school. As Edwin Waugh commented:

> Of the history of the island scarcely anything is known now, except what comes down in the shape of misty tradition – very misty and very scanty indeed – for even that has been almost entirely swept away in the wholesale emigration of the old inhabitants which took place in 1828. In that year all the inhabitants of Rum, with the exception of old Kenneth Maclean's father, who then lived at Carn an Dorian where his son now lives, were carried off in a body to America. So clean, indeed, was the sweep of the population, that a few families were afterwards brought over from Skye, to keep up the continuity of life upon the island.
>
> I am beginning to know the people here, in a friendly way, both old and young, and I will now take a stroll along the edge of the sea, amongst the cottages in which they dwell.

Beginning at the southern point of Loch Scresort Waugh discovered some ruins: 'a touching relic of the old population'. Walking back towards Kinloch he next encountered the cottage of old Kenneth Maclean, 'with its little byre close by, both standing end to end, at the head of a green field which slopes down to the rocky shore ... Its name is Carn an Dorian or The Otter Stones.' This field is now wooded but the ruins which sport gable, chimney and windows, sitting at the landward edge of the trees, must have been Kenneth's cottage. There is an older blackhouse in the middle of the wood nearby, which is in a fine state of preservation; it has a fireplace against the west wall and a separate byre in front. This may have been where the family lived before the newer cottage was constructed, and may have been the ruin with which Waugh began his account.

> Kenneth is strongly attached to this hereditary plot of ground; for as he tells you, it was granted to his forefathers as 'a free land', by one of the old Macleans, lairds of the island in former days ... He has seen four [*sic*] new lairds of Rum in succession in his own life-time; but he tells you with pride that his progenitors have lived upon the island for eleven generations.

Kenneth was considered 'a man of mark' locally, often acting as precentor for the church services. He had an interest in botany and 'knew more about the unwritten traditions of Rum than any man living'.

About half a mile further on, Waugh described the wandering pathway dipping down to a little creek called Reigan na Pol, or 'The Best of Pools'. On its shore stood the little church and three inhabited cottages. The first was the home of Malcolm Macleod, a lobster fisherman: 'a hardy good-looking young fellow; but a man of few words'. One day he and his comrade Donald Henderson took Waugh round to Kilmory by boat and he was coerced to sing a Gaelic song. His cottage, of stone roofed with a grassy thatch, stood on the edge of a rocky shelf overlooking the creek and commanded a fine view of the bay looking west up Kinloch Glen. Nearby, beside a pretty little rock ravine richly festooned with bright lush greenery and wild flowers, stood another thatched cottage occupied by old John Matheson from Bracadale, and his daughter Mary Ann. The eighty-eight-year-old was a short, square-built man, very strong in his time, with quite a sense of humour.

> Old John's cottage is only of one storey in height, yet it is somewhat more roomy than the rest of the shielings upon the shore of the bay. The schoolmaster of the island lodges there.

This is almost certainly what is now referred to as Foxglove Cottage, which served as a schoolhouse until the new bungalow was built in the 1960s near the school. John Matheson died in 1885 at the age of ninety-one.

> About one hundred yards walk over broken, rocky and miry ground brings us to the door of old Etty [Effie] Russell's cottage, which stands on the west side of the pool ... Etty is an aged widow ... Everything in her cot, from the earthen floor to the roof, is black with the smoke of the turf fire, which wanders round the inside of the little shieling, and lingers there ... until at last it finds an outlet by a hole in the thatch, or by the doorway ... But old Etty is not quite so poor and forlorn as a stranger might think from the appearance of her dwelling place. She has a cow of her own; and she has a croft and a cottage, and a byre for her cow, for which she pays nothing ... She is thrifty and industrious too. I noticed an old fashioned spinning wheel in a corner of her cottage. I have no doubt the old wheel is brought into play now and then. I know that she does a little weaving upon the handloom at so much per yard when she can get it to do. Mr Ferguson, the sheep farmer of the Isle of Rum, gives her work of that kind, now and again.

Young Donald Ferguson who leased the grazings in Rum then, was a merchant from South Uist.

> Old Etty weaves [tweed] when she can get a job. She has the milk of

her cow; she bakes a little oatcake by her turf fire; and she delights in tea, brewed and stewed and boiled till it is as black as ink ... She has a kindly old sister, Mary who is helpful and strongly attached to her. They are very thick together. When one of the sisters is unwell, the other attends to her ... I could never find out where old Mary lived; but she lives somewhere in the huts along the shore. I meet her now and then. She is always going to her sister Etty's and she has a kind of smile, and a kindly, inarticulate greeting, though she can hardly understand a word of English. But Mary is not the only kind neighbour that cheers old Etty's lonely hours, for the crones of the clachan creep into her cottage, and sit round her hearth, chatting among the smoke ...

Etty, or Effie as she was referred to in the census, lived in a cottage facing the church; it is now gone but must have been somewhere near the modern house called Bayview (where I once lived).

Although Salisbury's pier – 'a rude but substantial stone structure, about 55 yards long, with a flight of steps leading down to the water near its eastern end' – had depth enough for steamers from Oban to come alongside at high water, they only did so by special arrangement. Smaller boats tied up, however, when the tide allowed, including what Waugh referred to as 'the Pot boat', whose crew hawked earthenware pots among the inhabitants of the islands, and 'the Tinkers' boats'. The latter were laden with assorted utensils of tin for sale. McAlister, his wild gypsy-looking wife and their six children, travelled round the Inner Hebrides most of the year, sleeping in the open boats or camping ashore. They were full of gossip and in June 1882 brought the news that Canna had been sold for £23,000 to Mr Thom, a shipowner from Glasgow.

The haven at the pier had a Gaelic name which translated as 'The Port of the Priest's Rock'. Waugh explained:

Near the south-west corner of its shore there is a rock, in front of which there is a natural kind of seat, almost like an armchair. I understand that tradition points to this as the rock to which the boat of the priest used to be fastened in ancient times ... Coming shoreward from the pier, the first dwelling we pass is the cottage of old Norman Mackinnon, the gardener at Kinloch House; and adjoining that there is a small warehouse, of one storey, of the same rough and simple style as the gardener's cottage.

This was probably on the site of the present-day boatshed and fuel store.

Old Norman is as Highland as a peat, as they say hereabouts. He is a good gardener, and a careful industrious man. He takes as much pride in the things grown in his garden as if he had made them himself ... The old man is naturally civil and obliging; indeed when you chance to meet him upon the road, he seems so anxious to say something pleasing that, even in stormy weather, he is not at all unlikely to tell you that it is a fine day!

About 30 yards beyond was the cottage of Kenneth Campbell, like that of his neighbour the gardener, possessing one of the few slated roofs in the island. Kenneth was:

stout, good-looking ... of middle height and rather more than middle age. He has seen a good deal of life as a common sailor, for he has been long voyages to Australia and other distant parts of the world; and he has settled down here at last, with his comely-looking goodwife, and his seven fine children, as skipper of the yacht belonging to the island. A clear streamlet comes down by the end of the cottage, into the port, and Kenneth's wife does her washing in the bright running water; and she spreads her clothes upon the heathery slope behind the cottage to dry. Both Kenneth and his goodwife are 'houseproud' and their dwelling is kept in better trim, and contains more of the conveniences of household life than is common among highland cottages. There are generally logs of timber, broken masts, or other pieces of wreck, lying about Kenneth's cottage, which have been gathered from the shore. Kenneth has a cow and a free croft, like most of the cottars on this island; and he is looked upon, among his poor neighbours, as a man rather 'well-off' in the world.

Waugh noted the deserted limekiln near the pier:

quickly abandoned because it was found that the stones of which it was built would not stand fire ... And now, after our short walk along the foot of the hill, The Port of the Priest's Rock is clean out of sight; and here we are, at the cluster of huts which the inhabitants call The Town. There are six of these huts; and although separated from each other, they stand almost in a line, with their doorways and their tiny windows looking across the rocky shore on to the bay, and their backs within ten yards of our roadside. ... They are little and low, although they look strong; and their thatched roofs are crossed and re-crossed with ropes, from the ends of which heavy stones are slung, to keep the thatch on in stormy weather. Only two of them have each a little rude chimney, which have evidently been added a long time after the cottages were first built; from the rest, the smoke escapes by a hole in the roof, or by the doorway ...

The first cottage was inhabited by John McCaskill and his good wife and their seven children, ranging from six months to ten years old. John is not much more than forty years of age; and he is a man of some mark among his simple neighbours; for like 'the skipper' he has seen a good deal of the world as a common sailor. He was one of the crew of the good ship *Lesbia* of Newcastle upon Tyne, on her way from Quebec to Grimsby. He, with twenty-three others, spent seven days upon the mast-head; and were picked up in a state of great exhaustion on the eighth day, by the steamer *Arthur* on her way to London.

The McCaskill cottage was better appointed than some of its neighbours, with a little chimney and a skylight in the thatch, as well as the tiny window in the wall. Unusually light and cheerful, it formed a great resort for those in need of a friendly chat. Beside it lived the cheery, ruddy-faced spinster Mary Maclean. Her brother, Malcolm, had died in May 1881. Although somewhat proud, quick-tempered and eccentric, the wise old fisherman was much respected in the community. He ran the only shop on the island, doing a small trade in groceries among the islanders, as well as, it is said, 'a little sly traffic in the whisky line'. After his nefarious career he finally fell ill. He refused a doctor but instead made his will and paid off all his debts. He even laid aside three bottles of whisky to be consumed at his funeral. Then he died. His friends made a rough coffin from driftwood, 'pressed his poor remains into it and nailed him up'. Due to storms it was many days before they were able to sail round to the Kilmory burial ground with his body. He was interred in a shallow grave and while filling it in they found assorted fragments of mouldering bones and rotten bits of coffins. An old headstone with faint lettering on it served as a headstone; only then did the mourners sit down for a smoke and to consume the three bottles of whisky.

The late Archie Cameron, who was brought up in Rum early last century, has related to me another story whose exact date is uncertain. Two men were charged with taking the body of a child to Kilmory for burial. This involved a long walk of five miles or so along the old road, which at that time ran along the north side of Kinloch Glen. It proved a wet and stormy day and the men decided to bury the little coffin beside the road, not even half-way to Kilmory, thinking no one would ever know. In the end, however, one of them had to confess what they had done, and the grave was marked with a crude, unmarked stone. It can still be seen beside what is now a footpath, near where it crosses Allt Airidh Thalabhairt above Loch nan Eala in Kinloch Glen.

After old Malcolm's death Mary took possession of the forty shillings that her brother had left her, and of his cottage; formerly she had lived with her sister, Effie. These Macleans had come from Bracadale with the Port na Caranean families after the Clearances, but had set up home in Kinloch. In the 1850s Effie had married John Russell, the elderly widower from Argyll who had been gardener to the Salisburys. On 19 February 1869 he died, leaving Effie, in her fifties and a widow. It was one of her stepsons, also John Russell, who had been the schoolteacher in Salisbury's time. A younger son Archibald emigrated to New Zealand.

Alongside Mary Maclean's cottage was a byre for her cow; it was a dingy structure, no window, no chimney and the door almost always closed. Not far away was another byre, at right angles to the road, where the widow Sarah Mackinnon kept her cow. No one knew how old the widow was, not even her daughter; some said she must be nearly ninety although the census return for 1881 gives her age as seventy. Only once is she known to have deserted her smoky little hut. In November 1881 the tide rose so high in a storm that many of the cottages were flooded. Old Sarah had 'to be dragged out by force, screaming feebly and clutching frantically at anything she could lay hold of'. She and her beleaguered neighbours had to be given shelter in the Big House:

> And it was a strange scene in Kinloch House that night; for the place was crowded with old and young, who had been drowned out by the tide; and the disaster was of such an unusual kind that many of the poor folk believed that the end of the world was at hand.

Widow Mackinnon's daughter Ann (or Flora?), the island beauty, was married to Donald Henderson, the fisherman from Tobermory who shared a boat with Malcolm Macleod. Henderson and his family only spent the fishing season on Rum, and retired to Mull for the winter. The widow had a small plot or 'garden' beside her cottage. Waugh mused:

> Perhaps, in some time gone by, it may have been more of a garden than it is now, but I have many a time leaned upon the low wall of that little enclosure and have looked carefully round, and I must say that at present I cannot discover anything therein to justify the name it bears.

This 'tangled wild' marked the end of The Town, that lay on what is now the camp site on Rum; in early spring, before the grass grows long, the overgrown foundations of the old blackhouses can still be distinguished.

The remaining dwellings on the shore of Loch Scresort were of quite a different character. The first of these stood only a hundred yards beyond the old widow's garden:

> a plain substantial house of two storeys ... built a few years ago, by the laird of the island, for the accommodation of visitors during the shooting season. It is white-washed outside; and it is known amongst the people of Rum by the name of 'Tigh Ban' or The White House. Its doors were never locked.

Nowadays it is the residence and office of the nature reserve's chief warden, and is still known as The White House.

In a green field behind the house there is a well, strongly impregnated with iron and other matters, which are said to have a valuable medicinal effect. The well is sunk in a field, and there are some traces of rude masonry about its sides, as if it had been known and used by the old inhabitants of the isle.

Indeed it was mentioned in the *Old Statistical Account* of 1796:

In Rum is a well, called *Tobar Dearg* (Red Well), the water of which is highly mineral, but very little used by the natives.

Waugh related another story about an old well at Kilmory, but it could conceivably refer to Tobar Dearg. Long ago an islander had been exiled to Coll for some misdemeanour. But he pined constantly for his native Rum until he made himself ill, and had to take to his bed. His chief eventually came and asked what he might do to save the man's life. All the man wanted was a drink of water from the old well at Kilmory. A six-oared boat was duly despatched to Rum on the errand, but the weather turned so stormy that the boatmen, for fear of their lives, agreed to get any fresh water from the nearest spot on Rum's shore. They returned to Coll and offered the dying man a drink. But as soon as his lips touched the cup he cried out, 'Ah, this is not the water from the well of Kilmory.' He turned his face away and died.

Exile was the lesser of the punishments meted out on his Rum tenants by Maclean of Coll. According to Kenneth Maclean:

there is a place upon the shore down towards the south point of the bay which is very bad indeed for midges and flies. A man was once stung to death there, I assure you. I have often heard both my father and my grandfather tell the story; and it was well known to all the old people who lived on the island when I was a child. It happened in the time of the old Macleans, when they were lairds of the island. The man was a native of the island, and a clansman of the Maclean. He had committed some crime, and the laird ordered him to be stripped naked and tied to a stake, and then left exposed in the sun in that spot till he was stung to death by the gnats and flies. I can assure you the people do not like the place now; because it is haunted, and groans are heard there in the night-time.

Archie Cameron later came to link his story of the Child's Grave with this incident. As he had it, after the man confessed, his companion was the one who was pegged out and stung to death. This seems unlikely, however, for surely Waugh would have been told about the Child's Grave too?

To reach Kinloch House from The White House, one had to cross a small bridge, 'a very simple rustic contrivance' made of three narrow

planks with a wooden handrail along one side only. This bridge was
washed away in the storm of November 1881 – when the sea had risen
six feet higher than ever before – and was replaced by another 'so like the
old one that a careless observer might not have noticed any difference'.
Waugh went on:

> The other day, when this stream was swollen with heavy rain, old
> Mackinnon the gardener was trying to wheel a barrowful of dirty
> clothes across the bridge; and not daring to trust the wheel upon a
> cracked plank, he was compelled to tilt his barrow so much on one side
> that, at last, he overbalanced it, and down it went into the stream, with
> him after it. The fall was only about six feet; but it was quite enough
> at once, for an old man. He was crooning Gaelic verse when he came
> across the meadow; but, as he clambered up the bank out of that stream,
> he was talking prose!
>
> A few yards walk from the end of the bridge, and along the burn
> side, brings us to a rickety wooden gate, from which a good pathway
> leads across a meadow of about four acres, at the head of the bay ... The
> land at the north-east end of the meadow is occupied by Kinloch House,
> with its lawn and garden, and the cluster of trees which shades the rear
> and the ends of the building. These trees were planted about fifty years
> ago; and their fine, healthy appearance now is strong evidence of what
> might be done in these bare, mountainous Hebridean isles by plantation.
> This compact clump of wood at Kinloch House looks very striking, seen
> from the bay; and it looks all the more so because the rest of the island
> is as bare of trees as a lapstone ...
>
> I think the cluster of trees at the rear of Kinloch House does not
> cover more than an acre of ground altogether, and yet the natives
> of Rum speak of it as 'The Park' ... When the sportsmen started
> from Kinloch House in a morning, clad in their shooting gear, with
> their guns, and their gillies, and their deer-stalkers, and their dogs
> abounding around them, wild with delight, those who were not going
> to the hills used to follow them to the edge of this wood at the rear of
> the house, to see them off ...
>
> Under its shade there were three substantial wooden huts, each raised
> about two feet from the ground upon stone pillars, as a protection from
> rats and other vermin. One of these huts was better ventilated than
> the rest, being used as a meat safe or pantry; another was used as a
> storeroom for fishing tackle and other odd things; and in the third the
> churning was done ...

Waugh described Kinloch House as:

> a plain, strongly built stone house, with a steep roof, and with a porch,

and with a small wing at each end, one of which was used as a gun room, and the other as a kitchen ... The south side of the lawn is flanked by the garden, and the north side partly by trees and partly by a low-built, comfortable, whitewashed cottage, which is the second best house upon the island, and is the residence of Mr Donald Ferguson, who is the sheep farmer of the island.

In the census this building was named Ivy Cottage and has now been much altered into what is now the post office and shop. Kinloch House, of course, is now demolished and only a few gate-posts remain.

After we have passed the Big House, the only remaining building of any kind upon the rest of the shore are those belonging to the farmstead ... They stand around the four sides of a courtyard; and they are strongly built of stone, with slated roofs; and in the north-west corner of the square, Roderick Macleod, Mr Ferguson's chief shepherd, lives with his wife and family ...

I have now made the circuit of all the inhabited part of the shore of Scresort Bay, where the great majority of the inhabitants of the island dwell; the only other inhabited places being four or five small sheep farms in lonely nooks of the isle, separated from each other by several miles of wild mountain land ... The monks of Iona are supposed to have first settled at Kilmory, on the north side of the island, and built the ancient church there, the ruins of which still remain [*sic*], with a cluster of broken, weed-grown walls ... The ragged remains of these dwellings of the ancient inhabitants of the isle are scattered over a few acres of ground, in a quiet, sheltered vale, and close by a beautiful mountain stream ...

The cottage at Kilmory (which until 1875 had been occupied by the unfortunate Matheson family) was now tenanted by a Skye shepherd, Murdoch Nicolson, and his wife. They had six children; the eldest son Malcolm, although only fourteen years old, was mentioned in the census return as assistant shepherd. The old widow, William Macleod and his son Donald, now married, were still the shepherds at Harris. Dibidil was unoccupied in 1881 but another Skyeman, James Chisholm, still lived with his young family at Papadil. Their son, Kenneth, by then fourteen, was according to Waugh:

hardy and shaggy as a Highland colt ... He comes nine miles over the wild mountain track every Monday morning [to school at Kinloch], and sometimes in very rough weather; he gets his porridge and milk, two or three times a day [with Kenneth Maclean's family at Carn an Dobhran]; and he goes whistling back over the hills to his father's solitary homestead every Saturday morning, as content as a king;

carrying with him into that secluded spot all the news of the busy world upon the shore of Scresort Bay.

... The other day, a poor woman, the wife of the shepherd living in the lonely part of the island called Guirdil, opposite the Isle of Canna, came eight miles over the mountains to see if she could get any kind of a lodging on the shore of Scresort Bay, for her son, another lad of about 14 years of age who could scarcely speak a word of English, so that he might have the benefit of the week-day school here for a little while. Unfortunately, after spending the best part of a day in making enquiries among the huts along the shore, she could not get any kind of accommodation for the poor lad on whose account she was so anxious; and she went back over the hills at sunset, quite cast down. She was a comely, intelligent-looking woman, very cleanly and decently clad; her husband was only a poor shepherd; and they had nine children, the youngest of which were twins. She could read and write a little herself; and she had taught all her children the alphabet ... She was very sorry to see her children growing up and learning nothing ...

She confessed with a deep sigh to Waugh in the kitchen of Kinloch House

and in a place where there was no chance of their learning anything; and now, the twins and the house together took up so much of her time that she had no time to teach them as she used to do.

Her name was Catherine Macdonald and she had come to Rum, like her husband Alexander, from Duirinish in Skye. Waugh concluded:

Since the time of the Macleans the Isle of Rum has changed hands more than once. From the Macleans, I believe, it was purchased by the late Marquis of Salisbury, who made some expensive efforts to improve the isle, which proved of no avail. After the death of the Marquis, the widowed Marchioness lived in seclusion in 'The Big House' for some years. After this the island was sold to the late Captain Campbell, at whose death in 1882, his nephew came into possession of it. 'Tigh Mor' is now the temporary residence of Mr John Bullough, the eminent machinist of Accrington, who is the lessee of the island.

Rum thus passed from Captain Campbell of Ormsary to his nephew who lived in Ballinaby in Islay. Miss Marion Campbell of Kilberry knows of a local tale that the funeral of the last Campbell of Ormsary was a scandalous affair, because cousins from Islay came to claim the estate. The will could not be found, however. As the coffin was being carried out of Ormsary House, someone noticed another mourner nip back inside to continue the search. So the coffin was put down on the gravel and everyone rushed indoors. They did not find the will but they did find the whisky. The coffin was not remembered until ten o'clock that night, when they finally took it down to 'bury the poor man decent, and there was no good came of it'. Miss Campbell also recalls hearing of a young Farquhar Campbell who died at Ormsary, probably of tuberculosis, around 1885, leaving only sisters so he was succeeded by an unpopular kinsman from Ballinaby on Islay. Perhaps his was the unfortunate coffin abandoned in the rush for his inheritance although the story could conceivably refer to Archibald, a grandson of the first Campbell of Ormsary who died in the eighteenth century, an alcoholic or bankrupt or both and without offspring.

PART V

Modern Rum

It was no Utopia, and the islanders often had their own differences as could be expected where there is a confined mass of humanity; but they were, by and large, a happy lot in congenial surroundings, doing work they enjoyed ...

Archie Cameron, 1988

15   *From Clogs to Castle*

... a palladian mausoleum of pink marble whose voice of anomaly is
subdued to a bat's squeak by the vast hills and the moving sea.

Gavin Maxwell, 1952

Hanging in the smoke room of Kinloch Castle in the Isle of Rum is the
framed 'pedigree' of Sir George Bullough. It dates back, somewhat optimis-
tically, 700 years, revealing how, in the thirteenth century, the Bulloughs
were humble farmers around Fazakerley, Kirkdale, Walton and Anglesarke
in Lancashire.

The end of the eighteenth century found Richard Bullough tenant
at Little Halton in the parish of Deane. The founder of the prosperous
industrial line was his son James, baptised in 1803. At the age of seven he
was apprenticed to a West Houghton weaver, and worked at a variety of
local mills. Eventually he married Martha Smith by whom he had three
sons: the eldest, John (who eventually purchased the Isle of Rum), born in
1837, and four daughters.

These were troublesome times since the workers resented the increasing
mechanisation in the cotton mills. As a lad James had experienced the rise
of this crusade against the new machinery, when workers actually stormed
a West Houghton mill. He realised, however, that the path to prosperity lay
in this new technology and he himself had a distinct talent for invention.
Indeed, he was to do as much as anyone in perfecting the very machines
that were replacing the rioting weavers.

He patented several devices for improving the loom, such as the 'roller
temple' and the 'weft fork'. If the warp broke on the loom the roller or

self-acting temple saved valuable machine time by employing a hair loop that rang a warning bell. The prototype was constructed using strands of his own sister's locks. Later he invented the 'slasher', a system of sizing and starching the warp which trebled the output of older, outmoded machines. These innovative devices made him so unpopular with the local workforce that in 1841 he was, for a time, forced to quit his home town of Blackburn. The following year the workers petitioned him about 'the professed improvement of the new loom' for which 'the patent was considered to be an evil in all its bearings'.

A kindly soul, James weathered the storm, however, and soon became a man of some affluence. He was quiet and unassuming, shunning the limelight. Wearing wooden clogs and a top hat, he delighted in playing marbles with the local children, dispensing garden peas from his pocket like sweets. He also much preferred the company of his less-privileged friends than to associate with higher society.

In 1856 he joined the Globe Works at Accrington, a firm that had been founded by John Howard three years earlier with capital from a business associate called Bleakley. When Mr Bleakley withdrew his finance Howard sought a new arrangement with James Bullough whose twenty-year-old son John also became a partner. Howard & Bullough Ltd had a workforce of forty and specialised in the manufacture of machines for the preparation and spinning of cotton.

Howard & Bullough also experimented in the manufacture of looms and young John soon showed that he had inherited some of his father's mechanical flair. Between 1868 and 1888 he took out no less than twenty-six patents. At an American exhibition in 1876 he had witnessed a device called a 'Rabbeth spindle' and two years later travelled to America to purchase the patent – 'for a considerable sum of money'. The speculation paid off for the device revolutionised cotton-spinning and without it the whole of the Lancashire industry might have foundered. Increased output at the Globe Works necessitated an extension of the original Fountain Street plant to Ormerod Street nearby, making it 'the biggest hive of industry in the district, with a world-wide reputation'. The annual wages bill increased from £8000 in 1866 to nearly £40,000 by 1874.

Having been educated at Queenswood College in Hampshire and Glasgow University, John Bullough was a cultured man, fond of music and dogs, and with a literary bent. When his father died in 1868 John was already a prosperous businessman and prominent in public life. Two years earlier he had married Bertha, a daughter of a Swiss gentleman Eduard Emile Schmidlin of Thun, near Berne. The couple had two children, George, born in 1870 (who as inheritor of the Isle of Rum will feature prominently later), and Bertha, born in 1873, who, in 1891, married Charles Young of Melbourne, Cambridgeshire.

John founded the Globe Works Technical School and was the first Accrington employer to adopt a nine-hour working day – a move which won him an appreciative testimonial from his workforce. Dated 5 February 1876, the document acknowledged how his inventions, and those of his father, had conferred 'pecuniary advantages to mill owners and manufacturers, and inestimable blessings upon the working classes of this and other countries of the world'. Changed days indeed from the troubled apprenticeship of his father. But, as his obituary was later to admit, 'discipline was one of Mr Bullough's cardinal principles and the Globe Works was no place for the lazy or indifferent workman'.

Robust in health and full of vitality and determination John Bullough took an active part in the affairs of the town, both religious and secular, but shunned all honours that were thrust his way. He readily dipped into his pocket to assist struggling local churches and in 1873 was elected President of the Accrington Church Industrial Co-operative Society. A staunch Tory he was largely responsible for the founding of the Conservative Club in Cannon Street. John Bullough never stood for Parliament himself but 'was always ready with a speech', as three privately printed volumes of his letters and speeches testify. Bullough greatly admired the Tory Prime Minister, Lord Salisbury, whose father had bought the Isle of Rum. In a speech to local Conservatives in December 1884, he praised Salisbury as 'a man of profound learning, a man of the highest refinement; he is the personification of courtesy and urbanity, he is a model landlord universally beloved by those around him'.

One of Bullough's friends was a Lancashire poet Edwin Waugh, who was often a guest at his Accrington home, named The Laund, or his Oswaldtwistle residence called The Rhyddings. In 1882 Waugh even visited Kinloch Lodge in Rum, 'the temporary residence of Mr John Bullough, the eminent machinist of Accrington, who is the lessee of the island'. For several years Waugh's host had been paying £800 per annum for the shooting rights on the island once owned by his political hero.

Bullough first came to Scotland as a student in Glasgow and in 1883 he got the opportunity to purchase a Highland estate of his own, Meggernie in Perthshire. An avenue two miles long and lined with lime trees led to a sixteenth-century mansion, once the property of the Stuart kings. Here were laid the plans for the Glencoe massacre in 1692. The estate itself occupied some 50 square miles and contained some of the best grouse shooting, deer forest and sheep walk in the whole of Scotland. As the advertisement in *The Times* stated:

it seems the very place for a wealthy man of the world, who is doubtful as to whether or no he is weary of its vanities ... The real attraction would be that a man of taste might have carte blanche in his own private wilderness, where all the elements of the picturesque are mingled in the wildest profusion.

The following year (1884) John Bullough, aged forty-seven, married again, having parted – somewhat acrimoniously – from his first wife. This latest event must have created quite a stir amongst his influential friends for his new wife, Alexandria Marian, was nineteen, only five years older than his own son George. She was the daughter of Kenneth Mackenzie, a banker in Stornoway on the Isle of Lewis, so quite how they first met is hard to say. Before he died seven years later John and his young wife had two children. Ian (born 1886) was to become a captain in the Coldstream Guards and married Lily Elsie, the beautiful actress. Gladys, the other child (born 1888), married a Grenadier Guardsman during the First World War but he was killed in action on the Continent only two months later.

Soon after John Bullough had purchased Meggernie, the Isle of Rum itself came on the market. It was advertised in *The Times* on 5 June 1886 by J. Watson Lyall & Co., 15 Pall Mall, London:

Being the most picturesque of the islands which lie off the west coast of Scotland, it is altogether a property of exceptional attractions. Its sporting capabilities are unsurpassed, and as a sporting estate it has at present few equals. Besides the sporting amenities it yields a very handsome rental. The population, some 60 or 70 in all, is composed of shepherds and workmen and their families employed by the sheep-farmer on the estate. There are no crofts. The extent is about 27,000 acres, of which about 300 acres are arable, 150 acres lochs and rivers, 530 acres foreshore and about 26,000 acres forest and moorland. The game consists of red and fallow deer, grouse, partridges, woodcock, snipe and the great variety of wildfowl of the West Hebrides. The winter shooting is particularly good. The deer and sheep are both well known as being some of the heaviest in Scotland. The fishings are excellent, there being on the island numerous lochs fully stocked with trout, and streams affording capital sea trout fishing during the season.

The lodge is situated on Loch Scrisort (where there is a splendid anchorage) and in a most convenient locality for speedy access to the shootings and fishings. It is situated at the head of the harbour, which is very good and safe for any size of vessel at all seasons. There is a large stone pier. The lodge is in good state of repair. There is also another smaller shooting lodge about 300 yards distant. There are the usual farm steadings, with suitable offices, stable, etc. The garden is well stacked and extends to an acre. There are made bridal paths throughout the island. Steamers from Glasgow or Greenock call at

Rum weekly, and all supplies can be easily got. By a steam launch the daily steamer between Oban and Skye can be reached at any time, or the train got at Oban or Strome Ferry. The scenery of the island of Rum is magnificent and so unique a property is seldom seen in the market. The rental of the estate is about £2250 and the public burdens are £120.

The Prospectus gives more detail, although its flavour suggests that the author may never have actually visited Rum. Despite occasional lapses of accuracy it does, however, provide an interesting portrait of the island at the end of the Campbell ownership, so is worth quoting at length:

At the head of the Loch stands the Mansion House of Kinloch, built in the last century by Maclean of Coll, who acquired the island from Clanranald. A landing is made at the substantial stone pier built by the late Marquis of Salisbury, who succeeded Maclean by purchase, and spent much of his time and money on improvements in the Island. He was greatly attached to the place, and is believed to have spent about £20,000 in improvements, including building the Pier, forming pony roads round and across the Island in several directions, and in erecting a gigantic breastwork across a ravine for the purpose of uniting in one the current of two streams, to admit Salmon to several lochs in the centre of the island.

Leaving Kinloch House, the glen of that name runs Westward towards the centre of the Island. Down from the left, over the sheer face of the cliff, falls Allt-an-Eassain (or the River of Waterfalls), which, at most seasons, forms a most beautiful cascade – in the drought of summer a thin silver streak, in spring and winter and after rain a foaming sheet of falling spray. About three miles up this glen the watershed is reached where Lord Salisbury formed his Salmon dam. To the North lies, broad and open, Creag nan Steardean, or Kilmory Glen; to the South, that of Harris; while on the Western shore of the island towers 'Bloodstone Hill' (1272 feet) flashing in the sunset, green as an emerald from base to summit, in one smooth face down to the sea.

In fact, Creag nan Steardain is the proper Gaelic name for Bloodstone Hill, not Kilmory Glen. The pamphlet continues:

... Below it lies the Glen of Guirdale, one large and continuous stretch of the finest pasture and a magnificent Corrie for Deer, quite sheltered and evergreen. In contrast to this, Glen Shelister, which lies next to East of Guirdale, is covered throughout with heather, forming part of the best grouse ground. Turning down to the Harris Glen to the South-west, on the left lie the black and rugged cliffs of Pakival (1924 feet) and Tralival, guarding the sides of Harris Valley, at the end of which stand up in bold relief the rugged outlines of Haskeval and Scour-nan-Gilian. This Corrie is full of deer at times, and gives the perfect shelter from all winds. Farther on the left lies Sandy Corrie, another favourite haunt of Deer, with fine pasture, and with its picturesque Loch of Fiadhiennis at the entrance, close in to the side of Ruinnse-val (1606 feet). On the right are Oreval and Ard-Mheall, a Limestone [*sic*] hill covered with finest grass and well sheltered. On its slope lie 'The Ringing Stones of Ardnave', blocks of stone which, whether placed there by man or nature, give out a sonorous metallic ring when struck. If anyone is adventurous enough to try the ascent of Haskeval, he will be rewarded by one of the most beautiful and magnificent views in Scotland ...

There are no crofters on the island, nor have been for upwards of forty years. The Mansion House of Kinloch is well built and substantial. It contains three public rooms, five bedrooms, kitchen, scullery, bath-room and servants' accommodation. It is backed by a clump of well-grown Trees. To the left, and within 50 yards, the Kinloch River flows into Loch Scresort. In front, the Lawn and Flower Garden stretches about 80 yards to the shore of Loch Scresort; and to the right, hidden by a fringe of evergreens, is an early and productive Kitchen Garden. There is a Lodge called the White House, distant about 800 yards, also situated on the shore of Loch Scresort, containing seven apartments, kitchen, scullery, bath-room etc. This house was put in thorough repair about three years ago, with the intention of making it the Shooting Lodge, and has been since used as an overflow house when the guests were too numerous for Kinloch House.

Deer. The Shootings have hitherto been limited to ten Stags and two Hinds, and the effect of this small limit has been to increase the number of Deer. Fifteen Stags at least per season should now be killed. The Deer are well known as being among the heaviest bodied in Scotland, many weighing over 20 stones when gralloched; one killed recently was about 27 stones in weight; unlike all other Island Deer, except those of Arran, they have particularly fine and heavy heads. Several royals were seen last season, and the year before one Royal and two eleven-point Stags were killed. The whole ground is admirably adapted for the stocking and breeding of deer, and there is no doubt that if partially or entirely cleared of sheep it could be made a 60 or 70 Stag Forest, and one of the finest in Scotland for sport. The number of Deer at present is estimated to be about 600.

The Grouse are also rapidly on the increase, especially since the destruction of vermin, which have been systematically poisoned and trapped for the last three years, and from 400 to 500 Brace can be got each Season. There is a fair stock of Partridges, Snipe are very numerous, and in the Winter Season there is first-class Woodcock and Wild Duck shooting. There is also a Small Herd of Fallow Deer. There are no Hares or Rabbits or other four-footed vermin on the Island, but Otters and Seals are plentiful. The shores and cliffs abound with seabirds of every description. Thousands of Cormorants [Shags?], affording excellent sport, are to be seen at all times seated on the ledges of the Sea Cliffs where they breed. Great numbers of Manx Shearwater breed in holes about the top of Haskival and Halival, almost the only place where these birds are known to breed in the British Isles. A pair of Golden Eagles breed every year at Bridianoch, near Bloodstone Hill, and several pairs of Sea Eagles build their eyries on the Cliffs of Papidal and Dibidal.

There are about 30 Lochs on the Island, many of which are full of excellent Trout, running as high as four pounds in weight in some; and in others, where very large baskets of from ten to twelve dozen can easily be made, running about two to the pound. The best of these are Loch an Dornabac, Loch Sgathaig, Mor-and-Beag, Loch Gaìnmhich, Loch Fiadhiennis, Loch Papidal, etc. The last is a most lovely spot at the South end of the Island. Situated within a hundred yards of the Sea, yet completely hidden from it by a rocky ridge, nestling close by its edge, and at the base of the mountain, rising behind for upwards of 2000 feet, is a typical Shepherd's Cottage, with heather-thatched roof ... Large hauls of Sea-trout may at all times be netted.

The island is divided into three large divisions by about 20 miles of galvanised Bessemer steel 6-wire fencing, each hirsel having large reserve enclosures similarly fenced, varying from a half to three square miles in extent. Each Shepherd and Watcher's House has Hay and Potato Ground thoroughly fenced with Deer-proof Fencing. There are also two large enclosures surrounded by Deer-proof fencing near to Kinloch House, intended for planting; and in the centre of the Island there is a large tract of land suitable for planting. About half of the Island is let as a Sheep Farm to a thoroughly practical and enterprising tenant on a nineteen years' lease, of which there are eleven years yet to run. The other half includes all the higher Hills, some of the finest pasture, and the cream of the Deer Stalking Ground, and is in the Proprietor's own hands, partially grazed by a small stock of Sheep. The Farm House and Farm Steading have both been recently thoroughly repaired, and are in all respects suitable. Some new cottages have quite recently been built for a yachtsman and shepherds, of modern design, and prettily situated on the shores of Loch Scresort.

The School-house is used as a Church, where the Parish Minister of Small Isles, who lives in Eigg, holds services, one Sunday each month; and on the intervening Sundays the Resident School Teacher – a Divinity Student – officiates.

The stock of black-faced Sheep on the Island is famed in all the Scotch Markets ... There are no Cattle on the Proprietor's portion of the Island, except those required for the use of the manager and shepherds' families, but the Tenants have a good fold of well-bred West Highland Cattle. Like the Sheep, the Cattle thrive admirably on the Island. There is, on the portion of the Proprietor's occupancy, a herd of over twenty Ponies of the real old Highland Breed, now very rare. These Ponies are particularly suited for use on the Island. The Rum breed of Ponies, like those of Barra, were always famous for endurance, shape and style.

The Steamer *Hebridean* from Glasgow, via Oban and Tobermory, calls every week, summer and winter, with mails, passengers, and goods, and to receive livestock or whatever else may be sent from the Island. As the harbour is safe in all weathers, the communication is uninterrupted, as is frequently not the case at some West Highland ports of call. It is understood that a Post Office is to be established in the Island shortly ...

This was obviously a colourful sales pitch from the London estate agents. An extract from 'The West Coast Fisheries Investigation' in the *Glasgow Herald* (13 October 1886) was more realistic:

The island of Rum is one of the best known at a distance, and one of the least known in reality, of all the group known as the Small Isles. Compact and of quite considerable extent, it is yet of no great commercial value as, while the pasture is sweet and rich where it grows, the island is so mountainous, so precipitous and so covered with heaps of stone that no great stock can be carried ... [With 400 to 500 deer] no better position for a deer forest could be imagined than this wild, rocky island with mountains from 2300 to 2700 feet high, and so rough and precipitous that only the foot of a stag, a goat or a bold hunter would care to attempt them ...

At or near the head of [Loch Scresort] a good pier has been built, behind which the stout yacht of the proprietor lies safely at all times. The loch is well provided with fairly-sized cod, and plaice are numerous and large in winter. Saithe and large lithe were as plentiful here as in the other places we had visited ... but no one taps the resources of the waters around except the farmer or some other of the dilettante occupants.

The report goes on to mention two shepherds in different parts of the island and a few cottages round the quiet mansion house. Twenty-two children attended the mission school and the population, all more or less dependent upon the estate, were Roman Catholic.

We felt how aggravating it must be to the inhabitants to look from the summit of their hills towards a dozen telegraphic stations, to see the steamers speeding north and south, and yet to feel that communication with the outer world was a haphazard thing.

No post, properly speaking, exists and where, unless a small boat can make the neighbouring island of Eigg, letters cannot be ordinarily despatched or received ... There is no shop in the island, no rabbits, no hares and no clergyman! What a tale of negations. Only occasionally does the resident clergyman in Eigg come over to conduct worship, and if the weather is commonly what it has been for these latter months, the schoolmaster from the Free Church mission must be the de facto clergyman of the island.

The sale of the island did attract interest, and among the people looking at the property was the eminent Scottish naturalist John Alexander Harvie-Brown from Dunipace in Stirlingshire. Widely travelled, he knew the Hebrides intimately and was the author of several definitive volumes on the fauna of the Highlands. He had first called at Rum in 1881 aboard his private yawl *Crusader* and he considered it to be 'in the forefront of desirable properties'.

His agent Andrew Forester, who had been advised that it was worth not more than £35,000, thought otherwise:

I have read with much interest your memo as to Rum and I cannot find in it one redeeming feature. Roads bad. Peats ditto. Lochs inaccessible. Rivers spoilt by artificial endeavour to improve on nature. No salmon. Difficulty of access. Climate abominable and generally everything uncomfortable. Ugh, ugh. I wouldn't live on the place tho' you gave me it for nothing ... I hear there was an offer of £70,000 last year for it which was refused. I don't believe a word of it!

The proprietor, Farquhar Campbell of Aros, Mull, died in August 1886 before a sale was effected, so the island fell to a relative, James Hunter Campbell of Ballinaby in Islay. Despite the protestations of his agent, Harvie-Brown was still interested and intended visiting the island the following month. He was told that

Mr Walter Campbell, the son of the laird, goes to Rum from Oban on Tuesday and advises you to take gun, rod and rifle. He proposes taking a small hamper of groceries and bread to the island for himself and if you come, you had better do likewise. Other things can be got on the island.

Whatever the outcome of his expedition, Harvie-Brown decided against purchasing Rum. John Bullough, too, having leased the shooting rights, knew the island well and may have hesitated. Despite a public auction having been announced in *The Times* for 15 June 1886 'at two o'clock precisely' the sale of Rum did not proceed for two more years. Perhaps it was delayed by the death of the proprietor or else interest had been slow.

Finally on 18 May 1888 John Bullough became the proud owner of the Isle of Rum. There seems to be some debate as to how much he had paid. The extraordinary sum of £150,000 has been quoted and we have already seen how offers of £70,000 seem to have been turned down. But it is unlikely that Bullough was required to pay so much and the £35,000 mentioned in other accounts seems nearer the going rate. Indeed it is confirmed by the deed of 'Disposition by James Hunter Campbell in favour of John Bullough', dated 14 May 1888.

In 1886 6000 sheep (which Harvie-Brown reckoned were 1000 too many) were being grazed by a Mr John Ferguson of Bornish, South Uist and Donald Ferguson, Merchant, Lochboisdale at an annual rent of £900. Bullough, however, was more interested in the sporting potential of the island, which was valued at £1000 per annum. Game-books preserved in Kinloch Castle record the first stag shot on Boxing Day 1888 by Bullough's eighteen-year-old son George. The following year workmen were engaged to build a stone shooting lodge at Harris on Rum's south-west shore. An almost identical house was built by the remote Loch Papadil but sadly it is now ruinous. A less substantial shooting box of timber and corrugated iron was erected at Kilmory and only its concrete foundations survive.

Until his death John Bullough corresponded with Harvie-Brown, furnishing him with 'every facility we could desire to investigate the island'. In his *Vertebrate Fauna of Argyll and the Inner Hebrides* Harvie-Brown writes:

> Long famous for the fine Red Deer it carries, fresh introductions [to Rum] have lately been made from Windsor by the proprietor, [including] ten fine young stags, two of which died. He also sends 4 or 5 young deer from his Perthshire estate – Meggernie, Glen Lyon – every year, so that by this infusion of new blood he hopes to get very large stags in a few years. Mr Bullough also states his intention – January 1890 – to send in four more stags this coming year from England. Stags already introduced from the south of England took to the hill in October and proved more than capable of holding their own. They fought with and conquered the native wild stags.

Later in 1890 Bullough writes:

> I send 4 or 5 calves (mostly hinds) every year which I breed from my Meggernie herd. [Rum] yielded 18 stags this season; next year 25 may be got.

In fact, according to the Game Books only four were shot in 1891, perhaps because it was the year that John Bullough himself died.

Twenty-two were shot in 1892. At that time there were still a few fallow deer in Rum which frequented the area around Salisbury's Dam.

Harvie-Brown noted a fair stock of red grouse, boosted from time to time by an introduction of fresh blood from Meggernie and from Yorkshire.

> What is remarkable [commented John Bullough] is how they assume the characteristics of the native birds. One can always get within shot, while in Yorkshire and Meggernie they are so wild that one cannot get near them in winter ... The new blood has done wonders for the grouse. We could kill 600 brace any season now and three years ago the place would with difficulty yield 200 ... I am sending more grouse this year [1890] to the number of 100.

Bullough also introduced other game birds:

> It is interesting to see the pheasants adapting to their new conditions. They have no trees; there is no proper covert and yet they flourish. They roost on the ground in the heather and seem quite at home there. [The following year he added:] One may now see as many as eighteen pheasants at one time. This is a natural increase since we don't breed artificially by hatching eggs under common fowls ... The partridges are healthy and have big broods, but they keep to the coastline. They do not spread over the interior so they will never be plentiful. I am sending more partridges this year [1890].

A Mr Byles, who rented the shootings on Rum before Bullough, had said that a pair of ptarmigan 'had lately been introduced'. Another pair were sent to the island by Bullough in 1888. 'I thought these had died but they have increased and multiplied; a covey of seven was seen a fortnight ago' [November 1890].

Harvie-Brown considered all these introductions to be

> of great interest indeed both to the naturalist of today and to the sportsman of the future. But we trust the experiments will not be carried too far with other species, as even the capabilities of Rum are finite.

In his last communication, dated, 22 November 1890 – little more than three months before his death – John Bullough wrote:

> Last year I planted 80,000 trees; they are doing exceedingly well and in January 1891 we begin planting again at Kinloch, Kilmory and Harris, probably over 500,000. They will embellish the island, and [if they] pay a small interest in twenty years, I am satisfied.

No trees survive from this period, either at Kilmory or Harris, so it is likely that planting was abandoned after Bullough's death.

Bullough continued:

> the new houses for the shepherds are much appreciated by the men,
> being built of stone and slated, with good internal accommodation, hot
> water apparatus and ovens for baking ... It is all very expensive but it
> is a great pleasure to develop the island as it is worthy of it.

These houses were erected at Kinloch, Kilmory, Guirdil and Harris and
some survive almost intact to this day. The Harris bothy is now used as
a byre, the Guirdil cottage has recently been reroofed by the Mountain
Bothies Association while the Kilmory house is currently occupied by the
red deer research team from Cambridge University.

Sadly, John Bullough was only to reap enjoyment on his investment
for three years – the fulfilment, however brief, of a romantic dream, made
all the more worthwhile because he was following in the distinguished
footsteps of Salisbury. On his way home from Monte Carlo Bullough
contracted a lung infection, and died in a London hotel on 25 February
1891 at the age of fifty-three. Thousands of people gathered at the station
when his coffin arrived in Accrington. According to a newspaper report
at the time, of the 1600 people who attended his funeral, 200 were his
own loyal employees. The minister preached how John Bullough had
been 'master of men who made our town what it is', estimating how the
2250 employees at his 'mighty manufactory' represented no less than 1000
homes in Accrington.

Howard & Bullough then became a private limited company, of which
his son George remained Chairman, and later a public company with
capital exceeding three-quarters of a million pounds. It continued to
prosper until the First World War, employing 6000 people, but suffered
during the recession in the 1920s. It survived the Second World War by
manufacturing shells, mines and aviation components. With the cessation
of hostilities it reverted to producing cotton looms and is now known as
Platt Saco Lowell.

For the National Census in April 1891 Mrs Bullough was in residence
at the White House, 'a widow of private means', in the company of her
five-year-old-son Ian (no mention of little Gladys), and several guests
from Fife. Perhaps she lived on at Meggernie until she remarried (a
Lt-Col. John Robert Beech), for it seems to have been to her son Ian that
this highly desirable sporting estate and castle eventually fell heir. George
Bullough, eldest child of her late husband's first marriage, inherited Rum,
surely very much the lesser property and lacking any grand mansion
house.

Despite a veiled request in an earlier poem that his tomb be built on
the banks of the River Lyon, John Bullough was laid to rest in a rock-cut
mausoleum on the lonely shores of Harris in Rum. The entrance was

apparently an octagonal stone-built tower, not unlike the gazebo at Kinloch. The passage running into the cliff behind was lined with enamelled tiles and mosaics. Legend has it that one of Sir George Bullough's less tactful guests was moved to comment how it reminded him of a public lavatory in Waterloo Station. His father's sandstone sarcophagus was moved out soon afterwards and the offensive tomb dynamited. John's body was finally laid to rest in an even more bizarre Grecian-styled mausoleum nearby, where Sir George and his wife were eventually to join him.

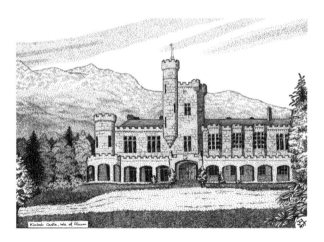

16   *No Utopia*

... a nightmare of an edifice. Into it Sir George and Lady
Bullough crammed the most ponderous and pompous articles of
furniture they could find ... In the plenishing of Kinloch nothing
of Edwardian ostentation, bad taste and sheer vulgarity was
overlooked.

Alasdair Alpin Macgregor, 1972

George Bullough had been born in Accrington on 28 February 1870. He
was educated at Harrow where he fast made a reputation for himself as
a sportsman and horse rider. Apparently at his father's insistence he had
served his time apprenticed to a blacksmith in order to learn the basics of
the family business.

Six foot eight, self-confident, handsome and only five years younger
than his stepmother, it is perhaps not surprising that this precocious
youth should find her an attractive companion. It is said that he had been
despatched on a round-the-world cruise with some friends to prevent any
clandestine relationship developing – though it was also the occasion of
his twenty-first birthday. This cruise could not have been made in the
Rhouma but it probably stimulated him to purchase the yacht four years
later. It was during his travels in 1891 that he learnt of his father's death,
and presumably of his inheritance.

There is little to suggest he was prepared to settle down, however. He
served as a Captain in the Scottish Horse. In addition he owned a 55-ft
sailing yacht called the *Mystery*, which was skippered by John MacAskill.
One account has it that she collided with the local mail boat in a fog and

was badly damaged before sinking in Loch Scresort. Another version was that she was merely broken up for scrap at the pier in Rum by a Glasgow firm and the copper from her hull was salvaged. MacAskill, a powerful but morose man with a beard, had eleven children, all of whom later found employment on the island. One of the four sons, James, was head keeper, two sisters kept the post office while the rest worked in the Castle or its grounds. The vessel had been purchased in February 1890 'with the purpose of establishing a more efficient steamboat service between the island of Rum and the mainland'. Built at Cowes almost thirty years earlier George registered her with the Royal Clyde Yacht Club in 1893.

In 1895, to replace his yacht *Mystery*, Bullough bought a 210-ft steam-screw schooner called the *Maria*. Built two years earlier by Napier, Shanks & Bell of Glasgow, the vessel had a gross registered tonnage of 670.54 tons. With an eye on his Scottish estate he renamed her *Rhouma* – an anglicisation of Rum and approximating to how it is pronounced in Gaelic. She was a twin-decked, single-screw, steel schooner which could be fully rigged with sails that had been made by the same company that, many years before, had supplied Nelson's HMS *Victory*.

In this handsome new yacht George Bullough continued to travel the world with his friends. His photographic albums run to twenty leather-bound volumes and contain now historic images of South Africa, Ceylon, India, Burma, China, Japan, Australia, New Zealand, Honolulu and California. Some of the more macabre prints reveal cruel punishments meted out to Chinese criminals, such as public beheadings by sword. Aboard, Bullough accumulated a bewildering array of expensive Oriental furnishings and souvenirs with which he would later adorn Kinloch Castle.

At the start of the Boer War, the *Rhouma* – at the behest of its owner, with a crew of forty and skippered by Captain Foxworthy – was despatched, in December 1899, to South Africa where she served as a hospital ship. Recruits for the British forces had been enlisted on the outgoing voyage, while 216 wounded men and 46 officers were treated on board until, a year later, the *Rhouma* returned to Britain with recuperating soldiers who were to become the first guests at the now completed Kinloch Castle. This gesture was both magnanimous and patriotic and did not go unnoticed. In October 1900 the Corporation of the City of Cape Town

> do hereby place on record their appreciation of the patriotic services which have been rendered to the Empire by Mr George Bullough, Island of Rum, by Oban, Argyllshire, North Britain, in placing at the disposal of the Imperial Authorities, for a period of upwards of a year, the steam yacht *Rhouma* for use as a recruiting station for soldiers invalided from the Front and for the numerous other actions which he

has taken for the alleviation of the suffering of those injured during the
campaign 1899–1900.

This elaborate and colourful testimonial is hanging in the smoke room
of Kinloch Castle, opposite the Bullough pedigree. That winter the
Rhouma underwent a refit before taking George, his future wife Monica
and a group of friends, to Madeira where he celebrated his thirty-first
birthday. On 10 December 1901, George was knighted, elevating the third
generation 'rags-to-riches' Bulloughs to the upper classes of British society.
He was finally created a baronet on 21 January 1916, reputedly for lending
the government £50,000; even though this is now considered to be the
equivalent of two and a half million pounds, it does seem to be a somewhat
unlikely reason. A coat of arms featured bulls' heads (for Bullough) and
motifs of bees (to represent industry). Sir George was a member of the
Royal Thames Yacht Club, which had been established by those aspiring
sailors who had made their fortune rather than inherited it and were unable
to join the highly prestigious Royal Yacht Squadron.

Merrick Rayner informed me that in 1912 the *Rhouma* was eventually
stripped and sold to the Italian government who renamed her *Giuliana* and
commissioned her as an 'armed yacht' into their Royal Navy. She served
for a year in the Italo-Turkish war with a complement of forty-six men
and four 6 lb guns. With a top speed of 12 knots her increased 934 tons
then consumed 180 tons of coal daily, until she was retired from sevice in
October 1928.

In the decade following his father's death, Sir George must have had
a residence in England but entertained his wealthy sporting friends at
the White House. Commander Frances Cadogan recalled a visit he made
there in 1898, as a thirteen-year-old, accompanied by his parents and a
Mr Hinton who was later to become his stepfather. (Cadogan's father died
in Rum in 1901.) Bullough had met them all in Madeira the year before.
Since the White House was already full the party stayed in the Lodge
at Kilmory where Cadogan shot his first stag, a seven-pointer. He also
remembers seeing a nesting pair of white-tailed sea eagles – 'perhaps the
last place for them to do so in Britain? Are they back?' he wrote to the
Nature Conservancy in June 1960.

The Cadogans returned the following year when the young Francis
and Ian Bullough, George's stepbrother, slept aboard the *Rhouma* but
came ashore for their meals. The two boys enjoyed a week's stalking with
the Head Keeper, John 'Hookey' Ashworth. (The nickname derived from
his youth in Lancashire when he was employed moving bales of cotton
with a hook. There is a loch on Rum which is still referred to today as
'Ashworth's Model Loch'.) Francis shot seven stags and Ian five, using a
single-barrel black powder .450 rifle. On one occasion they each bagged

two stags in the last ten minutes of the day, it not being allowed to fire after 4.30 p.m. because of the failing light. The game books record thirty-two stags shot in 1898 and an unprecedented thirty-eight the following year.

The house party [Cadogan recalled] consisted of Cole (a stockbroker), Costaker (a solicitor), J Homfray (in Welsh coal) and others, and were known as 'the Rum Brigade'. Mitchell was George Bullough's secretary, Jack Brown the Factor, Miss Campbell the housekeeper; I think she was related to the second Mrs Bullough, Ian's mother.

Cadogan returned to stalk deer in 1900, 1904 and 1909, his successes being recorded in the Kinloch Castle game-books. He kindly enclosed a copy of a letter from his stepfather, the forthright Harry Hinton, recounting his experiences on the island, which accurately reflects the type of house party in which the bachelor George delighted:

I met a house full of about ten sportsmen – none of whom I cared for very much except for Herman-Hedge – all the others spent their time sucking up to our host. The dinners were a very tedious matter and we sat round the table drinking until two in the morning. I did this for two nights and then got up and went to bed as soon as dinner was over. I never met such a set of sportsmen and they rarely killed anything. I had never seen a red deer but after the shooting of wild goats on the Desertas [off Madeira] for many years, a stag looked like a haystack to me.

After about a week I asked our host at dinner one night how long it would take to walk right round the island. He replied that he had never done it but his shepherds said it would take about 12 hours. I then said I could do it in much less time. One of the party asked me how long and I said about eight. He bet me a fiver I couldn't do it, which I accepted providing I could chose my day.

The next week I started off after breakfast on a lovely morning to meet a stalker at the halfway house [Harris?] an hour and a half later. He then showed me the route as there was only one sheep track. It came on dense mist and after walking for another one and a half hours I found myself at the halfway house again. Back home I was met with roars of laughter, headed by Cole who won my fiver. I then bet them all that I could do it in four hours ...

I started at 10 a.m. wearing only a pair of knickers, a singlet and a pair of shoes. It was a lovely morning but when I got to the top of the hill it came on to rain so hard that I got drenched. My shorts chafed my legs so much that I could not stop for a rest at the halfway house. The stalker then came on with me but as soon as there was a good road I left him far behind and reached home in under the four hours and won some hundred and twenty pounds. The laugh that night was on the other side although my legs suffered for a day or two! ...

And that is an account of my famous walk round the island. I forgot to say that the castle was being built then and there must have been a hundred workmen there. Most of them had bets on the result and I was met with great cheers when I got home.

Some years later George Bullough's head keeper, James MacAskill, was to break Hinton's record circuit of the island to win himself a considerable sum of money and a gold watch.

It may have been George's wild drinking companions that first suggested changing the spelling of Rum to 'Rhum'! Bullough continued to press for a post office which was duly opened in May 1891. According to James Mackay's *Islands Postal History No. 4* the name of the first postmaster is not known but in 1895 Donald Maclachlan was appointed. Two years later he was replaced by I. [or J.] MacAskill but only for a few months until S. Nash took over. After 1898 Nash received an allowance for taking the mailbags from the pier to the post office. George Bullough then demanded telegraphic facilities and the cable was laid in 1899 by SS *Monarch*. The proprietor then demanded that the island's name be changed and in June 1905 a new date stamp and mail bag seal using the 'Rhum' spelling became operational. (The spelling does, however, appear on a graveslab at Kilmory, dated 1843.)

Just as his parents had wed under 'somewhat romantic circumstances' Sir George's own courtship was not without complications. Details are rather obscure but the lady in question was a divorcee and – as Mrs Monica Charrington, her estranged husband one of the wealthy brewing family – had visited Rum with her father in October 1902. Her divorce was filed the following month citing Sir George as co-respondent and granted on 15 May 1903. On 24 June that same year Sir George married the said Monica Lily, a year his senior and eldest daughter of the fourth Marquis de la Pasture, Gerard Gustavus Ducarel, a French nobleman who could claim descent from Napoleon's sister Caroline, Queen of Naples; the family had fled to England in 1791 and no longer possessed any estate of worth. Perhaps lacking the approval of the bride's family, the marriage could not be an elaborate society event or else it was just that Rum offered a particularly romantic and remote setting. Whatever, the island folk thought it a very grand occasion when the wedding took place in the White House, with Major Hugh Tristram as best man and the Rev. John Sinclair (1825–1908) from the Isle of Eigg officiating. The minister emigrated to Nova Scotia that year, where he died a few years later.

Monica Bullough was regarded as somewhat daring for her day, and it has even been suggested that she formed the model for the oil painting by Galliac of a nude woman on a tiger skin, which still hangs discreetly in a dark corridor of Kinloch Castle. Apparently she was not unduly enthusiastic about Rum nor the sporting life it provided and the late Archie Cameron (one of her estate staff who subsequently wrote a delightful memoir of his time in Rum entitled *Bare Feet and Tackety Boots*) remembers her as more of a socialite, gracious and courteous, always ready for a friendly chat. She regarded Archie's mother, who was a cook in the White House, as a special confidante and as soon as she arrived in Rum for the season would pay her a visit to catch up on the news.

Sir George, too, was friendly enough and would pass the time of day with the estate staff whenever he went up to the farm steading to inspect his ponies. But to Archie he always maintained the rather austere air of a Highland laird, as he strutted around in Rum tweed or a kilt of Mackenzie tartan.

At that time Kinloch Lodge, overrun with rats, had already been demolished and the grand castle of Sir George's dreams was not yet finished. His plans were typically outrageous and ambitious: 'I want a castle as long as my yacht', but this had to be modified since the site he had chosen, between two small burns, did not allow it. The eminent London architects Leeming & Leeming were appointed. The firm had been founded in Halifax twenty-five years earlier and had made a considerable reputation in 1884 designing the Admiralty Buildings on Horse Guards Parade.

Sir George, shown two types of sandstone – one from Rum, the other from Arran 150 miles to the south – opted for the red Arran stone because the local material would not have been easy to work. All materials, including the sandstone blocks already cut to size, had to be brought to the island in puffers, flat-bottomed boats that could beach themselves at low tide to be unloaded. Construction began with a hundred or so masons and craftsmen being imported from Lancashire. Bullough apparently insisted that they all wore kilts, with local tradition adding how the reluctant workforce had to be sweetened with a bonus on top of their wages because of the blood-thirsty midges!

No expense was spared. The two-storeyed building was of a striking castellated design, surrounded by a covered colonnade where Sir George could take his early morning constitutional dryshod. The household was awoken at 8 a.m. by Neil Shaw playing 'Johnnie Cope' on his pipes. Shaw was a steward on the *Rhouma* and rowed ashore every morning to give his recital. The task later passed to Duncan Macnaughton, a stalker who came to Rum in 1918.

The four corners of the building were offset with small turrets which inside provided small dressing rooms for the upstairs bedchambers. Above the main door a large crenellated tower was topped with a tall turret – embellishments which strove to justify its claim to the title 'Kinloch Castle'.

The modest entrance hall, cluttered with antlers as coat hooks, leads to a spacious and impressive wood-panelled main hall, mutely lit in daylight through narrow stained-glass windows. Lion- and tiger-skin rugs litter its parquet floor between Oriental furnishings and grotesque bronzes. Two enormous portraits of Sir George and Lady Bullough painted by H. Riviere in 1909 dominate the hall. Monica Lily sits serene and beautiful to one side of the comfortable fireplace while her husband, in a kilt of Rum tweed, stares down from the first-floor gallery, viewed from the floor below, almost as if he were leaning on the sturdy timber balustrade of the balcony. Beside his portrait stands a seven-foot-high plum-coloured enamel vase, its twin on the opposite balcony outside the small tower bedroom directly over the castle's main door. Above that was the piper's room, accessed from the main stair, eventually leading out to the parapet of the main tower itself.

Along the balcony hang huge oils of the island commissioned from Bryan Cooper in 1900, and a sad row of mounted stags' heads. Three sets of antlers above the fireplace were a family effort: one shot by Sir George, another by Lady Bullough and a third by their only child Hermione 'on the north side against a bright sun'. A dark passage off to the left, with reproduction oils of Stuart kings, leads to the dining room and the kitchens, with the servants' quarters above. The original access for dinner guests was directly from the main hall through a 'secret' room to the right of the fireplace. A few years after the castle's completion, however, this was sealed off, leaving an alcove off the dining room where the piper would sit with a dram, waiting to give the household a post-prandial recital.

The panels of the airy dining room are panelled in lozenges of polished mahogany, large French windows out to the colonnade affording a fine vista across Loch Scresort to the Knoydart hills on the far horizon. Apparently this east-facing aspect to the dining room was not accidental since the evening sun on the west wing might overheat the room and dazzle the seated guests. A stern portrait of the patriarchal John Bullough hangs over the fireplace. On the opposite wall a painting of the *Rhouma* in full steam watches over the dining suite which originally came from her state rooms. The legs of the sixteen heavy mahogany chairs would have been screwed to her deck, the leather-padded seats swivelling to allow easier access.

After the meal the men would retire across the passage to the homely smoke room. Ample leather chairs huddle round the spacious fireplace, above which hangs a portrait of a black-and-tan setter as well as various medals won at Crufts, etc., by Bullough's hounds. Some of the leaded panes in this room ingeniously open both in and out at the same time to act as storm windows and prevent draughts. Otherwise wooden vents above the wood panelling draw away the cigar-tainted atmosphere. A full-size billiard table from Burroughs & Watts in Soho is the main feature of the smoke room but other entertainments on offer were roulette, mah-jong and playing cards.

The ladies withdrew to an elegant, pastel-painted drawing room on the sunny west wing, furnished in Jacobean style with hand-embroidered wall hangings of watered silk. French windows overlook both Loch Scresort and the pyramid peak of Hallival to the south. Next door is a more austere Empire Room with numerous etchings of Napoleon, recalling Lady Bullough's links with the French aristocracy. Doors open on to a stylish patio which formerly had been a conservatory, full of beautiful pot plants and brightly coloured tropical cage birds.

Across the passage from the Empire Room is a sumptuous ballroom, with highly polished sprung floors and a magnificent chandelier of cut glass. Around its panelled walls stand deep-buttoned sofas whose gold silk damask are protected under floral chintz coverings. Sweetmeats would be served through a tiny hatchway in one wall, below a recessed minstrels' gallery.

The south-west corner of Kinloch Castle was formerly George Bullough's work area, with an office and a huge locked safe with its key long since mislaid, and access to the workshops and gunroom. Lady Bullough quickly altered this layout and took over the office as a library to house over 2000 books; the complete works of Dumas, Sir Walter Scott and Tolstoy cheek by jowl with a motley assortment of stiff-backed 'penny-dreadfuls' of the day, richly bound sets of the *Brigade of Guards Magazine*, sporting journals, volumes on military history and the French court. Rather unkindly Derek Cooper observed how 'none of the books reveal even the remotest preoccupation with culture … the kind of ephemera that would have passed a mindless rainy afternoon for the kind of people who assembled in country houses in that carefree time'.

Shattering what would otherwise be the cosy, musty atmosphere of the shady library is a hideous monkey-eating eagle in bronze, glowering through white enamelled eyes from the dark recess of the turret alcove. This formidable creature is in stark contrast to a handsome, life-sized eagle of ivory which once graced the main hall. Each feather had been meticulously carved and screwed into position, a lifetime's work for some Oriental craftsman. It was one of a pair for which Sir George bid against the Emperor of Japan, who then gave his lonely eagle to the Tsar of Russia as a wedding present; it is in the Kremlin Museum. The Rum eagle has since been removed to the National Museum of Scotland in Edinburgh for safe-keeping along with other valuable objets d'art and antiques, including some silver, a set of seventeenth-century Brussels tapestries and a four-poster bed from Lady Bullough's chamber which was reputed to have belonged to Marie-Antoinette.

Lady Bullough's own boudoir was linked to that of her spouse by a private door. His is a more masculine bedchamber, remaining much as it was when he last vacated it, with riding boots by the hearth, their boot trees engraved with his personal monograph. Sir William Bass's and other guest rooms lie at the end of this corridor, from which another dark passage of oak leads into the back wing, directly above the double doors of the courtyard. Tiny windows, black timber beams and bulky four-poster beds combine with wine-red carpeting to present a gloomy almost haunted air. The end room is brightened by a large white wooden screen carved by Grinling Gibbons which came from Wandsworth Palace. From the same source came the skilfully painted wall paintings of cupids which aim their darts at you wherever you stand in the room.

But the highlight of the upper floor of the castle is the bathroom plumbing. One end of each bath is a hooded shower unit, with a bewildering array of brass knobs to direct the spray from almost any angle desired – douche (a deluge from a single opening overhead), wave (a ribbon of water ejected at neck level) or spray (needles of hot water from all directions). From below waste height one may choose plunge (a stream projected at knee height), sitz (a shower from around your feet) or jet (an alarming geyser of water directed between your legs). A mahogany door reveals the full ingenuity of lead plumbing from Shanks of Barrhead, a latter-day jacuzzi to rival any ship's engine room.

The novelty on the ground floor, near the Steinway grand piano, is undoubtedly the orchestrion, manufactured by Imhof & Mukle of Germany. Costing in excess of £2000 in its day, it is essentially an electrically driven barrel organ with serried ranks of tubular or trumpet-shaped pipes, and full percussion – drums, cymbals and triangle. A selection of perforated paper rolls activate quick marches, polkas and popular operettas of the time (such as *The Belle of New York, The Honeysuckle and the Rose* and *Ma Blushin' Rosie*) to more serious works such as *Lohengrin* and the *Ride of the Valkyries*. But it is the *William Tell Overture* which displays the full technology at its most frantic.

There were only ever three or four such instruments produced; one of them is now in the Victoria and Albert Museum, and only the one in Kinloch Castle is in pristine working order. (This is thanks mainly to the dedication of a retired telephone engineer and organ enthusiast from Edinburgh, called Craig Macpherson.) Typically, Sir George irreverently tucked his novel juke-box into a cupboard under the stairs.

The entire castle is lit by electricity, an exciting new innovation when the castle was built. It was generated by a turbine powered via a huge cast-iron pipe, from a reservoir 600 feet above sea-level in Coire Dubh on the slopes of Hallival. Its 110v DC current continued to function until 1983, when a new system was installed to provide 240v AC.

Kinloch Castle was finally completed around 1902. Its first occupants were the wounded officers convalescing after the Boer War, a magnanimous gesture on behalf of Sir George and his fiancée. In spare moments she noted down their reminiscences in a stiff-backed notebook, which is still in the castle library, but the Bulloughs themselves did not move in officially until after their wedding the following year. Even then they used the castle only during the stalking season, for a few weeks every year. This extravagant shooting lodge cost Sir George Bullough over a quarter of a million pounds, a considerable fortune at the turn of the century. Sir John Betjeman pointed out how, in the eighteenth century, a country house should be

> a luxuriant contrast with the rough simplicity of nature outside, and somewhere that was highly coloured in winter when all without was grey with mist and driving rain.

Thus the abominable climate of Rum would have particularly warranted this

> stone embodiment of good King Edward's reign, a living memorial to the stalking, the fishing and the sailing, the tenantry and plenty of the days before 1914 and the collapse of the world.

He praised it as

> an undisturbed example of pre-1914 opulence. Whatever people may think of the taste of their grandparents, at Kinloch Castle will be found nothing plastic or jimcrack. Good money was paid for good workmanship.

The Poet Laureate was as renowned for his delight in old fashion as he was for his distaste of things modern. But he was also writing his article for *Scotland's Magazine* (1959) with the widowed Lady Bullough looking over his shoulder. Clive Aslet was more detached in a recent number of *Country Life* (1984), also displaying an obvious knowledge of antiques:

> The interior furnishings in particular were done to a compellingly high standard, and Kinloch shows with near total completeness the seductively easy, at times sumptuous, look a top-quality London decorator would create for a country house – opulent, informal and richly coloured. Kinloch is a remarkable survival, but it is not an august house.

Alasdair Alpin Macgregor, on the other hand, was never one to mince his words when it came to disapproval – and there was much in the Highlands of which he did not approve! He saw Kinloch Castle as

> a nightmare of an edifice. Into it Sir George and Lady Bullough crammed

the most ponderous and pompous articles of furniture they could find ... In the plenishing of Kinloch nothing of Edwardian ostentation, bad taste and sheer vulgarity was overlooked.

Whatever one's opinion of his castle, no one could disapprove of Sir George's efforts with the surrounding policies. Rich soils were shipped from Ayrshire as the basis for his lavish gardens, rockeries and lawns. A small golf course and bowling green were laid out, even a racquets court. Two hundred yards of heated glasshouses nurtured every fashionable hothouse fruit: grapes, peaches, nectarines and figs. In its heyday Kinloch Castle required forty of a staff, no less than fourteen of them gardeners.

Machinery to heat indoor ponds by the mouth of Kinloch Burn was one of the responsibilities of Dugald Cameron, Archie's father. Turtles were kept more for the amusement of guests than to provide them with exotic soups. One day Sir George accidentally dropped a diamond ring into a tank and it was never recovered; one of the turtles must have swallowed an expensive if indigestible meal! In disgust the turtles were released at sea near the Isle of Canna. Alligators up to three feet in length were kept in a greenhouse, in special cages with bars as thick as a human thumb. One of the estate staff charged with looking after them recalled how, from time to time, they bit their way to freedom and had to be shot 'in case they interfered with the comfort of the guests'.

On the shore, beyond the front lawn with its elaborate fountain, stands a gazebo, empty now but when still glazed it contained a display of spears and shields from Africa, and relics from the Boer War such as empty shell cases. Many rotted away and had to be dumped in Loch Scresort but others were transferred to the castle, to join a collection of bizarre Oriental weapons.

The Bulloughs also possessed two luxurious four-wheeled, horse-drawn carriages with deep blue upholstery and their personal monogram on the doors. They could rarely be used, however, since a pair of horses had difficulty pulling them up the hilly road. Out of season two men were deployed maintaining the roads to Kilmory and Harris so that two Albion cars could transport guests on picnics to Kilmory. On special occasions the local children were bundled aboard with two carts following behind to transport hampers of strawberries, melons, grapes and other treats. The Albions rarely clocked up more than a hundred miles each year. Sir George preferred to walk while Lady Bullough had her own palomino called Pebbles which could pull a trap, always referred to as 'the machine'.

Trees and shrubs from all over the world were planted around the castle which have matured to provide a rich natural haven for wildlife – especially woodland flowers, insects (including midges), songbirds, cuckoos, even nesting herons and a pair of sparrowhawks.

The proprietors, like all those which had gone before, were not averse to trying to improve upon nature, however, more for sporting reasons than aesthetic ones. Frogs and hares were introduced to the island but none survived. A few blackcock were apparently set free but starved, since the trees had not yet established. Partridges persisted for a time around Kilmory and one of the last old cocks in Kinloch did battle with a hawk but died of its wounds. Mallards were reared and pheasants had spread into Kilmory, Shellesder and Kinloch Glens. Around Kinloch they became so much of a nuisance eating the crops that they had to be shot as vermin. Red grouse are the only gamebirds which still survive on the island today although they are no longer numerous. Early last century Rum provided annual grouse bags of several hundred brace, whilst woodcock and snipe provided additional sport over the winter.

Dinghies had been dragged on horse-drawn sledges to several freshwater lochs for the benefit of trout-fishing guests. Both sea and brown trout could be caught in the lochs and burns although numbers declined after 1918. Despite all Lord Salisbury's best efforts in the nineteenth century, salmon have always been rare. Estate staff such as Dugald Cameron, Archie's father, were charged with providing fresh sea fish and lobsters for the Castle kitchens; venison, of course, also figured regularly on the menu.

Sir George took great interest in the quality of his deer in Rum and, according to Kenneth Whitehead in his *Deer of Great Britain and Ireland*, 'by the introduction of park blood and artificial feeding did much to raise the level of an island race of deer'. Between 1925 and 1928, for instance, forty deer from Warnham Park in Sussex were released: nineteen stags and twenty-one hinds.

> The best stalking ground [Whitehead continues] was in the south of the island which is fairly high and rough with many fine corries. The north and north-west beats consist of two glens with grassy slopes which make for easy walking and spying. The ground to the north and north-east is mostly low lying, and not very good stalking ground ... About 1929 a young stag from Rum swam across to the Isle of Eigg, a distance of about 5 miles.

In 1895 there were reckoned to be about 800 red deer in Rum, but by then the fallow deer were probably extinct. As many as forty stags were being shot each season by the turn of the century, fewer thereafter until 1924, when a record fifty were shot. No hinds were ever culled or else were never recorded in the game-books until 1939. Deer numbers had by then increased markedly to an estimated 1700 or 1800, so the annual cull could also increase; 101 stags were shot in 1934 and the head stalker Duncan Macnaughton was presented with a new telescope to mark the event. Hundreds died during the hard winter of 1941.

Harvie-Brown had noted how the sheep were also being improved by importing good quality rams. In 1895 the grazings were let to a Mr Mackay, who ran some 3000 head together with a herd of Highland cattle; there were also a few dairy cows. Shepherds and their families lived at Kilmory, Guirdil, Harris and sometimes Dibidil. The farm manager and head shepherd, with an assistant or two, stayed at Kinloch. Several fields of Kinloch Farm were cultivated for seeds, oats and potatoes, with hay gathered in for the livestock. A few pigs were also kept from time to time.

In addition to Kinloch Castle Sir George also had a house in Hertfordshire called Bishopwood where, in 1908, he became Master of the Ledbury Hounds. Twenty-four noisy black and tan hounds were kept on Rum and had to be exercised every morning. Occasional fox hounds and beagles from the south accompanied the Bullough shooting parties 'on holiday'. Estate staff were not allowed to keep pet dogs or cats.

Another property, Warren Hill in Moulton near Newmarket, allowed Sir George to indulge in his passion for racing. He owned two studs and raced with some success, winning the 'War' Grand National in 1917 with Ballymacad and the 1000 Guineas in 1934 with Campanula. On 24 June 1922 the magazine *Sport Pictures* carried the headline 'Sir George Bullough's Golden Ascot' when Golden Myth won the Gold Cup and the Gold Vase. An ex-Cavalry officer, he was a member of the Jockey Club and the National Hunt Committee.

He took particular pride in the Highland garrons that have survived in Rum for hundreds of years. The blood line had almost died out by 1888 but John Bullough re-established the stud with a stallion named Skye and two mares (Fanny and Dolly) from the New Forest. At various times George Bullough despatched some of his mares to be served by one of Lord Arthur Cecil's Highland pony stallions, which still represented the old Rum strain. He also purchased appropriate stallions including Claymore from Strathaird and Rory o' the Hills, even a pure-bred white Arab, policies which won him first prize at one of the Highland shows. Most of the year the ponies ranged free but were gathered in once a year so that surplus could be selected for sale in Oban; ponies which had already been broken in fetched higher prices. The prime function of the stocky Rum ponies was to carry deer carcasses off the hill during the stalking season.

With the completion of Kinloch Castle Sir George's shooting parties became more organised and even more exclusive. They usually brought personal servants from the south, including a French chef. Nigh on a hundred men, women and children lived on the island throughout the year to maintain the services – housekeepers, handymen, boatmen, gillies, gamekeepers and gardeners – under the watchful eye, and all too often the thumb, of a Factor. In his autocratic position this lonely figure frequently made himself distinctly unpopular. 'It was no Utopia,' said Archie Cameron in his extremely entertaining book, and the islanders often had their own differences as could be expected where there is a confined mass of humanity; but they were, by and large, a happy lot in congenial surroundings, doing work they enjoyed.

Archie was one of seven children. His father Dugald was from Acharacle in Moidart, and had first worked as a galley boy aboard a ship, and then as a cattle drover. He came to work in Rum when he was nineteen and lived there for forty-six years. There he met and married his wife Annie, from Tolsta in Lewis. In contrast to her staunch Prebyterianism, Dugald was a very out-going character, ever ready with an amusing story or a Gaelic song and would readily turn his hand to anything that needed doing about the island. As ferryman he had to rise at 3 a.m. to meet the steamer on its way back to Oban from Canna. Once he even had to row across to Eigg to retrieve his daughter, marooned there on her way back from Oban High School.

The gentry seldom ventured beyond the confines of the castle policies to mingle with the islanders; the gentlemen only when stalking or fishing, and the ladies hardly at all.

The whole setup within the barrier [Archie Cameron recalled] resembled a beehive with the Queen Bee and her attendants sacrosanct within, the workers humming and buzzing about continually while we, in the lower echelon scurried hither and thither ensuring that the inner sanctum was secure and provided for.

We would sometimes catch a glimpse of the maids, temporarily relieved of their duties, lingering about the massive white gates making vain attempts to defend themselves from the ubiquitious and savage midges ... If any of the other occupants did venture out we, the workers, were obliged, even expected, to scurry into whatever refuge we could find until the entourage had passed. If we were not smart enough and an unexpected encounter did take place, Lady Bullough was always very friendly and gracious, and would stop and have a short chat with us ...

During the social events such as picnics, Highland Games and school prize-givings, when the White Gates and the policies were open to everybody, socialising and fraternising were the order of the day and we all mixed freely, gentry and commoner alike. These were days to be remembered and talked about for a long time. Meeting outside the White Gates again we reverted to our proper status, realising that the party was over, we tied up our hair and showed due respect to the gentry. We did not resent this and accepted THEM as ethereal from another world.

Whenever Sir George arrived with his sporting friends, newcomers had to demonstrate their proficiency with a rifle on an iron cut-out of a stag just outside the policies. Even then some of them proved quite a liability for the stalker who might have to chase a badly wounded beast until darkness, and then resume the pursuit next morning. After a successful first kill tradition demanded that the shooter was 'blooded' by having a fistful of congealed stag's blood dashed in his face. Nor were the ladies exempted but they were usually more concerned for their new tweeds than the gore dripping from their chins.

After a really successful day three stags might be carried back to Kinloch, one per pony. 'The arrival of the ponies carrying the carcasses was always a welcome sight to us young followers,' recalled Archie Cameron.

> We hung around savouring the aroma of hot leather saddles, sweating horses and the smell of the deer themselves which, of course, meant venison – our main diet in the stalking season and salted or dried for the winter ... After a quick bite the gillies commenced their work, which often carried them late into the night ... There was no electricity at the kennels where the skinning and dressing was carried out ... The carcasses prepared and hung, the whole place was then hosed down and we youngsters were sent off, carrying home a stag's liver. The gillies would then make their way to the gunroom at the castle to enjoy a well-earned jolly evening, to relate and regale each other with tales ... Beer was on tap and the supply was lavish ...

The gentry meantime had repaired to the castle for a hot bath and dinner.

> After the port and cigars had done their rounds and the day's activities recounted, the gentlemen would join the ladies and make their way to the ballroom to dance the night out under the heavenly blue ceiling with its astral decoration, to the sound of the electric organ.

Hermione Bullough, the couple's only child, had been born on 5 November 1906 and instructions were sent from England for the gamekeeper in Rum, Calum Sinclair, to collect a bottle of water from the waterfall in Coire nan Grunnd, so that the Rev. J. Sinclair (who had originally married the couple) could take it south for the baptism. Archie Cameron remembered her as a tall but delicate-looking girl. A white nanny goat was brought to Rum in the hope that its milk would benefit Hermione's constitution. The little girl accompanied her mother on walks around the policies and repeating her every word and gesture, perhaps as a training for her future social life. The goat was ultimately turned loose in Harris Glen to fraternise with its own kind, creatures which went feral after the island was cleared a hundred years earlier.

Calum Sinclair had been a shepherd at Meggernie until Sir George offered the job as stalker in Rum. During the winter, while the Bulloughs were in the south, he used to take his meals in the castle kitchen. One day he was joined by a shepherd, fresh off the steamer from Tobermory and well in his cups. The maid set a place for him but the shepherd had to ask Calum what the two spoons were for. 'Wheesht,' joked Calum, 'don't let on your ignorance. When you get the soup you fill the big spoon with the little spoon.' This he duly did, much to the hilarity of the kitchen staff! Calum Sinclair left Rum for Sunart in 1910 but is remembered to this day by 'Malcolm's Bridge' on the road to Harris.

The *Rhouma* had been sold in 1912 but two smaller boats were purchased, one called the *Triton* (later renamed *Rhouma II*) and the *Saonara*. The *Triton* was 147½ ft long and 337 gross registered tonnage, built of steel as a twin-screw sloop by the Ailsa shipyard in Troon in 1902 and formerly owned by James Coates, the cotton magnate. Sir George had little time to enjoy her since the First World War broke out and the *Rhouma II* was requisitioned for five years and armed with a 6 lb cannon and a 6 lb anti-aircraft gun. Sir George sold her after the war in 1919 to Vincent Grech of London, who sold her on in 1924 to Oswald Liddell, who renamed her *Osprey*. A later owner reinstated her name to *Rhouma* until she became the *Hiniesta* in 1939 under Sir Frederick Preston, who gave her to the Second World War effort as a calibrating vessel before selling her on, with several other name changes: *President Roberts, Hiniesta* again and finally *Madiz*. Flying the Panamanian flag she ended her days as a charter vessel in the Mediterranean until ultimately scrapped at a venerable age of seventy-three in October 1975. In addition, between 1903 and 1908 the Rum estate had been running a 43-ft, 18-ton wood screw steamer built in Greenock and called *Kinloch*. This was sold and replaced by a 1904 Lowestoft fishing boat, an 80-ft, 64-ton wood screw ketch, called *Magnificent* which Sir George renamed *Kinloch II* and kept for eleven years.

There is a painting in Kinloch Castle of a large four-masted merchant ship under full sail with the name *Kinloch Castle* on her bow; but there is no record that such a ship ever existed and, according to George Randall, it seems to have been a flight of pure fantasy on Sir George's part. While on the subject of ships it is worth recording, too, that an 823-ton Norwegian barque, *Midas*, was wrecked in severe gales near Kilmory on 27 December 1896, while *en route* from Londonderry to the USA. Furthermore a drifter, *Bounteous*, ran aground on the north shore of Rum on 4 December 1917. There seems to be no record of the vessel (or vessels) that came to grief at Wreck Bay and Schooner Point, although Archie Cameron recollects one incident where the crew made it back to Kinloch, leaving their vessel reduced to matchwood in Wreck Bay.

When a shooting party wished to stay at Papadil Lodge they were taken round on the estate boat. The servants meanwhile had gone on ahead by pony to open up the house and light fires. New shepherd families at

Guirdil were also installed using the boat. George Macnaughton, the son of the stalker Duncan, remembered when one unlucky family and their belongings could only be landed on a rock; they were told they would be able to get ashore when the tide went out.

On the outbreak of the First World War Sir George became a major supervising the Remount Department. In preparation for the war the Albions and horse carriages were packed away under dust sheets. All the young men in Rum were mustered and given riding lessons on the ponies. 'They then disappeared like a cloud of midges in a breeze', commented Archie Cameron, 'to display in the mud of Flanders what they had learned from a quick canter round the castle on Rum. Most are still in Flanders.' The gardeners never came back and a skeleton staff of boys too young for the war, including young Archie – in his own words 'employed just to feed the midges' – were supposed to maintain the gardens until, eventually, they slid into a wilderness of weeds and broken glass. Duncan Macnaughton, the stalker, survived the hostilities to return and caretake the island as a much-respected Factor. Britain was never to be the same again. The Great Depression struck during the 1920s and the Bulloughs' finances, and therefore their interest in Rum, gradually waned. Any visits the family made had to be by private charter or by mailboat from Oban.

In 1932 Hermione Bullough married the fifth Earl of Durham – a 46-year-old widower – and both continued to visit Rum for the stalking. Captain the Honourable Claude Lambton recorded the stags he shot between 1935 and 1938 in the Kinloch Castle game-books. The Countess of Durham herself shot a stag in 1936. Her son John (born 1932) was often left on the island with Duncan Macnaughton in the hope that he would become interested enough to take up where his grandfather had left off, but to no avail. He celebrated his twenty-first birthday in the ballroom of Kinloch Castle just before the island was sold to the Nature Conservancy. Hermione herself died in 1992.

Sir George, aged sixty-nine, died of heart failure while out playing golf near Boulogne in July 1939 and Rum passed into the hands of trustees. His funeral took place at Moulton near Newmarket where the immediate mourners were his widow, the Earl and Countess of Durham, Mrs Young (Sir George's sister) and her husband, and the Marquis de la Pasture – presumably by this time Lady Bullough's brother rather than her father. Bullough left a gross estate of £710,037 with net personalty of £661,679. To his widow were left £25,000, his horses, stables, furniture, motor cars, farming stock, yachts, boats, household and personal effects,

> feeling sure but without creating any Trust in the matter, that she will carry out any wishes informally expressed to him with regard to friends and servants.

The residue of his property was left in trust for his wife for life,

> with remainder to his daughter Hermione, Countess of Durham, with remainder to her husband and children as she may appoint, or to her children in equal shares.

His body was taken to Rum for interment in a huge granite sarcophagus in the family mausoleum at Harris. A place was reserved for his wife although she was to outlive him by nearly thirty years. She stayed on at Newmarket, only occasionally visiting Rum with small shooting parties, even as late as 1954 when, at eighty-five, she valiantly drove her old Austin to Harris to pay her respects to her late husband. The next time she made that journey was one cold and stormy day in early June 1967, to her last resting place in the Rum mausoleum, having died in London on 22 May at the age of ninety-eight. Her coffin had to make the bumpy ride to the Harris mausoleum in the back of a long wheel-base Land Rover, since the road no longer allowed the passage of a more salubrious vehicle. The mourners accompanying it, together with staff of the Nature Conservancy who by then owned the island, got very wet and cold. The island – if not the weather – had changed much since Lady Bullough first came there nearly seventy years ago.

> There they rest [concluded Derek Cooper] incongruous in death as they most assuredly were in life. The opulent richness of Kinloch Castle, the cigar smoke and the champagne, was as out of place in Rum as indeed it might have been if set down in the slums of Accrington from whence the wealth came to sustain this Hebridean mirage.

Perhaps the last word is more appropriate to Archie Cameron, who himself died only a few years ago:

> All that is gone now. There is no more dancing in the ballroom ... The electric organ is silent, no longer required for dancing but occasionally set in motion for the amusement of tourists ... The castle is now open to boarders who rampage through what was at one time to us sacred ... I don't intend to get involved in discussion about the rights and wrongs of big estates. Really that is quite pointless, since there are so few of them left. But this I know: the estate of Rum employed about a hundred people, and they were better off there than they would have been almost anywhere else. Of course it was a patriarchal and even tyrannical society in which we grew up, but I would rather have grown up there, with all the freedom and beauty of the island, than in some Gorbals slum.

17 *How Strange a Cycle*

How strange a cycle. Uninhabited originally save by wild animals,
it became at an early age the home of men ... The island lost all its
inhabitants on a wool and mutton speculation. And now yet another
change was on the eve of ensuing, and the island was to return to
its original state, as a home of wild animals ...

Hugh Miller, 1845

In 1872 only Eigg, amongst all the Small Isles, boasted a parish school,
which had been established nearly a century previously. After the efforts
of the SSPCK some of the proprietors chose to finance schooling for
their tenants themselves, with intermittent assistance from the Free
Church or the Gaelic Schools Society. In Rum Lord Salisbury wanted no
truck with the Free Church so ran the school from his own pocket, but
this arrangement lapsed once the island was sold in 1870.

The Education Act (Scotland) of 1872 made schooling compulsory for
children aged from five to thirteen. It also attempted to bring some sort
of system to bear on a complex assortment of schools which were being
run by private landowners: the Church of Scotland, the Free Church, the
United Free, the Roman Catholic Church, or the Episcopalian. However,
the non-sectarian, publicly financed institutions the Act advocated were
slow to reach the remoter outposts of the Kingdom, and were to be run
by locally elected School Boards through a Scotch Education Department
based in London.

The Small Isles parish was fortunate to enjoy the tireless efforts of its
then minister, the Rev. John Sinclair. The first School Board foundered

by 1875 but the Rev. Sinclair served as the new Chairman from 1876 (until his death in 1908, attending no less than 158 of its 161 meetings in that period). Under threat of legal proceedings, the School Board finally coerced Norman Macleod of Orbost, Captain Campbell's tenant in Rum, to begin paying school rates in 1876. Previous to this Campbell seems to have shown no interest in the education of the island children, despite the presence of Salisbury's old schoolhouse at Kinloch. MacNeill agreed to provide a site for a school building on Canna. Together with Captain Swinburne of Muck, these island proprietors were asked to serve on the School Board but not one of them attended any of the meetings. Teachers were finally installed in both Canna and Muck by 1877 but Rum remained a problem.

The Muck teacher, Colin Campbell from Jura, had three-quarters of his £40 annual salary paid by the SSPCK and was expected to spend three months of his year teaching in Rum. But this was far from satisfactory, with few children being taught and 'want of order being maintained'. There was a lack of accommodation in Rum and the School Board approached the proprietor and tenant 'with a view to lodging the teacher for 6 months in the year at Kinloch to which parents might send their children in the summer months'. Eventually the island Factor replied that 'the present practice of itinerating among the families of the island was preferable'. By April 1880 Captain Campbell was prepared to pay the teacher's accommodation as he travelled between Kinloch, Kilmory and Harris.

That summer a student from New College taught at Kinloch under the sponsorship of the Free Church Ladies Association. The remit of this august body was to encourage schools to be set up in neglected localities, to be taught – invariably through the medium of Gaelic – from April through summer and autumn by students from the Highlands who, during the winter should attend college in the south. Although the Society had long passed its peak of effectiveness, with schools functioning in 133 different localities, it still supported a few after the Parochial School Boards were instituted. The Free Church provided a teacher in Rum for a whole year, at a cost to the School Board of £20 per annum, and William Henry MacDougall was appointed. In 1881 nineteen-year-old Andrew Nicolson from Colinton in Edinburgh is mentioned in the census as teacher substitute, presumably while MacDougall was attending college. MacDougall was the teacher whom 'the Limping Pilgrim' Edwin Waugh met in 1882.

But the Rum teacher possessed no actual qualifications and had to take his scholars to Eigg for annual inspection. His teaching was deemed to be 'very indifferent' and the School Board justified his continued employment to the Education Department thus:

How very peculiar the condition of the island is, how difficult to secure a certificated teacher or a pupil teacher for such an insular and sparse population.

By October 1883 the proprietor in Rum was building several cottages at Kinloch, including one for the teacher which would serve 'to accommodate those pupils who are a long distance from Kinloch' and the School Board promised to pay a reasonable rent for the use of such a building. Presumably this was the long, roomy cottage, now referred to as Foxglove, above the present school and schoolhouse. The post of permanent teacher was advertised several times, with 'Gaelic and Psalmody a recommendation'. Only when this was excluded from the remit were any applications received, but both young ladies declined the post, one because of the expense in shipping her luggage to the island. So the existing arrangement had to continue for a further four years.

Finally, in October 1889, seventeen years after the Education Act had come into force, Mr James Robertson, an Aberdonian, moved from Oban to take up the position as the island's first permanent and fully certificated teacher. He alternated his efforts between Kinloch and Kilmory, but since neither school met the statutory number of openings the Kilmory children came to be boarded out at Kinloch. Robertson was sixty-eight and lived in Rum with his sister; he was dismissed in 1893. His successor, Miss Helen Stewart, stayed only a year, and a Miss Macfee nearly three years. In May 1897 Miss Janet Cameron was appointed but soon a motion was before the School Board 'in connection with the Rum teacher'. By the end of the following year two island families, the Camerons and the Mackinnons, had withdrawn their children from the school. In the spring the School Board had to concede:

> that the state of education under the present teacher, Miss Cameron, so far as the feelings of the people of Rum are concerned, is not conducive to progress or harmony.

They declined to dismiss her even though she had become – it may be through inadvertence – 'obnoxious to the majority'. By the end of 1899 Miss Cameron agreed to quit the island if a suitable post was found for her on the mainland but no action was taken for a further two years. By February 1902 the School Board finally accepted that the islanders' complaints were well founded and resolved to dismiss Miss Cameron. Although a new teacher, Miss Macrae, was appointed in November, she could not begin teaching until Miss Cameron vacated the schoolhouse and yielded up both the school log-book and register. Solicitors finally resolved the deadlock in March 1903 but the School Board were faced with a bill for fifteen weeks' lodgings at Kinloch for their new incumbent. In August they discovered that 'Miss Janet Cameron, late teacher of the school at Rum, is now an inmate of an asylum owing to insanity'. Whether this was the root cause of her problem in Rum, or brought on by it, is not clear.

As soon as Miss Macrae resigned in December 1903, the proprietor of Rum, Sir George Bullough, expressed a desire to take the matter of schooling 'under his full control'. He offered to build a new schoolhouse – presumably the present church-cum-school – and wished to deal directly with the Education Department rather than the School Board. This seems strange since it was only a matter of months after the indefatigable Chairman of the School Board, the Rev. Sinclair, had officiated at Sir George's wedding in Rum.

Mr Keil was appointed as interim teacher until, in March 1904, the School Board transferred 'either wholly or in part, the school of Rum to the proprietor of the island, provided a legally qualified teacher be employed'. Miss Gaw took up the position in August and the Rum school passed into private hands; this unprecedented move reflects both the determination of the island's domineering owner and the relief of the School Board in getting shot of the Rum school and its associated problems. After the Rev. Sinclair died in 1908 the School Board lost its prime driving force. Mr Thomson, owner of Eigg and Muck, took his place until he died in 1913 when Mr Allan Thom of Canna was elected instead.

In fact, Bullough failed to run his school any better than the Board. He appointed Mr Peter Jopp (who had once been turned down for the post by the School Board) as his first teacher in Rum. Bullough had more success with Miss MacNab and Miss Margaret Forgan, as we learn below from Archie Cameron's reminiscences. In October 1915 Bullough relinquished control again, school and cottage (Foxglove) 'for all time coming free of rent'. Like the Salisbury structure which preceded it, Bullough's school also functioned – as it still does today – as the island church. A partition, installed in 1959, can be moved across to divide the interior into two separate rooms. The church pews are removable but the impressive pulpit is a permanent fixture. Like all schools of its day, the windows are set high in the walls (to discourage daydreaming) and without colourful decorations by the pupils the interior would be rather austere. But at least the toilets are indoors.

Archie Cameron vividly recalled his schooldays there around 1913:

> Miss Forgan was a real darling who, after administering a dose of the strap, would hold the recipient back at closing time. She then took him or her up to her cottage where she handed out a big slab of delicious, homemade tablet, sometimes with an apologetic kiss on the cheek.

Prim little Miss Macnab was another favourite of Archie's while some of her replacements were particularly friendly and easy-going. He recalled:

One so much so that she went off on holiday and returned a lot slimmer than when she left. Well, who can blame the girl. Entertainment was almost non-existent, and the occasional visit of a Naval patrol boat was an event to be taken advantage of!

Another successor was quite a likeable man but his wife had to stand in when he himself was the worse for drink. On our way to school we would sometimes meet this unfortunate man, unshaven and collarless, making his round of the village begging drink.

This tragic figure was replaced by another alcoholic who lived alone with his addiction and his faithful Sheltie dog. A friendly, helpless and lonely man when sober, Archie remembered him as 'a fiendish genius', he would appear in school wearing large tackety boots and knickerbockers, which only helped to emphasise his diminutive stature. His shirt was usually smeared with brose, egg yolk and blood from his attempts to shave. Armed with a pointer, Archie recalled:

> he would leer at us, his large hooked nose quivering with venom, beneath his piggy eyes. He would approach me with an evil grimace, crook his finger and snarl in his Aberdeen accent, 'Come in aboot, Erchie, come in aboot.' In this state, my mind and brain were completely immobilised and blank, and I was consequently unable to feel any pain as I was furiously assaulted, bounced off desks and beaten with the pointer. At last I was hurled to my seat, my collar and jacket torn ... The 'ringmaster' would be foaming at the mouth and collapse into his seat completely exhausted, while with my sleeve I would remove most of his spittle from my face ... Meanwhile he would sit there, making little gasping sounds as he tried to regain his breath and recharge his batteries for the assault on his next victim.

The memories and imagination of a schoolboy may be running into excesses here. An entry in the school log-books, dated November 1913, noted that 'two of the older boys were inclined to disorder' – perhaps one of them was Archie, mischievous even into old age. These irregular diaries were kept by the teacher, with quarterly assessments of the class by school inspectors. Some of the entries were incidental; in 1914, for instance, 'the children were naturally excited by the war' and several were delegated to knit socks for the soldiers. At intervals the school roll was mentioned; in September 1913, for example, there were twenty-two pupils but usually some were absent due to illness. One teacher complained that progress in class was made more difficult if the children arrived cold and wet during a storm. Another entry ungraciously recorded how 'the stupid children remain stupid, generally speaking they are lazy'. And again:

> a certain number of children have the greatest objection in learning

lessons at home or indeed in school either. I expect the atmosphere of home is not conducive to study, and in school the number of different classes prevent proper supervision on the part of the teacher.

Most of the derogatory comments in the log-books emanate from one particularly unpopular Factor, who regularly inspected the pupils as a representative of the School Board and rarely saw eye to eye with the incumbent schoolmaster. Mr John Johnston was appointed in January 1916, at a salary of £80 per annum, with £7 to his wife to take sewing classes and to clean the school. In February 1917, he is on record as falling foul of the Factor, Mr Brebner, who was inspecting the school for the Board:

> time keeping very bad … found children away from home for dinner at 11.45 am. Mr Johnston (since I wrote the above) has come in and shows me his watch which is 15 minutes ahead of Post Office time.

Two days later Johnston announced:

> leaving here today to take up duties in Eigg Public School. Mrs Johnston takes charge of school till another teacher is appointed. Regarding above entry as to correct time, Post Office people admit time very unreliable.

Even after the resignation of Johnston, the Rum Factor persisted. On his next visit to the school on 13 April he added:

> With regard to Mr Johnston's remarks about my entry on 26th February, even allowing for his time being correct the children were out of school twenty to twenty-five minutes before time, as was admitted by him on the 28th February. This practice was very common which was the reason for my entering it in the logbook.

Mrs Johnston presided over the Rum school while the Board advertised for a new teacher. They had two refusals and eventually Johnston had to come over from Eigg in his own boat to retrieve his wife and her belongings. This move greatly annoyed the School Board and Miss Sarah Campbell had to be brought over from Muck as interim teacher, until Miss Johann Munro was appointed in January 1917. Mr Johnston is still remembered with affection on Eigg as *An Sgoilear Ban*. And the School Board must have had a high opinion of his capabilities as a teacher because, as the only fully qualified teacher in their parish, they won full exemption for him from military service in the First World War. He finally left Eigg in 1923, transferring to Bracora on the mainland, his boat beached and decaying at the head of Loch Morar until quite recently.

In 1919 the Small Isles School Board became part of the Glenelg, Arisaig, Moidart and Small Isles School Management Committee. Schooling did improve in the Small Isles as a result. Although the powers of the new

Committee were less than the old School Board, it had more resources available and was better able to install relief teachers. Mr Brebner was again delegated to check the registers of the Rum school; an important task, for one teacher on Eigg was dismissed for falsifying them. Soon he was sniping at another teacher:

> Her first entry criticises the English grammar of the pupils. Her own grammar as used throughout the Log would appear to indicate that she was incapable of judging it.

According to the log-books, schoolwork was surprisingly varied considering the isolation. Lady Bullough sometimes contributed sewing materials for the girls, while Mr Johnston taught navigation to the boys. Physical exercise had to be performed outside but 'although the children enjoy it, because of persistent bad weather, they are on the whole ignorant of the least elementary things in connection with the subject'. The pupils were also very interested in nature study, but in winter the three Rs adhered to a more rigorous timetable: 'beginning work at 9.30 am and finishing at 3.30 in order to get the full benefit of the light'. Elsewhere we read 'winter weather having set in, the children are just allowed half an hour at dinnertime and thus they are able to get away at 3.30 instead of 4 pm'.

Absenteeism was a constant problem, not just because of ill health or bad weather – 'one boy was absent two days this week. Excuse given that he was watching cows'. Some pupils were deemed hopeless cases:

> Attendance broken today [12 September 1941] by the absence of one girl who, as far as I can see, should make a very determined effort to come to school regularly in order to assimilate even a small fraction of the knowledge she should have assimilated years ago ... She is amazing in her inability to comprehend even the simplest thing asked her ... A most difficult and exacting pupil.

On the whole, however, with a small roll and such individual attention, the level of education imparted by the island school was commendable. In November 1916 an inspector observed how:

> this school has made marked progress in all branches since the last visit ... The older children are distinctly intelligent and show to much advantage under examination.

In September 1929 another visitor found:

> a pleasant little school of five pupils. The children speak out with confidence, and read and answer readily, distinctly and accurately. The various subjects receive their due attention; the geography of the oldest boy was unusually good.

Some pupils were able to make exceptional progress but unfortunately not all were able to take advantage of it. On 31 August 1938:

> Jean Mitchell, who was awarded a county bursary, is back at this school again as her parents were unable to find lodgings for her, within their means, in Fort William where she was to attend the secondary school.

Responsible for nearly thirty schools in remote and inaccessible localities, the School Management Committee introduced a system of 'side schools' in 1918. In Rum, for instance, children of outposted shepherds, and who were too young to board in Kinloch, would not have received any education at all were it not for side schools. Scholars, ready to leave the Rum school and not yet in employment or in attendance at a secondary school on the mainland, were appointed as pupil teachers; Katie Macrae, Angus Thwaite, Marion Ferguson and Chrisannie Mackinnon were taken on in Rum. They visited the cottages at Harris or Guirdil week about, where they lodged with the family during the week and taught the infants. Getting there was not always an easy task as the young Guirdil teacher's entry for 8 November 1918 indicated: 'unable to proceed here on Monday owing to severe weather conditions and the state of the hill footpath'. The class was opened the following day, however, and time made up after hours. This particular shepherd family left the island in May 1919 and the Guirdil side school closed.

The family at Harris left a year later but were immediately replaced so that by June 1920:

> Reopened school here on 7th inst. and found pupils to consist of two boys aged, respectively, slightly over five, and six and a half years. Found pupils to possess Gaelic language solely and to have received no previous schooling. Immediately started instruction in first simple rudiments of knowledge.

The main school at Kinloch supplied textbooks, jotters, slates and pencils, and the headmaster or headmistress occasionally hiked over to check up on things. In May 1921 Mrs Mary Macrae discovered serious irregularities and had to dismiss the young itinerant teacher. She reported:

> closed school until further notice. Entries for Monday 2nd and Monday 9th are false, as the teacher had not opened the school on these dates!

In May 1926 the side school had to close for good 'as a result of the children leaving the place'.

In 1923 the Rum school produced the Small Isles' first bursary success when Mary MacInnes was able to attend secondary school on the mainland. Others were to follow. In 1930 Inverness County Council assumed the running of local schools. The post of parish minister, based on Eigg, was abandoned in 1945, being replaced until 1982 by a part-time missionary; the last resident priest left in 1952.

The school at Kinloch had to close on 25 May 1945 when its last two pupils departed the island, not to reopen again until November 1956 with a roll of six. Although the castle had been provided with DC electricity from an innovative hydro scheme installed at the beginning of the century, this facility was not extended to the school – situated at the far end of the village – until January 1958, soon after the Nature Conservancy had bought the island. The new owners even erected a temporary electric fence around the school flower border to keep the deer out! The plumbing was upgraded, a new wash-hand basin was fitted and the old fireplace was replaced by a stove; this finally expired in April 1973 and gas heaters were installed. These in turn had to be renewed again in 1982 when carpeting was also laid over the wooden floor. By this time the school curriculum was rich and varied, with such educational aids as television, video and computer. The children either took packed lunches or else returned home for their midday meal. Sometimes on a wet day they were given a lift in one of the estate vehicles; otherwise they walked since bicycle tyres did not stand up very well on the rough road.

The school roll had peaked in May 1958 with fifteen pupils but thereafter hovered between six and eleven – though not always with an even sex ratio. For a short time in 1977, when only four families were living on the island, the school had only one pupil. Scottish Natural Heritage (SNH) likes to encourage young families with children but again, in 1991, with only one of several island children old enough to attend school the continued existence of the school became precarious. Otherwise SNH strive to maintain six or eight families in Rum, a population of some 30–40 people. Only the school-teacher is employed outwith the organisation, by the Education Authority, which itself transferred from the County Council to Highland Region in 1976. Nearly all of the teachers have been women (one of them, Mrs Mabel Maclean, later, as Mrs Anderson, taught me for two years, 1957–8, in the Central School, Inverness) and few stay longer than two years; in 1933 one lady lasted only three days. The longest spells have been five, six and eight years. A new schoolhouse, a Dorran bungalow, was erected beside the school in the 1960s.

When John Bullough bought Rum in 1888 he seems to have taken over some of the sheep stock, writing to Harvie-Brown about his efforts to rehouse his shepherds. It seems that the Bulloughs eventually concentrated the sheep enterprise at Kilmory and reduced the overall numbers accordingly – to about 1000 ewes – until finally doing away with them altogether in 1926. After Sir George died, Lady Bullough's inclination was to retain the existing regime in Rum unless a very strong reason for change could be demonstrated. She maintained that this was more because of the dislocation and confusion which would result, rather than any fundamental preference of her own.

During the Second World War the Government formed the Agricultural Executive Committee to assess how all farms and crofts in the country could increase their productivity. One of the members for Lochaber was Donald Cameron, son of a Fort William auctioneer. In his book *Where Wild Geese Fly* Cameron related how many locals had objected to the proprietor of Rum refusing sheep to graze there. The farm had been let for a time during the First World War so eventually in 1940 Sir George's widow consented to let the AEC advertise it. At first there were no takers.

One of Cameron's shepherds had worked on Rum as a young man and recalled the size and vigour of some of the wedders and stags. On an impulse Cameron himself offered £50 annual rent, which was gratefully accepted. Only then did he visit the island to look over his new investment. He was met off the steamer, the old *Lochmor*, and shown around by the head stalker – presumably Duncan Macnaughton. Cameron was not impressed with what he saw:

> The greater part of the island was rocky and sour-looking and there were deer everywhere, especially on the few grassy areas. The stalker said that there were over two thousand and at that the island was fully stocked, with a herd of some 20 semi-wild ponies – of the Highland type but thicker set and immensely strong-looking. A few of these were broken in to carry deer carcasses off the hills.
>
> There was a stone-walled fank near the Kilmory road. It was in fair condition but had no dipping tank and all the gates had rotted away since it was last used some twenty years before when the previous sheep stock had been cleared off. There were several empty houses at Kinloch, the landing place, and the huge castle with its disused walled garden, a derelict bathing pool [*sic*] and aquarium. The castle itself had been kept in good condition. Across the burn was a good farm steading used only for the several milk cows belonging to the estate, and the stalkers' vans etc.
>
> There were some 15 of a population, being two stalkers, a cowman, a boatman, the castle housekeeper and their families, plus a teacher ... I learned that permission to land was required and often refused unless it was someone – fishing boat crews etc – wanting to send messages from the little post office which had the only telephone on the island. The lady owner would be really annoyed that I was about to break the spell and could not be expected to welcome my sheep, my shepherds or myself.

Cameron's contract was to extend for seven years, with his stock not to exceed 1000 sheep and 100 cattle. He recalled:

I could have houses for myself and two shepherds at Kinloch, a share of the steading and two fields, one a meadow for hay and the other a deer park to hold sheep at handling.

That first winter he began with 600 sheep, letting them range over most of the island, but the mortality was high and lambing poor. His shepherds put this down to overstocking by the deer and the AEC recommended a higher cull. Lady Bullough disapproved of Cameron's interference and refused to let the estate boat handle his stock; so he had to use a private charter. For an extra £50 rent Cameron was given permission to double his stock numbers, buying in 1000 gimmers over the next two years. In his book Cameron kept his cards close to his chest, however, for, according to W. J. Eggeling, there were almost 5000 sheep on Rum in 1941, over 5500 in 1942, about 6750 in 1943, over 6400 in 1944 and about 3300 in 1945. In addition Cameron kept at least twenty cross-Highland stirks. Not surprisingly, Cameron had to employ an extra shepherd:

> With three families of shepherds, the social life on the island blossomed. Occasional dances were held in the steading, when everyone turned up and danced to the ancient gramaphone or a wheezy old accordion, which all seemed able to manipulate. The school roll was doubled and the girl teacher had some five or six classes for little more than that number of pupils.

But regardless of deer numbers, the climate and underlying geology precluded any quality grazing and the sheep were required to eat seaweed for extra minerals. Cameron's venture provided meagre reward and he came out with little profit; in 1946 he decided not to renew the lease. His successor took over on Martinmas 1947 but did not offer Cameron enough for his stock so they had to be removed for sale on the mainland.

The new tenant was Walter Mundell from Tarradale, near Muir of Ord on the Black Isle. Despite initial setbacks he apparently built up his sheep stock to nearly 3000, with 100 head of cattle. Hirsels were retained at Harris, Guirdil and Kilmory, with the wether hoggs being fattened away on the Black Isle and the gimmers retained on Rum. Mundell had the let of the White House for his own use but rarely went there. His shepherds lived at the Kinloch farmhouse, at Kilmory and at Harris (where the Lodge was occupied for a time). The shepherds were expected to help the estate in the upkeep of the roads and in muir burning; in the latter they tended to be rather indiscriminate and occasionally fires got out of hand.

In 1957 Lady Bullough sold the island to the Nature Conservancy. Mundell decided not to renew his lease and for his part, he seemed reluctant to divulge much to his new landlords about his stock numbers. It is thought that he removed 1100 Blackface ewes, 564 lambs and thirty-five tups; fifty more sheep were missed and gathered up later. In addition he took off forty or so cattle, including twenty-seven pure and cross Highland cows, nine pure and cross Highland bulling heifers and one bull. Four milk cows and a heifer calf were left behind, together with twenty-two ponies (including a stallion and four geldings), a lorry, a van and two old Austin cars. The human population stood at twenty-eight, including six children attending the island school under Mrs Katie Macgregor the teacher.

According to *The Scotsman* (5 April 1957):

> Heavy taxation had obliged Lady Bullough to make her decision. Her one fear, she confided to her factor, was that the Government would take over Rum for a rocket range or other scheme. She wanted it to remain unspoiled for all time.

So Rum passed into the hands of the Nature Conservancy, the Government conservation body, on 1 March 1957, at a knock-down price of £23,000 (with a gift of the castle and its contents), the island 'to be used as a nature reserve in perpetuity and Kinloch Castle maintained as far as may be practical'. England already had National Parks but due to pressure from influential landlords such parks were rejected out of hand in Scotland. Thus the responsibility for countryside conservation in Scotland fell largely to the Nature Conservancy and its national nature reserves (NNRs). In 1951, two years after the body came into existence, Beinn Eighe became its very first reserve, bought outright from the public purse. The Cairngorms, established in 1954, is still the largest NNR in Britain but relies heavily upon private agreements with appropriate landowners. The important island reserves of Rum and St Kilda were both declared on the same day, 4 April 1957, the first acquired by purchase and the second by lease from the owners, the National Trust for Scotland.

Throughout the Bullough ownership, landing by casual visitors was discouraged and Rum soon gained the reputation for being the 'Forbidden Island'. In the 1930s, for instance, Robert Atkinson, that pioneering island-goer, knew of yachtsmen in Loch Scresort who tried to get ashore for freshwater but were turned away by the island gamekeepers or estate staff. In an unpublished account of the incident he recalled:

> I knew of one yachtsman whose burly crew equalled in number the defence squad; they landed in defiance – you're not stopping us from getting freshwater and if any of you lay so much as a finger on that boat etc. – they got the water, which they did not really need, and left again, dogged but, by force of numbers, unmolested. You can buy a steamer ticket to Rum but you must stay on board the steamer. I have also heard, but I don't know if it has any truth, that once a shipwrecked crew was turned off Rum ... One would like to think that behind the

screen of prohibition and taboo, Rum hid some secret or subversive activity ... But apparently only deer; and all the fence of restriction was to preserve the deer so that they might live undisturbed until they were required to be shot, but exclusively at the invitation of the proprietor.

In fact, in his manuscript, which Atkinson had hoped to publish as a book, he and two companions confessed to staging a clandestine raid on Bullough's private estate and sailing away with the antlered head of one of his stags as a trophy – certainly not the first and unlikely to be the last. In true Highland poaching tradition, the deer in Rum's remote shores have long attracted interest from local fishing boats. A sad consequence of such activities, however, is when a wounded beast escapes to die a lingering, agonising death.

In contrast the botanist John Raven was granted permission to visit Rum in early August 1948 (although not confessing to his mission of investigating a series of unlikely plant records by Professor Heslop Harrison). He paid her a visit in the castle and 'when Lady Bullough eventually appeared, not even the presence of a vast ivory eagle brooding over [his companion] Creighton's head could detract from the friendliness and charm with which she received us. We found it hard to believe that she resented the presence of strangers on her island so strongly as the Professor led us to suppose' (as quoted in *A Rum Affair* by Karl Sabbagh). The two young botanists were then given a dram by Duncan Macnaughton and he later provided them with some cooking pots since they had lost their own on the steamer.

In 1949 Alastair Dunnett and a companion boldly landed by canoe at Kinloch without permission. While they were putting up their tent they were accosted by a local in tweeds, with a gun and two dogs, who sent them to see Lady Bullough. The old widow declined to give them an audience but instructed her stalker to dispense both permission and a complimentary haunch of venison! Some visitors maintain that a polite request for permission to land was rarely refused, but the unwelcoming reputation of Rum, perhaps first established at the time of the Clearances, lingers on even to this day.

Now, with its passing from private to public ownership, Rum was once again at the centre of controversy. There was considerable resentment from the farming community about the loss of valuable sheep grazing. The concept of national nature reserves was a new one and at first the media totally misrepresented it. The *Daily Herald*, for instance, reported how:

Government-financed mouse lovers have taken over a Hebridean island – and banned the islanders from buying meat and groceries. The mouse lovers say food for sale would encourage trippers. And trippers would disturb the mice. The island is Rum, just bought for a fortune from public funds. It is the only place where the giant Rum mouse lives ... Mr E M Nicolson, director of the board [*sic*] in Scotland, holding a stuffed giant Rum mouse in his hand, told me: 'Rum is a real find for us. The way Lady Monica ran it suits us admirably. There is no proper shop – and things will stay that way. We will permit visitors to land, but they must not wander far from the jetty. We don't want hikers disturbing the mice and the deer and the pygmy shrews.'

Being a respected provincial broadsheet, the *Inverness Courier* (27 August 1957) could take a more rational view. They reported how the Northern Pastoral Club were complaining about the loss of the sheep grazings, farmers claiming that this was 'a damaging blow to Britain's food production'. In fact, the *Inverness Courier* admitted, the tenant Mr Walter Mundell of Tarradale had voluntarily decided to quit. According to one more enlightened farmer, John Robertson of Castlecraig, Nigg, Mundell's 1000 ewes represented only one-third of 1 per cent of the sheep population of Scotland: 'the sacrifice we are making may well be worth it in the future. Let the Conservancy get on with their research, and help us improve our farms.' The *Inverness Courier* added:

> the island was in private ownership for years, and it is rather amusing to hear people who have probably never been in Rum in their lives and have no desire or intention to go there now – protesting about the possibility of access to the island being restricted.

As long ago as 1797 Edward Daniel Clarke considered that Rum offered 'a treasure to the naturalist, which I trust will in future be less neglected'. In 1845, just as Lord Salisbury was about to take over the island as a sporting estate, Hugh Miller wrote:

> How strange a cycle. Uninhabited originally save by wild animals, it became at an early age the home of men ... The island lost all its inhabitants on a wool and mutton speculation. And now yet another change was on the eve of ensuing, and the island was to return to its original state, as a home of wild animals ...

Its acquisition by the Nature Conservancy completed that strange cycle. With a final ironic twist even the sheep were to be removed, and the island reverted to a state of nature, with only a few human families remaining to steward the wildlife and visitors.

In 1943–4, as a member of the Ramsay Committee on Scottish National Parks, the late Frank Fraser Darling had recommended that a large research nature reserve be set up on Rum for the study of red deer and their environment. Indeed, in the 1930s Darling had approached Sir George

Bullough to approve just such a research project on Rum but he was refused. Only then did Darling look to the Dundonnell estate in Wester Ross for the material for his classic book *A Herd of Red Deer.* He later lamented to J. Morton Boyd:

> Two of the great advantages of Rum over a mainland forest are the fact that Rum is an island and the deer cannot move out, and island isolation cuts down disturbance. I'd have given all I had to have been allowed to work on Rum then.

The project was ultimately taken up by the Nature Conservancy themselves, and later, a team of scientists from Cambridge University.

The Nature Conservancy's charter required it to provide scientific advice on the conservation and control of the natural flora and fauna of Great Britain; to establish, maintain and manage nature reserves in Great Britain, including the maintenance of physical features of scientific interest; and to organise and develop the scientific services thereto. The Nature Conservancy had been formed upon the recommendation of the two Wildlife Conservation Committees, one for England and Wales and the other for Scotland. In their 1949 Report the latter advised setting up fifty national nature reserves in Scotland, including the Isle of Rum, of which it wrote:

> Isolated, yet within easy reach of the mainland, it would make an outstanding station for research, and indeed is the most suitable island for this purpose in Scotland.

In the first management plan for the new island reserve, W. J. Eggeling concluded:

> the great although unbalanced diversity of habitat on the reserve, combined with island isolation and the absence of competing land uses, makes Rum an especially favourable centre for studying ecological and reserve management problems including those concerned with the floristic enrichment of mountain and moorland vegetation, the ecology and management of red deer, and elucidation of the effects of a considerable range of climate, soil, elevation and exposure on plant and animal life ... The variety and scientific interest of the geology of the island surpasses that of any area of comparable size in Britain, and the inter-relationships of rock, soil and vegetation can be studied in a wide variety of conditions.

Initial research was directed towards identifying the basic wildlife resource on the island with surveys of plants, animals and geology. The range of animal habitats was to be diversified by re-creating the devastated scrub woodland. Finally a major project into the red deer population and its management was initiated. Deer numbers were to be reduced by an annual cull, which, together with the removal of the sheep, would immediately relieve grazing pressure. In addition, the practice of muirburn was ceased immediately. Advice was sought from other organisations which might have an interest in the agricultural and forestry potential of the island. The response was disappointing. The Hill Farming Research Organisation, the Department of Agriculure and Fisheries for Scotland and the North of Scotland College of Agriculture all deemed Rum unsuitable for grazing research which could more easily be carried out elsewhere. Aside from the farm fields and gardens around Kinloch, the Forestry Commission could identify only some 500 acres suitable for commercial planting. This liberated the Nature Conservancy from commercial constraints, so research, other than that on the island's red deer, could be directed towards conservation management. The woodland recreation scheme continued and the results of the deer study were already beginning to have management implications for estates on the mainland.

As regards the estate, the Nature Conservancy began renovation of buildings, bridges and roads. Camp sites, toilets, shelter and seats were provided for the general public, and a nature trail laid out. A herd of thirteen Highland cattle were introduced in 1971 as an additional grazing impact to the sward at Harris and Guirdil. The concept of a fully equipped field station never came to fruition and in 1973 the research arm of the Nature Conservancy, now to be the Nature Conservancy Council (NCC), became devolved into an independent body called the Institute of Terrestrial Ecology. None the less, two years later NCC established an innovative project on the island to reintroduce the white-tailed sea eagle. This was how I came to live in Rum (having first visited it as a student in 1969) and I have described the project at length in my book *The Return of the Sea Eagle* (1983). The human story of Rum, and indeed of the Highlands and Islands in general, played a part in the demise of the sea eagle in Britain, sheep farmers, landowners and gamekeepers being intolerant of predators, and of scavenging eagles in particular. The Salisbury papers are eloquent testimony to the treatment of what were referred to as 'vermin', hence the need for the reintroduction of sea eagles, with Rum, appropriately enough, being chosen as the locus for this innovative conservation project.

A critical review of the estate in 1976 necessitated a cutback in staff and facilities to make financial savings, and some of the work, such as planting trees in the new South Side enclosure, was instead undertaken by parties of volunteers. In 1982 work began to upgrade the ageing hydroelectricity scheme from 110 volt DC to 240 AC. In 1991 NCC itself devolved into three separate organisations, one each for England, Wales and Scotland, leading to yet another metamorphosis in April 1992 when the embryonic Nature Conservancy Council for Scotland merged with the Countryside Commission for Scotland to become Scottish Natural Heritage.

The full implications for Rum are only now beginning to emerge but the 'new vision' for the island – launched on the fortieth anniversary of the nature reserve – does not seem to me to be offering anything startlingly new. There is formal recognition that Rum has to function as one of the Small Isles but its own inhabitants have never enjoyed long-term security or continuity. In this 'new vision' no consultation was made with previous 'islanders'. Each successive community in Rum prefers to reconstruct a fresh identity and then, unwittingly, sets about reinventing the wheel. None seems to wish to make contact with anyone who has ever lived there before, nor indeed do the owners, to see what the recurring social and practical problems have been. While fresh ideas are vital to any situation, so too is experience, local knowledge, continuity and kinship, things that have always been denied folk living in Rum for nigh on two centuries. Many of the ideas in this 'new vision' have been thought of before so it remains to be seen whether any progress will actually be made this time.

At the turn of the millennium thoughts of some of the more radical employees of SNH on the island turned to the fashionable 'community ownership' idea that had been so successfully pursued by the Eigg folk. Rum has not had a native population since old Kenneth Maclean died in the 1880s, and has had a regular turnover of staff (and therefore inhabitants) since it came into ownership of the Nature Conservancy in 1957; few remain for tours of more than five or six years. Miller saw the island as a landscape without figures and to some extent it still is, and has been ever since the Clearances.

It is true that Rum, Eigg, Muck and Canna have long had separate histories and, since the Lordship of the Isles, they have been under distinct and often eccentric ownership. Rum is unusual in the Small Isles in having no indigenous islanders so it has not always been easy to maintain accord within its community; it is virtually bereft of continuity in culture and tradition. It has, however, enjoyed a relatively long period of stability, first under the Bulloughs and latterly under Scottish Natural Heritage and its predecessor bodies. Canna, too, belonged for many years to the noted Gaelic scholar Dr John Lorne Campbell, who recently gifted the island to the National Trust for Scotland. The Isle of Muck has long been owned by the hard-working, sympathetic and benevolent MacEwen family. Until recently, however, Eigg has had a succession of short-term owners, few of whom have left the place in good heart or offered the islanders much hope for the future. Community ownership, however, should at least offer Eigg the security and the continuity that the resilient islanders need and deserve.

A common ferry service is vital to maintaining effective links not only with the mainland but also between the four islands themselves. They may yet share a doctor, priest and minister but the latter two are now domiciled on the mainland. Otherwise the four communities have had little encouragement to co-operate. Periodic threats or changes to the ferry service usually remind the islanders that they can function more effectively in social and political matters by acting together. This was evident when the Small Isles Community Council pitted the wishes of the four islands against the four owners to ensure a suitable replacement for the Islands' steamer. (Indeed, of the four, only John Lorne Campbell of Canna really understood the needs of the community.) Now that Eigg is under community ownership the four Small Isles are better placed to function as a unit, possibly holding some more formal status such as a 'natural heritage area', national park or whatever. Rum's future should no longer be viewed in isolation but instead as integral amongst that of the four Small Isles.

Catechist's List: Census for the Small Isles, 1764–65

In Edinburgh University Library, with a copy at the Clan Donald Centre Library, Sleat, Isle of Skye

> Rum is an island ... inhabited by protestants but [for] two men and four women. But they come to hear the minister and catechist when either of them is here. These papists are none of the natives of the island of Rum. They come here from Eig and Canna. The priests do not come here to officiate. The protestants there would not allow any of them to after the death of three worthys? there two years ago. The priest was forced in there by contrary winds on his way from Canna to Eig on a Saturday. He took his lodging in a protestant house. The landlady being of his religion he offered to say mass on Sunday but the good man of the house would not allow him to officiate .... within his dwelling house or any other house belonging to him. His wife now is one of the converts in Rum.
>
> ... I subscribe the former ... at Canna, 20th March 1765
> Neill McNeill, Catechist

Kilmory

1 Murdo Maclean	60	Donald Maclean, his son	13
Marion MacQuarrie, his wife	42	John Maclean, his son	8
Rory Maclean, his son	16	Rorry Maclean, his son	5
Allan Maclean, his son	13	Margaret Maclean, his daughter	6
Lauchlan Maclean, his son	10	Mary Maclean, his daughter	2
Neill Maclean, his son	7		
Hector Maclean, his son	5	4 John MacQuarrie	32
		Margaret Maclean, his wife	7
2 John Fraser	44	John MacQuarrie, his son	5
Effie Maclean, his wife	42	Ketty MacQuarrie, his daughter	2
Alexander Fraser, his son	10		
Charles Fraser, his son	6	5 Hector MacQuarrie	37
Elizabeth Fraser, his daughter	1	Mary MacQuarrie, his wife	30
		John MacQuarrie, his son	9
3 Donald Maclean	54	Hector MacQuarrie, his son	7
Mary MacQuarrie, his wife	40	Mary MacQuarrie, his daughter	4

Catherine MacQuarrie, his daughter	3	
Donald MacQuarrie, his son	1½	

6 Donald MacQuarrie	39
Marion Maclean, his wife	34
Lauchlan MacQuarrie, his son	7
Donald MacQuarrie, his son	5
John MacQuarrie, his son	1
Effie Maclean, widow	60

7 Hector Mackinnon	56
Christina Maclean, his wife	51
John Mackinnon, his son	20
Catherine Macleod, servantmaid	23

8 Donald MacQuarrie, senior	54
Flora MacQuarrie, his wife	42
Flora MacQuarrie, his daughter	12
Hector MacQuarrie, his son	9
John MacQuarrie, his son	7
Christina MacQuarrie, his daughter	5

9 John MacQuarrie, senior	81
Marion MacQuarrie, his daughter	49
Catherine MacQuarrie, his grandchild	12

10 Murdo Maclean	30
Christina Campbell, his wife	37
John Maclean, his son	6
Anna Maclean, his daughter	4

11 Cathrina MacInnes, widow	47
Marion Maclean, her daughter	14

Allan Maclean, her son	10
Rachel Maclean, her daughter	7
Anna Maclean, her daughter	6

12 Cathrina MacInnes, widow	42
Angus Maclean, her son	8
Marion Macdonald, widow	64
Flora Maclean, widow	67

13 Neill Maclean	30
Marion Mackinnon, his wife	27
Margaret Maclean, his daughter	4
Donald Maclean, his son	3
Christina Maclean, his daughter	1½

14 Malcolm Maclean	64
Rachel Maclean, his wife	52
Rorry Maclean, servant	17

15 Rorry Maclean, senior	37
Christina Maclean, his wife	26
Cathrina Maclean, his daughter	7
Marion Maclean, his daughter	4
Archibald Maclean, his nephew	12

16 John Mackinnon, convert	34
Marion MacQuarrie, his wife	32
Neill Mackinnon, his son	9
John Mackinnon, his son	7
Mary Mackinnon, his daughter	2

17 John Maclean, junior	21
Marion Maclean, his wife	20
Margaret Maclean, widow	60

Sandynessia

18 Neill Macdonald	42
Anna Maclean, his wife	36
Marion Macdonald, his daughter	15
Anna Macdonald, his daughter	7
Hector Macdonald, his son	6

19 Allan Maclean	28
Anna MacQuarrie, his wife	26

20 Donald Mackay	40
Gunnet [Janet] Mackinnon, his wife	44

John Mackay, his son	12	
Hector Mackay, his son	10	
Donald Mackay, his son	9	
Peter Mackay, his son	7	
Angus Mackay, his son	3	
Cathrina Mackay, his daughter	2	

21	John MacInnes	50
	Mary Mackay, his wife	52
	Lauchlan MacInnes, his son	16
	Caristina MacInnes, his daughter	18
	Cathrina MacInnes, his daughter	11
	Margaret MacInnes, his daughter	9

22	John Maclean	48
	Anna Mackay, his wife	43
	Margaret Maclean, his daughter	12
	Angus Maclean, his son	9
	Anna Maclean, his daughter	6

John Maclean, his son	2	

23	Malcolm Mackay	50
	Margaret Maclean, his wife	27
	Anna Mackay, his daughter	21
	Mary Mackay, his daughter	17
	Lauchlan Mackay, his son	9
	Archibald Mackay, his son	7
	Mary Mackay, his daughter	3
	John Mackay, his son	1¼

24	Norman Maclean	37
	Cathrina Campbell, his wife	34
	Allan Maclean, his son	15
	Murdo Maclean, his son	12
	Flora Maclean, his daughter	10
	Cathrina Maclean, his daughter	8
	Marion Maclean, his daughter	6
	Isabella Maclean, his daughter	2

Loch: *at the harbour*

25	Allan Maclean	19
	Mary Mackay, widow	50
	Donald MacInnes, servant	20
	Donald Maclean, his [Allan's] brother	7
	Mary Maclean, his sister	3
	John Maclean, lunatick	17

26	Neill Campbell	63
	Flora Macleod, his wife	60
	Duncan Campbell, his son	30
	John Campbell, his son	26
	Donald Campbell, his son	24
	Marion Campbell, his daughter	19
	Mary Campbell, his daughter	17
	Cathrina Campbell, his daughter	2

27	Allan Maclean, senior	60
	Cathrina Campbell, his wife	56
	John Mackay, her son	22

28	John Macgillvray	63
	Cathrina Macdonald, his wife	57
	Rorry Macgillvray, his son	25
	Anna Macgillvray, his daughter	19
	Mary Macgillvray, his daughter	15

29	Marion Maclean, widow	52
	Mary Campbell, her daughter	28
	John Campbell, her son	19
	Marion Campbell, her daughter	17
	Mary Kennedy, her mother	89

30	Allan Maclean	40
	Flora MacQueen, his wife and a convert	27
	Flora Maclean, his daughter	3
	John Maclean, his son	1¼
	Angus MacQueen, convert	20

31	John Mackinnon	70
	Archibald Mackinnon, his son	34

Mary MacInnes, his [Archibald's] wife	26
Neill Mackinnon, his son	5
Archibald Mackinnon, his son	3
Donald Mackinnon, his son	2
Mary Campbell, servantmaid	22

32 John Mackinnon, junior	47
Anna Maclean, his wife	33
Donald Mackinnon, his son	9
Mary Mackinnon, his daughter	7
Neill Mackinnon, his son	4
Flora Mackinnon, his daughter	4

Harris

33 John Maclean, elder	40
Rachel Campbell, his wife	39
Allan Maclean, his son	24
Florry Maclean, his daughter	19
Margaret Maclean, his daughter	12
Neill Maclean, servant	27
Cathrina MacQuarrie, servantmaid	30
34 Hugh Macdonald	40
Mary Maclean, his wife	38
Hector Macdonald, his son	8
Neill Macdonald, his son	5
Donald Macdonald, his son	2
35 Donald Mackay	30
Margaret Campbell, his wife	27
Margaret Mackay, his daughter	6
Peter Mackay, his son	1¼
36 Donald Campbell	70
Mary Maclean, his wife	62
Lauchlan Campbell, his son	22
Mary MacQuarrie, his wife	20
Mary MacQuarrie, servantmaid [no age given]	
37 Hector Campbell	29
Effie MacArthur, his wife	27
Mary Campbell, his daughter	1½
Mary Campbell, servantmaid	16
38 Angus Campbell	67
Florry Mackay, his wife	61

Malcolm Campbell, convert	29
Mary Macdonald, his [Malcolm's] wife	30
Hector Campbell, his son	3
Angus Campbell, his son	½
39 Hector MacQuarrie	24
Gunnet [Janet] Maclean, his wife	23
Marion Campbell, widow [his mother?]	64
40 Neill MacQuarrie	74
Cathrina Macdonald, his wife	62
Effie MacQuarrie, his daughter, blind	29
Allan Macgillvray, his grandson	17
Rachel Macgillvray, his granddaughter	12
41 Allan MacQuarrie	37
Mary Maclean, his wife	32
Cathrina MacQuarrie, his daughter	5
Anna MacQuarrie, his daughter	4
John MacQuarrie, his son	2
Marion MacQuarrie, servantmaid	26
42 Donald MacQuarrie	32
Carylin?? MacQuarrie, his wife, convert	27
Mary MacQuarrie, his daughter	4
Marion MacQuarrie, his daughter	2
Florry MacQuarrie, his daughter	1¼
Mary MacQuarrie, his sister	18

43 John MacQuarrie	32	Marion MacQuarrie, his daughter	17
Mary Mackay, his wife	28	Angus MacQuarrie, his son	15
Mary Maclean, widow		Allan MacQuarrie, his son	11
[his or her mother?]	52	Annabella MacQuarrie, his daughter	7
		Guliann ? MacQuarrie, his daughter	5
44 Alexander MacQuarrie	21	Neill MacQuarrie, his son	2
Cathrina Mackay, widow			
[his mother?]	60	46 John MacQuarrie	36
Marjory Cameron, servantmaid	35	Florry Maclean, his wife	31
		Donald MacQuarrie, his son	6
45 Lauchlan MacQuarrie	40	Mary MacQuarrie, his daughter	5
Ann Macdonald, his wife	37	Malcolm MacQuarrie, his son	1
John MacQuarrie, his son	19		

Papadil *village or town*

47 Alexander Maclean	32	Cathrina MacInnes, servantmaid	19
Anna Mackinnon, his wife	27	49 Rorry Maclean	40
Mary Mackay, maidservant	18	Cathrina Maclean, his wife	36
		Lauchlan Maclean, his son	16
48 Lauchlan Macgillvray	37	Donald Maclean, his son	8
Mary Campbell, his wife and		Effie Maclean, his daughter	4
a convert	33	Marion Maclean, his daughter	2

Guirdil

50 Allan Maclean, elder	37	Cathrina Lamond, widow	60
Mary Maclean, his wife	30		
Allan Maclean, his son	10	52 John Macdonald	50
Gunnet [Janet] Maclean,		Carylin? Macdonald, his wife	50
his daughter	3	Donald Macdonald, his son	21
Margaret Maclean, his daughter	1½	Ann McEachen, his mother	97
Mary Maclean, servantmaid	19		
		53 Mary Macdonald, widow	50
51 Charles Maclean	27	Cathrina McQueen, convert	21
Florry Maclean, his wife	29		
John Maclean, his son	2	54 Neill MacInnes	27
Mary Maclean, widow	76	Margaret MacArthur,	
Neill Mackay, servant	27	his wife and papist from Canna	26
Carylin? Maclean, servantmaid	19	Cathrina MacInnes, his daughter	1

Cove *in Rum*

55	John Maclean, elder	57		Lauchlan MacQuarrie, his son	15
	Marion MacQueen, his wife	58		Rachel MacQuarrie, his daughter	10
	Hugh Maclean, his son	25		John MacQuarrie, his son	7
	Unna Maclean, his daughter	16			
	Mary Maclean, servantmaid	36	57	John Maclean	80
	Charles Macpherson	5		Mary Maclean, his wife	50
	Flora Macleod, servantmaid	23		Rachel Maclean, his daughter	16
	Donald Campbell, servant	56		Donald Maclean, his son	15
	John Mackay, servant	25		Archibald Maclean, his son [1st wife?]	50
56	John MacQuarrie	40		Gunnet [Janet] Maclean,	
	Margaret Nicolson?, his wife	37		his? daughter	¼

SUMMARY OF APPENDIX I

Surnames on the Catechist's List

Maclean	106 (36%)	Fraser	5 (2%)
MacQuarrie	65 (22%)	Macleod	2 (1%)
Campbell	33 (11%)	MacQueen	2 (1%)
MacKay	23 (8%)	Macpherson	1 (0.3%)
MacKinnon	20 (7%)	Cameron	1 (0.3%)
MacDonald	16 (5%)	Lamond	1 (0.3%)
MacInnes	11 (4%)	Kennedy	1 (0.3%)
MacGillvray	10 (3%)		

Total   297

Wives and widows are listed under their maiden surname and in these totals these have been changed to their married name where it is obvious.

Population of Rum's Townships according to the Catechist's List

Kilmory	84	Guirdil	22
Harris	71	Cove	20
Kinloch	45	Papadil	12
Sandenesia	43		

Total   297

Age Distribution of Rum's Population on the Catechist's List

Infant	14	51–55	7
2–5	43	56–60	13
6–10	44	61–65	8
11–15	19	66–70	4
16–20	30	71–75	1
21–25	17	76–80	2
26–30	33	81–85	1
31–35	14	86–90	1
36–40	24	91–95	0
41–45	8	96–100	1
46–50	12		

Total   297

APPENDIX II

Muster Rolls of the Rum Island Company of Inverness-shire Volunteers or (from 1805) Rum Island Company of Volunteer Infantry

Captain	1	Donald Maclean enrolled 30 Sept. 1803
Lieutenant	2	Alexander Maclean enrolled 30 Sept. 1803 until
	3	John Maclean promoted from ensign 19 May 1804 and Lieutenant commanding in 1810 and 1811
Ensign	3	John Maclean enrolled 30 Dec. 1803
(2nd Lt)		(prom. to Lieutenant 25 March 1804)
	86	Hector Maclean promoted from ranks 19 May 1804
Paymaster	3	John Maclean in June 1805 and Sept. 1808
Sergeant	4	Donald Maclean
(on permanent pay)		
Sergeants	5	Donald Mackinnon until June 1810
	6	John MacQuarrie
	7	John Maclean from June 1810
Corporals	8	Charles Maclean
	9	Malcolm MacQuarrie
Drummer	10	Hector Morrison (on permanent pay – until Dec. 1806)
Drummer	11	Norman Maclean (on permanent pay June? 1806 until June 1810)
	12	Donald MacKay from June 1810
	47	Donald Maclean from June 1810
Privates	13	Angus Cameron enrolled 9 Dec. 1803
	14	Donald Cameron from c.1810
	15	Donald Campbell from Sept? 1805 until 1809
	16	John Campbell from Sept? 1805 except 1808/09
	17	John Campbell from c.1810
	18	Lachlan Campbell until 1809
	19	Neil Campbell enrolled 17 Dec. 1803 until 1808
	20	Alexander Kennedy from 1810
	21	Angus MacArthur until 1809
	22	Colin MacArthur from 1810
	23	John MacArthur

24   Lachlan MacArthur from 1810

25   Malcolm MacAskill from 1810

26   Neil MacAskill until 1809

27   Allan MacDonald from 1810

28   Archibald MacDonald

29   Donald MacDonald

30   Hector MacDonald enrolled 12 Dec. 1803 until 5 May 1806

31   Hugh MacDonald 1808/9 only

32   Neil MacDonald until 1808

33   Alexander MacInnes until 1809

34   Angus MacInnes until 1809

35   Donald MacInnes

36   Lachlan MacInnes until 1809

37   Lachlan MacInnes until 1805

38   James MacInnes from 1810

39   John MacInnes

40   John MacInnes 1805 until 1809

41   Lachlan MacInnes 1806/7 and 1810/11

42   Allan MacIsaac until 1806

43   Donald MacIsaac from 1810

44   Malcolm MacIsaac from 1810

45   Donald MacKay except 1806

46   Donald MacKay enrolled 17 Dec. 1803 until 1809, when
      promoted drummer?

47   Donald MacKay until 1807

48   Hector MacKay to 1809

49   James MacKay from 1810

50   Lachlan MacKay from 1810

51   Malcolm MacKay 1805 only

52   Neil MacKay

53   Peter MacKay

54   Peter MacKay from 1810

55   Allan MacKinnon enrolled 17 Dec. 1803

56   Allan MacKinnon from 1806 until 1808

57   Angus MacKinnon enrolled 17 Dec. 1803 until 1808

58   Archibald MacKinnon from 1810

59   Charles MacKinnon enrolled 12 Dec. 1803 until 1809

60   Donald MacKinnon

61   Donald MacKinnon enrolled 17 Dec. 1803 until 1808

62   Donald MacKinnon enrolled 15 Dec. 1803 until 1808

63   Hector MacKinnon enrolled 12 Dec. 1803

64   Hugh MacKinnon enrolled 14 July 1807

65   John MacKinnon

66	John MacKinnon
67	John MacKinnon until 1809
68	John MacKinnon enrolled 25? June 1806 until 1809
69	Lachlan MacKinnon except early 1806
70	Malcolm MacKinnon enrolled 17 Dec. 1803 until discharged 12 March 1804, same person 1810/11?
71	Neil MacKinnon
72	Neil MacKinnon enrolled 14 July 1807
73	Neil MacKinnon from 1807
74	Norman MacKinnon enrolled 9 Dec. 1803
75	Rory MacKinnon until 1809
76	Allan Maclean
77	Allan Maclean
78	Allan Maclean until 1809
79	Angus Maclean from Dec. 1808
80	Archibald Maclean from Dec. 1808
81	Charles Maclean enrolled 12 Dec. 1803 to 1809
82	Donald Maclean promoted drummer 1810?
83	Donald Maclean enrolled 12 Dec. 1803
84	Donald Maclean enrolled 12 Dec. 1803, discharged 9 April 1804.
85	Donald Maclean from 1810
86	Hector Maclean promoted Ensign 19 May 1804
87	Hector Maclean
88	Hector Maclean from 1809
89	Hugh Maclean
90	Hugh Maclean from 1810
91	James Maclean 1809 only
92	John Maclean
93	John Maclean
94	John Maclean
95	John Maclean
96	John Maclean enrolled 17 Dec. 1803
97	John Maclean except part 1805/6
98	Lachlan Maclean enrolled 14 July 1807
99	Malcolm Maclean
100	Murdoch Maclean
101	Murdoch Maclean until 1807
102	Neil Maclean
103	Neil Maclean
104	Neil Maclean except 1807 and 1809
105	Rory (Roderick) Maclean from 1806
106	William Maclean enrolled 9 April 1804 until 1809
107	Donald MacMillan enrolled 12 March 1804, except 1809

108	Hector MacMillan from 1810	
109	Malcolm MacMillan enrolled 17 Dec. 1803 to 1807	
110	Allan MacQuarrie	
111	Allan MacQuarrie from 1809	
112	Charles MacQuarrie enrolled 18 July 1804	
113	Donald MacQuarrie	
114	Donald MacQuarrie until 1810	
115	Guary MacQuarrie	
116	Hector MacQuarrie	
117	Hector MacQuarrie until 1810	
118	Hector MacQuarrie until 1808	
119	John MacQuarrie	
120	John MacQuarrie	
121	John MacQuarrie	
122	John MacQuarrie	
123	John MacQuarrie	
124	John MacQuarrie	
125	John MacQuarrie until 1810	
126	John MacQuarrie until 1810 except 1806/7	
127	Lachlan MacQuarrie discharged 18 July 1804	
128	Malcolm MacQuarrie until 1810	
129	Neil MacQuarrie until 1810?	
130	Archibald Stewart from 1810	
131	Donald Stewart from 1810	

Date	Duty	Total pay allowance	Clothing
1803	9 days	£48 3s. 9d.	
1804	85 days	£523 6s. 2d.	£134 2s. 3d.; £5 15s. carriage and freight from Edinburgh Castle for 80 muskets etc.
1805	83 days	£524 12s. 8d.	£5 7s. 3d. including 30 days' permanent duty at Kinloch 17 June to 17 July
1806	56 days	£305 4s. 7d.	£5 7s. 3d.
1807	26 days	£109 4s. 0d.	
1808	26 days	£204 16s. 5d.	including 13 days' permanent duty at Kilmory, 26 Sept. to 8 Oct.
1809	26 days	£109 4s. 0d.	
1810	18 days	£75 12s. 0d.	
1811	18 days	£75 12s. 0d.	

Rates of Pay and Clothing Allowance

Captain	9s. 5d. per day		
Lieutenant	5s. 8d. per day		
Ensign	4s. 8d. per day		
Sergeant		1s. 6d. per day	£3 3s. 9d.
		per man	
Corporal		1s. 2d. per day	£1 12s. 0d.
		per man	
Drummer	1s. 0d. per day	£2 3s. 6d. per man	
Private	1s. 0d. per day	£1 10s. 0d. per man	

SUMMARY OF APPENDIX II

Surnames on Muster Rolls

Maclean	38	MacIsaac	3
MacQuarrie	22	MacMillan	3
MacKinnon	22	MacAskill	2
MacKay	11	Stewart	2
MacInnes	9	Cameron	2
MacDonald	6	Morrison	1
MacArthur	4	Kennedy	1
Campbell	5		

Total   131

APPENDIX III

Passenger List of the Ship Saint Lawrence

Tobermory

In the port of Greenock:

Know ye that Jonathan Cram hath here entered certain passengers' luggage free. In the *Saint Lawrence*, Jonathan Cram, Master, for Ship Harbour in Cape Breton. Dated this 12th July 1828 in the ninth year of King George the Fourth.

Free.

Signed. John MacDougall P.C. Office

Two hundred and fifty chests

Twenty trunks

Fifty barrels

Forty bags

Port of Leith

List of passengers going in the ship *Saint Lawrence* of New Castile, Burthern per register —tons. Navigated with men including Jonathan Cram, the Master, bound for Ship Harbour, Cape Breton.

1 Hugh Maclean	49	
farmer, Rum, Gut of Canso		
2 Marion Maclean	45	
3 Flory Maclean	19	
4 John Maclean	13	
5 Angus Maclean	10	
6 Mary Maclean	6	
7 Catherine Maclean	4	
8 Hector Maclean	3	
9 Allan Maclean	infant	
10 Lauchlin Maclean	45	
farmer		
11 Mary Maclean	45	
12 Marion Maclean	24	
13 Hugh Maclean jr.	27	
14 Catherine Maclean	60	
15 Donald Maclean	48	
16 Mary Maclean	40	
17 Hector Maclean	60	
18 Effie Maclean	60	
19 Angus Campbell	19	
20 Neil MacQuarrie	55	
21 Marion MacQuarrie	50	
22 Simon Dalgleish	62	
23 Penny Dalgleish	23	
24 Donald MacKay	27	
25 Neil MacKay	30	
26 Charles MacKay	24	
27 Catherine MacKay	60	
28 Jean MacKay	22	

29 Catherine MacKay	13	71 Margaret Maclean	10
30 John MacKay	19	72 John Maclean	6
31 Peter MacKay	35	73 Alexander Maclean	5
32 Flory MacKay	32	74 Ann Maclean	3
33 Lauchlin MacKay	5	75 Donald Maclean	infant
34 Donald MacKay	3	76 Rory MacIsaac	85
35 Angus MacKay	2	77 Mary MacIsaac	40
36 John MacKay	infant	78 Peggy Maclean	80
37 Jonathan MacKinnon	30	79 Donald MacPhaden	54
38 Archie MacKinnon	28	80 Flory MacPhaden	50
39 Ann MacKinnon	60	81 Hector MacPhaden	19
40 Mary MacKinnon	26	82 Ann MacPhaden	13
41 Ann MacKinnon	5	83 Donald MacPhaden	10
42 John MacKinnon	3	84 John MacPhaden	8
43 Flory MacKinnon	infant	85 Angus MacPhaden	6
44 Alexander MacKinnon	28	86 Hector Maclean	32
45 Margaret MacKinnon	60	87 Catherine Maclean	29
46 Marion MacKinnon	28	88 Mary Maclean	infant
47 Jessie MacKinnon	26	89 Malcolm MacKinnon	45
48 John MacKinnon	24	90 Bell MacKinnon	35
49 Catherine MacKinnon	16	91 Catherine MacKinnon	18
50 Charles Maclean	30	92 Christina MacKinnon	15
51 Flory Maclean	62	93 John MacKinnon	13
52 John MacQuarrie	65	94 Marion MacKinnon	10
farmer		95 Peggy MacKinnon	6
53 Marion MacQuarrie	60	96 Flory MacKinnon	4
54 Allan MacQuarrie	30	97 Bell MacKinnon	2
55 Donald MacQuarrie	28	98 Margaret MacKinnon	60
56 Rachel MacQuarrie	26	99 Flory MacKinnon	30
57 Margaret MacQuarrie	24	100 Catherine MacKinnon	28
58 Bell MacQuarrie	20	101 Lauchlin MacKay	28
59 Lauchlin MacInnes	55	102 Mary Maclean	50
60 Mary MacInnes	48	103 Donald MacKinnon	47
61 Penny MacInnes	25	104 Margaret MacKinnon	46
62 Allan MacInnes	23	105 Jessie MacKinnon	21
63 Hector MacInnes	21	106 Lauchlin MacKinnon	20
64 Mary MacInnes	19	107 Donald MacKinnon	16
65 Donald MacInnes	17	108 John MacKinnon	13
66 Marion MacInnes	10	109 Catherine MacKinnon	10
67 Flory MacInnes	8	110 Angus MacKinnon	6
68 Jessie MacInnes	6	111 Peter MacKinnon	3
69 Neil Maclean	40	112 John MacKinnon	48
70 Mary Maclean	30	113 Ann MacKinnon	45

114 Bell MacKinnon	20	157 Angus MacMillan	38
115 Donald MacKinnon	18	158 Marion MacMillan	40
116 Mary MacKinnon	15	159 Ann MacMillan	28
117 Neil MacKinnon	12	160 Neil MacMillan	24
118 John MacKinnon	6	161 Marion MacMillan	17
119 Donald MacKinnon	3	162 Ann MacKay	40
120 Hugh Maclean	29	163 Duncan MacKay	20
121 Marion MacKinnon	28	164 Mary MacKay	25
122 Rachel MacKinnon	infant	165 Neil MacKay	18
123 Allan Maclean	89	166 Donald MacMillan	57
124 Ann Maclean	62	167 Marion MacMillan	52
125 Peggy Maclean	40	168 John MacMillan	67
126 Peggy MacArthur	12	169 Catherine MacMillan	26
127 Hector MacArthur	6	170 Mary MacMillan	24
128 Donald MacKay	54	171 Ann MacMillan	23
129 Christine MacKay	49	172 Neil Stewart	26
130 Mary MacKay	20	173 Marion Stewart	20
131 Flory MacKay	18	174 Flory MacMillan	17
132 John MacKay	15	175 Neil MacMillan	13
133 Donald MacKay	10	176 Donald MacMillan	48
134 Neil MacKay	6	177 Catherine MacKinnon	50
135 Jean Cameron	48	178 Marion MacMillan	88
136 Peggy MacKinnon	20	179 Flory MacKinnon	18
137 Roddy? MacKinnon	17	180 Marion MacKinnon	16
138 Catherine MacKinnon	15	181 Ann MacKinnon	12
139 Mary MacKinnon	13	182 Allan MacKinnon	18
140 Archie MacKinnon	10	183 Neil MacKay	60
141 Lauchlin MacKinnon	40	184 Mary MacKay	57
142 Marion MacKinnon	35	185 Mary MacKay	35
143 Lauchlin MacKinnon	12	186 Donald MacKay	23
144 Catherine MacKinnon	10	187 Peggy MacKinnon	30
145 Archie MacKinnon	8	188 Neil MacKay	28
146 Donald MacKinnon	6	189 John MacKay	26
147 Mary MacKinnon	infant	190 Christina MacKay	21
148 Donald MacKay	65	191 Jessie MacKay	33
149 Christina MacMillan	60	192 Ann MacKay	infant
150 Alexander Maclean	26	193 Duncan MacKinnon	63
151 Neil Maclean	28	194 Mary MacKinnon	58
152 Catherine Maclean	33	195 Alexander MacKinnon	30
153 Archie MacMillan	27	196 Ann MacKinnon	25
154 Jessie MacMillan	28	197 Lauchlin MacKinnon	24
155 Donald MacMillan	2	198 Ann MacKinnon	20
156 Neil MacMillan	infant	199 Catherine MacKinnon	15

200	Donald MacKinnon	19	205	Christina Maclean	42
201	Flory MacKinnon	40	206	John Maclean	13
202	Margaret MacKinnon	38	207	Malcolm Maclean	11
203	Allan MacKay	12	208	Flory Maclean	9
204	Allan Maclean	58			

Surnames of the Saint Lawrence Passengers

MacKinnon	71	MacArthur	2
Maclean	44	MacIsaac	2
MacKay	37	Dalgleish	2
MacMillan	20	Stewart	2
MacInnes	10	Cameron	1
MacQuarrie	9	Campbell	1
MacPhaden	7		

Age Distribution of the Saint Lawrence Passengers

Infant	9	46–50	13
2–5	14	51–55	5
6–10	23	56–60	14
11–15	19	61–65	6
16–20	27	66–70	1
21–25	18	71–75	0
26–30	31	76–80	1
31–35	8	81–85	1
36–40	10	86–90	2
41–45	6		

Total   208

Bibliography

Anderson, A. Orr, *Early Sources of Scottish History: AD 500–1286*, Oliver & Boyd, Edinburgh, 1922.

Anderson, James, *An Account of the Present State of the Hebrides and Western Coasts of Scotland*, Elliot, Edinburgh, 1785.

Anon, 'Finding of Norse gaming piece on Rum', *Proc Soc Antiq Scot*, vol. 78 (1944), p. 139.

Aslet, Clive, 'Kinloch Castle, Isle of Rum' (2 parts) *Country Life*, 9 Aug. 1984, pp. 380–4; 16 Aug. 1984, pp. 446–9.

Atkinson, Robert, 'A Stag from Rum: an essay on poaching'. Unpublished manuscript (?1940) from the author.

Baird, R., *Shipwrecks of the West of Scotland*, Nekton Books, Glasgow, 1995.

Banks, N., *Six Inner Hebrides*, David & Charles, Newton Abbot, 1997.

Barclay, William, *Contra Monarchomachos*, n.d.

Betjeman, John, 'Kinloch Castle', *Scotland's Magazine*, Dec. 1959, pp. 16–21.

Bingham, Caroline, *Beyond the Highland Line*, Constable, London, 1991.

Boswell, James, *The Journal of a Tour to the Hebrides with Samuel Johnson LL.D.* (1786); Reprinted by Oxford University Press, Oxford, 1974.

Boyd, J. Morton, *Fraser Darling's Islands*, Edinburgh University Press, Edinburgh, 1986.

Bray, Elizabeth, *The Discovery of the Hebrides: voyagers to the Western Isles 1745–1883*, Collins, London, 1986.

Bristol, Nicholas Maclean, *Hebridean Decade: Mull, Coll and Tiree 1761–1771*, Society of West Highland and Island Historical Research, Isle of Coll, 1982.

British Fisheries Society, *Unpublished Report* (1788), ed. Lord Mount Stewart; from Dr John Lorne Campbell of Canna.

Brown, Olive and Whittaker, Jean, *A Walk around Tobermory*, privately published, Oban, 1988.

Bryden, J. and Houston, G., *Agrarian Change in the Scottish Highlands*, Martin Robertson/Highlands and Islands Development Board, Inverness, 1976.

Buchanan, Robert, *The Land of Lorne*, Chapman & Hall, London, 1871.

Bumstead, J. M., *The People's Clearance: Highland emigration to British North America*, Edinburgh University Press, Edinburgh, 1982.

Burke, Sir B. and Burke, A. P., *A Genealogical and Heraldic History of the Peerage and Baronetage, the Privy Council and Knightage*, 81st edn, London, 1923.

Burt, Ed. (1754), 'Letters from the North of Scotland', extracts ed. by A. J. Youngson, in *Beyond the Highland Line*, Collins, London, 1974.

Cameron, Archie, *Barefeet and Tackety Boots: a boyhood on Rhum*, Luath Press, Ayrshire, 1988.

Cameron, Donald, *Where Wild Geese Fly*, privately published, Glen Nevis, 1985.

Campbell, John Lorne, *Canna: the story of a Hebridean island*, Oxford University Press, Oxford, 1984; 3rd edn, Canongate, Edinburgh, 1994.

Carmichael, Alexander, *Carmina Gadelica*, vol. 1, Edinburgh, 1900.

Cecil, Lord David, *Hatfield House: a guide*, St George's Press, London, 1973.

Cecil, Lady Gwendoline, *Life of Robert, Marquis of Salisbury, vol. 1: 1830–1868*, Hodder & Stoughton, London, 1922.

Clarke, Edward Daniel, 'Journal 1769–1822', in W. Otter's *Life and Remains of the late Rev. E. D. Clarke*, 1825, pp. 321–40.

Clutton-Brock, T. H. and Ball, M. E, *Rhum: the natural history of an island*, Edinburgh University Press, Edinburgh, 1987.

Cooper, Derek, *Hebridean Connection*, Routledge & Kegan Paul, London, 1977.

Cooper, Derek, *Road to the Isles: travellers in the Hebrides 1770–1914*, Routledge & Kegan Paul, London, 1979.

Cumming, C. F. Gordon, *In the Hebrides*, London, 1883.

Darling, F. Fraser, *West Highland Survey*, Oxford University Press, Oxford, 1955.

Dawson, J. H., *An abridged Statistical History of Scotland*, Edinburgh, 1853.

de Saussure, L. A. Necker, *A voyage to the Hebrides or Western Isles of Scotland: vol. 8*, Sir Richard Phillips & Co., London, 1822.

Dobinson, J., 'Rhum Expedition, 1967', *Schools Hebridean Society Annual Report*, 1967, pp. 36–51.

Donaldson, M. E. M., *Wanderings in the Western Highlands and Islands*, Alexander Gardner, Paisley, 1923.

Donaldson, M. E. M., *Further Wanderings – mainly in Argyll*, Alexander Gardner, Paisley, 1926.

Dressler, Camille, *Eigg: the story of an Island*, Polygon, Edinburgh, 1998.

Dunn, Charles W., *Highland Settler: A Portrait of the Scottish Gael in Nova Scotia*, University of Toronto Press, Toronto, 1958.

Eggeling, W. J., 'A Nature Reserve Management Plan for the Isle of Rhum', *Journal of Applied Ecology*, vol. 1, 1964, pp. 405–19.

Emeleus, C. H. and Forster, R. M., *Field Guide to the Tertiary Igneous Rocks of Rhum, Inner Hebrides*, Nature Conservancy Council, Peterborough, 1979.

Fairrie, A. A., 'The Militia, Fencibles and non-regular forces of Inverness-shire, from the Napoleonic War to 1914', in *Loch Ness and Thereabouts*, ed. Loraine Maclean of Dochgarroch, Inverness Field Club, Inverness, 1991, pp. 74–90.

Gilbey, W., *Ponies, past and present*, Vinton & Co., London, 1900.

Grant, I. F., *Lordship of the Isles*, Moray Press, Edinburgh, 1935.

Gregory, Donald, *The History of the Western Highlands and Isles of Scotland* (1881), reprinted by John Donald, Edinburgh, 1975.

Groome, F. H., *Ordnance Gazetteer of Scotland*, 3 vols, London, 1903.

Harker, A., *The Geology of the Small Isles of Inverness-shire*, Geological Survey, Glasgow, 1908.

Harrison, J. W. H., 'The Flora of the Islands of Rhum, Eigg, Canna, Sanday, Muck, Eilean nan Each, Hyskeir, Soay and Pabbay', *Proc Univ Durham Philos Soc*, 10, (2), 1939, pp. 87–123.

Hart-Davis, Duff, *Monarch of the Glen*, Jonathan Cape, London, 1978.

Harvie-Brown, J. A. and Buckley, T. E., *A Vertebrate Fauna of Argyll and the Inner Hebrides*, David Douglas, Edinburgh, 1892.

Knox, John, *A Tour through the Highlands of Scotland and the Hebride Isles in 1786*, Gordon & Elliot, Edinburgh, 1787.

Hunter, James, *The Making of the Crofting Community*, John Donald, Edinburgh, 1976.

Irish Franciscan Mission to the Hebrides 1619–46, unpublished translation by Dom Denys Rutledge, from Dr John Lorne Campbell of Canna.

Jenkins, Belinda, 'The Forbidden Island – but Sir George Bullough made it his Scottish sanctuary', *Accrington Observer*, 4 Aug. 1984.

Johnson, Dr Samuel, *A Journey to the Western Islands of Scotland* (1775), reprinted by Oxford University Press, Oxford, 1974.

Lloyds Register of Yachts, (1915). Additional material on *Rhouma* from Mr Merrick Rayner, Chiswick.

Love, John A., 'Deer traps on the Isle of Rum', *Deer*, vol. 5, (3) (1980), pp. 131–2.

Love, John A., 'Shielings on the Isle of Rhum', *Scottish Studies*, vol. 26 (1981), pp. 39–63.

Love, John A., *The Isle of Rum: a short history*, privately published, Fort William, 1983.

Love, John A., *The Return of the Sea Eagle*, Cambridge University Press, Cambridge, 1983.

Love, John A., *The Birds of Rhum*, Nature Conservancy Council, Inverness, 1984.

Love, John A, 'Rhum's Human History', in *Rhum: The Natural History of an Island*, eds T. H. Clutton-Brock and M. E. Ball, Edinburgh University Press, Edinburgh, 1987, pp. 27–42.

MacAskill, Roderick, 'The Parish of the Small Isles', in *The Third Statistical Account of Scotland, vol. 16*, ed Hugh Barron, Scottish Academic Press, Edinburgh, 1985.

MacCulloch, John, *The Highlands and Western Isles of Scotland, vol. IV*, Longman, London, 1824.

MacDiarmid, Hugh, *The Islands of Scotland*, Batsford, London, 1939.

MacDonald, James, *General View of the Agriculture of the Hebrides*, Board of Agriculture, Edinburgh, 1811.

MacDonald, J. M., *Highland Ponies and Some Reminiscences of Highlandmen*, Eneas Mackay, Stirling, 1937.

MacDougall, J. L., *History of Inverness County*, Nova Scotia, n.d.

MacGregor, Alasdair Alpin, *An Island Here and There*, Kingsmead Press, Bath, 1972.

MacKay, J. A., *Islands Postal History Series No 4: Skye and the Small Isles*, privately published, Dumfries, 1978.

Mackenzie, Alexander, *The History of the Highland Clearances* (1883), reprinted by Alex Maclaren and sons, Glasgow, 1966.

Mackenzie, W. C., *The Highlands and Isles of Scotland*, Moray Press, Edinburgh, 1949.

Maclean, Rev. Donald, *The (Old) Statistical Account of Scotland, vol. 17* (1796), ed. Sir John Sinclair, Edinburgh; reprinted as vol. 20, EP Publishing, Wakefield, 1983.

Maclean, Rev. Donald, 'Parish of the Small Isles, January 1836', in *New Statistical Account, vol. 14*, Edinburgh, 1845.

Maclean, Sir Fitzroy, *West Highland Tales*, Canongate, Edinburgh, 1985.

Maclean, J. P., *A History of the Clan Maclean*, Cincinatti, 1889.

McLean, Marianne, *The People of Glengarry: Highlanders in transition, 1745–1820*, McGill-Queen's University Press, Montreal, 1991.

Macleod, Donald, Extract from a letter written by Donald Macleod, Drynoch, to his mother at Kinloch, Isle of Rum and dated 24 Sept. 1876. Copy in SNH files, Rum, 1876.

Macleod, Finlay, *Togail Tir*, Acair, Stornoway, 1989.

Macleod, Kenneth, *The Road to the Isles*, Grant & Murray, Edinburgh, 1927.

MacPhail, J. R. N., *Highland Papers, vol. IV*, Scottish History Society, Edinburgh, 1934.

MacQuarrie, John R., 'Laughlan MacQuarrie – amazing family', *Mac-Talla*, vol. 4(1) 1984, pp. 4–6. Clan MacQuarrie Association of Atlantic Canada.

McQuary, Roderick L., *A Book about MacQuarries*, Paupers' Press, Nottingham, n.d.

Mactavish, D. C., *Minutes of the Synod of Argyll, 1639–1651*, Scottish History Society, Edinburgh, 1943.

Magnusson, M., *Rum: Nature's Island*, Luath Press, Edinburgh, 1997.

Martell, J. S., *Immigration to and emigration from Nova Scotia 1815–38*, publ. no. 6, Public Archives of Nova Scotia, Halifax, 1942.

Martin, Martin, *A Description of the Western Islands of Scotland, circa 1695* (1703); 4th edn,
    Eneas Mackay, Stirling, 1934.
Matheson, E. H., *Matheson 1875–1975: an Otago family history*, privately printed, 32 pp,
    n.d.
Maxwell, Gavin, *Harpoon at a Venture*, Adventure Library, London, 1955.
Miller, Hugh, *The Cruise of the Betsey: or a summer holiday in the Hebrides*, 7th edn,
    William P. Nimmo, Edinburgh, 1869.
Miller, R., 'Land-use by summer shielings', *Scottish Studies*, vol. 11(2) (1967), pp. 193–221.
Mitchell, Sir Arthur, *Geographical Collections relating to Scotland made by Walter Macfarlane*,
    vol. 2, Edinburgh University Press for the Scottish Historical Society, 1907.
Monro, Sir Donald, (High Dean of the Isles), *A Description of the Western Isles of Scotland
    called Hybrides* (1774), William Auld, Edinburgh; reprinted by Eneas Mackay, Stirling,
    1934.
Muir, T. S., *Ecclesiological Notes on some of the Islands of Scotland*, David Douglas,
    Edinburgh, 1885.
Murray, Sarah, *A Companion and Useful Guide to the Beauties of Scotland*, 1803.
Nature Conservancy Council, *Isle of Rhum National Nature Reserve Handbook*, Nature
    Conservancy Council, Inverness, 1974.
O'Dell, A. C. and Walton, K., *The Highlands and Islands of Scotland*, London &
    Edinburgh, 1962.
Pennant, Thomas, *A Tour in Scotland and Voyage to the Hebrides, 1772*, Benjamin White,
    London, 1776; extracts ed. by A. J. Youngson, in *Beyond the Highland Line*, Collins,
    London, 1974.
Richards, Eric, *A History of the Highland Clearances: vol. 1: agrarian transformation and the
    eviction 1746–1886*, Croom Helm, London, 1982.
Richards, Eric, *A History of the Highland Clearances: vol. 2: emigration, protest, reasons*,
    Croom Helm, London, 1985.
Richardson, Robert, *The Book of Hatfield*, Barracuda Books, Chesham, Bucks, 1978.
Ritchie P. R., 'The stone implement trade in third millennium Scotland', in *Studies
    in Ancient Europe*, ed. J. M. Coles and D. D. A. Simpson, pp. 117–136, Leicester
    University Press, 1967.
Royal Commission on the Ancient and Historical Monuments of Scotland, *Ninth Report:
    The Outer Hebrides, Skye and the Small Isles*, HMSO, Edinburgh, 1928.
Royal Commission on the Ancient and Historical Monuments of Scotland, *The
    Archaeological Sites and Monuments of Scotland no. 20: Rhum, Lochaber District, Highland
    Region*, RCAHMS, Edinburgh, 1983.
Royal Scottish Geographical Society, *The Early Maps of Scotland*, Edinburgh, 1936.
Royal Scottish Geographical Society, *The Early Maps of Scotland: vol. 1*, Edinburgh, 1973.
Rum Island Company of Volunteer Infantry, *Muster Rolls 1803–1811* ref. no. WO13/4383,
    Public Record Office, Kew, Surrey.
Rum School log-books, in Inverness Library; Side School log-books in Rum School.
Sabbagh, K., *A Rum Affair*, Allen Lane, The Penguin Press, London, 1999.
Salisbury Rum papers, 1845–62, Archives of Hatfield House, Hatfield, Herts; letter
    books and account books with correspondence between Lord Salisbury and his Factor
    in Rum.
Scott, Hew, *Fasti Ecclesiae Scoticanae: vol. 7*, Oliver & Boyd, Edinburgh, 1928.
Scott, W. L., 'Excavation of Rudh' an Dunain cave, Skye', *Proc Soc Antiq Scot*, vol. 68
    (1934).
Select Committee on Emigration, *Third Report*, QQ 826,2907,2986, Scottish Record
    Office, 1827.

Shaw, Frances J., *The Northern and Western Islands of Scotland: their economy and society in the seventeenth century*, John Donald, Edinburgh, 1980.

Shaw, Margaret Fay, *From the Alleghenies to the Hebrides*, Canongate, Edinburgh, 1993; Birlinn, Edinburgh, 1999.

Simpson, W. Douglas, *Portrait of Skye and the Outer Hebrides*, Robert Hale, London, 1967.

Sinclair, Rev. A. Maclean, *Clan Gillean*, Haszard & Moore, Charlottetown, 1899.

Skene, William F., *Celtic Scotland: A History of Ancient Alban*. 3 vols (1876), reprinted by Books for Libraries Press, New York, 1971.

Smith, J. Drew, 'The economic and agricultural history of the Island of Rhum', unpubl. thesis (1949), copy in SNH library, Rum.

Smout, T. C., *A History of the Scottish People 1560–1830*, Collins, London, 1969.

Smythe, Alfred P., *Warlords and Holy Men: Scotland AD 80–1000*, Edward Arnold, London, 1984.

Society for the Propagation of Christian Knowledge, Unpublished Committee Minutes, (IV 396) (1731), from Dr John Lorne Campbell of Canna.

Steven, C. R., *The Island Hills*, London, 1955.

Stone, Jeffrey C., 'Timothy Pont and the first topographical survey of Scotland c.1583–1596: an informative contemporary manuscript', *Scottish Geographical Magazine*, vol. 99(3), 1983, pp. 161–8.

Stone, Jeffrey C., *The Pont Manuscript Maps of Scotland: Sixteenth century origins of a Blaeu atlas*, Map Collector Publications, Tring, 1989.

Swire, Otta F., *The Inner Hebrides and their Legends*, Oliver & Boyd, Edinburgh, 1966.

Taylor, J., *The Penniless Pilgrim and other pieces*, 1618.

Tyrie, Father John, unpublished report (1737), translated from the Italian by Rt Rev. Colin Macpherson, Bishop of Argyll and the Isles. 'Scritture Referite nei Congressi – Scozia: vol. 1, folio 24'. From Dr John Lorne Campbell of Canna.

Walker, Rev. Dr John, *Report on the Hebrides of 1764 and 1771*, ed. Margaret M. Mackay, John Donald, Edinburgh, 1980.

Watson, William J., 'Aoibhinn an Obair an t-Sealg', *Celtic Review*, vol. 9(34) (1913), pp. 156–68.

Waugh, Edwin, *The Limping Pilgrim on his wanderings*, John Heywood, Manchester, 1883.

Webster, Alexander, 'An Account of the number of people in Scotland in the year one thousand seven hundred and fifty five', in *Scottish Population Statistics*, ed. J. Gray Kyd, Edinburgh, 1952.

Whitehead, G. K., *The Deer Stalking Grounds of Great Britain and Ireland*, Hollis & Carter, London, 1960.

Whitehead, G. Kenneth, *Hunting and Stalking Deer in Britain through the Ages*, Batsford, London, 1980.

Wickham-Jones, Caroline, *Rhum: mesolithic and later sites at Kinloch: excavations 1984–1986*, Society of Antiquaries of Scotland Monograph Series, no. 7, 1990.

Wickham-Jones, Caroline, 'A round-bottomed vessel from a new archaeological site at Papadil, Rum', *Glasgow Archaeological Journal*, vol. 18 (1993), pp. 73–5.

Williams, Ronald, *The Lords of the Isles*, Hogarth Press, London, 1984.

Williamson, Kenneth and Morton Boyd, J., *A Mosaic of Islands*, Oliver & Boyd, Edinburgh, 1963.

Wormell, P., 'Establishing woodland on the Isle of Rhum', *Scottish Forestry*, vol. 22(3) (1968), pp. 207–20.

Index

a'Bhrideanach 6, 24, 225
Accrington 220, 221, 230, 232, 249
Agricola 26
agriculture 24, 49, 61, 64, 66, 67, 71, 78,
    85, 86, 88–90, 95, 115, 123, 127, 139,
    141, 142, 145, 163, 166, 183, 222, 244,
    262, 265
Ainshval 4
Aisgobhall 67
Albion 181, 195
alder 9, 23, 24
Alexander II 37
Alexander III 37, 38, 44
Alexander of Islay 39
Allan nan Sop 44
allivalite 6
Allt Airidh Thalabairt 209
Allt an Eassain 223
Allt na Ba 5
Am Ministear Laidir 75
am Piobair Mor 56
amphibians 14
an Cleirach Beag 45
an Dornabac 100
Anderson A. O. 28
Anderson, James 121, 140
Anderson, Mrs Mabel 258
Angus Mor of Islay 37, 38
Angus Og of Islay 38, 42
animals 8, 13, 20, 24, 65, 264
an Sgoilear Ban 255
archaeology 18, 19, 21, 23, 24, 36
Ard Mheall 224
Ard Nev 3, 6, 110
arrowhead 16, 17, 18, 19, 21, 22
Arthur Cecil, Lord 184, 195, 244
asses 184
ash 139
Ashworth, John 204, 234
Ashworth's Model Loch 234
Askival 6, 35, 48, 67, 83, 97, 105, 198,
    224, 225
Aslet, Clive 241
aspen 9, 24
Atkinson, Robert 261, 262
Auckland 200

Australia 128, 132, 133, 139, 155, 176, 207
axe head 19

Bagh na Uamha 20, 30, 31, 36
bagpipes 56, 72
Balliol, John 38
Banker, the 131, 132
Barkeval 100, 105, 223
Barra 38, 43, 118, 147, 163, 184, 226
basking shark 104
Bass, Sir William 240
bathrooms 240
Bayview 181, 207
Bealach a'Bhraigh Bhig 17, 141
Beatson, Rev. David 200
Beatson, Rev. H. 147, 200
Beccan, St 27, 28, 31
beech 139
Ben Mor 48
Benbecula 108
Betjeman, Sir John 242
Betsey 140–142, 144
birch 9, 23, 24, 66, 84
birlinn 37, 43, 45
Bishop of Argyll/Isles 39, 47, 49, 53, 121
blackcock 243
Black Valley 110
Black Watch 116
Blaeu, Joan 48
bloodstone 7, 8, 16, 17, 18, 21, 22, 23, 66,
    68, 141, 142, 187
Bloodstone Hill 7, 13, 17, 22, 141, 186,
    187, 193, 223, 225
Blundell, Dom. Odo 56, 80
boats 160, 163, 164, 166, 173, 176, 178–81,
    184, 202, 203, 206, 207, 211, 227, 232,
    243, 247, 248, 260, 262
Boer War 233, 242
Boswell, James 41, 43, 51, 69–73, 75, 90,
    122, 124
Bounteous 247
bowl, prehistoric 25
Boyd, J. Morton 264
Bracadale, Skye 142, 143, 157, 164, 199,
    209
Breacachadh Castle 42, 69, 70, 71

Breadalbane 133
Brebner, Mr 255, 256
British Fisheries Society 55, 74, 75, 140, 196
Bronze Age 9, 18, 19, 22, 24, 25, 26
Bruce, Robert 38, 42
Buail' a Ghoirtein 22
Buchanan, Robert 198, 199, 204
Bullough, Alexandria 222, 230, 235
Bullough, Bertha 220–2
Bullough, Gladys 222, 230, 248
Bullough, Hermione 238, 246, 248, 249
Bullough, Ian 222, 230, 234
Bullough, James 219, 220
Bullough, John 85, 107, 203, 204, 214, 219–22, 227–33, 238, 258
Bullough, Lady Monica 231, 232, 234, 236–45, 249, 256, 258–63
Bullough, Sir George 85, 219, 220, 222, 228, 230–49, 253, 258, 264
Bullough, William 204
Bulloughs 192, 196, 219, 253, 261, 266
burial cist 36
burial ground 29, 30, 127, 156, 160, 166, 177, 200, 209

Cadogan, Francis 234
cairns 24
Calgacus 26
California 172
Camas Pliascaig 22, 36
Cameron, Alexander 143
Cameron, Annie 237, 246
Cameron, Archie 126, 143, 209, 211, 217, 237, 243–9, 253, 254
Cameron, Donald 259
Cameron, Dugald 242–5
Cameron, Janet 252, 253
Cameron, Kirsty 165, 172
Camerons 42, 44, 252
Campbell, Captain 146, 177, 197, 214, 251
Campbell, Colin 251
Campbell, Donald 124
Campbell, Farquhar 197, 198, 204, 214, 215, 227, 251
Campbell, Hector 164, 173, 174, 175, 194
Campbell, James Hunter 227, 228
Campbell, John Lorne 40, 53, 54, 59, 68, 77, 104, 128, 266, 267
Campbell, Kenneth 142, 143, 163, 172, 207
Campbell, Marion 214, 215
Campbell, Walter 227
Campbells 40, 50, 59, 69, 71, 74, 123, 223
Campbells of Ballinaby 214, 223, 227
Campbells of Kilberry 197, 214
Campbells of Ormsary 197, 214, 215

Canada 122, 129–33, 171, 172
Canna 7, 8, 10, 12, 14, 17, 22, 30, 36, 46, 48, 53, 55–9, 65, 67, 68, 70, 72, 74, 75, 80, 81, 85, 88, 89, 91, 92, 104–6, 113, 118, 121, 126, 137–139, 166, 169, 171, 173, 179, 186, 199, 203, 207, 214, 242, 245, 251, 253 266
Cape Breton 120, 127–133, 139
Carmichael, Alexander 98
Carn an Dobhran 143, 205, 213
carriages 242, 248
cars, Albion 242, 248
Catholicism 14, 48, 50, 53–8, 60, 68, 72, 76, 77, 80, 108, 121, 137, 140, 226, 250
cats 244
cattle 10, 13, 66, 71, 74, 79, 84, 88–92, 94–100, 114–15, 121, 127, 139, 144, 145, 164, 165, 171, 175, 176, 183, 197, 198, 206, 207, 210, 226, 244, 259, 261, 265
caves 20, 30, 41, 56, 67, 80, 100, 137
Celtic crosses 29, 30, 31, 160, 161
chapel 29, 64, 68, 204, 213
Charles II 113
Charlie, Prince 59, 68, 115
Charrington, Monica 236
Child's Grave 209, 211
Chisholm, Alexander 144, 169
Chisholm, James 199, 213
Chisholm, Kenneth 199, 213
church 137, 169, 204, 205, 207, 213, 225, 253
Church of Scotland 54, 64–6, 71, 75, 76, 130, 133, 140, 250
Clach Cuid Fir 126 (see Rocking Stone)
Clan Donald 37, 39
Clan Ruari 37, 38
Clancy, T. O. 28
Clanranald 39, 41, 43, 47, 48, 50, 51, 54, 59, 60, 80, 123, 126, 222
Clarke, Edward Daniel 77–9, 103, 104, 106, 108–11, 263
Clearances 94, 95, 102, 113, 116–22, 124–35, 141–3, 145, 162, 170–2, 184, 209, 262, 266
Clement, D. 189–91
climate 9, 10, 12, 19, 24, 66, 88, 90, 94, 95, 151, 227, 260, 264
clipping 147, 149
coal 7
cockles 20
cod 226
Coire nan Grunnd 9, 17, 106, 246
Coll 37, 42, 43, 44, 45, 46, 49, 50, 51, 59, 69–71, 74, 75, 90, 114, 123, 124, 211
College of Agriculture 265
Columba, St 14, 26, 27, 28, 35

Comet, Donati's 161, 162
Community Council 267
community ownership 266
Comyn, John 38
conservation 261, 264, 265
Cooper, Derek 239, 249
copper 25
cormorants 225
corn 10, 183, 196
corncrakes 107
cottages 67, 77, 78, 82, 83, 85, 86, 137, 141–3, 145, 164, 176, 182, 186, 198, 204–10, 212, 213, 225, 226, 230
cotton mill 219–21, 230, 234
Courier, Inverness 154, 164, 178, 263
Cowan, Francis 156, 160
Cowan, Walter 143, 155–61, 181
crab apple 24
crabs 20
Creag nan Steardan 16, 223 (see Bloodstone Hill)
Creidimh a'bhata bhuide (see yellow stick religion)
crofting 119, 183, 197, 198, 206, 207, 222, 224, 259
Cromwell 113
crops 88, 89, 95, 196
crows 15, 104, 193
Crusader 227
cuckoo 15, 242
cull, deer 243, 264

dairy produce 90, 94–100, 198, 207
Dam, Salisbury's 187–92, 196, 223, 229
Darling, F. Fraser 96, 150, 263, 264
David II 38
Davison, Capt. W. 113
Dawson, J. H. 10
De Saussure, Necker 79, 92
Dean of the Isles 44, 67
deer trap 78, 109–112
deer, fallow 161, 182, 183, 195, 196, 202, 222, 225, 229, 243
deer, red 13, 14, 15, 18, 20, 24, 36, 47, 49, 64, 66, 72, 95, 108–12, 144, 178, 185, 195, 196, 202, 203, 212, 221, 222–4, 226, 228, 234, 235, 238, 243, 244, 246, 259, 260, 262–5
de la Pasture, Marquis 236, 248
Department of Agriculture 265
Dibidil 6, 9, 11, 15, 35, 145, 150, 177, 182, 185–7, 199, 213, 225, 244
disease/accidents 66, 68, 88, 162, 165, 166, 173, 174, 176, 179–81, 200, 204
doctor 204

dogs 161, 183, 186, 187, 205, 212, 244, 254, 262
dogwhelks 104
Donald Dubh 40, 42
Donald of Islay 37, 39, 42
Donaldson, M. E. M. 14, 56
Donnan, St 27
dotterel 78, 108
drainage 169, 186, 193
dress 72, 77, 114, 171, 172, 237
Dressler, Camille 56, 126
Drumfin (Aros House) 51
ducks 107, 183, 193, 222, 225, 243
Dugan, Father 54
Dumna 26
Dunnet, Alastair 262
Durham, Countess 248, 249

eagle, golden 15, 109, 194, 195, 225
eagle, ivory 239, 262
eagles 193, 194, 195, 239
eagle, white-tailed sea 15, 194, 195, 225, 234, 265
Earl of Ross 37, 39
Education Act 1872 250, 252
Edward II of England 38
Eggeling, W. J. 260, 264
Eigg 5, 6, 10, 12, 14, 17, 21, 22, 27, 31, 36, 38–41, 46–8, 54–9, 65, 70, 72, 75–7, 79–81, 96, 97, 100, 105, 107, 116, 118, 121, 126, 130, 131, 137, 138, 140, 147, 151, 166–9, 171, 175, 184, 189, 195, 200, 203, 204, 225, 227, 236, 243, 245, 250, 251, 253, 255, 256, 266, 267
electricity 240, 241, 258, 265
Elizabeth I of England 43, 46, 47
Ellen Lewis 133
Elliott, Christina 200, 201
Elliott, William 164
elm 9
emigration 115, 118, 119, 121, 122, 125–35, 143, 144, 170–2, 176, 205
environment 23
Eriskay 92
erratics 8
excavation 18, 21, 22, 23, 24, 36

Faithfull, John 17
fank 186, 259
faults 4, 6, 7, 8
fencing 225
Fencible Regiment 51, 75, 116
Ferguson, Donald 206, 213, 228
Ferguson, John 228
Ferguson, Marion 257

ferryman 245, 259
fertiliser 183
fiddle 80–82
Finch, Alfred 178
Fionchra 7, 12, 13, 17, 64, 108, 141
fish 20, 61, 79, 92, 101, 102, 163, 165, 178,
　　183, 188, 226, 243
fish ladders 102, 192
fish traps 20, 101, 102
Fisher, Ian 30
fishing 102–4, 114, 157, 163, 164, 173,
　　178, 199, 200, 206, 209, 210, 212, 222,
　　262
fishing nets 20, 102, 173, 196
flax 21, 182
Fletcher, Angus 175
flooding 11, 166, 186, 193, 210
Florida 46
flowers 13, 183, 206, 242, 258
fog 12, 161, 166
Forbidden Island 261
Forester, Andrew 227
Forestry Commission 265
Forgan, Margaret 253, 254
fort, promontory 25, 100
fossils 4, 5, 7, 8, 65, 78
Foxglove Cottage 206, 252, 253
Franciscans 53
Fraser, Duncan 143
Fraser, Marjory Kennedy 203
Fraser, Rev. W. 80
Free Church 41, 140, 144, 167, 168, 227,
　　250, 251
frogs 14, 243
frost 11, 161, 182, 183
fruits 182, 183, 242
Fullerton's *Gazeteer* 10
fulmar 15

Gaelic 53, 57, 63, 64, 69, 79, 104, 116,
　　134, 140, 168, 198, 202–4, 206, 212,
　　233, 245, 251, 252, 257, 266
Gaelic Schools Society 79, 80, 81, 138, 250
gales 12, 164, 179–82
gamebooks 107, 235, 248
gamekeeper 204, 233–5, 244, 246, 261,
　　265
gaming piece, Norse 36
gannets 106
garden 181–3, 193, 204, 207, 210, 212,
　　213, 222, 224, 242, 244, 248, 259, 265
Garmoran 37, 38, 39
Gascoyne, Francis Mary 153
gathering 145–7, 175
Gaw, Miss 253
gazebo 231, 242

Geikie, Sir Archibald 6
geology 3, 140, 260, 264
Gertrude 133
Giblin, Father C. 54
Gilbey, Sir Walter 92, 184, 185, 195
Gille Riabhach 43
Gillean 42
Gilles, Angus 171
Gilles, Flora 172
Gilles, John 142, 143, 157, 163, 164, 172
Gilles, Neil 165
Gillis, Rev. A. 81
Giuliana 234
glaciation 8, 12, 19, 23, 126
glasshouses 242
Glen Duian 110, 111
Glen Guirdil 17, 23, 77, 141, 223
Glenharie 48, 49
Globe Works 220, 221
gneiss 4, 6
goats 15, 20, 25, 94, 96, 151, 184, 185,
　　226, 235, 246
Gordon, Seton 109
granary 181, 183
granite 6, 13
Grant and sons 21
Grant, Rev. Peter 169
grasses 12, 13, 90, 92, 151
grave 143, 161, 200, 209, 211
Gregory, David Maclean 132
Griffiths, Moses 67
grouse, red 15, 66, 107, 193, 202, 221,
　　223, 224, 229, 243
Grulin, Eigg 56
Gualann na Pairc 86
guillemot 15
Guirdil 22, 24, 77, 78, 82, 102, 141,
　　144–7, 149–51, 164, 166, 174, 175, 177,
　　182, 183, 186, 194, 195, 199, 203, 214,
　　223, 230, 244, 248, 257, 260 265
gulls 15, 183

Haakon of Norway 37, 38
Hallival 6, 9, 17, 35, 83, 105, 106, 198,
　　225, 239
Hammersley, John 178
hare, brown 14, 225, 227, 243
Harman, Mary 20
Harmony, Dove of 128, 129
Harris, Rum 9, 11, 12, 17, 23, 24, 25, 48,
　　85, 86, 107, 143, 145, 146, 149–51, 164,
　　165, 166, 170, 175, 177, 186, 187, 193,
　　199, 213, 223, 229, 230, 235, 242, 244,
　　247, 249, 251, 257, 260, 265
Harris bothy 182, 230
Harris Glen 13, 49, 188, 192, 246

Harris Lodge 228, 260
Harrisite 7
Harvie-Brown, J. A. 191, 192, 196, 227–9, 243, 258
Hatfield House 145, 152–4, 158, 161–3, 173, 176, 184, 185, 187, 189, 190, 192
hawks 193
hawthorn 24
hay 161, 225, 259
hazel 9, 23, 24
hazelnut shells 18, 19, 20, 24
heather 12, 13, 193, 229
Hebridean 204, 226
Hector Allanson 46
Hector Mor 42, 45, 50
Hector Roy 42, 45, 50
Hector the Stern 42
Henderson, Catherine 143, 156, 161
Henderson, Donald 206, 210
Henry VIII 40
heron 242
Heslop Harrison 30, 262
Highland Laddie 128, 129
Highland Lass 133
Hill Farming Research Organisation 265
hirsels 145–49, 171
holly 24, 66, 84
horses 20, 89–94, 184, 242, 244, 246
Howard and Bullough 220, 230
hounds 244
houses 181, 230
Hugh's Brae 24
Hunter, Alexander 51, 116, 126–9
hut circles 24

Ice Age 8, 12, 19
Inbhir Ghil 8
inscribed slab 20
insects 13
Inverlochy, Battle of 44, 50
Inverness 147, 166, 257, 258
Inverness County 131, 132
Iona 27, 28, 35, 53, 65, 67, 70, 72, 213
Iron Age 9, 25
Ivy Cottage 213

Jacobite Risings 50, 56, 59, 64, 65, 68, 69, 72, 75, 77, 100, 114, 115, 124
James Cecil 144, 153–5, 176
James I of England 47, 49
James II 39
James IV 40
James V 40, 42
James VI 42, 44, 46, 47, 49, 53, 108
Jenny Lind 178–80
jetty 263

John Abrach 44, 45
John Garbh 42, 43, 44, 49, 50, 52
John of Fordun 44
John of Islay 39, 40, 42, 44
John of Lochaber 44
Johnson, Dr Samuel 51, 55, 63, 68–73, 75, 90, 92, 113, 114, 119, 122–4
Johnston, John 255, 256
Jopp, Peter 253
Juan de Sicilia 46
juniper 9, 23

Kaming 48
Keil, Mr 253
kelp 79, 118–21, 123
Kennedy, Father A. 56
Keppie, J. 30
kerb cairns 24
Kildonan, Eigg 27, 56, 75, 80
Kilmory 11, 12, 14, 24, 25, 29, 30, 48, 49, 64, 82, 85, 86, 105, 107, 117, 127, 128, 132, 144–6, 149, 150, 156, 160, 166, 169, 174, 175, 177, 186, 195, 199, 200, 206, 209, 211, 213, 229, 230, 242–4, 251, 252, 258–60
Kilmory bothy 182, 200, 230
Kilmory Glen 8, 12, 23, 142, 191, 193, 223, 243
Kilmory Lodge 228, 234
Kilmory River 102, 187, 188, 191–3
King of England 38, 39, 40, 59
King of Man 38
Kinloch 247
Kinloch II 247
Kinloch 11, 14, 18, 23, 24, 25, 67, 85, 86, 117, 129, 143–5, 147, 149, 150, 160, 164, 166, 169, 171, 175, 177, 181, 182, 185, 195, 196, 199, 203, 204, 213, 229, 230, 243, 246, 247, 251, 252, 257–9, 262
Kinloch Castle 247
Kinloch Castle 13, 85, 219, 228, 233, 236–49, 258, 259, 261
Kinloch Farm 18, 181, 183, 213, 222, 225, 244, 259, 260, 265
Kinloch Glen 6, 11, 12, 126, 166, 186, 193, 206, 209, 223, 243
Kinloch Lodge (House) 85, 138, 181, 182, 192, 193, 204, 207, 210–13, 221, 222–6, 237
Kinloch River 102, 187, 192, 204, 242
Kinloch Woods 15
kittiwake 15
Knox, John 74, 75, 86, 103

Lachlan Bronnach 42, 43
Lachlan Lubanach 42

Lachlan Mor 42, 43, 45, 46
Lachlan Og 42
Laird of Coll see Macleans of Coll
lambing 147, 149, 150, 173, 193, 194, 260
Lauder, Adam 144
lava 7, 12, 13, 23
lazybeds 85, 86, 143
Lesser Isles 81, 121
lightning 12
lime 179, 181
lime kiln 181, 207
limpets 20, 22, 25
lithe 226
Little Ice Age 11
Livingston, Colin 204
Livingston, David 204
Livingston, Duncan 144
Livingston, Hugh 204
lizards 14, 141
Loch a'Ghille Reamhra 110
Loch Dornabac 7, 225
Loch Fiachanius 224, 225
Loch Gainmhic 225
Lochmor 259
Loch nan Eala 209
Loch Papadil 225
Loch Scresort 4, 12, 18, 22, 33, 38, 48, 64, 67, 74, 78, 79, 85, 102–4, 127, 129, 138, 141, 142, 160, 163, 166, 178, 192, 198, 204, 205, 210, 213, 214, 222–6, 233, 238, 239, 242, 261
Loch Sgathaig 225
Long Loch 8, 12, 23, 188, 189, 192, 193, 196
longevity 66, 101
Lordship of the Isles 36, 39, 40, 41

Mac Iain Abrach 44
Mac Neil of Canna 55
MacAskill, Kenneth 58
MacAskill, James 233, 236
MacAskill, John 208, 232, 233, 236
MacAskill, Rev. M. 75
MacCulloch, John 1, 10, 81, 90, 121, 141, 160
Macdonald, Alexander 81, 143, 214
Macdonald, Anne 172
Macdonald, Catherine 214
Macdonald, Charles 176, 177
Macdonald, Donald 175
Macdonald, Duncan 194
Macdonald, Father A. 80
Macdonald, Flora 68
Macdonald, James 11, 90, 93, 121–4
Macdonald, John 199

Macdonald, Norman 142, 143, 157, 163, 164, 170–2, 174, 177
Macdonald, Una 116
Macdonalds 40, 41, 46, 47, 64
MacDonnell of Keppoch 114
MacDonnell, Father F. 54
MacDougall, Ewen 37
MacDougall, H. M. 155–9, 169, 181, 184, 185
MacDougall, Hugh 176
MacDougall, Lachlan 175, 177, 199
MacDougalls of Lorne 37, 38
MacDougall, William Henry 204, 251
MacEwens of Muck 266
Macfarlane, Walter 48, 90, 108
Macfee, Miss 252
MacGillivray, Neil 177
MacGillivray, William 93
MacGregor, A. Alpin 232, 241
MacGregor, Donald 143
MacGregor, Katie 261
MacGregor, tenant 155, 160
machair 12, 16
MacIans 49, 50
MacInnes, Mary 257
MacInnes 115
MacIntyre, John 175, 177
MacIntyre, Peter 174–7
MacIvor, Richard 18
Mackay, Donald 80
Mackay, James 236
Mackay, Margaret 66
Mackenzie, Alexander factor 159–77, 179, 180, 182–96, 200
Mackenzie, Alexander shepherd 174, 175
Mackenzie, Elizabeth 162, 168
Mackenzie, Isabella 139
Mackenzie, Kenneth 222
Mackenzie, Sarah 159, 162
Mackenzie tartan 237
MacKerran, Lachlan 68
Mackinnon, Alexander 143
Mackinnon, Angus 176
Mackinnon, Bill 129
Mackinnon, Chrissie 257
Mackinnon, Flora 172, 199, 210
Mackinnon, Hector 144, 169, 199
Mackinnon, Hugh 75, 126
Mackinnon, Iain 186, 187
Mackinnon, John 143, 163, 172, 175
Mackinnon, Margaret 131, 172
Mackinnon, Norman 199, 207, 212
Mackinnon, Sarah 172, 173, 177, 198, 199, 210
Mackinnon, William 175, 176
Mackinnons 47, 115, 252

Mackintosh, Mary 131
MacLachlan, Donald 236
Maclean of Ardgour 42
Maclean of Coll 14, 33, 42–4, 47–52, 54–6, 64, 67, 69–72, 74, 75, 92, 103, 108, 118, 119, 123, 127–9, 132, 205, 211, 214, 222
Maclean of Crossapol 71, 75, 124, 128, 131
Maclean of Duart 33, 41, 42, 44, 45, 47
Maclean of Gallanach 124, 128, 129, 131
Maclean of Grishipol 45
Maclean of Lochbuie 42
Maclean, Alasdair 132
Maclean, Alexander 51, 52, 79, 91, 114, 117, 122, 124, 125
Maclean, Allan 45, 58, 124, 128, 129, 131–33, 143, 166, 170, 172, 177, 182
Maclean, Angus 142, 143, 163, 172, 177
Maclean, Anne 172
Maclean, Archibald 143, 166, 170–2
Maclean, Catherine 170, 172, 177, 199
Maclean, Charles 124, 131
Maclean, Christy 131, 132, 172
Maclean, Daniel 128, 139
Maclean, Donald 50, 51, 54, 55, 69, 70, 90, 92, 117, 120, 122, 124, 131, 132, 163, 172
Maclean, Dr Lachlan 124–126, 128, 129, 137–40, 145
Maclean, Fitzroy 43
Maclean, Hector 42, 44, 45, 49, 50, 54, 59, 69, 131
Maclean, Hugh 50, 51, 52, 59, 69, 122–6, 197
Maclean, James 128, 131
Maclean, Janet 116
Maclean, John 117, 131–4
Maclean, John Mor 132
Maclean, John Norman 52
Maclean, John the Banker 131, 132
Maclean, John, bard 72, 119, 124, 128, 130
Maclean, J. P. 41, 45, 46, 52, 131
Maclean, Kenneth 33, 143, 163, 170, 172, 173, 177, 193, 199, 205, 206, 213, 266
Maclean, Lachlan 42, 46, 49, 50, 59, 64, 69, 120, 124, 132
Maclean, Miss Mabel 258
Maclean, Malcolm 199, 209
Maclean, Margaret 143, 172
Maclean, Marigold 132
Maclean, Marion 132
Maclean, Mary 131, 132, 199, 207, 209, 210
Maclean, Molly 68
Maclean, Murdoch Mor 132, 133

Maclean, Neil 124, 163, 164
Maclean, Peggy 82, 83
Maclean, Peter 163, 164, 172
Maclean, Rev. Donald 71, 75, 76, 78, 79, 116–18, 124–5, 129, 130, 131, 137
Maclean, Rev. Hector 70
Maclean, Rev. Neil 80, 81
Maclean, Roderick 120, 128, 131
Maclean, Sarah 131
Maclean, Sir John 72
Maclean, William 52
Maclean's Point 120
Macleans 41
Macleans of Muck 50
Macleod, Angus 142, 143, 163
Macleod, Capt. Norman 198, 202, 203, 251
Macleod, Donald 188, 199, 202, 203, 213
Macleod, Dr (Dunvegan) 200, 202
Macleod, Malcolm 206, 210, 213
Macleod, Rev. A. 81
Macleod, Rev. Kenneth 203
Macleod, Rev. Norman 133, 134
Macleod, Roderick 199, 213
Macleod, William 199
Macleods 40, 41, 47, 64, 70, 75, 113
MacMaister, John 122, 127
MacNab, Miss 253
Macnaughton, Duncan 237, 243, 248, 259, 262
Macnaughton, George 18, 187, 248
MacNeil of Barra 43
MacNeill of Canna 126, 139, 169, 251
MacNeill, Donald 126
MacNeill, Neill catechist 60
Macpherson, Dr Hugh 126
Macpherson, James 68
Macpherson, Prof. N. 17, 204
Macphie, Mr 189, 192
MacQuarrie, Allan 116
MacQuarrie, Angus 116
MacQuarrie, Donald 56
MacQuarrie, Lachlan 56, 115
MacQueen, Rev. D. 57, 75
Macrae, Allan 172, 174
Macrae, Donald 169
Macrae, Katie 257
Macrae, Mairi 174
Macrae, Malcolm 163
Macrae, Miss Mary 252, 253, 257
Macrae, Murdoch 142, 166
Macrae, Norman 165
Macrae, William 144
MacRuari, Alan 38
MacRuari, Amy 39
MacRuari, Ranald 38, 39

MacSweens 37, 70, 71
Magnificent 247
Malcolm's Bridge 17, 247
mammals 14, 15
management plan 264
maps 26
Margaret 133
Margaret, Maid of Norway 38
Margaret, Regent 39
Maria 233
marigold cross 29, 30
Martin, Martin 29, 63, 84, 85, 96, 102, 107, 108
Mary Queen of Scots 40, 46
Massacre in Eigg cave 41, 80, 137
Maternity Hollow 64
Matheson, Alexander 200, 201
Matheson, Allan 165, 166
Matheson, Archibald Duncan 200
Matheson, Christina 172, 200, 201
Matheson, Christina-Anne 200
Matheson, Donald 142, 143, 163, 165, 172, 185, 187
Matheson, Dougald 200, 201
Matheson, Elliot Hugh 201
Matheson, Helen 201
Matheson, James 200, 201
Matheson, Jesse Margaret 200, 201
Matheson, John 142, 163, 165, 166, 172, 173, 181, 199, 200, 206
Matheson, Lake (NZ) 201
Matheson, Matthew 200, 201
Matheson, Margaret 172
Matheson, Mary Anne 206
Matheson, Murdo(ch) 175, 177, 182, 199, 200, 201
Matheson, Murdo 200
Matheson, Neil 165
Matheson, Rebecca 200
Matheson, Robert 200, 201
Matheson, William John 200
Mathesons 142, 213
mausoleum 86, 219, 230, 231, 249
Maxwell, Gavin 104, 112, 219
mead 21
meal 164, 165, 175, 183, 198
Meggernie 221, 222, 228–30, 246
Melville, Herman 129
merlin 15
Mesolithic 19, 20, 21, 22
microliths 19, 21, 22
Midas 247
middens 19, 25
midges 13, 14, 211, 237, 242, 248
Miket, Roger 98
Miller, David 25

Miller, Hugh 3, 4, 5, 13, 16, 41, 84, 96, 101, 104, 112, 135, 137, 140–2, 144, 163, 250, 263, 266
Miller, Prof. R. 94, 95
Minch 5
minerals 7, 13, 66, 68, 78, 79, 141, 142, 145, 260
Minishal 110
Mitchell, Jean 257
Monadh Mhiltich 110
Monro, Dean 44, 67, 106–9, 111
moon rock 7
mouse, field 14, 15, 262, 263
mouse, house 14
Muck 6, 12, 14, 23, 46, 49, 50, 51, 54, 57, 60, 70, 71, 76, 77, 80, 81, 92, 104, 118, 121, 123, 126, 128–31, 137, 138, 147, 151, 179, 251, 255, 266
Muir, T. S. 29, 160
muirburn 260, 265
Mull 51, 72, 74, 104, 124, 139, 140, 146, 155, 156, 159, 166, 174–6, 189, 197, 199, 210, 227
Mundell, Walter 260, 263
Munro, Johann 255
Murray, John 138, 167, 168
Murray, Mrs Sarah 74, 76, 78, 91, 123
Museum of Scotland 16, 17, 36
muster rolls 117
Mystery 232, 233

Napoleonic wars 116, 120
narwhal 36
Nash, S. 236
National Parks 261, 263, 267
National Trust for Scotland 261, 266
Nature Conservancy 18, 78, 234, 248, 249, 258, 260, 261, 263–6
nature reserve 261–4, 266
nature trail etc 265
NCC 18, 265
Neil Mor 45
Neolithic 19, 21, 22, 24, 25
Newmarket 244, 248, 249
New Loch 191
newts 14
New Zealand 133, 134, 165, 176, 200, 201, 210, 233
Nicholson, Andrew 251
Nicholson, E. M. 263
Nicholson, Malcolm 213
Nicholson, Murdoch 213
Nova Scotia 124, 128, 129, 132, 236

oak 9, 23, 24, 66, 84
oats 183

olivine 7
Orchestrion 240, 249
Origines Parochialis 38
Orval 6, 7, 13, 17, 78, 108, 110, 111, 141, 224
Ossian 68, 69, 73
otter 15, 105, 193, 225
Otter, William 77
owl, short-eared 15
oysters 20, 104

Padding, John 178
Pakival (Barkeval) 223
Palaeolithic 19
Papadil 6, 11, 25, 28, 29, 31, 35, 82, 143, 145, 147, 149–51, 162, 175, 177, 182, 184–7, 194, 195, 199, 213, 225
Papadil Lodge 145, 228, 247
partridges 107, 183, 193, 222, 224, 229, 243
paths 185, 186, 222, 235, 257
peat 9, 12, 23, 24, 143, 161, 169, 176, 197, 198, 206, 227
Pennant, Thomas 10, 12, 61, 65–9, 85, 86, 88–92, 94, 106, 107, 109
peridotite 6
pheasants 107, 229, 243
photographic albums 233
Pictou 130
Picts 26, 35
pier 74, 103, 147, 198, 207, 208, 222, 223, 226, 236
piggery 181, 183
pigs 124, 178, 183, 198, 244
pine 9, 23, 85
piper 237, 238
pipits 15
plagioclase 7
plaice 226
plantations 229, 265
plants 8, 13, 65, 262, 264
ploughs 86
plover, golden 15, 78, 108
poaching 262
poems/songs 68, 69, 72, 119, 120, 124, 130, 131, 203, 206
poikilo-macro-spherulitic feldspars 7
poison 193
pollen 21, 23, 24
ponies 92, 93, 184, 223, 226, 244, 246–8, 259, 261
Pont, Timothy 48, 106
Port na Caranean 142, 143, 157, 164, 199, 209
post office 85, 138, 180, 181, 203, 213, 226, 227, 233, 236, 255, 259

potatoes 88, 115, 128, 139, 161–4, 170, 176, 183, 225, 244
pottery 16, 21, 22, 25
poultry 89, 198
Prebble, John 114
Presbyterianism 49, 57
Priest's Rock, Port of 207, 208
Prince Edward Is. 130
Privy Council 46, 48, 56
Protestantism 14, 48, 50, 54, 60, 64, 65, 67, 76, 108
ptarmigan 78, 107, 108, 229
Ptolemy 26
puffins 105–7

quarry 17, 18, 187
quay 74, 103, 147, 174, 181, 182, 195, 198, 207, 208, 222, 223, 226
Quebec 172, 209
Quinish, Mull 46, 49, 51, 70, 71

rabbit 14, 225, 227
radiocarbon dating 18, 19, 21, 24
rain 10, 11, 12, 212
raised beach 9, 23
Ramsgate Packet 148, 178, 193
Ranald MacRuari 37, 38, 39
Randall, George 247
Raonapol 102, 206
rat, brown 14, 15, 105, 193, 212, 237
Rauney, Isle of 38
raven 15
Raven, John 262
Raynor, Merrick 234
razorbill 15
razorfish 104
RCAHMS 18, 20, 24, 25, 29, 30
reindeer 195
research 263–5
Rhouma 232–4, 237, 238, 247
Rhouma II 247
Rhum 156, 161, 236
Ringing Stones of Ardnave 224
Ringing Stone, Tiree 8
Riogachd na Forraiste Fiadhaich 84, 108
roads 162, 187, 227, 242, 247, 258, 260
Robert Bruce 38
Robert Cecil 154, 155, 177, 197, 221
Robert II 39
Robertson, Charles 175
Robertson, James 252
Robertson, John 263
Robertson, Rev. Dr 112
Rockery Burn 204
rocket range 261
Rocking Stone 126, 224

Romans 26
Ronin 67
Rose, Hugh 119
Ross, Murdo 81
Ross, William 199
rowan 24, 66, 84
Ruari 37
Rudh'an Dunain, Skye 17, 75
Rudha nam Feannag 22
Ruinsival 224
Rum Cuillin 13
Rum population 47, 56, 58–60, 66, 67,
  72, 74, 77, 81, 123, 125–7, 129, 137,
  142, 166, 170, 172, 174, 177, 197, 222,
  258–60
Rum riabhach na sithne 108
Rum Volunteers 76, 116, 117
run-rig 67, 86, 88, 115
Russell, Archibald 176, 210
Russell, Effie 172, 173, 176, 177, 199, 206,
  209
Russell, Hugh 170, 185, 186, 187
Russell, John jr 167–9, 176, 210
Russell, John snr 143, 163, 166, 172, 173,
  176, 177, 180–2, 209
Russell, William 177
Rutledge, Dom. D. 54

Sabbagh, Karl 262
saithe 226
saitts 109
Salisbury, 1st Marquess 152
Salisbury, Lord or 2nd Marquess of 85,
  92–4, 102, 104, 143–6, 151–79, 181,
  183–197, 200, 214, 223, 230, 243, 250,
  253, 263, 265
Salisbury, 3rd Marquess 154, 155, 177,
  221
sallows 24
salmon 64, 102, 173, 188, 189, 193, 196,
  223, 227, 243
salt laws 103, 104
Samhnan Insir 12, 16, 18, 143, 145, 147,
  149–51, 166, 175
San Juan Bautista 46
Sandy Corrie 48, 224
Saonara 247
schist 4
School Board 250–2, 255–7
school logbooks 254, 255
schools 56–8, 71, 79–81, 137, 166–9, 176,
  182, 203–6, 213, 214, 225, 226, 227,
  244, 250–8, 260, 261
Schools Hebridean Society 16
Schooner Point 247
Scotch Militia Act 116

Scott, Sir Walter 41, 78, 82
Scott, W. Lindsay 17
Scottish Natural Heritage 18, 85, 258,
  265, 266
Scuir (Sgor) Mor 17, 67, 141
SDD 18
seabirds 20, 225
seals 20, 105, 225
seashells 12
seaweed 79, 88, 92, 94, 118, 119, 123, 139,
  183, 260
Select Committee 119, 126–8
settlement 21, 23, 36
Sgurr nan Gillean 224
shag 15, 20, 225
Shaw, Neil 237
shearing 147, 149
shearwater, Manx 13, 14, 15, 36, 49, 66,
  105–7, 225
sheep 20, 71, 74, 84, 89, 90, 91, 95–100,
  115, 119–23, 126, 127, 135, 139, 140,
  142, 144–9, 156–8, 160, 161, 173–5,
  183, 184, 187, 193, 197, 206, 221, 222,
  224–6, 228, 243, 244, 258–61
sheep mortality 146–51, 157, 158, 173–5,
  184, 185, 260
sheep numbers 148, 149, 173–5, 228,
  258–61, 263
Shellesder 15, 20, 25, 223, 243
shellfish 20, 25, 104, 243
shellsand 178, 183
shepherds 145, 146, 149, 156, 157, 162,
  164, 165, 169, 170, 172–6, 179–83, 186,
  187, 194, 196, 199–201, 203, 213, 214,
  222, 226, 235, 244, 246, 247, 257–9, 265
shielings 24, 94–100
shop 209, 213, 227
Short Isles 54
shrews 14, 15, 263
Sibbald, Robert 64
side schools 257
Simpson, Ian 16
Sinclair, Calum 246, 247
Sinclair, Rev. John 204, 236, 246, 250,
  251, 253
Sinclair, Rev. A. Maclean 51, 120, 124, 125
Sinclair, Rev. D. Maclean 128, 129, 139
Sinclair, Sir John 76, 115, 121
Sliochd Iain Garbh 52
Small Isles 5, 12, 46, 48, 49, 54, 56, 57,
  66, 71, 76, 80, 86, 104, 105, 115, 116,
  129, 137, 140, 203, 225, 226, 250, 255,
  257, 266, 267
Small Isles population 58–60, 76, 77, 81,
  115, 137, 139
smearing 145, 146, 149, 151, 158, 175

Smith, Drew 20, 36
smithy 181, 184, 187
snipe 15, 161, 202, 222, 224, 243
snow 11, 151, 161, 164
Snowden of St John's 166
soil 10, 12, 13, 18, 22, 23, 66, 95, 181, 183,
    198, 242, 264
Somerled (Somhairle) 36, 37, 39
songbirds 15, 242
songs 72, 245
souming 91
South Side 85, 142, 143
Spanish Armada 46, 92, 93
sparrowhawk 15, 242
Spray 133
Sron an t-Saighdeir 6, 9
SSPCK 56–8, 65, 79, 250, 251
St Kilda 57, 64, 261
St Lawrence 129
Stable Flats 12
stalker 235, 237, 243, 246, 259
Statistical Account (New) 88, 102, 103, 110,
    125, 129, 130, 137, 145
Statistical Account (Old) 10, 71, 76, 79,
    84–6, 88, 90–2, 96, 102–6, 109, 125,
    129, 137, 211
Statutes of Iona 47, 53
steamer 147, 148, 160, 170–2, 178, 179,
    187, 202, 204, 207, 222, 223, 226, 227,
    233, 244, 247, 261, 262, 266
Steven, Campbell 13
Stevenson, R. L. 12
Stewart, Helen 252
Stewart, John 58
stock grazing 88, 90, 91, 94–100, 114–15,
    121, 139, 140, 144, 150, 164, 206, 222,
    225, 244, 259, 262, 265
Stoddart, James 174
stone stripes/polygons 9
stone tools 16, 17, 18, 19, 20, 21, 22
stonechat 15
storms 161, 164, 166, 179, 208–12, 249,
    257
Strone 151, 184–7
Stuart, Lord Mount 55
sunfish (basking shark) 104
Swann, Bob 105
swans 193
Swanson, Rev. John 41, 140, 144
Swinburne, Capt. T. 126, 251
Swire, Otta 17
sycamore 139

Tacitus 26
tales/traditions 64, 68, 72, 75, 108, 126,
    205, 211, 266

tanning 68, 85
teaching 56–8, 71, 79–81, 137, 166–8,
    206, 214, 227, 250, 252–8, 260
temperatures 11
Tern 198
Tertiary period 5, 7, 9, 17
The Park 212
The Town 204, 208, 210
Thom, Allan 253
Thom, Robert 207
Thompson, Kate 106
Thomson, Mr 253
Thwaite, Angus 257
tinkers 207
toads 14
Tobar Dearg 211
Tobermory 51, 72, 74, 104, 124, 139, 140,
    155, 159, 181, 185, 197–9, 204, 210,
    226, 247
Tobermory galleon 46, 92
Torridonian sandstone 4, 13
tradesmen 77, 114, 139
transhumance 94–6
traps 193
Treaty of Perth 38
trees 9, 23, 28, 84, 85, 138, 205, 213, 224,
    229, 242, 243, 265
Tristram, Hugh 236
Triton 242
Trollval 36, 105, 223
trout 102, 193, 222, 225, 243
tupping 146, 147
turnips 183
turtles 242
tynchell 109
Tyrie, Father 54, 56

Uist 38, 39, 93, 95, 111, 112, 115, 118, 163,
    184, 206, 228

vegetables 182
vegetation 8, 9, 12, 13, 23, 24, 145, 262,
    264
Victoria, Queen 154, 187
Vikings 9, 14, 28, 35, 36, 37, 93
villages 67, 77, 82, 85, 86, 90, 96, 137
volcano 5, 6, 7, 17
voles 15
volunteers 116

Waipu, NZ 133, 134
Walker, Rev. J. 7, 10, 59, 64, 65, 69, 79,
    84–6, 88, 90, 91, 93, 94, 101, 106–9,
    117, 151, 184
Ward, Father C. 14, 53, 54
Ward, Capt. William 178, 179, 194

Watson Lyall & Co. 222
Watson, W. J. 112
Waugh, Edwin 13, 33, 102, 196, 197, 204, 205, 207, 210–14, 221, 251
weather 10, 11, 12, 24, 25, 70, 80–3, 88, 141, 146, 148, 149, 151, 161, 175, 179–81, 208–13, 248, 257
Webster, Rev. A. 59
well 211
Welsh miner 162, 185–7
Welshman's Rock 162, 185
West Coast Fisheries Investigation 226
wheatear 15
Whitehead, Kenneth 243
White House 196, 204, 210, 211, 222, 224, 230, 234, 236, 260
Wickham-Jones, C. 18, 19, 20, 25

William 113, 114
willow 9
wind 12
woodcock 161, 222, 225, 243
woodland 9, 10, 23, 24, 48, 64, 66, 84, 85, 138, 205, 212, 222, 224, 229, 242, 264, 265
wrasse 22
Wreck Bay 110, 247
wrecks 78, 161, 166, 179–81, 200, 207, 209, 232, 247, 261
wych elm 139

yellow stick religion 50, 54, 55, 64
Young Coll 43, 50, 69–73, 90, 122, 124

Zoo, London 194